Western GRIT

A rock climbing guidebook to
selected routes on the
western gritstone edges
and quarries
of the Peak District,
south Lancashire
and Cheshire

This page: Colin Binks on
Bachelor's Left-Hand (HVS 5b)
at Hen Cloud. *Page 87*

Cover: Colin in a superb
position on *East Rib* (HVS 5a)
at Shining Clough. *Page 162*

This book belongs to

Text, topos, photo-topos, maps
Chris Craggs and Alan James.

Photos by Chris Craggs unless otherwise credited

Original ROCKFAX design
Ben Walker, Mick Ryan and Alan James.

Printed by Clearpoint Colourprint, Nottingham.
Distributed by Cordee
(Tel: (+int) 44 (0) 116 254 3579)

Published by ROCKFAX Ltd. May 2003
© Chris Craggs © ROCKFAX Ltd. 2003

ISBN 1-873341-80-6

ROCKFAX

rockfax.com

Sheffield, UK and Bishop, CA, USA
E-mail UK: alan@rockfax.co.uk
E-mail USA: mick@rockfax.com

RRP £18.95 (*about* $30, = 30)

ROCKFAX

PEAK GRITSTONE EAST (2001)
- rockfax.com/peak_gritstone/
The most popular UK guidebook ever covering the magnificent eastern gritstone edges of the Peak District. Full colour throughout, 288 pages, nearly 2000 routes and 50 action photos.

"..this book is as close to perfect a guidebook as we are likely to get."
- Ed Douglas, Climber, February 2002
"It's a breath of fresh air. It's a revolution. Never has a guide book been so inspiring. You can now look at a crag that you have never been to and take a fairly educated guess as to whether you will enjoy the style of climbing it has to offer."
- Matt Heason, Planetfear.com

COSTA DAURADA (1998 and 2002) - rockfax.com/costa_daurada
Winter sun destination near Barcelona in northern Spain. Single pitch sport climbing on perfect limestone. Now full colour with 172 pages, 1000+ routes and all major areas.
"It is the most comprehensive and up-to-date guide available for this area, superseding the Spanish guide." - John Adams, Climber, March 1999

COAST BLANCA, MALLORCA, EL CHORRO (2001) - rockfax.com/spain
Third edition of the most popular ROCKFAX guidebook to three brilliant climbing areas in Spain. Sport and some trad climbing. Now with 360 pages and nearly 3000 routes.
"This easily lives up to the very high standards that we have come accustomed to from the ROCKFAX range over the past eleven years" - Ben Heason, Planetfear.com

YORKSHIRE GRITSTONE BOULDERING (2000)
- rockfax.com/yorkshire_bouldering
All the bouldering on the brilliant gritstone outcrops of Yorkshire, England. 320 pages, nearly 3500 problems over 17+ locations.
"..one day all guidebooks will look like this" - Simon Panton, Climber, February 2001

DORSET (2000) - rockfax.com/dorset
Sport climbing, trad climbing, deep water soloing and bouldering on the south coast of England. 1500 routes on 272 pages including 32 pages of colour.
"Mighty fine; a job well done" - Mike Robertson, OTE, May 2000

PEAK BOULDERING (1998 and 2000) - rockfax.com/peak_bouldering
Gritstone bouldering in the Peak District, near Sheffield, England. The only guidebook available. 2nd Edition - 224 pages, 38 locations and 1600+ separate problems.
"Having had a chance to use the guide for myself, plus liaising with others, it has become apparent that it is pretty damn good." - Neil Bentley, High, August 1998

NORTH WALES LIMESTONE and NORTH WALES BOULDERING (1997)
rockfax.com/north_wales_limestone
Sport and traditional climbing found on the spectacular Ormes of Llandudno. Also includes a bouldering guide to North Wales. 224 pages, 800+ routes, 34 separate crags.

ISLANDS IN THE SKY - VEGAS LIMESTONE (2001) - rockfax.com/vegas
A guidebook to the rock climbing on Las Vegas and Great Basin limestone in the USA. 224 pages, 652 routes.

RIFLE - BITE THE BULLET (1997)
Sport climbing on the limestone of Rifle Mountain Park in Colorado. 72 pages, 200+ routes.

PEMBROKE (1995)
Traditional climbing on the Pembrokeshire Coast of South Wales. All the important routes are included. 112 pages, 450+ routes.

BISHOP BOULDERING SURVIVAL KIT (1999)
All the information you need for bouldering around Bishop in California.

ORDERING
All books are available from your local retailer
or Cordee *(3a DeMontfort Street, Leicester, LE1 7HD. UK.*
Tel: (+int) 44 (0) 116 254 3579)
or by credit card using the safe online ordering at:
rockfax.com/shop.html

CONTENTS

INTRODUCTION ___

Fine views from Alderman in the Chew Valley.

This new volume covers a huge sweep of gritstone from the magnificent pink hued cliffs of north Staffordshire, through the high and wild outcrops of Kinder and Bleaklow, on through the quiet gems of the Chew Valley and into the extensive quarries of south east Lancashire. At the last minute we decided to add the best of the Cheshire sandstone outcrops, although most definitely not gritstone they were first described in John Laycock's 1913 guide, *Some Gritstone Climbs*, and the most recent guide is out of print. Added to this is the fact that the routes are in the same style as those in the rest of the book, putting them here didn't feel too revolutionary.

The cliffs described here are not the elegant and extensive outcrops of the Eastern Edges, but a set of more retiring venues. They are less accessible and take some effort to get to know but of course, being gritstone, the effort is always well worth it. I first climbed on western grit two thirds of a lifetime ago in 1968. We visited The Roaches where we grabbed *Via Dolorosa* (VS 4c) and *Pedestal Route* (HVD 4a) between impressive towering clouds shedding heavy showers. A couple of years later we were back as college freshers for what were then considered the big three classics and at the the end of the day we left, suitably pleased, having done *Valkyrie* (VS 4c), *Saul's Crack* (HVS 5a) and *The Sloth* (HVS 5a). In the intervening years I have climbed over the whole area, and would be the first admit there area some less than memorable routes on the Western Edges. On the other-hand there are some real hidden gems that are all the more worthwhile because of their unsung quality. As a few samples go and try *Zigzag Climb* (VDiff) at Kinder Downfall, *Pedestal Route* (HVD 4a) at the Roaches, *Route 1* (HS 4b) at Wimberry, *Tower Face* (VS 5a) on Laddow, *Pisa Direct* (HVS 5a) on Shining Clough, *Paradox* (E1 5b) at Wilton 1, *The Arete* (E2 5c) at Tintwistle, *True Grit* (E3 5c) at The Ravenstones, *Renaissance* (E4 6a) at Upperwood, *Pigs on the Wing* (E5 6b) at Wilton 2 and *Wristcutter's Lullaby* (E6 6c) at Wimberry: put simply, all are as good as any routes on Eastern Grit.

Colin Binks and Dave Gregory climbing *The Crank* (VS 4c) on an atmospheric day at Ramshaw. *Page 93*

THE AREAS

The south west corner of the Peak is in Staffordshire; far and away the most popular of the main areas covered in Western Grit. Here are the peerless tiers of The Roaches, with the castellated edge of Hen Cloud, a superb 'second best' and also the delights of Ramshaw. Around Whaley Bridge is a trio of smaller crags, Windgather is immensely popular and justly so, with a glorious setting and many lower grade climbs. Nearby Castle Naze is also pleasant, but remains much quieter. The steep shady walls of New Mills Tor see even less traffic, despite having some excellent pumpy climbing and staying dry in wet weather.

The great swath of moor that is the Kinder Scout plateau has a ring of rock protruding from it edges and facing in virtually all directions. The cliffs are a coarse, rugged grit and are all an hour or so from the road. Meeting another team on these high and wild cliffs it unusual - this is Peak climbing as it used to be, and it is perfect if you want to get away from it all.

Amelia McMahon climbing *Great Chimney* (Sev 4a) at Hen Cloud. *Page 88* Photo: Alex Ekins

The Bleaklow/Longdendale area is stark and neglected, except for the popular and easily accessible quarry of Hobson Moor. Shining Clough is a summer-only cliff whereas both Laddow and Tintwistle Knarr Quarry have a longer season and would benefit greatly from a little more traffic.

The Chew Valley might be considered as the Peak's 'Lost World'; a whole array of fine cliffs perched above the reservoirs, superb settings, good rock and no crowds. Unfortunately the best venue - Wimberry - faces north, though if this is out of condition the sunnier outcrops such as Alderman or Standing Stones should allow you to get something done.

Lancashire is an enigma; there is some excellent climbing here but outside visitors are rare. The quarries have a bit of a rogue reputation but they are home to some excellent routes, it's just a matter of choosing your time and venue to match the prevailing conditions.

Hopefully the small selection offered here will tempt you to sample the place and then go on to explore the delights of the Red Rose County more fully. From the fierce cracks of the Wilton Quarries to the sheltered bouldering of Brownstones, from the popular Anglezarke to the neglected Littleborough area, there is certainly plenty to tempt.

The sandstone outcrops of Cheshire and Merseyside have a long history with Helsby being climbed on since the start of the 1900s. Frodsham gives excellent bouldering and Pex Hill is one of the most popular crags in the book despite its diminutive size. Helsby has also been neglected over the years, at least in part because it looks so grotty when glimpsed from the motorway below. Despite this, call in on a mild summer's evening and I guarantee that you will be pleasantly surprised.

Mike Appleton on the Ravenstones' classic *True Grit* (E3 5c). *Page 206.* The Standing Stones can be seen in the middle distance.

BOULDERING

 There are plenty of bouldering areas in this book and these are located on the maps with the adjacent symbol. The idea behind including this information is to cater for those who like to indulge in a bit of bouldering from time to time, but don't require the more in-depth approach provided by a bouldering guide. The ROCKFAX guidebook to Peak Bouldering covers selected areas in greater.

In addition there are three crags not included in Peak Bouldering that are primarily of interest to boulderers; Brownstones, Frodsham and Pex Hill. At these crags we have given bouldering grades (see page 14) to most of the problems.

WEB SITE

The section of the ROCKFAX web site at the address www.rockfax.com/western_grit/ contains extra information relating to this book. As things develop we will be posting pdf updates and free pdf downloads of other crags (Portable Document Format - a universal format which can be viewed and printed out on all modern computers using the free application Adobe Acrobat Reader).

ROCKFAX ROUTE DATABASE

www.rockfax.com/databases/

The ROCKFAX Route Database contains a listing of every route in the book with the possibility for you to lodge comments and vote on grades and star ratings. This information is essential to help us ensure complete and up-to-date coverage for all the climbs. We can then produce updates and make sure we get it right in subsequent editions. To make this system work we need the help of everyone who climbs on Western Grit. We can not reflect opinions if we have not got them so if you think you have found a big sandbag of a route, or discovered a hidden gem that we have only given a single star to, let us know about it. We also want to know your general comments on all other aspects of this book. Basically if you have anything to say about Western Grit, don't just say it to your mates down at the pub, say it to ROCKFAX. Use the forms at www.rockfax.com/feedback/

THE BOOK

Photographing and documenting the Eastern Edges was a pleasant diversion; pick a sunny afternoon and walk along the base of the cliff, snapping away with the digital camera and a couple of hours later the images are on the screen ready to be manipulated and edited into the document. The Western Edges have been more of a challenge; many are remote from the road, often face north and are at the top of impressively steep slopes. As an example the superb cliff of Wimberry took four visits to get some usable photographs, and then one more, just to finish the place off!

In the process of compiling this book we have continued to developed the techniques established in Peak Gritstone East particularly with respect to the photography of the crags, which is key to the ROCKFAX guidebooks. Since Peak Gritstone East, the feedback we have had from the vast majority of users has been extremely positive and there is little doubt that Peak Grit East has changed British guidebooks for ever. Here we present Western Grit, the next step along the road - please enjoy.

Chris Craggs and Alan James, May 2003

ACCESS

Much of the high moorland areas covered in this guidebook do not have a historical right of access. Sections of the heather moors that back the Staffordshire and Chew cliffs, and cover Kinder and Bleaklow, have been used for rearing grouse for well over a century and the characteristic environment here has developed through this use. We are fortunate to be on the receiving end of the work done on our behalf over the years. Continued access requires a responsible approach, the freedoms already won could be so easily lost, and this is all our responsibility. Crags with access arrangements are detailed in their introductions. If you do encounter access problems contact the BMC, Tel: 08700 104 878 access@thebmc.co.uk. For information on the ACT see page 28.

CLOSURES

Infrequently access restrictions do occur (signs will be posted) mainly due either to nesting birds, or through potential fire hazards.

Group use on *Heather Slab*.

GENERAL BEHAVIOUR

A little Country Code sense is all that is required, no fires, leave no litter, close gates after you, park sensibly and avoid disturbing farm animals.

Please use the designated parking areas whenever possible and be aware of the increased incidence of car crime. The tell-tale sign of broken glass in any car park means it is a good idea to leave nothing of value in the car. If you park away from the recognised areas the car needs to be right off the road or you stand a good chance of getting ticketed.

All the moors in Derbyshire are grazed by sheep and as such make an unsuitable destination for domestic dogs. If you really must take your best friend on a climbing trip it should be tied up and kept quiet. The place should be cleaned up before you leave!

TOP ROPING/GROUPS

The development of indoor walls has introduced a new generation to climbing who enjoy it for the physical/technical aspect and do not feel the urge to seek the adrenaline high generated when leading climbs. Unfortunate this often leads to the monopolisation of certain (usually very accessible) routes at busy times as a line of unfortunate souls are introduced to outdoor climbing on a bow-taught top rope. This can be a selfish and unreasonable approach, please be aware of the needs of others, remove ropes that are not in use and avoid popular climbs at busy times. Consider leading easier routes rather than top-roping harder ones, this will spread the load and ultimately is much more rewarding.

The wear and tear that climbs are suffering is another growing problem; a visit to Windgather Rocks will reveal the damage that can be done through over-use.

If you must visit the cliffs in a large group, please consider other climbers. What feels like good-natured banter and horseplay can seem like yobbish behaviour to others on the cliff who are there for a bit of peace and quiet. Keep your kit in one area and try to avoid monopolising classic climbs for extended periods of time.

Valkyrie (VS 4c) on the Lower Tier of the Roaches. Page 52

INTRODUCTION

ETHICS

Climbing is an anachronistic pastime and one of its great attractions is the lack of rules and structure. Despite this there is a long history of ethical purity; the way individuals climb a piece of rock is up to them, although the way they report the ascent is a more public affair. For example preplacing gear, hanging on a runner whilst clipping it, taking tension from the rope, are all regarded as forms of cheating. There remains only ONE pure form of ascent but if you want to tick the route having sat on half a dozen runners then so be it. The best form of ascent is a ground-up lead, placing the gear as you go, in a single push. On the harder and more serious routes, the individual moves are often practiced extensively and then the route led or soloed in what has become known as a 'headpoint'. Traditionally the expression 'practiced on a top-rope first' was used. In reality nobody really cares how you do the route as long as the rock doesn't suffer.

There is no reason for adding fixed protection (pegs or bolts) or attempting to improve holds on any of the routes in this

Ben Bransby on the upper wall of *Painted Rumour* (E6 6a) on the Roaches Upper Tier. *Page 64.* Photo: John Henry Bull

guide and if you think otherwise then you are wrong. Wire brushing on the harder routes needs to be done with great care as even iron-hard gritstone can be damaged by over-zealous cleaning. Most modern damage to the crags in this book has occurred when climbers have attempted to retrieve stuck gear. Equipment that gets stuck is invariably gear that is badly placed, so think before you place it. If it does get well and truly jammed it may be better leaving it for someone who can get it out without damaging the route.

GEAR

The flared breaks and cracks make gritstone an ideal place for Friends and other camming devices. Many old routes which were bold and unprotected leads in their day are now relatively safe with the modern protection devices available. A typical gritstone rack consists of a single set of wires, a few hexes and a full range of Friends. One or two slings will also be found useful on some routes and often on the cliff-top belays. For harder routes, micro-wires and more-advanced camming devices may be found essential. Most grit routes are short enough to be climbed on a single 10mm or 11mm rope. The only exceptions to this are routes which wander around, in which case you may need to consider 2 x 9mm ropes. Other useful items are; tape for bandaging your hands before, or after, they are wrecked by some savage crack, a toothbrush for cleaning the smaller holds on the harder routes and a bouldering mat for those unprotected starts. The only other thing you need is this book!

MiniGUIDES

from rockfax.com

Downloadable PDF guides to areas all over the World

Kalymnos - Cala Gonone - Inland Sardinia
Bishop Bouldering - Eastern Sierras
Margalef - Montgrony - Tenerife
Peak Bouldering - Langdale Bouldering
Skye Ridge - Lofoten Island
and more being added all the time

This is gritstone, the home of British climbing, so as you would expect we are using the British trad grade. The table below is an attempt to compare the grades with several other systems across the world. It is a slightly different table from the ones in previous books, and the one on the ROCKFAX web site, because of the unique nature of gritstone routes.

BOLD ROUTES - Many of the gritstone and sandstone routes covered in this book have limited protection and you can find yourself in some very serious situations, especially on the harder climbs. This should be clear from the text but please make sure you use your own skill and judgment as to whether you will be able to safely complete a chosen climb. A bold E2 may only feel like a Sport grade 6a on a top-rope but it is a very different proposition as a lead or solo.

BRITISH TRAD GRADE

1) **Adjectival grade** (Diff, VDiff, Severe, Hard Severe (HS), Very Severe (VS), Hard Very Severe (HVS), E1, E2,.... to E9).
An overall picture of the route including how well protected it is, how sustained and a general indication of the level of difficulty of the whole route.

2) **Technical grade** (4a, 4b, 4c,..... to 7a).
The difficulty of the hardest single move, or short section.

COLOUR CODING

The routes are all given a colour-coded spot corresponding to a grade band.
GREEN ROUTES - **Everything at grade Severe and under.** Mostly these should be good for beginners and those wanting and easy life.
ORANGE ROUTES - **Hard Severe to HVS inclusive.** General ticking routes for those with more experience.
RED ROUTES - **E1 to E3 inclusive.** Routes for the experienced and keen climber. A grade band which includes many of the Peak's great classics.
BLACK SPOTS - E4 and above.

BOULDERING

The boulder problems in this book are given a UK tech grade and a V-grade.

ROUTE GRADES

BRITISH TRAD GRADE (See note on bold routes)	Sport Grade	UIAA	USA
Mod (Moderate)	1	I	5.1
Diff (Difficult)	2	II	5.2
VDiff (Very Difficult)	2+	III	5.3
HVD (Hard Very Difficult)	3-	III+ / –IV–	5.4
Sev (Severe)	3	IV+	5.5
HS (Hard Severe) 3c 4b SAFE BOLD	3+	V–	5.6
VS (Very Severe) 4a 5a SAFE BOLD	4	V	5.7
HVS (Hard Very Severe) 4b 5b SAFE BOLD	4+	V+	5.8
E1 5a 5c SAFE BOLD	5	VI–	5.9
E2 5a 6a SAFE BOLD	5+	VI	5.10a
E3 5b 6a SAFE BOLD	6a	VI+	5.10b
E4 5c 6b SAFE BOLD	6a+	VII–	5.10c
E5 6a 6c SAFE BOLD	6b	VII	5.10d
E6 6b 6c SAFE BOLD	6b+	VII+	5.11a
E7 6c 7a SAFE BOLD	6c	VIII–	5.11b
E8 6c 7a SAFE BOLD	6c+	VIII–	5.11c
E9 7a 7b SAFE BOLD	7a	VIII	5.11d
E10 7b SAFE BOLD	7a+	VIII+	5.12a
	7b	IX–	5.12b
	7b+	IX–	5.12c
	7c	IX	5.12d
	7c+	IX+	5.13a
	8a	X–	5.13b
	8a+	X	5.13c
	8b	X+	5.13d
	8b+		5.14a
	8c	XI–	5.14b
	8c+	XI	5.14c
	9a		5.14d
	9a+	XI+	5.15a

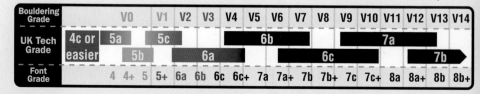

Bouldering Grade	V0	V1	V2	V3	V4	V5	V6	V7	V8	V9	V10	V11	V12	V13	V14
UK Tech Grade	4c or easier	5a		5c		6b					7a				7b
		5b		6a			6c							7b	
Font Grade		4	4+ 5	5+	6a	6b	6c	6c+	7a	7a+	7b	7b+	7c	7c+	8a	8a+ 8b 8b+

Route Symbols

 A good route

 Technical climbing involving complex or trick moves

Fingery climbing - small holds!

 A very good route

Powerful moves requiring big arms

Fluttery climbing with big fall potential

 A brilliant route

Sustained climbing, either long and pumpy or with lots of hard moves

A long reach is helpful/essential

Rounded holds typical of gritstone

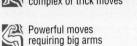

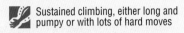

Photo-topos

Descent

2

4

Alternatives for the same route

1

3

Next area

Crag Symbols

 Approach - Approach walk time and angle
10 min

 Sunshine - Approximate time when the sun is on the crag
Afternoon

 Green and damp in the winter with lichen and moss
Green

 Sheltered from the wind
Sheltered

 Bouldering spots - Marked on the maps and described in the text
Bouldering

Grade Colour Codes

The colour-coded route numbers correspond to the following grade bands:

❶ - Grade Severe and under

❷ - Grade Hard Severe to HVS

❸ - Grade E1 to E3

❹ - Grade E4 and above

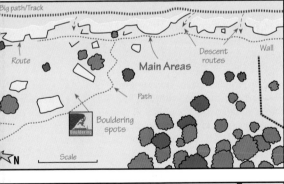

Big path/Track

Route

Main Areas

Descent routes

Wall

Path

Bouldering spots
Bouldering

N   Scale

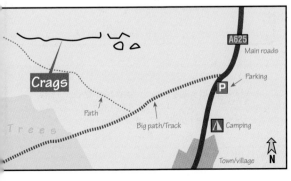

A625

Main roads

Crags

Parking

P

Path

Big path/Track

Camping

Trees

Town/village   N

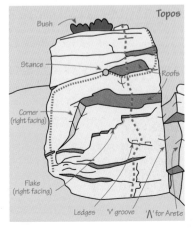

Topos

Bush

Stance

Roofs

Corner (right facing)

Flake (right facing)

Ledges   'V' groove   '∧' for Arete

INTRODUCTION (Français)

Le Peak District est connu par ses falaises de grès, dont beaucoup sont comprises dans le topo-guide ROCKFAX très populaire Peak Gritstone East. Western Grit est le topo-guide qui va de pair, qui étend la couverture géographique au reste du Peak District et aux Pennines et qui comprend certaines des falaises de grès les plus belles, les plus exposées aux intempéries et les plus sauvages. Commençant par le sud il y a le Roaches, toujours populaire, et les autres falaises de Staffordshire, qui sont prèsque aussi célèbres que Stanage comme site d'escalade. Plus au nord existent d'autres belles falaises sur les landes de Kinder, Bleaklow et la Vallée de Chew, et à l'ouest se trouvent les belles carrières de Lancashire. Finalement on a les falaises de grès au sud de Liverpool, en Cheshire.

Les voies sur toutes ces falaises sont principalement courtes, d'une longeur, et demandent de la protection naturelle. Il n'existe même pas une seule voie protégée par spits dans ce livre (il y a quelques spits anciens mais on conseille de se méfier de son utilisation!). Le rocher, du grès, a une texture rugueuse et offre des formations fabuleuses avec des lignes naturelles et une adhérence sans pair. Même après des années d'escalade, bien des voies ne sont pas patinées, tellement le grain est rugueux.

Les falaises ci-décrites se trouvent pour la plupart dans un très beau cadre, sur les landes sauvages et attirantes de Staffordshire et Derbyshire et sur le paysage onduleux de Lancashire et Cheshire.

LE GUIDE

Ce guide contient tous les renseignements nécessaires pour trouver les meilleures voies sur les falaises décrites. Il y a des plans de situation, des photo-topos et des descriptions pour pouvoir localiser les voies. On utilise aussi beaucoup de symboles avec les voies pour donner une idée du type d'escalade : vous les trouverez tous en face avec des explications.

L'ÉQUIPMENT

Toute la protection sur les voies est naturelle, et vous en aurez besoin d'une bonne séléction. Ce qui est le plus utile c'est les friends car ils s'adaptent bien aux fissures qui se trouvent fréquemment sur les falaises. Vous aurez besoin également d'un jeu de coinceurs et de quelques sangles. Pour bonnes promotions sur le matériel, consulter **www.rockrun.com**

COTATIONS

Toutes les voies dans ce livre ont une cotation "traditionnelle" qui comprend deux éléments:
1) La note qualificative (Diff, ..., Very Severe (VS ou "très difficile"), ... E1, E2, ... jusqu'à E9). Ceci vous donnera une vue d'ensemble de la voie, y compris son niveau de protection, d'intensité, ainsi qu'une indication du niveau de difficulté de l'ensemble de la voie.
2) La note technique (4a, 4b, 4c, 5a, ... jusqu'à 7a). Ceci fait référence au niveau de difficulté du mouvement individuel ou de la portion la plus ardue de la voie.
Il y a une table de conversion à la page 14.

INFORMATION SUPPLÉMENTAIRE

Pour en savoir plus sur le grès du Peak District, consulter ce website spécialisé:
www.rockfax.com/peak_gritstone/

ROCKFAX

ROCKFAX consiste d'Alan James au Royaume-Uni et de Mick Ryan aux États-Unis. Ça fait depuis 1990 que nous faisons des guides d'escalade sur des endroits situées dans le monde entier. Vous trouverez des renseignements sur toutes nos publications sur notre website **www.rockfax.com**

E-mail (Royaume-Uni): alan@rockfax.co.uk E-mail (États-Unis): mick@rockfax.com

Bonne voie

 Très bonne voie

 Voie majeure

 Escalade technique nécessitant des mouvements complexes ou astucieux

 Requiert des bras solides pour des mouvements de force

 Escalade de continuité, longue et avec bouteilles garanties ou bien avec beaucoup de mouvements durs

Escalade à doigts – prises coupantes!

Escalade angoissante avec possibilité de grandes chutes

Les grands seront avantagés.

Prises arrondies ou inclinées

Photo-topos

- - Descente

Alternatives pour la même voie

Secteur suivant

 Approche - Temps de marche d'approche et pente.

 Soleil - Heures approximatives auxquelles la paroi est exposée au soleil.

 Couvert de lichen et mousse en hiver.

 Protégé du vent

 Secteurs de bloc – signalés sur les plans et décrits dans le texte

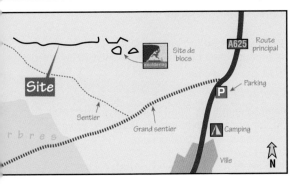

Grand sentier

Voie

Sites

Voies de descente

Mur

Sentier

Site de blocs

Echelle

N

Les numéros des voies en couleurs différentes correspondent aux bandes de cotations suivantes:

❶ - Niveau 3+ ou au-dessous

❷ - Niveau 4 à 5+.

❸ - Niveau 6a à 6c.

❹ - Niveau 6c+ et au-dessus

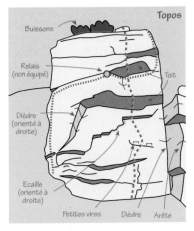

Topos

Buissons

Relais (non équipé)

Toit

Dièdre (orienté à droite)

Ecaille (orienté à droite)

Petites vires

Dièdre

Arête

Site

Sentier

Grand sentier

Site de blocs

A625 Route principal

P Parking

Camping

Ville

N

EINFÜHRUNG

Der *Peak District* ist wohlbekannt für seine Kanten aus grobem Sandstein (Gritstone). Viele von ihnen wurden im sehr beliebten ROCKFAX Kletterführer *Peak Gritstone East* dokumentiert. *Western Grit* ist das Begleitbuch, das die Abdeckung auf den Rest von *Peak Gritstone* und *Pennines* und damit einige der besten, exponiertesten und wildesten Sandsteinfelsen im Umkreis ausdehnt. Im Süden beginnend, befinden sich die ständig beliebten *Roaches* und die anderen *Staffordshire* Felsen, die als Kletterziel fast so berühmt sind wie *Stanage*. Weiter im Norden befinden sich noch viel mehr gute Felsen bei den Heidemooren von *Kinder*, bei *Bleaklow* und dem *Chew Valley*. Im Westen liegen die guten Steinbrüche von *Lancashire*. Schließlich finden wir südlich von *Liverpool* die beliebten Sandsteinfelsen von *Cheshire*. Die Aufstiege an all diesen Felsen sind hauptsächlich kurze selbst zu sichernde Einseillängen-Routen. Im ganzen Buch wird kein einziger Haken beschrieben (Es existieren zwar einige alte Bolts, von denen aber nicht ernsthaft anzunehmen ist, daß Sie diese benutzen würden!).
Der Fels, Gritstone, ist eine Art grober Sandstein, der fantastische Felsformationen mit großartigen natürlichen Linien und hervorragender Reibung bietet. Viele Routen sind, obwohl sie schon seit Jahren viel geklettert werden, wegen der groben Felsstruktur dennoch nicht speckig.
Die Felsen befinden sich hauptsächlich in schönen Gegenden bei den reizvollen Mooren von *Staffordshire* und *Derbyshire* sowie in der sanften Landschaft von *Lancashire* und *Cheshire*.

DER KLETTERFÜHRER
Dieses Buch beinhaltet alle Informationen, die nötig sind, um die besten Routen an den Felsen zu finden. Dies umfaßt Zustiegsskizzen, Phototopos und Beschreibungen, die die Routenfindung erleichtern. Außerdem werden viele Symbole benutzt, um zu verdeutlichen, von welcher Art Kletterei eine Route ist. Diese Symbole sind auf der nächsten Seite erklärt.

AUSRÜSTUNG
Alle Sicherungen in diesem Gebiet sind selbst zu legen und eine gute Auswahl an Material ist nötig, um hier zu klettern. Am nützlichsten für Gritstone sind Friends, die hervorragend in die sehr häufig auftretenden Risse passen. Ein Satz Keile und einige lange Schlingen sind ebenfalls nötig.

SCHWIERIGKEITSBEWERTUNG
Alle Routen sind traditionell britisch bewertet, d.h. zweiteilig:
1) Eine adjektivische Bewertung wie "Diff" (schwierig), "Very Severe" (sehr ernst), [...], "E1, E2, ..., bis E9" (Extreme Schwierigkeiten). Diese stellt eine Gesamtbewertung der Schwierigkeiten der bezeichneten Route dar, wie sie abgesichert, wie anhaltend schwer sie ist.
2) Die klettertechnische Bewertung 4a, 4b, 4c, 5a, ... bis 7a. Sie bezieht sich auf die Schwierigkeit des härtesten Einzelzuges (der härtesten Einzelstelle) der Tour. Eine Umrechnungstabelle befindet sich auf Seite 14.

ZUSÄTZLICHE INFORMATION
Zusätzliche Informationen zum WesternGritstone befinden sich auf der ROCKFAX Webseite **www.rockfax.com/western_gritstone/**

ROCKFAX
ROCKFAX sind Alan James in Großbritannien und Mick Ryan in Amerika. Seit 1990 schreiben wir Kletterführer für Gebiete in der ganzen Welt. Informationen zu unseren Publikationen befinden sich auf unserer Webseite www.rockfax.com.

E-mail (UK): alan@rockfax.co.uk E-mail (USA): mick@rockfax.com

Lohnende Kletterei

 Sehr lohnende Kletterei

Brilliante Kletterei

 Technisch anspruchsvolle Tour mit trickreichen Zügen.

Heikle Kletterei mit hohem Sturzpotential, aber nicht allzu gefährlich.

Durchgehend anstrengende Tour; entweder anhaltend schwer oder mit einer Reihe harter Züge.

Kleingriffige, rauhe Kletterei - nichts für zarte Hände.

Anstrengende Züge. Erfordert kräftige Oberarme.

Lange Arme sind hilfreich.

Abgerundete und abwärtsgeneigte Griffe

Photo-topos

Abstieg

Alternativen für dieselbe Route

nächstes Gebiet

Felsymbole

 Zugang - Zeit und Steilheit des Zugangsweges.

 Sonnenschein - Zeit, zu der der Felsen in der Sonne liegt.

 Grün, im Winter mit Flechten und Moos bedeckt

 windgeschützt

 Bouldergebiete - auf den Karten eingezeichnet und im Text beschrieben

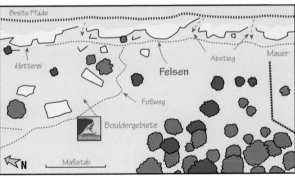

Breite Pfade

kletterei

Felsen

Abstieg

Mauer

Fußweg

Bouldergebiete

N   Maßstab

Farbig markierte Routennummern

Die farbigen Routennummern entsprechen den folgenden Schwierigkeitsbereichen:

1 - Grad IV+ und darunter
2 - Grad V bis VI
3 - Grad VI+ bis VII+
4 - Grad VIII und darüber

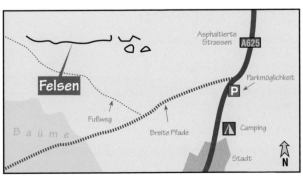

Felsen

Asphaltierte Strassen   A625

Parkmöglichkeit   P

Fußweg

Bäume

Breite Pfade

Camping

Stadt   N

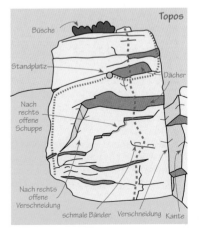

Topos

Büsche

Standplatz

Dächer

Nach rechts offene Schuppe

Nach rechts offene Verschneidung

schmale Bänder   Verschneidung   Kante

INFORMATION

MOUNTAIN RESCUE
In the event of an accident requiring the assistance of Mountain Rescue:

Dial 999 and ask for 'POLICE - MOUNTAIN RESCUE'
Quote the grid reference given at the top of the page.

All mountain rescue incidents in the Peak District area fall under the responsibility of Derbyshire Constabulary. If in any doubt request Derbyshire Police Operations Room.

MOBILE PHONES
Most of the crags described in this book have good mobile phone coverage across the major networks. The exceptions are the remote moorland crags where coverage is sporadic and unpredictable. Often a signal can be found by walking to a high point or simply by changing direction.

BRITISH MOUNTAINEERING COUNCIL
British Mountaineering Council, 177-179 Burton Road, West Manchester, Manchester, M20 2BB.
Tel: 08700 104 878 www.thebmc.co.uk

TOURIST INFORMATION OFFICES
If you are short of ideas of what to do on a wet day, need some accommodation, looking for camp sites, want some tickets for the theatre or are just interested in local history; take a look at the **Tourist Information Offices**. They contain much more useful information than we have on these pages.
Buxton - Tel: 01298 25106 tourism@highpeak.gov.uk
Leek - Tel: 01538 483741 tourism.services@staffsmoorlands.gov.uk
Manchester - Tel: 0161 234 3157 manchester_visitor_centre@notes.manchester.gov.uk
Macclesfield - Tel: 01625 504114 informationcentre@macclesfield.gov.uk
Saddleworth - Tel: 01457 870336 ecs.saddleworthtic@oldham.gov.uk
Bolton - Tel: 01204 334400 tourist.info@bolton.gov.uk
Preston - Tel: 01772 253731 tourism@preston.gov.uk
Runcorn - Tel: 01928 576776 tourist.info@halton-borough.gov.uk
Warrington - Tel: 01925 632571 informationcentre@warrington.gov.uk
St Helens - Tel: 01744 755150 sthelenstic@yahoo.co.uk
More information and other travel tips are at - www.travelengland.org.uk

ACCOMMODATION
For short stays the following camp sites are well-positioned for the climbing in some of the areas. More campsites and huts can be found on the following web sites -
www.ukclimbing.com/listings/campsites.html - www.derbyshirecamping.co.uk
www.ukcampsite.co.uk/sites - www.highpeak.gov.uk/tourism/accom/
www.thebmc.co.uk/outdoor/huts/huts.asp

Staffordshire Area
Don Whillans Memorial Hut - Rockhall Cottage, The Roaches. Bookings - Tel/Fax: 01433 639 368 mike@cdmsconsultancy.co.uk
Hen Cloud Campsite - Small site on the right, just before Hen Cloud.
Kinder Area
Edale - Newfold Farm, Grindsbrook, Edale, Hope Valley, S33 7ZD. Tel: 01433 670372
There are many other camp sites near Edale.
Bleaklow and Longdendale Area
Crowden Campsite - Hadfield, Glossop, Derbyshire. Tel: 01457 866057

Youth Hostels - There are YHAs in Buxton, Edale, Gradbach Mill (near Staffs crags) and Crowden.
Check - www.yha.org.uk

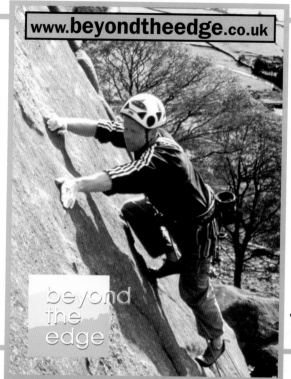

INFORMATION

GETTING AROUND

The easiest way to get to most of the areas covered in this book is by car and the approach descriptions are written assuming you have access to a car. However if you are trying to get to the crags by public transport here is a list of useful contacts which may help.

Trains - There is a regular service from Sheffield and Manchester to Edale from where the Kinder crags are within walking distance.

Buses - There is no one location to go for reliable information about buses, however most of the operators have reasonably efficient web sites.

National sites - www.pti.org.uk - www.firstgroup.com

Staffordshire - www.firstgroup.com/firstpmt

Derbyshire - www.derbysbus.net

South Yorkshire - www.sypte.co.uk

Merseyside - www.merseytravel.gov.uk

Manchester - www.stagecoachmanchester.co.uk - www.gmpte.gov.uk

CLIMBING SHOPS

The main cities of Manchester and Liverpool have big city centre outdoor shops like Cotswolds, Ellis Brigham and Blacks. More shops listed at - **www.ukclimbing.com/listings/shops.html**

Mountain Fever - Stoke-on-Trent. Tel: 01782 266137 **www.mountainfever.co.uk**

Alpenstock - Stockport. Tel: 0161 480 3660

Hitch 'n' Hike - Hope Valley. Tel: 01433 651013

Paul Braithwaite - Oldham. Tel: 0161 620 3900

Fell and Mountain - Accrington. Tel: 01254 390986

Outdoor Action - Blackburn. Tel: 01254 671 945

Adapt Outdoors - Liverpool. Tel: 0151 709 6498

Rocksport - The Edge, Sheffield. Tel: 0114 272 9733 and Banner Cross, Sheffield. Tel: 0114 266 7333 **www.sheffield-climbing.co.uk**

PUBS

There are many pubs in the areas covered by this book. The following is a selection of the favourite après-climb pubs contributed by readers of ROCKTALK. More pubs listed at - **www.pub-explorer.com**

Staffordshire Area

The Lazy Trout - In Meerbrook, which is the little village by the Tittesworth Reservoir Visitor Centre.

The Wilkes' Head - In Leek on St. Edward Street - first left after Market Square towards Macclesfield.

The Rock - Upper Hulme. Not as popular with climbers as one might expect.

Whaley Bridge Area (map page 108)

The Bee Hive - In Coombes below Castle Naze and Windgather.

The Navigation - In Whaley Bridge just by the Canal Basin.

The Walzing Weasel - In Hayfield (on the road between the main junction in Hayfield and New Mills). Excellent food and drink.

Kinder and Bleaklow Areas

The Nag's Head - In the centre of Edale. Good beer but ordinary food.

The Globe - High Street in Glossop. Live music, Pale Rider on tap.

Chew Area

The Church - Above Uppermill and near Running Hill Pits (map page 182). Wide selection of ales.

The King William - On the main road through Greenfield and has a good variety of real ales.

Lancashire Area (map page 232)

The Black Dog - Drive north up the A675 from Wilton 1 to Belmont. Turn left in the middle of the village at the signpost for Horwich.

Bob's Smithy - Continue past Brownstones from Wilton to the next junction.

The Dresser's Arms - In Wheelton (near Anglezarke and Denham) on the east side of the A674 between Chorley and Blackburn. Good range of guest beers.

Cheshire Area

The Unicorn - Just past the lights in Cronton village (map page 288). Good beer but no decent real ales.

CLIMBING WALLS

This book covers a very wide area of the country with many walls. Included on the list below are the best of these. More walls can be found on the UKClimbing web site at - www.ukclimbing.com/walls/

- Lead routes
- Bouldering
- Showers
- Cafe
- Shop

BLACKBURN

Boulderuk.com
10 Heaton Street, Blackburn. Tel: 01254 693056
Dedicated bouldering facility with every angle of board including 6m roof and 6m prow. Winter bouldering league. Coaching, masterclasses and 'Introduction to Bouldering' courses available. Drinks, snacks, chalk and accessories. Open Mon - Fri 10am - 10pm, Sat - Sun 10am - 8pm including bank holidays. www.boulderuk.com
ROCKFAX Rating - ★★★★ - Dedicated bouldering centre run by experts.

GLOSSOP

Glossop Leisure Centre
High Street East, Glossop. Tel: 01457 863223
Moulded concrete bouldering wall. Given a face lift in 1997 with new discs and 50 colour-coded problems. Open Mon - Fri 9am to 10:30pm, Sat 10am to 8pm, Sun 10am to 9pm.
ROCKFAX Rating - ★★ - Cramped little wall but with surprisingly good bouldering.

HUDDERSFIELD

Huddersfield Sports Centre
Southgate, Huddersfield. Tel: 01484 223630
Dedicated room in sports centre. Panelled leading wall and curved-resin bouldering wall. Open Mon to Fri 7:15am-10:30pm, weekends 9am-9pm.
ROCKFAX Rating - ★★★ - Good extensive centre with interesting bouldering feature.

LEEDS

The Leeds Wall - see advert on page 21
100a Gelderd Road, Leeds LS12 6BY Tel: 0113 234 1554
Large dedicated Climbing Centre. Gear shop with extensive range of boots, harnesses, ropes and hardwear. Variety of climbing walls for all ages and abilities. Taster sessions, beginner and improver courses available. Lizard Club for kids at weekends and during school holidays. Cafe and vending on site. Open Monday to Friday 10am till 10pm, weekends and bank holidays 10am till 8pm. www.theleedswall.co.uk
ROCKFAX Rating - ★★★★ - An excellent and extensive wall. Superb main steep lead wall but plenty of easier-angled walls as well and lots of quality bouldering.

LIVERPOOL

Awesome Walls Climbing Centre - see advert 293
St. Albans Church, Athol Street, Liverpool. Tel: 0151 2982422
Large dedicated Climbing Centre. Major 16.5m lead wall plus 12m free-standing pillar. Four separate bouldering areas with marked problems. Courses, gear hire, cafe and shop. Open Monday to Friday 12am-10pm, weekends and bank holidays 10am-6pm.
ROCKFAX Rating - ★★★★ - Excellent centre with superb steep lead wall which always has quality hard routes, plus extensive bouldering.

www.ep-uk.com

info@ep-uk.com

E/P Bolt-on holds

E/P Climbing Accessories

E/P Training Tools

Entre-Prises - Official Climbing Wall Supplier to the British Mountaineering Council

CLIMBING WALLS

PRESTON

West View Leisure Centre ▮ ▧ ▨ ▩ ▤

Ribbleton, PR1 5EP. Tel: 01772 796788
Dedicated room in sports centre. 10m leading wall and bouldering
wall. Major extensions planned. Open Mon - Fri 9am to 10:30pm,
weekends 8am to 10:15pm.
ROCKFAX Rating - ★★★ *- Good lead wall but current bouldering is*
poor however this will be improved with the new developments.

▮ - Lead routes

▨ - Bouldering

▤ - Showers

▧ - Cafe

▩ - Shop

SALFORD

Broughton RC ▨ ▤ ▧

Camp Street, Broughton. M7 9ZT. Tel: 0161 792 2375
Bencrete bouldering wall and DR free-standing boulder. Woodie. Open Sun - Fri 9am to
10pm, Sat - 9am to 3pm.
ROCKFAX Rating - ★★★ *- Thought by some to have the best hard bouldering around.*
Less to offer for the low-grade boulderer and no lead climbing.

SHEFFIELD

The Edge ▮ ▨ ▤ ▧ ▩ **- see advert opposite**

John Street, Sheffield. Tel: 0114 275 8899
Dedicated Climbing Centre. Up to 15m lead and top rope climbs with two articulating walls.
Extensive featured curved-resin bouldering area. Regular route changing. Popular winter
bouldering league. Huge Woody with 10m roof, stepped and 10/30/45 degree boards. Open
all week 10am-10.30pm (8pm weekends and bank holidays). Cafe and ROCKSPORT gear
shop open until 8:30pm weekdays and 6pm weekends.
www.sheffieldclimbing.co.uk - online gear ordering.
ROCKFAX Rating - ★★★ *- Excellent centre with good range of routes which are changed*
regularly and a quality bouldering room.

STOCKPORT

Rope Race ▮ ▨ ▤ ▧ ▩

Goyt Mill, Upper Hibbert Lane, Marple. Tel: 0161 426 0226
Dedicated Climbing Centre. Built and added to by various people since 1993. Curved resin
bouldering wall and separate cellar-style area. One 18m lead featured wall and plenty of
other panel lead walls. Open Mon - Fri 10am to 10pm, weekends 10am to 7pm.
ROCKFAX Rating - ★★★ *- Complex arrangement of walls. Good small bouldering section.*
Lead routes suit lower grade climbers.

WARRINGTON

The North West Face ▮ ▨ ▤ ▩ ▧

St. Anns Church, Winwick Road, Warrington, WA2 7NE. Tel: 01925 650022
Dedicated Climbing Centre. A 14-rope, 15m lead wall. Livingstone bouldering wall and lead
wall. Woody and campus board. Instruction available. Open all week 10am-10pm (Saturday
to 8pm only).
ROCKFAX Rating - ★★★★ *- Very popular centre with fine lead walls and bouldering.*

BMC GUIDEBOOKS

This book is a selective guidebook which means that it only covers the major buttresses, on the major crags, on the western side of the Peak District, up into Lancashire and across as far as Cheshire. A more-complete list of routes on many of these crags, and other smaller venues, is provided by the BMC with their series of guidebooks. For any frequent visitor to the area, these books will be found to be indispensable and will compliment the coverage given here.

STAFFORDSHIRE (2003)

The much-anticipated new guide to the Staffordshire crags is due to be published in 2003. The Roaches, Hen Cloud, Ramshaw, Newstones, Baldstones and The Churnet Valley, plus many other minor venues.

KINDER (1991)

Covers Windgather and Castle Naze, all the crags around the Kinder plateau and the Bleaklow and Longdendale areas.

CHEW VALLEY (1988)

Covers Wimberry, Rob's Rocks, Dovestones, Ravenstones, Standing Stones, Upperwood Quarry, Alderman, Running Hill Pits and Den Lane, plus half a dozen other crags in the Chew area.

LANCASHIRE (1999)

Covers Wilton, Brownstones, Anglezarke, Denham and Littleborough crags in greater detail than in this book, plus many more cliffs across Lancashire and Cumbria.

ON PEAK ROCK (1995 and 2002)

An attractive selected climb book covering the whole of the Peak District. Nothing from Lancashire and Cheshire.

There is no other current guidebook for the Cheshire Area crags.

ACCESS VOLUNTEERS

Access to crags is often something we take for granted; just turn up, park our cars and walk up to the crags without giving it a second thought. In reality a great deal of painstaking negotiation and effort is often needed to ensure that we climbers can enjoy unrestricted access to our favourite crags. This work is usually carried out by the BMC and its many volunteers who have spent countless hours over a period of years attending meetings, writing letters and generally presenting the case on behalf of all climbers. Please keep the efforts of these people in mind if you are contemplating ignoring the access advice given in this book, or on the BMC web site (**www.thebmc.co.uk/outdoor/rad/rad.asp**). One ignorant action by a single climber can undo years of volunteer effort.

Special thanks need to be made to Dave Bishop, Henry Folkard and Les Ainsworth who have all put many years of effort into negotiating access for the areas covered in this book.

ACT - The Access and Consevation Trust

A contribution is made from the proceeds of this guidebook to the ACT which supports access and conservation work across all the crags in the country.

Brian Rossiter and Dave Spencer climbing *Rhododendron Buttress* (E2 5c) at Hoghton Quarry. This quarry has regretably suffered from access restrictions in the last few years. *See page 260 for more details.*

ACKNOWLEDGEMENTS

Thanks to all the climbers I have visited these great cliffs over the years; early days with Pete Ackroyd, Colin Binks (still keen 30 years on), college times with Steve Warwick, Nigel Baker and Rich Watkinson, an on down the years with Martin Veale, Pete O'Donovan, Jim Rubery, Mike Appleton, Graham Parkes, Dave Spencer and Brian Rossiter.
Special thanks to Dave Gregory, who despite being a long-standing member of 'the establishment', saw the value of our guides and was supportive throughout. Whilst checking for the guide he took a ground fall from *Central Route* at the Roaches and without the superb efficiency of the Staffordshire Air Ambulance would probably not survived the experience. Happily he has bounced back into the rudest of rude and continues to enjoy these fine climbs!
Many thanks to Alan James - again. Having made the not inconsiderable efforts to 'negotiate' our right to produce these guidebooks we have moved forward again. His dedication and vision are the reason these guides are as good as they are, and without his manning of the 24 hour help-line we would still be some months away from the printers.
And last but far from least Sherri Davy has been supportive throughout the whole project, helping with the laborious work of checking first ascents etc... tramping into some of the more remote cliffs in the Peak and egging me on when long sessions in front of the Mac have begun to get a bit wearing - thanks for everything.

Chris Craggs - May 2003

This book brings together information from 5 separate areas all of which have long climbing and guidebook histories. The documenting of the information in these areas has been carried out by many people over the years and we would like to thank all of those that have made a contribution. We would also like to acknowledge the role of the BMC in co-ordinating the work of the Guidebook Committee since 1971.
We have received hundreds of comments and votes via the Gritstone Route Database as well as masses of other feedback. I would like to thank all those who have taken an interest in the Internet side of this guidebook and hope that you will continue to let us know what you think in the future. Thanks also to those who posted messages of support and encouragement during the great guidebook debate.
Thanks also to the following:
Carl Dawson and Graham Hoey for their excellent and diligent proof reading; to John Read for feedback on Hen Cloud, the Roaches and many hard routes; to Ben Tye and Martin Kocsis for feedback on the Whaley Bridge Area, Kinder and Bleaklow; to Kevin Thaw for his Chew comments; to Ian Fenton, Gareth Parry and Phil Kelly for their Lancashire feedback; to Pete Chadwick, Dave Ranby, Andy Farrell and Mark Hounslea for their Cheshire comments; to Karsten Kurz and Juan Varela-Nex for their translations; to Pete Chadwick, Ian Parnell, Alex Ekins, Chris Fryer, Mark Sharratt, John Henry Bull, Dave Clay, tom Briggs and Airlie Anderson for their excellent photographic contributions; to Nick Smith for his superb work on the Gritstone Route Database; to Andy Hyslop for business advice and feedback; to Mick Ryan for his many and varied contributions to Rocktalk and for his work in the US, and to my mother Liz James and father Mike James for their general help and support.
Once again Chris Craggs has proved that he can produce the goods both prolifically and efficiently and his dedication to make sure we got it right was superbly illustrated by his repeated trips to the most far-flung and highest spots of Western Grit. My thanks are due to him for once again being an excellent person to work with.
Finally thanks once again to my family. Hannah, Sam and Lydia have had to put up with Daddy's many extended sessions in front of the computer when really he should have been playing with them and special thanks to Henriette.

Alan James - May 2003

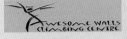

Damascus Crack (HS 4b) on the Upper Tier of the Roaches. *Page 61*

Upper Tor Wall (HS 4b) on Upper Tor, high above Edale, Kinder South. *Page 136*

Region	CRAG	No. of ROUTES	Mod	Diff	VDiff	HVD	Sev	HS	VS	HVS	E1	E2	E3	E4	E5	E6	E7
Staffordshire	The Roaches	282	3	13	21	14	29	16	35	33	24	19	17	26	13	15	
Staffordshire	Hen Cloud	94		1	6	1		1	16	12	13	4	5	9	8	8	
Staffordshire	Ramshaw	129		1	7	8	2	13	17	13	16	10	6	11	7	3	
Staffordshire	Newstones and Baldstones	43			3	5	4	3	7	6		3		2	1		
Whaley Bridge	Windgather	58	6	9	7	9	11	3	10	2	1						
Whaley Bridge	Castle Naze	61		1	12	3	11	5	11	9	6		1	2			
Whaley Bridge	New Mills Tor	17						1	2	2	5	1	3	4	2	2	
Kinder	Kinder South	103		5	9	2	8	7	19	6	15	10	5	6	7		2
Kinder	Kinder North	87		1	5	3	12	9	19	10	10	7	2	8			1
Kinder	Kinder Downfall	68		1	4	5	1	6	11	15	6	6	5	7			1
Bleaklow and Longdendale	Shining Clough	72		1	5	10	11	3	13	13		4	3	4	4		1
Bleaklow and Longdendale	Laddow	53		3	2	10	3	9	8	5	4	3	4	1	1		
Bleaklow and Longdendale	Tintwistle	23							5	6	2	1	4	3	2		
Bleaklow and Longdendale	Hobson Moor Quarry	39			3			1	2	4	5	4	7	3		6	4

proach walk	Sunshine or shade	Access	Green	Sheltered	Bouldering	SUMMARY	Page
10 min to 20 min	From mid morning		Green		Bouldering	The best of the west; hundreds of routes on superb rock in a magnificent setting. There is enough here to last most folks a lifetime. **Best feature:** the hand-jam on the lip of *The Sloth* and knowing it is almost in the bag.	46
10 min	From mid morning	Restrictions	Green			Towering battlements, high on the hill and with a great selection of crack and arete climbs. Often looks greener than it actually is. **Best feature:** the exciting exit from the groove of *Delstree* - not too rounded but a great teaser!	80
3 min to 10 min	Morning		Green			East facing and easy of access with plenty of wide cracks and rounded exits – a great venue for the proficient. **Best feature:** *Ramshaw Crack* – the classic man-eater!	90
5 min to 10 min	Morning				Bouldering	A couple of idyllic east facing venues, more famous for bouldering than climbing. **Best feature:** *Ray's Roof*, you loose skin just looking at it!	102
2 min	Afternoon					A delightful little outcrop, the most popular in the book. It faces the evening sun and is a great spot for a little gentle after-work action. **Best feature:** Being taken up *High Buttress Arete* as the perfect introduction to our sport.	110
5 min	Afternoon					A quiet crag with a nice set of crack climbs. A good place for pushing your grade. **Best feature:** the *Scoop* and the associated sense of history as you tiptoe across it.	117
5 min	Shade from trees			Sheltered	Bouldering	The Peak's attempt at an outdoor climbing wall and a great place for a workout. **Best feature:** the town is close enough for a brew when you get bushed.	124
60 min	Lots of sun				Bouldering	The sunny side of Kinder, big blobby outcrops of coarse rock in a lovely setting. It is possible to link several cliffs in one day by a walk along the rim. **Best feature:** *Upper Tor Wall*, a classic moorland experience.	130
60 min	Late summer evening only		Green			The dark side of Kinder, as remote as any in the area, with an hour's approach and a good chance of having the place to yourself. **Best feature:** Brother's Buttress; having made the effort to get here, do them all.	140
60 min	Afternoon		Green			Wild and windy, a place enjoyed by the pioneers and still well worth a visit. **Best feature:** a well-frozen Downfall - a once in a blue-moon event though!	150
60 min	Late summer evening only		Green			Bleaklow's finest, a set of tall buttress a long way from the road and facing north. A great hot weather retreat. **Best feature:** the crack of *Phoenix Climb*, Harding's finest offering on the high moors this side of the Peak.	160
50 min	Morning					Lofty and neglected buttresses, once at the cutting edge but now seeing little traffic. **Best feature:** the towering face of *Tower Face*.	168
20 min	Lots of sun					A neglected and grassy quarry with a good selection of climbs, most of which are hard, and all of which need more traffic. **Best feature:** *The Arete*, a real gem, balancy and bold; and well worth the walk up.	174
1 min	Afternoon			Sheltered	Bouldering	Western Grit's roadside cliff, catching the afternoon sun, it's great for a quick fix. **Best feature:** it is one minute from the car.	178

Region	CRAG	No. of ROUTES	GRADE RANGE													
			Mod	Diff	VDiff	HVD	Sev	HS	VS	HVS	E1	E2	E3	E4	E5	E6
Chew Valley	Wimberry	72		2	5	3	4	3	11	2	5	9	9	6	5	4
	Rob's Rocks	17	1		5	1	2	3	2	1		1	1			
	Dovestones Edge	83	2	6	11	4	12	5	19	5	6	7	1	2	2	
	Ravenstones	64	2	4	8		7	6	9	8	8	3	5	2	2	
	Standing Stones	53				3	7	1	9	8	8	7	5	5		
	Upperwood Quarry	25					1		3	5	4	1	3	4	4	
	Alderman	13		1	2		3	1	1	2	2	1				
	Running Hill Pits	88			1	2	5	8	14	15	13	10	5	7	6	1
	Den Lane Quarry	25					1	1	11	4	4	1		1		
Lancashire	Wilton 1	40					1	3	7	4	4	3	3	7	3	1
	Wilton 2 and 3	76	1	5	13		6	2	11	8	7	7	9	2	2	2
	Brownstones	43		1	4		2	2	7	6	8	6	5		2	
	Angelzarke	39			1		2	5	7	6	3	2	2	5	4	2
	Denham	15			1		2		2	2	3	3	1	1		
	Littleborough Area	69		1	4	3	2	6	19	9	6	9	2	2	3	
Cheshire	Helsby	94	2	2	8		10	3	12	7	6	12	11	11	8	1
	Frodsham	67			3	6	2	5	4	9	12	12	7	2	3	
	Pex Hill	120		2	5		3	3	18	21	16	20	14			7

Approach walk	Sunshine or shade	Access	Green	Sheltered	Bouldering	SUMMARY	Page
30 min	Shade all day		Green		Bouldering	A great cliff with soaring cracks and grooves as well as some intimidating blank faces. **Best feature:** *Route 1*, an historic classic, do it whatever grade you climb at.	184
40 min	Lots of sun					A short sunny outcrop in a wild setting and with a good collection of lower grade climbs. **Best feature:** finishing off the day with a trip up *Wilderness Gully East*.	192
30 min	Afternoon					A bit of a hike but a fine set of lower and middle grade climbs that catch the evening sun. Gritty after rain. **Best feature:** *Hanging Crack* - possibly the best of its genre in the Peak	194
25 min	Shade all day		Green			North-facing, green and miles from the road! The good side? A cracking set of climbs. **Best feature:** The arete on *True Grit*, set above acres of open moor.	202
10 min	Lots of sun					Sunny of aspect and easy of access, yet strangely neglected. **Best feature:** The unsung VS gem of *Fairy Nuff* - fair enough?	208
3 min	Morning	Restrictions				An east-facing quarry, high and cool and best used as a retreat on hot days. The climbs are generally hard. **Best feature:** the vast bulk of *Renaissance*.	214
15 min	All day					A tiny and very pleasant outcrop set above a massively steep slope. **Best feature:** the magical setting, with views as good as those from Bamford.	218
10 min	Afternoon		Green	Sheltered	Bouldering	A small series of quarries with some great rock. Unfortunately the aspect means that the place is often green. Best on warm summer evenings. **Best feature:** some hyper-technical offerings.	220
25 min	Morning			Sheltered		Only minutes from the road, an east facing quarry, with some steep jamming cracks and tough grades. **Best feature:** if you don't like the place it's not far back to the car!	228
5 min	Morning		Green	Sheltered		An impressive and imposing quarry with climbs to rival its Peak counterparts. Mostly hard routes. **Best feature:** *Cameo*, a superb introduction to the quarries, balancy and sustained, with just enough gear.	234
3 min	Morning	Restrictions		Sheltered		The friendly side of Lancashire quarries with many lower-grade climbs. **Best feature:** the rock-over by the peg on *Shiver's Arete*.	242
3 min	Afternoon			Sheltered	Bouldering	Roadside bouldering, short and sunny and on excellent rock. **Best feature:** an evening doing a bit of bouldering with a few mates.	250
5 min	Sun and shade			Sheltered		An easy accessible quarry with rock of variable quality. Popular with groups but plenty of good climbing if you seek it out. **Best feature:** *Golden Tower* in the evening sun.	254
1 min	Afternoon					A west-facing quarry, seconds from the road and with some pleasant climbs. **Best feature:** the striking groove of *Mohammed*...	260
20 min	Afternoon					Three venues, which are close enough together to be visited in the same day. **Best feature:** a warm evening sampling the delights of Blackstone Edge.	264
10 min	Afternoon		Green			Cheshire's finest, an excellent sandstone cliff that is sadly neglected. **Best feature:** *Flake Crack* is not too be missed.	272
10 min	Afternoon		Green		Bouldering	Strenuous bouldering in a wooded setting, a great place for a full body work out (reaches the parts that Pex Hill doesn't). **Best feature:** ambling back down to the car with sore fingers and weary forearms.	282
5 min	Sun and shade			Sheltered	Bouldering	Merseyside's own outdoor climbing wall, and a cracker it is too. A place designed to hone technique and sharpen finger strengthen. **Best feature:** choose your traverse and pump till you drop!	288

THE TOP 200

The following list contains 200 of the best routes on the Western edges and quarries arranged in a very approximate order of difficulty. This should provide you with hours of entertainment as you see how high up the list you can tick.

1st Class (GOLD AWARD)
A clean lead, on-sight, bottom up, no pre-placed gear, no weighting the gear.
2nd Class (SILVER AWARD)
Led with a fall but returned to the ground.
Led after pre-practice on a top-rope (headpoint).
Followed the route (seconding or top roping) first try without weighting the gear or rope.
3rd ....
"Covered the ground". Sat on a runner, top-roped with falls, winched, human pyramid, stood in slings, used a ladder.

Alan James contemplating *Black Magic* (E5 6b) at Pex Hill. *Page 296*

Jon Burnsall on *Commander Energy* (E2 5c) on the Roaches Lower Tier. *Page 57* Photo: Chris Fryer

Mike Appleton on *Turtle* (E1 5b) at Upperwood Quarry. *Page 217*

Dave Spencer climbing *Berties Bugbear* (S 4a) at Wimberry. *Page 188*

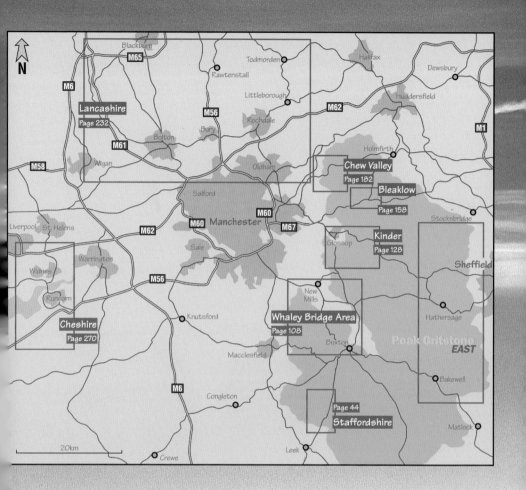

N

M65

M6

Lancashire
Page 232

M56

M61

M58

M62

M60 Manchester

M60

M67

M56

M6

20km

Blackburn

Rawtenstall

Todmorden

Halifax

Dewsbury

Littleborough

Huddersfield

M62

Rochdale

Bury

Bolton

Holmfirth

Oldham

Chew Valley
Page 182

Bleaklow
Page 158

Stocksbridge

Salford

Sale

Glossop

Kinder
Page 128

Sheffield

Liverpool St. Helens

Widnes

Warrington

New
Mills

Runcorn

Knutsford

Whaley Bridge Area
Page 108

Hathersage

Peak Gritstone
EAST

Cheshire
Page 270

Buxton

Macclesfield

Bakewell

Congleton

Page 44

Matlock

Staffordshire

Crewe

Leek

End of a great day. Climbers walking off *Valkyrie* at the Roaches.

STAFFORDSHIRE

Buxton

Baldstones

Newstones

A53

Ramshaw

Five Clouds

Roaches

Hen Cloud

The Rock (pub)

Campsite and cafe

Upper Hulme

Leek

About 1km

N

THE ROACHES

The Roaches is the finest and most popular of all of the Western Edges and with good reason; there are hundreds of routes on offer of every imaginable style. Here are climbs from the most amiable of ambles through to some of the hardest routes around.

The cliff splits easily into sections. The **Lower Tier** is partly sheltered by a stand of ancient pine trees and is home to some great crack climbs and a superb set of pebbly walls and slabs. Up the steps there is the **Upper Tier**; big and brassy, throwing down a challenge that is hard to resist, with a host of fine climbs, many of a reasonable grade - and many harder ones too. Straggling away leftwards is the series of isolated buttresses known as **The Skyline**. Most climbers arrive here quite late in their Roaches career and then wonder what took them so long. Although relatively 'small beer' compared to the rest of the cliff, the rock is superb, the setting is great and the outcrops are normally much quieter than elsewhere in the area. In front of and below the rest of the cliffs, is the bumpy ridge of **The Five Clouds**. Again, the amount of climbing here is limited but this is more than made up for by its quality. Individual recommendations at the Roaches are largely a matter of choice but for starters do *Pedestal Route* (HVD 4a), *Black and Tans* (Sev 4a), *Valkyrie* (VS 4c), *Saul's Crack* (HVS 5a), and *The Sloth* (HVS 5a) and you should go away well satisfied and with just a little idea of the quality of the climbing available on this superb cliff.

BOULDERING - There is plenty of bouldering at the Roaches. Some spots are indicated on the crag maps. Full coverage is given in the 1998 Peak Bouldering ROCKFAX.

APPROACH Also see map on page 44

There is parking for 75 cars on the roadside lay-by under the cliff. If this is full (it happens very early on fine summer weekends), there are two alternatives. Option 1 is to leave the car at the Park and Ride scheme based on the extensive parking at Tittesworth Reservoir (drive towards Leek and keep an eye out for the signs). The other option is some limited parking below the towers of Hen Cloud where there is usually space (about 25 cars in two spots) and take the 15 minute walk to the cliff, either via the road or following the track across the fields. The astute will realise there are easier ways to reach the far end of The Skyline other than the long walk from the regular parking spot. More details are given with the individual sections in the following pages.

WARNING - If you can't park in the designated spots below the Roaches, and you attempt to squeeze the car onto a grass verge, then you will be ticketed.

CONDITIONS

The Lower Tier tends to be green after rain or in the winter partly because of the trees, and partly because of it being at a lower altitude than the rest of the cliff. By the same logic, it is sheltered from the worst of the weather and offers shade (at least at the base of the wall) in high summer. The Upper Tier and The Skyline are clean and rapid-drying but can get a bit blowy when the weather is wild.

OTHER GUIDEBOOKS - A more complete list of routes at The Roaches is published in the BMC *Staffordshire* guidebook.

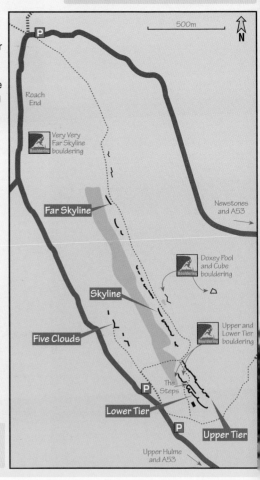

Descent down steps

From mid morning | **10 min** | **Green**

Teck Crack Area

Side tabs: Staffordshire | Whaley Bridge | Kinder | Bleaklow | Chew | Lancashire | Cheshire | Newstones | Ramshaw | Hen Cloud | Roaches

SLIPPERY JIM

To the left of the steps is a series of short undercut walls with good (and popular) bouldering and some worthwhile though hard climbs. On the far left is the open groove of *Slippery Jim* with half a dozen good pebble-pulling offerings to either side.

❶ Apache Dawn **E5 6c**
8m. The pebbly wall on the left, starting at the small cigar-shaped pod and scratching a way to a rounded finish. The weather cornice may need pushing back. Probably uses some of the same holds as *Catastrophe International*. High in the grade.
FA. Julian Lines 1993

❷ Catastrophe Internationale **E5 6c**
8m. From the right-hand end of the long elongated slot, climb straight up the steep wall by hard pulls on pebbles and desperate friction. The landing is hard. *Apache Internationale* is probably the easiest method of getting up the wall and *Catastrophe Dawn* the hardest!
FA. Nick Dixon 1985

❸ Slippery Jim . . . . **HVS 5b**
8m. The awkward and often rather green groove is squirmed to a rounded exit. The route is not popular, partly because of where it is and partly because it's hard! Usually feels like E1.
FA. Don Whillans 1958

❹ Bareback Rider **E4 6b**
8m. Climb the rounded arete on its right-hand side by technical laying away to a grasping exit. Despite the name, an *'a cheval'* approach is not a good idea, though a cavalier one might help!
FA. Dave Jones 1980

❺ K.P. Nuts **E7 6c**
10m. A desperate bouldery Nadin route. Safe with a good spotting team and there is some gear in the break for the crux. Start left of *Ascent of Man* and climb to the break (pre-placed wires on first ascent). Undercut up and pull over, using whatever pebbles you can find, to the finish of *Ascent of Man*.
FA. Simon Nadin 1989

❻ Ascent of Man **E3 6a**
10m. A mini-classic, intense and varied, packing a lot of climbing into a short distance. Gain the undercut flake with difficulty and follow it to its end where scary friction moves lead leftwards up a ramp to easy ground. Best climbed when the boggy area below the route is in prime condition, making falling off even more undesirable than normal.
FA. Andrew Woodward 1974

❼ Ascent of Woman **E3 6a**
10m. The right-hand start and direct finish to *Ascent of Man* goes at about the same grade although it is less popular.

❽ Days of Future Passed **E3 6b**
10m. The rounded arete leads by laybacking to a tough, though well-protected, mantelshelf finale.
FA. Andrew Woodward 1974

❾ The Aspirant **E3 5c**
8m. Climb the centre of the left-hand side-wall of the gully, passing a useful flake to an exit on the left.
FA. Gary Gibson 1978

47

TECK CRACK AREA
The tallest buttress left of the steps has a couple of reasonably graded routes (as long as you like awkward cracks) and more desperate climbing on slopers and pebbles.

Crystal Grazer Area

The Upper Tier

From mid morning | 10 min | Green

---

① Ackit . . . . **HVS 5b**
14m. Follow the right-trending flake by awkward laybacking (good gear is available but it is tricky to place) to bulges, which are crossed by a steep pull and an exit out left. A good line.
FA. Don Whillans 1958 Direct Finish Tony Barley 1967

② Just For Today **E6 7a**
16m. The wall and slab. The crucial huge stretch for a sloper is protected by a side runner in *Ackit*, placed on route. Finish direct.
FA. Paul Clark 1994

③ Barriers in Time **E6 6b**
16m. The elegant arete is superb but slightly harder for shorties. Make a tricky start to reach the first break then tackle the arete above by some hard laybacking. Friends in the second break may permit a long scraping fall to be taken. The last reach will remain in your memory for a long time! Said to be low in the grade.
FA. Simon Nadin 1983

④ Sunday at Chapel **E6 6c**
10m. The steep right-hand side of the arete is bold and slappy to a final crack. A distant side runner in *Ackit* was used on the first ascent. Finish up *Barriers in Time* if you want an even more intense experience.
FA. Nick Dixon 1988

⑤ Ant Lives . . . . **V6 (6c)**
8m. Start by a 'fun' mantelshelf then make a powerful move to the ledge before galloping off rightwards.
FA. Nick Dixon 1987

⑥ Inertia Reel **V6 (6c**
Attain a small flake and the rounded ledges above from a minute undercut in the low break. Escape right or jump off!
FA. Johnny Dawes 1986

⑦ Teck Crack Direct . . **V5 (6b**
Reach the thin crack from the left by hard moves and then a rapid hand-traverse.

⑧ Teck Crack Super Direct **V7 (6c**
Gain the thin crack from directly below making a hideous pull on a poor crack and pebbles.

⑨ The Dignity of Labour . . **V5 (6b**
From the right-hand arete, move left to holds and yet another fearsome mantelshelf finish. Virtually a route.
FA. Nick Dixon 1983

⑩ Teck Crack **E1 5c**
1) **4a, 10m.** Climb the grotty gully and cross the slab leftwards to a stance at the foot of the steep crack.
2) **5c, 14m.** Jam and layback the crack (5b to grit gurus?) to a pleasant, seated stance by a plaque that explains the route's name, which is not to do with it being technical!
FA. Joe Brown 1958

⑪ Inertia Reel Traverse **V11 (6c**
The well-chalked low-level traverse is a classic. About as pump and as rounded as they come.
FA. Jerry Moffatt 1980s

From mid morning | 10 min | Green

Descent

Teck Crack Area

CRYSTAL GRAZER
An immaculate hanging slab which has one of the hardest and blankest routes in the area. With the buttress being so close to the steps, you might expect the routes to be popular - well they aren't!

Staffordshire · Whaley Bridge · Kinder · Bleaklow · Chew · Lancashire · Cheshire

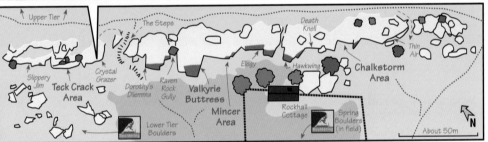

Upper Tier
The Steps
Death Knell
Thin Air
Slippery Jim | Crystal Grazer | Teck Crack Area | Dorothy's Dilemma | Raven Rock Gully | Valkyrie Buttress | Elegy | Hawkwing | Chalkstorm Area
Mincer Area
Lower Tier Boulders
Rockhall Cottage
Spring Boulders (in field)
About 50m
N

⑫ Lightning Crack . . . . . **HVS 5b**
1) 5b, 10m. Quickly gain the thin hanging crack with difficulty and follow it to ledges and a belay.
2) 4c, 15m. The wall on the left is climbed via a rounded mantelshelf. The pitch can be improved by hand-traversing the rounded pod that runs out towards the arete just below the top.

⑬ Mushin' **V12**
The direct start to *Pindles Numb* is one of the hardest boulder problems in the Peak. Use a glued undercut above the break to reach a cluster of shallow pockets. Pull up on these into the groove above.
FA. Ben Moon 1990s

⑭ Pindles Numb **E4 6b**
10m. Climb leftwards from the 'welcoming' holly via a finger traverse and pull into the leaning corner with difficulty. Once established, finish easily.
FA. Nick Dixon 1984

⑮ Crystal Grazer **E5 6a**
10m. Gain the lip of the roof from the diagonal crack on the right then foot traverse left to a shallow groove. Climb the left-hand side of this to finish. Thought by some to be 6b.
FA. Phil Burke 1982

⑯ A Fist Full of Crystals . . . **E6 6b**
12m. Follow *Crystal Grazer* to the groove and balance up this with some trepidation and nothing in the way of gear. Very blind.
FA. Nick Dixon 1983

⑰ Doug **E8 6c**
12m. Start as for the last two routes but climb the right-hand edge of the buttress to a delicate finale up a shallow scoop. Popping pebbles haven't helped. Named after cottage's most famous resident.
FA. Nick Dixon 1986

⑱ Fred's Cafe . . . . **VS 5a**
10m. The right-slanting crack leads awkwardly to an easy slab. Well-protected but a thrash and often choked with pine needles.
FA. Gary Gibson 1978

Newstones · Ramshaw · Hen Cloud · Roaches

DOROTHY'S DILEMMA

To the right of the stone steps the Lower Tier thrusts forward with one of the finest buttresses on grit. The big names are further right, but the left-hand area is home to many routes which are only marginally less classic.

1 Yong Arete . . . . **S 3c**
8m. The scooped arete just to the right of the steps is climbed on well-scratched holds after a precarious start. Delicate and without too much protection.

2 Poisonous Python . . . . **HVS 5b**
8m. Although short-lived, the thin snaking-crack on the front of the buttress has good moves and good runners.
FA. Gary Gibson 1978

3 Yong . . . . **HVD 4a**
10m. The mild jamming crack has good hidden layaway holds. Western Grit's answer to Froggatt's renowned *Heather Wall*.

4 Something Better Change **E2 5b**
10m. The centre of the delicate slab on small but improved holds. The exit is very rounded and avoiding the crack to the left requires will-power especially near the top. A (sensible?) side runner in *Yong* lowers the grade a couple of notches.
FA. Gary Gibson 1978

5 Wisecrack . . . . **VS 4b**
8m. The steep diagonal crack in the face.

6 Hypothesis . . . . **HVS 5b**
10m. Small wires protect the delicate left-hand arete.
FA. Colin Foord 1968

7 Destination Earth **E7 6b**
12m. The slab is bold and precarious; a side runner (placed on route) may stop you repeating the first ascensionist's bouncing trick but then the route is only really worth E4.
FA. Simon Nadin 1984

8 Cannonball Crack . . . . **S 4b**
12m. The wide crack is awkward to start and leads to a left-wards exit over a chockstone. Trivia Question: how many other *Cannonball Cracks* are there in the Peak?

9 Graffiti **E1 5b**
16m. Start up the arete and move left to a groove and crack which used to be the **Direct Finish** to *Cannonball Crack* before it was usurped.
FA. Gary Gibson 1978

10 Dorothy's Dilemma . . . **E1 5a**
18m. The fine delicate arete is not over endowed with gear and requires commitment and neat footwork. Start on the left, move onto the front face (wires) then press on and stay cool.
FA. Joe Brown, Slim Sorrell, Dorothy Sorrell 1951

From mid morning | 10 min | Green

Descent down steps

Valkyrie Area

RAVEN ROCK GULLY

The deep dark rift that splits the buttress has some worthwhile if gloomy climbs from the constricted struggles of the *Raven Rock Gully* routes to the glorious jamming of *Crack of Gloom*. From here on, we have grit on a grand scale.

---

⑪ Bengal Buttress . . . . **HVS 4c**

28m. Climb the left arete of the buttress past holes to a ledge then trend right via a grassy ledge to the right-hand arete. Up this delicately (poor protection) then step left to finish up a short flake crack. Mild at the grade but with a serious crucial section that requires a careful approach.
FA. Ivan Waller 1930

⑫ Schoolies **E3 5c**

20m. Good bold climbing though escapable. Climb the bulges (reachy) then straight up the centre of the face to the final crack of *Bengal Buttress*.
FA. Phil Burke 1978

⑬ Crack of Gloom . . . **E1 5b**

20m. The ever-leaning crack in the left-hand side of the gully would be a mega-classic in a more open setting. Here it is well-named, moody and magnificent. Jam the never-ending series of overhangs to the great boulder blocking the rift then make a tricky traverse left to a difficult exit where big fists sure help.
FA. Joe Brown 1958

⑭ Raven Rock Gully Left-hand . . . **VS 4b**

20m. The back of the great rift has a crack/groove in each angle. The long steep groove on the left leads by sustained climbing to an exit through the small gap.
FA. Dave Salt 1969

⑮ Raven Rock Gully . . . . . . **Diff**

20m. The deep and gloomy rift to a tight and scruffy exit through the manhole. A worthwhile and atmospheric route that is a lot easier than it looks from below.
FA. JW Puttrell 1901

⑯ Swinger . . . . **VS 4c**

20m. The steep and neglected crack in the right wall of the gully leads to the upper section of *Via Dolorosa*.

⑰ Sidewinder **E5 6a**

24m. A devious oddity that grapples with the left-hand edge of the great roof. From the base of the crack of *Swinger*, ape right and climb a groove to a possible stance under the giant overhang. A flake on the left leads past the lip then stretch right, passing a flake, to climb the arete.
FA. Phil Burke 1980

⑱ Via Dolorosa . . . . **VS 4c**

32m. A long and wandering trip up the huge buttress, which can be split into three pitches if required. Start below a battered holly and climb glazed rock (**4c**) to the roof. Escape out left passing the holly to ledges (**4a** - possible stance) then climb to the left-hand corner of the huge roof (choice of ways). Continue to runners (big Hex up and left) then reach a flake on the right wall of the gully with difficulty. Once established, finish out right on the front of the buttress (**4c**).
FA. Morley Wood early 1920s!

VALKYRIE BUTTRESS

A huge Easter Island statue of a buttress, perhaps the single most imposing bit of grit in the country, with routes to match. *Valkyrie* may just be the best VS on grit, the *Direct* is only marginally inferior and the sustained jamming on *Matinee* is glorious, especially for the uninitiated who usually get mauled!

① Valkyrie Direct . . . . [icons] **HVS 5b**
28m. A long and elegant pitch up the steep jamming cracks in the arete. Climb the crack and the bulges to a rest at the base of the flake on the regular climb. Finish leftwards up this.
FA. Joe Brown, Don Whillans (The Dream Team) 1951

② Matinee . . . . [icons] **HVS 5b**
24m. The lower crack is almost always damp and usually smelly. Ignore this fact and jam up it to a (possible) stance on the giant flake. The continuation is awkward, especially the fist-grinding belly-flop into the wider finishing section.
FA. Brown and Whillans 1951, named after the astounded audience.

③ Valkyrie . . . . [icons] **VS 4c**
A wandering climb of great quality - the archetypical 'must-do'!
1) 4b, 15m. Climb the slabby groove to its top then traverse left to a stance on giant jammed blocks with a variety of belays.
2) 4c, 25m. Climb on to the tip of flake (a sling on it stops the rope jamming down its back) and descend its edge (scary) until a hidden foothold gives some respite. Gain a narrow crease on the left and teeter along this to access the front face of the buttress. One tricky move leads to the slabby finish. Great care is needed with the rope to avoid it jamming and to protect the second adequately. Thought by many to be HVS. *Photo page 11.*
FA. Peter Harding 1946

④ Northern Comfort . . [icons] **E6 6c**
14m. From the tip of the *Valkyrie* flake, climb the wall past some useful flakes to a finish up the left arete; bold and very reachy.
FA. Niall Grimes 1996

⑤ Licence to Run . . . . . . [icons] **E4 6a**
12m. The right-trending flakes in the wall above the *Valkyrie* stance are pumpy though good gear is available if you can stop!
FA. Gary Gibson (1 rest) 1980 FFA. Pete O'Donovan 1980

⑥ Licence to Lust . . . . [icons] **E4 6a**
12m. A counter-diagonal across the wall, utilising the same holds and runners in the central section at *L2R*.
FA. John Allen 1987

MINCER AREA

⑦ Eugene's Axe . . . . . . [icons] **E2 5c**
20m. Climb the rounded arete from a big flake to steeper rock then take the wall above, left then right, then finally left again.
FA. John Codling 1979

⑧ Pebbledash . . . . [icons] **HVS 5a**
1) 5a, 10m. Head up the steep rock then pad left at the limit of HVS friction and move left to a stance in the corner.
2) 4b, 8m. Finish up the main groove or the flake to its left.
FA. Dave Salt 1969

⑨ Secrets of Dance . . [icons] **E4 6a**
20m. Follow the groove of *Pebbledash* then climb the disap-pearing crack in the steep wall until a right-trending ramp can be followed rapidly to easy ground.
FA. Simon Nadin 1984

Change in viewing angle

MINCER AREA

Named after the classic (and awkward) crack climb, the area is now better known for its superb collection of slab climbs. Technical in all cases and bold in most, you are unlikely to have to queue for these particular gems.

10 Against the Grain . . 🎱🕸️🔣 ☐ **E6 7a**
20m. Intense. Climb the easy flake and thin curving crack to where it withers then move left and climb the wall on tiny holds (each move is a touch harder then the last) to finish, grasping just a little, up the ramp of *Secrets of Dance*. E5 for gurus.
FA. Simon Nadin 1986

11 Thing on a Spring . . 🔣🕸️🔳 ☐ **E6 7a**
20m. Another desperate route up the wall above the traverse of *The Swan* with a safe fall-out zone beneath very hard wall climbing up a slight ramp. From the thin crack, teeter across the wall diagonally rightwards using a crucial pebble (which did come off but has been glued back on) and a ramp for the feet to desperately rounded ledges and a final easy crack.
FA. Simon Nadin 1986

12 The Swan . . . . . . 🔣🗡️🔳▌ ☐ **E3 5c**
26m. An elegant pitch requiring commitment on the traverse. Climb thin cracks to where they fade, place a high runner, then tiptoe round the bulge and traverse right until a stiff pull is needed to reach the continuation crack. A runner on the tree to the right can be used to shorten the pendulum if you muff the crux. Swing right and finish up the excellent jamming crack.
Up the Swanee, E4 5c. As for *The Swan* but make the traverse with your feet in the break instead of your hands. Twice as gripping as *The Swan* and especially so for the tall.
FA. John Gosling (why didn't he call it The Goose?) one peg 1969
FFA. Ron Fawcett 1977. FA. Up the Swanee John Yates 1970

13 Swan Bank . . . . . . 🔳🔘▌ ☐ **E4 5c**
20m. Start up *The Mincer* to below the roof then step left to a flake and make bold and stretchy moves up to the end of the traverse of *The Swan*. Finish rapidly up this.
FA. Gary Gibson 1981

14 The Mincer . . . . 🔳🗡️ ☐ **HVS 5b**
24m. Boulder up into the hanging groove then mince rightwards awkwardly (especially if you're long-legged) to pass the nose and climb the excellent gradually-widening cracks above.
FA. Joe Brown, Don Whillans 1981

15 Smear Test . . . . . . 🔳🔳🕸️🔳 ☐ **E3 6a**
12m. Approach via the hanging groove (actually *Mincer Direct*) then from a chockstone runner - or belay - sketch right across the slight weakness in the slab, to reach the finger crack and a short sprint to safety. Sticky rubber is a big help on this one!
FA. Gabe Regan 1977

16 Pincer . . . . 🔳🔘🕸️ ☐ **VS 5a**
20m. Climb the short steep wall (bouldery crux) to a rest below the bulges then move rightwards to the shrubby gully. Up this to a traverse out left leading to a short finger and hand crack. Sadly, after the start, the route is only about Severe.

17 Kicking Bird . . . . 🎱🕸️ ☐ **E4 6a**
20m. Good but devious, and hard! Pull through the bulge then cross the overhang by baffling moves to access the base of the slab. Climb *The Mincer* a short distance, step back onto the slab as for *Smear Test* but climb up and right (almost as far as the crack – side runner) then finish back leftwards.
FA. Al Simpson, Dave Jones (alts) 1978

18 Bloodstone . . . . . . 🎱🕸️🔳 ☐ **E5 6b**
18m. Avoids the loop on the previous climb by a direct ascent of the desperate slab which eases with height. Kit under the overlap and a large Friend low in *The Mincer* is all you get.
FA. Simon Nadin 1983

19 Bloodspeed . . . 🎱🗡️🕸️🔳 ☐ **E6 6b**
18m. Start as for *Kicking Bird*, pull through the overlap then climb the slab to the right to the base of the thin crack on *Smear Test*. Gear under overlap and low in *The Mincer* are all that protect you as you shuffle rightwards on poor smears and minimal handholds, trying not to think of your rope sawing on the lip in the event of a fall. A bit easier for the tall, but still 6b!
FA. Simon Nadin 1984

Staffordshire

Whaley Bridge

Kinder

Bleaklow

Chew

Lancashire

Cheshire

Newstones

Ramshaw

Hen Cloud

Roaches

←- - Descent down steps

From mid morning | 10 min | Green

Hawkwing Area

ELEGY
A magnificent slab route or two to get the heart pounding and a selection of awkward and arduous crack climbs. Also worthy of note are two tough offerings, one with the longest name on gritstone and one with the hardest mantelshelf anywhere on the planet - allegedly!

① **Guano Gully** .... ☐ **S 4b**
14m. The narrowing crack leading to an open groove up and right is a less smelly experience than you might be expecting. Once past the crucial overhang, things ease dramatically.

② **Mousey's Mistake** .... ◤☐ **E2 5b**
14m. Climb the right-hand side of the gully to the roof then step out above the overhang and climb the delicate left-hand side of the *Elegy* slab. Side runners lower the stress factor.
FA. Dave Jones 1978

③ **A Little Peculiar** .... ▨◲☐ **E6 7a**
14m. The direct over the imposing roof features the hardest mantelshelf in the world - a free hanging one-armed flip, with no footholds!! Good holds lead to the lip but above there is precious little with which to make progress. If you manage the desperate gymnastics, casually saunter up *Elegy* to finish, or more in keeping step right and pad up *Clive Coolhead*. Protected by side-runners, (a chockstone in the crack) and RPs low down. Votes on the database suggested the route might be E6 7b, but as it has only had one ascent - who would know?
FA. Paul Higginson 1990s

④ **Elegy** .... ▨◲☐ **E2 5c**
16m. Perhaps the best slab route in Western Grit! Climb the awkward overhanging corner to the base of the upper crack and large cams. Balance left to the tantalising flake and if you are completely baffled, try a bit of lateral thinking. Follow the creaky flake to its end (slightly dubious runners) then weave a way up the final bald slab connecting a set of small 'blisters' by brilliantly intense climbing. *Photo page 21.*
FA. Mike Simpkins (tension to start) 1960. FFA. John Yates 1969

⑤ **Clive Coolhead Realises the Excitement of Knowing You May be the Author of Your Own Death is More Intense Than Orgasm** ☐◲▨☐ **E5 6b**
14m. Strange name - good route! The right side of the *Elegy* slab is at the limit of friction and the grade varies from E4 to E6 depending on how high you put the side runner in *The Bulger*. A wire in *Elegy* can also be used to reduce the swing potential.
FA. Nick Dixon 1983

⑥ **The Bulger** .... ▨◲☐ **VS 4c**
14m. The leaning corner (as for *Elegy*), and the awkward wide crack above, give an unsatisfying struggle. Bridge the lower section and swim up the final bit - all very graunchy.
FA. Joe Brown, Don Whillans 1951

⑦ **Fledgling's Climb** .... ▨◲☐ **HS 4a**
14m. Starting in the gully, traverse left above the overhang then climb the wall and the well-positioned rib. Not well-protected, rather polished, and can be green; care required by fledglings.

⑧ **Little Chimney** .... ☐ **Mod**
10m. The little chimney in the back left-hand corner of the bay is quite unremarkable but offers a blocky quick tick.

Descent down steps

Elegy Area

Change in viewing angle

HAWKWING

Another fine jutting buttress, with a couple of belting classics and some rather tricky crack climbs. *Hawkwing* is the real gem here, though the awkward fissure of *Kestrel Cracks* sees (many) more ascents. The enticing pockets of *Logical Progression* are for the hard-core only.

⑨ Battery Crack . . . . **VS 4b**
10m. Climb the awkward crack rising from the recess and head into the groove above. A successful ascent will leave you beached and battered below the final section of *Lucas Chimney*. A great route for masochists!

⑩ Lucas Chimney . . . . **S 4a**
10m. The narrow rift in the main angle is a well-protected struggle and the leftward exit is a pig; the best advice is to try staying high. Often green early in the season or after rain, in which case it is worthy of a manky HS 4c.

⑪ Hawkwing **E1 5b**
22m. An fine route up an elegant buttress. Start at the left arete then spiral up and right following cracks to the opposite arete. Place small wires before following the parallel diagonal cracks to an exposed and awkward finale back on the left-hand arete. Excellent throughout and very varied climbing.
FA. Gary Gibson 1978

⑫ Carrion **E3 5c**
18m. Climb the centre of the front face direct, starting over the butch overhang, crossing the diagonal cracks and finishing with a flourish at a notch in the final narrow wall. A bit of a non-line but with some fine climbing if you are strict!
FA. Gary Gibson 1980

⑬ Kestrel Crack . . . . . . **VS 4b**
20m. A well-rounded 'classic' though too much of a struggle to be a real three star outing. The striking hanging fissure has a brace of awkward starts (easiest on the left) and a wide awkward exit. A couple of tricky-to-thread chockstones help protect the main difficulties of the route.

⑭ Headless Horseman **E1 5b**
20m. Climb *Kestrel Cracks* to the first thread then traverse out to the arete and teeter up this, heart in mouth.
FA. Jonny Woodward 1978

⑮ Logical Progression . . . **E7 6c**
20m. The hanging lower arete just right of the *Headless Horseman* traverse is reached via a very hard traverse from the right to the enticing pockets (crux) and a lovely balancy move to stand up in them. The arete above is much easier. Good Friends under the roof protect the crux (back-rope useful) and a very poor Friend in the right-hand pocket serves the rest.
FA. Sam Whittaker 1998

⑯ Flimney . . . . **S 4a**
18m. The flake and groove passing to the left of the rhododendrons is approached via the gymnastic bulge or flake just right. Plough through the vegetation to the final dirty groove. It should perhaps have been called *Floove*!

Staffordshire

Whaley Bridge

Kinder

Bleaklow

Chew

Lancashire

Cheshire

Newstones

Ramshaw

Hen Cloud

Roaches

Logical Progression arete

From mid morning | 10 min | Green

Descent either way

Chalkstorm slab

DEATH KNELL

One of the less popular sectors of the Lower Tier, though the superb and harrowing *Death Knell* is worth seeking out if you are up to the challenge. *Flake Chimney* gives a memorable beginner's route that requires consideration to protect ones second on the rope if you want them to climb again!

❶ Amaranth **E4 5c**
12m. Climb the blunt arete (as for *Death Knell*) and step left onto the slab and balance carefully up this, avoiding the shrubs.
FA. Gary Gibson 1979

❷ Death Knell **E4 5c**
14m. A classic frightener. Climb the blunt rib above the rhododendrons delicately to the bulges and make committing moves up and right to reach a crack, runners and easy ground - phew.
FA. John Yates 1970

❸ Rhodren .... **HVS 5b**
12m. A mini-*Mincer* and popular, though this one is easier for the tall. From the foot of the odd perched flake, climb the grungy groove to the overhang and layback rightwards round this to easy ground.
FA. Joe Brown 1958

❹ Flake Chimney .... **Diff**
14m. Traverse the crest of the huge perched flake (walk across or ride it - the choice is yours) to reach an easy groove. Awkward to protect so be wary of scaring beginners!

❺ Straight Crack .... **HS 4a**
10m. Bridge the leaning corner (don't push too hard on the flake) and then step left to reach the eponymous fissure, thankfully above the wide and potentially awkward lower section.

❻ Punch **E3 6b**
14m. Force a way into the hanging groove with great difficulty (overhead gear) then finish more easily through the shrubbery.
FFA. Jonny Woodward 1978

❼ Choka **E1 5c**
12m. Pull through the roof using the thin crack and continue up its wider extension.
FA. Joe Brown (1 point of aid) 1958

ROCKHALL COTTAGE

The quaint little house just below the cliff is built into the boulders and for some years was the home of Doug, self-styled Lord of the Roaches. After he moved out the place was bought by the BMC and named the *Whillans' Memorial Hut* in memory of one of the greatest gritstone pioneers. See booking information on page 20.

CHALKSTORM AREA

Sadly the very popular easy routes here have been rather battered to death by never-ending top-roping sessions, simply because they are so close to the road.
Of the harder offerings, both *Commander Energy* and *Hunky Dory* are well worthwhile and you have the added extra of baffled school kids saying "Sir, sir, sir, can we do that one next, can we, can we, please?"
The route after which the area is named has generated more hot air on the issue of grading than probably any other in the country. It is graded E4 for an on-sight ascent and no other, only then can you truly offer an opinion!

⑧ Circuit Breaker 🔝🎏 ☐ E3 6a
10m. Climb the fingery, bulging arete then the flake above to the final delicate slab perched on the front of the buttress.
FA. Gary Gibson 1980

⑨ Hunky Dory 🔝🎏 ☐ E3 6a
10m. The thin twisting cracks in the side-wall give a technical and sustained pitch to a good rest which gives you time to psych up for the tricky mantelshelf finale.
FA. Gabe Regan 1975

⑩ Prow Corner 🔝 ☐ VDiff
12m. The awkward corner in the left-hand edge of the recess is worthwhile. Avoid stepping right if you want the full tick.

⑪ Prow Corner Twin Cracks 🔝 ☐ HVD 4a
12m. The twin cracks just right are trickiest at the overlap. Surprisingly popular, especially with Outdoor Centres.

⑫ Chalkstorm 🔝🎏 ☐ E4 5c
14m. The slab has thin unprotected moves to pass the overlap. It is often climbed with a side runner (E1 to HVS depending where you put it). Arguments about the grade rage on, mostly by folks who have top-roped the climb - so what do they know? Often dirty from the top-roping/abseiling hordes' muddy boots.
FA. Ian Johnson 1977

⑬ Prow Cracks 🔝🎏 ☐ VDiff
10m. Climb the left-hand crack then transfer right at the level of the bulges. An excellent introduction to jamming.

⑭ Prow Cracks Variations 🔝 ☐ HVD
10m. The obvious counter-diagonal is also well worth doing and is just a touch harder, especially the final wide section.

⑮ Commander Energy 🔝🎏 ☐ E2 5c
12m. The flying fin is approached up the bulging arete. Hand-traverse a flange out left then rock onto it and layback smartly, heart in mouth, up the impressive arete. *Photo page 41.*
FA. John Allen 1975

Staffordshire

Whaley Bridge

Kinder

Bleaklow

Chew

Lancashire

Cheshire

Newstones

Ramshaw

Hen Cloud

Roaches

Descent

Commander Energy

THIN AIR

The final section of the Lower Tier doesn't see too much traffic, mainly because the tough trio of three star routes don't have a single runner between them. The collection of easier climbs makes for a decent venue when things are too busy further left. On the far right, the *Roaches Ridge* makes a good scrambling approach to the Upper Tier.

1 Rocking Stone Gully . . . . ☐ HVD
8m. The groove with wobbly chockstones is short-lived. If you are feeling technical, elegant semi-laybacking can avoid the worst of the grovelling. The rocking stone has recently been vandalised and is now only a shadow of its former self.

2 Captain Lethargy . . . . ☐ HVD
8m. The crack in the slab, trending left where it finishes. Packs a punch for its diminutive size and requires confident foot-work.

3 Sifta's Quid Inside Route . . . . . ☐ S 3a
10m. Interesting; this variation avoids the crux of the regular route by some speleological lunacy. Climb towards the slot beneath the boulders then get squirming. Helmet, harness and runners will all impede your progress on what is Western Grit's answer to *Helfenstein's Struggle*.

4 Sifta's Quid . . . . ☒☐ HS 4b
10m. The tricky bulging crack-line was named after a bet that the crag was worked out; well it wasn't then and it isn't now!
FA. John Amies 1968

5 Obsession Fatale . . ☒☒☒☐ E8 6c
10m. The ultra-sketchy slab left of *Piece Of Mind* is easy (ish) on a top-rope, but a mighty-bold solo. Some say it is only E7 6b but only those who have done it on-sight are really allowed to comment.
FA. Julian Lines 1992. Julian fell off it and was unharmed before he made the first ascent. Kevin Thaw was less lucky (see photo opposite).

6 Piece of Mind . . . . ☒☒☒☐ E6 6b
12m. The unprotected blunt rib with the crux at the top was an astounding ascent before sticky rubber and remains a bold and infrequently climbed pitch. Sadly top-roping it is polishing the crucial holds just below the top - do you really have to?
FA. Jonny Woodward 1977

7 Thin Air . . . . ☒☒☐ E5 6a
10m. Heart-stoppingly precarious! The crescent-shaped ramp is gained by a hard rock-over. Once established pad carefully up and right to glory. The route is as unprotected as it looks, the finish is very fluffable and the landing truly awful.
FA. Gary Gibson 1980

8 The Roaches Ridge . . . . . . ☒☐ Diff 3a
70m. Popular with Outdoor Centres and their lines of penguins, the long rambling ridge at the right-hand end of the cliff gives a pleasant scramble with multifarious variations. It is low in the grade and offers a good intro to 'rock-hopping', though the many more direct variations increase the grade and the quality. Fontainebleau meets The Roaches!

Kevin Thaw, moments before losing it, on *Obsession Fatal* (E8 6c) on the Roaches Lower Tier. *Opposite* Photo: Airlie Anderson

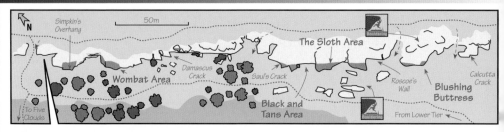

Staffordshire | Whaley Bridge | Kinder | Bleaklow | Chew | Lancashire | Cheshire | Newstones | Ramshaw | Hen Cloud | Roaches

SIMPKINS' OVERHANG

The far left-hand side of the Upper Tier has a couple of contrasting venues, the popular and battered slab hidden on the far left and the great jutting flat roof of *Simpkins' Overhang*. The easier routes here are popular, and although not quite of the quality of the climbs to either side of *The Sloth*, they are still excellent and the area tends to be quieter.

① Rooster . . . . **VDiff**
12m. Climb straight up the unprotected face to a ledge then continue up a mild jamming crack above.

② Chicken Run . . . . **HVD**
12m. From blocks below the slab, trend right to a slot then climb straight up (well-polished chips!) to a good ledge. Start on the right but trend left (crux) to an exposed exit.

③ Fern Crack . . . . **S 4b**
18m. Excellent. A boulder problem start gains the crack right of the arete, then follow this (thread) to a ledge on the left - and mantel onto a higher ledge, stance. Move left round the arete and climb the easy green groove on shelving holds.

④ Demon Wall . . . . **VS 5a**
1) 4b, 10m. Climb into the hanging groove on the right passing a bulge early on, to a stance out right. Scary but less so than...
2) 5a, 6m. Move out left and climb the wall on polished slopers and without much protection. Keeping calm in a crisis is useful.
FA. Bowden Black 1945

⑤ Perverted Staircase . . . . **VS 5a**
12m. Climb the fearsome crack through the left-hand side of the roof by gymnastic manoeuvres to reach easier ground.
FA. Geoff Sutton 1958

⑥ Simpkins' Overhang . . . **E4 5b**
14m. Approach the roof with trepidation then follow the main flake rightwards to the lip and a difficult final move to sensibly angled ground. Escape up and left to finish or climb a shallow groove - **The Fantasy Finish, 5b**.
FA. Phil Burke 1979, though futuristically top roped by Mike Simpkins in the 1960s. Fantasy Finish, Dave Jones 1979.

⑦ Inverted Staircase . . . . **Diff**
1) 14m. Climb the pocketed wall left then right into the groove to the right of the big roof and follow this to a leftward exit to a big ledge and thread belays.
2) 8m. Move left and squirm through the boulder-choked chimney to the top.
FA. Fred Pigott 1931

⑧ The Tower of Bizarre Delights . . **E3 5c**
10m. Steep and imposing. Climb directly to the ledge above the first pitch of *Inverted Staircase* then continue boldly up the hanging crack and finish more easily out right.
FA. Dave Jones 1978

⑨ Heather Slab . . . . **S 3c**
16m. The once heathery slab that forms the back of the recess is followed directly and is worryingly difficult to protect, especially on the upper wall. The groove on the left is **Diff**.

WOMBAT AREA

A superb roof climb or two and a small but good collection of lower grade climbs away from the crowds that inhabit the areas further to the right. The combination makes this a good venue for strongmen and shy beginners!

10 Capitol Climb . . . . **HS 4a**
20m. A worthwhile climb. Get into the hanging groove and exit right below the overhang to reach a short crack that leads to ledges. Climb the face above, finishing up a short crack.
FA. R Handley 1954

11 Wombat **E2 5b**
20m. A classic piece of roof climbing, pumpy and bold though not especially technical. Climb the wall to a thread then traverse the flake to its end and make a couple of strenuous pulls on less generous holds to reach easy ground. All very antipodean.
FA. Mike Simpkins 1960

12 Live Bait **E4 5c**
20m. Climb the wall using a small flake, skip right to the block then cross the roof leftwards with hard moves to pass the lip. Finish much more easily up the heathery face above.
FA. Gary Gibson 1981

13 West's Wallaby . . . . **VS 4c**
14m. Climb the awkward diagonal crack to the huge block tucked under the roof, then hand-traverse this (it's OK, the thing is well-jammed) and continue round the arete to a rest. Climb up then back leftwards to access the front face and finish easily.
FA. Graham West 1960

14 Walleroo **E2 5c**
20m. Start up *West's Wallaby* then from the right-hand edge of the jammed block climb leftwards on small flakes to difficult moves around the lip and easy terrain.
FA. Mike Simpkins 1960

15 Wallaby Direct . . . . **HVS 5a**
20m. Follow *West's Wallaby* to the middle of its traverse then climb steeply to an improving crack and easier ground.
FA. Mike Simpkins 1960

16 Late Night Final . . . . **S 4a**
20m. The undercut chimney that bounds the buttress on the right (thread) can be a tortuous struggle - how good is your gritstone udging? The upper section is an amble.

17 The Valve **E4 5c**
16m. Climb the arete on the left then the right wall via a ramp, finishing back left on the crest. Exposed and poorly-protected.
FA. Gary Gibson 1978

18 Beckermet Slab . . . . **S 4b**
14m. Mild but bold. Bridge up the gully then hand-traverse out left (crux - very hard for the short) to gain the front face which is climbed leftwards to a finish up the delicate slabby groove (poorly-protected), then the arete on the right.

19 Maud's Garden . . . . **S 4a**
1) 4a, **14m.** Balance up the crux slab then follow the crack to a stance below the bulges.
2) **8m.** Move right and squirm up the groove to outflank the overhangs then finish direct up the arete or the face to its left (8m). A left-hand start drops the grade a notch.
FA. Bowden Black 1945

20 Runner Route . . . . **HS 4b**
14m. Bold and delicate. Climb the slab to the break (and runners) then crimp on to find a finish up the flaky crack above.
FA. Nat Allen 1955

21 Damascus Crack . . . . **HS 4b**
12m. Sustained but well-protected climbing up the crack, with a flaky exit to the right or a good steep and juggy finish up the tower above and left (**VS 4c**). *Photo page 33.*
FA. Geoff Pigott 1955

22 Libra . . . . **HVS 4c**
10/14m. The well-scoured crack left of the sharp arete is sustained and precarious. Escape at the top or belay then move left and climb the juggy tower (not marked on topo).

Scramble descent

10
8
The Pipe Stance
3
4
The Sloth
1 2
3
5
6 7 8 9 10

From mid morning — 12 min

← Wombat - 50m

---

❶ Rotunda Buttress . . . . . . 🔲🔲 **VS 4c**
18m. Climb the wide crack then trend left to a ledge. From here, climb right and then left again following the best holds to an airy finish up the final section.
FA. Bowden Black 1945

❷ Rotunda Gully . . . . 🔲 **Mod**
14m. The open gully provides an awkward descent route for the competent and a suitably mild outing for timid beginners.

❸ Bachelor's Buttress . . . 🔲🔲 **HVS 4c**
18m. Low in the grade but serious and with a bold finale. Once thought "only suitable for married men and others accustomed to taking risks". Climb the slab to the left edge of the overhang; move up then trend back right crossing the side-wall on polished holds to the airy arete and a finish up a short crack. It is also possible to climb the side-wall direct until an awkward move reaches holds and gear at a more consistent HVS.
FA. Fred Pigott 1913

❹ Gypfast . . . . 🔲🔲 **E4 5c**
16m. The large triangular overhang is a bit of a one-move-wonder. Fix runners to left and right then cross the flakes rightwards to hard moves round the lip and an anticlimactic finish.
FA. Phil Gibson 1979

❺ Saul's Crack . . . . 🔲🔲 **HVS 5a**
18m. A Roaches' classic and a good test of your jamming technique. Climb into the groove then thug up the polished corner crack to the overhang and exit rapidly rightwards to easier ground. The crack is renown for 'eating' poorly placed gear, care required lest you lose your prized possession. *Photo page 69.*
FA. Joe Brown 1947

SAUL'S CRACK
To the right, the cliff becomes ever more impressive and is home to a truly great series of climbs, long and involving, but often of a very reasonable grade. The major classic of *Saul's Crack* is a bit harder and will doubtless seek out any weaknesses in your jamming ability.

❻ Humdinger . . . . 🔲🔲 **E1 5b**
18m. Climb the narrow buttress to the roofs and pull through these powerfully (hard for the short who will have to stretch), eventually trending rightwards. Low in the grade.
FA. Mick Guilliard 1969

❼ Jeffcoat's Chimney . . . . . 🔲 **VDiff**
A classic of considerable antiquity.
1) 18m. Climb the well-scratched chimney passing an overhang on the left (polished) then continue rightwards past the holly to a good stance.
2) 6m. Move left to outflank the overhangs, or for something harder finish up the steep corner (**VS 4c**).
FA. Stanley Jeffcoat 1913

❽ Jeffcoat's Buttress . . . . 🔲🔲 **HS 5a**
A route with an arduous (and avoidable) start. Using the chimney start lowers the route to a more amenable **HS 4b**.
1) 5a, 18m. Climb the fingery polished scoop by a long reach, or avoid it by the chimney on the left. Weave up towards the overhangs, pulling over a bulge with difficulty to enter a groove Trend right below the huge roofs to the 'pipe' stance.
2) 3c, 10m. The pleasant jamming cracks on the right are awkward to enter and soon lead to the cliff top.
FA. Stanley Jeffcoat 1913

The Sloth Area

Simpkin's Overhang
Wombat Area
Damascus Crack
Saul's Crack
Roscoe's Wall
Blushing Buttress
Calcutta Crack

To Five Clouds

Black and Tans Area

From Lower Tier

Descent

Staffordshire
Whaley Bridge
Kinder
Bleaklow
Chew
Lancashire
Cheshire
Newstones
Ramshaw
Hen Cloud
Roaches

BLACK AND TANS AREA

Home to *Black and Tans*, one of the very best Severes anywhere on grit, plus a host of routes from VDiff to E2 that are well worthy of attention. The impressive stature of these climbs makes them especially worthwhile.

⑨ Hanging Around . . . . . . 🔒🔑⬜ **HVS 5b**
6m. A direct pitch to the 'pipe' stance tackles the large and trenuous bulges on a right-trending line. Finish much more asily up *Jeffcoat's Buttress*.
A. Gary Gibson 1978

⑩ Ruby Tuesday . . . . 🔒🔑⬜ **E2 5b**
mini-expedition, devious and with some excellent climbing.
) 5b, 12m. Climb to the block overhang and pull over to the ase of a short ramp. Exit rightwards from the top of this to oin *Black and Tans* which is followed to its stance.
) 4b, 6m. Climb out left then up the short rib to a small tance. Pull onto the right edge of the wall above and traverse ft (gripping) to climb the exposed rounded rib.
A. Mick Guilliard, John Yates (alts) 1970

⓪ Black and Tans . . . . 🔒⬜ **S 4a**
classic expedition weaving up the impressive buttress.
) 4a, 14m. Climb *Hollybush Gully* and move out left to climb a roove to its top, step left across the side-wall then mantelshelf nto a small stance.
) 4a, 16m. Continue up the groove then step left and tackle e bulges by a trio of awkward, and poorly-protected semi- antelshelves, mild but bold. It is also possible to start up *effcoat's Chimney* then follow ledges rightwards via a long averse to the base of the groove, at the same grade.
A. Fed Pigott 1922

⑫ Black Velvet . . . . 🔒⬜ **HVD 4a**
24m. Another fine climb, less popular than its near neighbour but not really much less worthy. Follow *Black and Tans* to its first groove. Climb this to its top, move left then back right to outflank the overhangs then finish up the well-positioned crack above. A big pitch at the grade.

⑬ Diamond Wednesday . . . . . 🔒⬜ **HVS 5a**
24m. A bit of an eliminate though with good positions, some interesting moves and low in the grade. Start up *Hollybush Crack* until above the prickly beast then climb the arete on the left passing a tricky overhang to gain the final exposed rib.
FA. Gary Gibson 1978

⑭ Hollybush Crack . . . . 🔒⬜ **VS 4b**
26m. Bridge up the wide lower section of the gully until it is possible to transfer into the crack to the right. Continue up this, passing a possible constricted stance, to the left-hand end of the great roof. Pull over the bulge then either finish easily, or if you are up to it, climb as far as a thread, descend a couple of moves and shuffle rightwards on rounded holds out into space to the final exposed (and thankfully easy) rib.

Staffordshire | Whaley Bridge | Kinder | Breakow | Chew | Lancashire | Cheshire

THE SLOTH

The overhang is the single most recognisable feature of the whole cliff. It looks huge from the path and even bigger up close! Of course *The Sloth* is one of the best know grit routes anywhere, though the roof is home to some much harder offerings. For more normal mortals, the slabs here have some of the best lower-grade routes anywhere.

Descent

Roscoe's Wall Area
routes 1 to 3

From mid morning | 12 min

---

1 Technical Slab .... **HS 4a**

24m. Despite the name, not very technical but bold in its central section. Climb straight up the slab (harder for the short and unprotected where it matters) until you join the traverse of *Pedestal Route*. Finish as for *Pedestal Route*, or more in keeping, out right as for *Hollybush Crack*.

2 Gilted **E5 6a**

28m. An odd and wild outing based on the left edge of the roof. From *Hollybush Crack*, hand-traverse the lip wildly to swing round the arete to a poor rest in a shallow cave in the middle of nowhere. Head up and right for one more impending move.
FA. Phil Burke 1979

3 Painted Rumour **E6 6a**

24m. Probably the biggest roof pitch on grit and truly magnificent. From directly above *Technical Slab*, place loads of gear at the back of the roof then attack it at its widest point, using the fragile glued flake with care. From the hole (spike runner and hands-off rest possible), pull back to the vertical using tiny rugosities (crux) and climb the wall more easily. *Photo page 12.*
FA. Simon Nadin 1985

4 Pedestal Route .... **HVD 4a**

28m. A great outing through some impressive territory. Climb the flake-crack up the right-hand side of the huge flake of The Pedestal to a sitting stance (low belays) on its top. Reverse off the end of the ledge then traverse left and up to the left-hand corner of the great roof. To stop the rope jamming, try fixing a runner out left to direct it away from the crack, then pull over the bulge and finish up the deep groove. Starting up the left-hand side of the flake ups the overall grade to **S 4a**.
FA. Morley Wood 1922

5 Loculus Lie **E5 6a**

28m. Another arduous and devious roof pitch. From the stance on *Pedestal Route*, climb to the Cheese Block runner on *The Sloth* then 'yard' leftwards and arc back right to the lip. Hand-traverse left until a long stretch reaches the tiny cave under the roof. Finish direct as for *Painted Rumour*.
FA. Simon Nadin 1983

6 The Sloth .... **HVS 5a**

24m. The crack that splits the enormous roof is a total gripper. The climbing is quite straightforward although mighty harassing and the route feels like E1. Climb to a sitting position on The Pedestal then step right and climb the short tricky wall to the roof (big sling on the massive spike of the Cheese Block). Lean right to get the first of the creaking juggy flakes then launch across these to the lip where solid jamming helps the pull over into the final easy crack. The old roof climbing adage of 'keep your feet on the rock at all costs' is worth bearing in mind. *Photo page 67*
FA. Don "It's OK if you use yer loaf" Whillans 1954

7 Central Route .... **VS 4b**

16m. The centre of the poorly-protected (medium Friends) slab has delicate and unprotected moves at 10m (harder for the short) before it eases off. Traverse right to a stance on the crest of the buttress and walk off, or finish as for the next route.

8 Right Route .... **VDiff**

24m. A classic up the slanting flake that bounds the right edge of the main slab; mild at the grade. Reach the flake via polished pockets then keep left (more polish) until is possible to outflank the roof and reach a stance on the right. Trend left above the big overhang (awkward to start) and finish up the crack.
FA. Morley Wood 1922

Newstones | Ramshaw | Hen Cloud | Roaches

MOUNTAIN
EQUIPMENT
DEFINING A WORLD OF FREEDOM AND MOVEMENT
www.mountain-equipment.co.uk
For a free colour brochure call 01457 854424

ROSCOE'S WALL

To the right of the 'main event' is a shorter bulging buttress and right again a taller wall. The best offering here is the desperate roof climb of *Paralogism*. At a lower grade *Crack and Corner* is especially worth seeking out and proves to be a bit of a shocker for 1922!

❶ Right Route Right . . . . 🔟 ▢ **HS 4b**
14m. Follow *Right Route* to the overhang then pull over this to gain the hanging groove just above and follow this to the top.

❷ Kelly's Direct . . . . 🔟 🔟 ▢ **E1 5b**
14m. From the shelf (see below), climb the crack on the left to a flake and follow this, and then rounded pockets, to the crest.

❸ Kelly's Shelf . . . . 🔟 🔟 ▢ **S 4b**
16m. The bulging face has a narrow ramp cutting through it from left to right. Climb on to this (an ungainly struggle for most) and follow it to the base of a crack. Finish up this, or the similar, but more exposed, face just to the left (**HS 4b**).

❹ Paralogism . . . . . . 🔟 🔟 🔟 ▢ **E7 6c**
14m. The large roof under the right-hand side of the buttress is taxing. Climb leftwards across the overhang to the lip then trend back right and pull onto rock of a saner angle. Pre-placed wires to left and right protected the first ascent though it has been done without.
FA. Simon Nadin 1987. On-sighted by Sam Whittaker 2003.

❺ Antithesis . . . . 🔟 🔟 ▢ **E5 6b**
14m. The right-hand edge of the scooped wall to the right is traversed leftwards with considerable difficulty. A side-runner in the next route is normal.
FA. Jonny Woodward 1980

❻ Easy Gully Wall . . . . 🔟 ▢ **S 4a**
20m. Climb to a block to the right of the gully then continue leftwards to a ledge. Move up and left to a higher one then take the flake to the overhangs and escape leftwards under these.

❼ Jelly Roll . . . . 🔟 ▢ **VS 4b**
22m. Follow the strenuous thin crack in the wall to a possible stance and block belay. Pull boldly over a bulge and climb a groove and follow this to a capping roof, which is climbed on 'surprising' holds. Save some big gear for the final section.

❽ Roscoe's Wall/Round Table . 🔟 ▢ **HVS 5**
20m. A good combination up the steep wall; the lower pitch sees plenty of attention, the upper one less so. Climb the centre of the wall (poor gear) to a flake, step right and take the steep face to ledges (stance?). Climb the wall leftwards (bold) to the wide crack. Climb this to its top and a finish out right.
FA. Don Roscoe 1955. FA. (Round Table) John Allen 1974

❾ Crack and Corner . . . . . 🔟 🔟 ▢ **S 4c**
An exciting expedition up an unlikely line at the grade.
1) **4c, 20m.** Climb into the crack with difficulty then follow it to a ledge, before moving left to a block belay.
2) **4a, 18m.** Take the wall to a good ledge then the groove to the final imposing overhang. Fortunately this has massive jugs.
FA. Morley Wood 1922

❿ Babbacombe Lee . . . . . . 🔟 ▢ **E1 5b**
10m. From the foot of the crack, climb the buttress rightwards to a good rest and a finish up a crack and awkward bulge.
FA. Dave Jones 1978

⓫ Hangman's Crack . . . . ▢ **S 4a**
10m. Start up the bank on the right and trend left to below the flake crack that splits the roof. Finish awkwardly up this.

The Sloth (HVS 5a) on the
Upper Tier of the Roaches.
Page 64

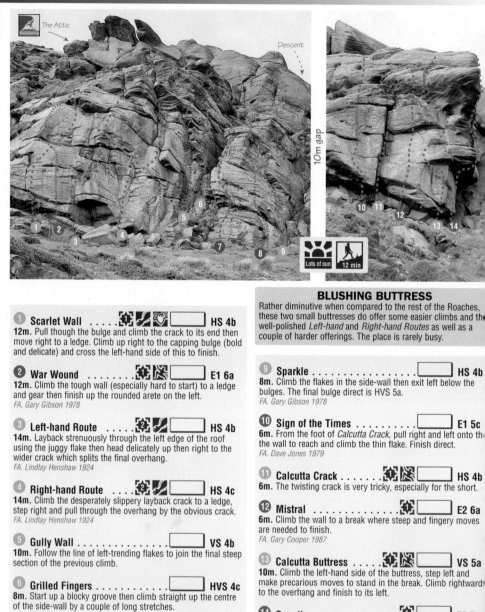

The Attic

Descent

10m gap

Lots of sun   12 min

 Staffordshire

Whaley Bridge

Kinder

Bleaklow

Chew

Lancashire

Cheshire

Newstones

Ramshaw

Hen Cloud

Roaches

1 Scarlet Wall . . . . . 🔲🔲🔲 **HS 4b**
12m. Pull though the bulge and climb the crack to its end then move right to a ledge. Climb up right to the capping bulge (bold and delicate) and cross the left-hand side of this to finish.

2 War Wound . . . . 🔲🔲 **E1 6a**
12m. Climb the tough wall (especially hard to start) to a ledge and gear then finish up the rounded arete on the left.
FA. Gary Gibson 1978

3 Left-hand Route . . . . . 🔲🔲 **HS 4b**
14m. Layback strenuously through the left edge of the roof using the juggy flake then head delicately up then right to the wider crack which splits the final overhang.
FA. Lindlay Henshaw 1924

4 Right-hand Route . . . . 🔲🔲 **HS 4c**
14m. Climb the desperately slippery layback crack to a ledge, step right and pull through the overhang by the obvious crack.
FA. Lindlay Henshaw 1924

5 Gully Wall . . . . 🔲 **VS 4b**
10m. Follow the line of left-trending flakes to join the final steep section of the previous climb.

6 Grilled Fingers . . . . 🔲 **HVS 4c**
8m. Start up a blocky groove then climb straight up the centre of the side-wall by a couple of long stretches.
FA. Dave Jones 1979

7 The Rib . . . . 🔲 **Diff**
8m. The right-hand edge of the gully is pleasant enough. Starting up the gully to avoid the bulges is quite a bit easier.

8 Rib Wall . . . . 🔲 **VDiff**
8m. The hard wall (4b direct) to a ledge, trend left to *The Rib*.

BLUSHING BUTTRESS
Rather diminutive when compared to the rest of the Roaches, these two small buttresses do offer some easier climbs and the well-polished *Left-hand* and *Right-hand Routes* as well as a couple of harder offerings. The place is rarely busy.

9 Sparkle . . . . 🔲 **HS 4b**
8m. Climb the flakes in the side-wall then exit left below the bulges. The final bulge direct is HVS 5a.
FA. Gary Gibson 1978

10 Sign of the Times . . . . 🔲 **E1 5c**
6m. From the foot of *Calcutta Crack*, pull right and left onto the wall to reach and climb the thin flake. Finish direct.
FA. Dave Jones 1979

11 Calcutta Crack . . . . . . 🔲🔲 **HS 4b**
6m. The twisting crack is very tricky, especially for the short.

12 Mistral . . . . 🔲 **E2 6a**
6m. Climb the wall to a break where steep and fingery moves are needed to finish.
FA. Gary Cooper 1987

13 Calcutta Buttress . . . . . 🔲🔲 **VS 5a**
10m. Climb the left-hand side of the buttress, step left and make precarious moves to stand in the break. Climb rightwards to the overhang and finish to its left.

14 Genetix . . . . 🔲 **E3 6a**
10m. Cross the roof with difficulty and climb the right-hand side of the arete to a grasping finish.
FA. Gary Gibson 1979

The next route is about 90m down the slope from the steps, or a lone boulder facing Hen Cloud.

15 Ou Est Le Spit? . . . . . 🔲🔲🔲 **E6 6b**
A gem of a route up the front of the boulder. Great moves, terrible landing and insecure throughout. It is worth brushing the nightmare sloping top before you try the on-sight.

Paul's Crack (HVS 5a) on the Roaches Upper Tier. *Page 62*

HARD VERY and VERY FAR SKYLINE

A remote and exposed series of small buttresses with a collection of great climbs on some of the very best rock around.

APPROACH - From the left-hand end of the Upper Tier, follow the cliff-top path past the Doxey Pool and on for about 500m (30mins from the main parking.) Or, from the limited parking on the minor road from Roach Grange to Hazel Barrow, it is about 10 mins to the Hard Very Far Skyline buttress. See map on page 46

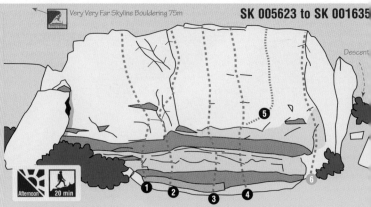

Very Very Far Skyline Bouldering 75m

SK 005623 to SK 001635

Descent

Afternoon 20 min

HARD VERY FAR SKYLINE

❶ Willow Farm . . . . . 🎭👊🗞 ▭ **E4 6a**
10m. The elegant slab on the left edge of the buttress is approached steeply. Small wires protect, low in the grade.
FA. Chris Hamper 1977

❷ Track of the Cat 🎭📊👊🗞🐱 ▭ **E5 6a**
12m. A powerful start and a technical groove (pull out right as soon as you can) culminate in an insecure, smeary reach for the top. On the final crucial section, the gear is a little too far away for comfort. Harder for the short.
FA. Jonny Woodward 1977

❸ Nature Trail . . . 🎭🗞🐱👊 ▭ **E5 6b**
10m. Make a hard pull onto the slab (Friends in low pocket to avoid gear in *Wings*) and blast up the slab with the last smeary move being the crux.
FA. Simon Nadin 1985

❹ Wings of Unreason . . .🎭👊 ▭ **E4 6a**
10m. The centre of the slab to a runner slot and a leap/stretch for the top. Again the tall have an unfair advantage (**E2 5c-ish**). *Photo opposite.*
FA. Jonny Woodward 1977

❺ Counterstroke of Equity . . . . 🎭🗞👊🐱 ▭ **E6 6c**
10m. A delicate combination of intense smearing and frantic scratching topped off with a dynamic finish. Use the *Wings of Unreason* pocket for much-needed protection.
FA. Richard Davies 1985

❻ Prelude to Space . . . . .🎭🐱 ▭ **HVS 4c**
10m. The delicate right-hand arete forms a pleasant contrast to the tough offerings further left. As expected, it is unprotected.
FA. Andrew Woodward 1977

VERY FAR SKYLINE

❼ Triple Point . . . . . .🎭🗞🐱 ▭ **E1 5c**
8m. Pull over the flat roof as for *Wild Thing*. Step up to a good wire slot, then head left to the arete and sprint up this. A **Direct Start** up the undercut arete is **6b**.
FA. Jonny Woodward 1982

← Track of the Cat 60m via the top

Descent

Art Nouveau - 100m

❽ Wild Thing . . . .🎭🗞 ▭ **HVS 5c**
6m. Enter the groove by fingery moves (or use the jugs!) and balance up it delicately. All over after the first move - unless of course you are soloing.
FA. Andrew Woodward 1977

❾ Entropy's Jaw . .🎭🗞🖋🐱 ▭ **E5 6b**
8m. Start up *Wild Thing* but follow the impossibly-thin seam up the smooth slab to the right. Good but hard-earned small wires protect and the fall from the top has been tested (and definitely isn't to be recommended).
FA. Andrew Woodward 1982

❿ Script for a Tier . . .🎭🗞🖋🐱 ▭ **E6 6c**
8m. Step out from the flake of *Mild Thing* to access the face left of the undercut arete and sketch up this.
FA. Simon Nadin 1985

⓫ Mild Thing . . . .🎭 ▭ **Diff**
6m. Use the flake to gain the floral cracks. Well-named.
FA. Andrew Woodward 1977

100m right is a solitary block below the path, see map page 73.

⓬ Art Nouveau . . .🎭🖋🐱 ▭ **E6 6c**
6m. A brilliant undercutting exercise on the rising diagonal overlap. The main small wire placement has gone west so it is solo only now, although the landing can be padded - still E6!
FA. Simon Nadin 1985

Dave Clay on the fine slab of *Wings of Unreason* (E4 6a) on Hard Very Far Skline Buttress. *Opposite* Photo: Dave Clay collection

Staffordshire | Whaley Bridge | Kinder | Bleaklow | Chew | Lancashire | Cheshire

ALPHA BUTTRESS
A pleasant slabby buttress in the middle of nowhere, always quiet and a good place to escape the crowds.
APPROACH - From the left-hand end of the Upper Tier follow the main path up to the top of the crag. Head left until you reach a pond - The Doxey Pool. Skyline Buttress is below here and Alpha Buttress is a little further along.

Far Skyline Buttress 550m

① Melaleucion **VS 4c**
8m. The front of the first buttress through a bevy of shelving overlaps.
FA. Steve Dale 1976

② Devotoed .... **VS 5a**
8m. Tackle the crack in the arete and then the bulges leftwards.
FA. Gary Gibson 1979

③ Alpha .... **VDiff**
8m. The shallow groove is awkward but the gear is good.

④ Alpha Arete .... **S 4a**
8m. The arete left of the scruffy corner on mostly good holds.

⑤ Breakfast Corner .... **Mod**
6m. The main groove is about as easy as they come.

⑥ Formative Years **E3 6a**
8m. The narrow slab is also thin! Blinkers advised.
FA. Howard Tingle 1982

⑦ Breakfast Problem .... **VDiff**
8m. The pair of cracks in the left-hand edge of the slab fuse as they rise. A bit close to its neighbour - good moves though!

⑧ Days Gone By .... **S 4a**
8m. The continuous crack just right is barely independent.
FA. Gary Gibson 1978

⑨ San Melas **E3 5c**
8m. The precarious centre of the slab with a move right at half height and a delicate finish. The start is bold but the upper slab is well-protected by bomber gear (small Friends) in the break.
FA. Andrew Woodward 1977

⑩ Hallow to our Men **E4 6b**
8m. Effectively a direct start to *San Melas* up the shallow groove.
FA. Gary Gibson 1981

⑪ Mantis ... **HVS 5b**
8m. The elegant arete on its right then left.
FA. Andrew Woodward 1974

⑫ Sennapod .... **VDiff**
8m. The corner named after its more famous Welsh counterpart. It is better that it looks with some good bridging moves.
FA. Gary Gibson 1978

⑬ 39th Step **E2 6a**
8m. The groove right of the corner and the slab above. An easily-placed side runner is normal at the grade.
FA. Gary Gibson 1979

⑭ Wallaby Wall .... **S 4b**
10m. The crack (huge gear helps) in the centre of the slab leads via excellent moves and a short traverse to the left-hand flake on the upper wall, or finish direct at a higher grade.

⑮ Definitive Gaze **E1 5c**
10m. Artificial but with some good moves. Climb through a scoop and up the indefinite flaky crack directly above.
FA. Gary Gibson 1979

⑯ Right-hand Route .... **S 4a**
12m. Worth seeking out. Climb into the crack on the right then pull out left to reach a well-positioned flake. Finish up this.

⑰ Looking for Today .... **HVS 5b**
8m. The thin crack and short face just right.

Skyline Buttress

Newstones | Ramshaw | Hen Cloud | Roaches

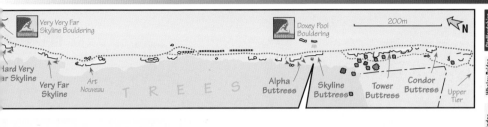

SKYLINE BUTTRESS

Rather remote but with a good selection of lower grade climbs. There is usually a team or two here although the crowds of the Upper and Lower Tier will not be present.
APPROACH - From the left-hand end of the Upper Tier follow the main path up to the top of the crag. Head left until you reach the pond of The Doxey Pool. Skyline Buttress is below the edge here.

1 Pinnacle Crack . . . . ☐ **Diff**
m. The obvious crack on the left is over far too soon.

2 Split Personality . . . . ☐ **E1 5b**
m. The centre of the face of the block, starting up the right-and arete and finishing up a thin crack-line.
. *Gary Gibson 1979*

3 Pinnacle Arete . . . . . . ☒☐ **VS 4c**
m. The arete of the block is easier than its Cloggy namesake.
. *R Desmond-Stevens 1945*

4 Pinnacle Slab . . . . ☐ **HVD**
4m. The long rib sticking out of the shrubbery gets steeper.

5 Mantelshelf Slab . . . . ☒☐ **VS 4b**
2m. From the arete, trend left and climb the slab, using the ponymous move at least once. Bold in the middle then easing.

6 Enigma Variation . . . . ☒☒☐ **E2 5b**
2m. The arete is followed past the overlap, then trend left up e slab. Excellent sport, delicate and not too well-protected.
. *Andrew Woodward 1976*

7 Karabiner Chimney . . . . . ☒☐ **HVD**
10m. The right-facing cleft is a mini-classic - of its type.
FA. R Desmond-Stevens 1945

8 Karabiner Slab . . . . ☒☐ **VS 4c**
10m. The slab just right is climbed direct.

9 Karabiner Cracks . . . . ☐ **Diff**
12m. The scruffy crack system to 'fields' and a chimney finish.
FA. A Simpson 1947

10 Slab and Arete . . . . ☒☐ **S 4a**
18m. Reach the ascending traverse from the left (awkward) avoiding the scruffy crack if possible. Follow it out to the right arete and a nicely exposed finish. The direct start is **Slips, E3 6a.**
FA. G Stoneley 1945. FA. Slips, Gary Gibson 1982

11 Drop Acid . . . . ☒☐ **E4 6a**
14m. Climb the left-hand side of the slab and difficult overhang - a runner on the left is sensible to protect the roof; contrived.
FA. John Allen 1987

12 Acid Drop . . . . . . ☒☒☒☐ **E4 5c**
16m. Delicate dancing, then butch and bold. Trend rightwards up the slab following an undercut flake. Pull over this then tackle the centre of the overhang. Unprotected and reachy.
FA. Jonny Woodward 1987

13 Skytrain . . . . ☒☐ **E2 5b**
14m. Climb the left-trending crack (hard) then the delicate (and avoidable) slab left of the easy upper section of *Slab and Arete*.
FA. John Peel 1977

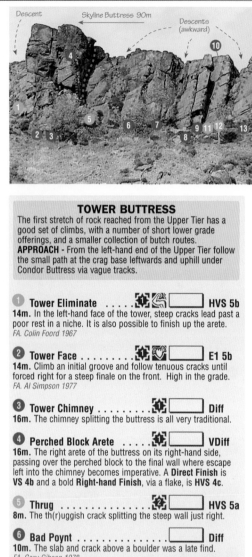

Skyline Buttress 90m

Descent

Descents (awkward)

Descent

Afternoon | 20 min

TOWER BUTTRESS

The first stretch of rock reached from the Upper Tier has a good set of climbs, with a number of short lower grade offerings, and a smaller collection of butch routes.
APPROACH - From the left-hand end of the Upper Tier follow the small path at the crag base leftwards and uphill under Condor Buttress via vague tracks.

1 Tower Eliminate . . . . . **HVS 5b**
14m. In the left-hand face of the tower, steep cracks lead past a poor rest in a niche. It is also possible to finish up the arete.
FA. Colin Foord 1967

2 Tower Face **E1 5b**
14m. Climb an initial groove and follow tenuous cracks until forced right for a steep finale on the front. High in the grade.
FA. Al Simpson 1977

3 Tower Chimney . . . . **Diff**
16m. The chimney splitting the buttress is all very traditional.

4 Perched Block Arete . . . . . **VDiff**
16m. The right arete of the buttress on its right-hand side, passing over the perched block to the final wall where escape left into the chimney becomes imperative. A **Direct Finish** is **VS 4b** and a bold **Right-hand Finish**, via a flake, is **HVS 4c**.

5 Thrug . . . . **HVS 5a**
8m. The th(r)uggish crack splitting the steep wall just right.

6 Bad Poynt . . . . **Diff**
10m. The slab and crack above a boulder was a late find.
FA. Gary Gibson 1978

7 Oversite . . . . **HVDiff**
10m. The slabby (and mildly bold) arete was also over-looked.

8 Ogden . . . . **VDiff**
8m. The pleasant left-trending crack on polished footholds.

9 Ogden Arete . . . . **S 4b**
8m. The worthwhile arete with a powerful start. Pleasant above.

10 Ogden Recess . . . . **VDiff**
8m. The wider fissure is a bit of a grunt. Finish direct.

11 Black Pig . . . . **VS 4c**
8m. The thin crack in the right wall of the chimney deserves its name if you don't use the footholds behind you!

12 Spare Rib . . . . **VS 4b**
8m. The right arete of the wall is serious but worth doing.
FA. Jonny Woodward 1977

13 Bad Sneakers **E2 5c**
8m. This attempt to climb the smooth slab almost gets forced into the gully before looping back right to finish.
FA. Dave Jones 1977

14 Spectrum . . . . **VS 4c**
8m. The pleasant right-hand side of the slab to a short crack.
FA. Jonny Woodward 1977

15 Middleton's Motion . . . . **VS 4b**
10m. Climb straight to and through a short roof crack. Not quite as stiff a problem as you might be expecting.

16 Strain Station **E4 5c**
12m. Climb the rib then attack the roof leftwards with conviction to a finish up the bold hanging arete above the lip.
FA. Gary Gibson 1981

17 Topaz **E2 5b**
10m. The slanting crack on the right-hand side of the overhang is approached via the rib and has a moment or two of interest.
FA. Gary Gibson 1979

18 Safety Net **E1 5b**
10m. The centre of the buttress leads over an overhang to another that caps the wall, and is cleaved by an excellent flake. Finish up this with gusto. *Photo page 23.*
FA. John Allen 1975

19 Shortcomings **E1 5c**
10m. The flake that runs up the right edge of the buttress is th substance of the route. Reach it with difficulty (hard for everybody and especially so for the short - **E2**) and sprint up it by quality 'barn-door' layback moves.
FA. Gary Gibson 1978

20 Left Twin Crack . . . . **HS 4b**
10m. The twin cracks in the left wall of the recess via a groove.

21 Square Chimney . . . . **Diff**
8m. The mild angle in the left-hand corner of the recess.

Tower Buttress 40m

Descent

Upper Tier 100m

Descent

Staffordshire
Whaley Bridge
Kinder
Bleaklow
Chew
Lancashire
Cheshire

CONDOR BUTTRESS

Being home to several worthwhile lower and middle grade routes makes this the most popular destination on the Skyline - that and the fact that it is the closest buttress to the road!
APPROACH - From the left end of the Upper Tier, follow the small path under the crag leftwards and uphill above the fence.

② Trio Chimney . . . . ⬜ **VDiff**
m. The right-hand angle is better than it looks. Start inside!

③ Substance . . . . ⬜ **VS 4c**
m. Despite the name, the left-hand arete of the next buttress is
no great substance.
Gary Gibson 1978

④ Lighthouse . . . . 🔲 ⬜ **VDiff**
Jm. The centre of the face has a polished and perplexing start.

⑤ Ralph's Mantelshelves . . . . . ⬜ **S 4a**
m. From the right toe of the buttress mantel-a-way up the face
eading leftwards. A more direct version is the same grade.

ONDOR BUTTRESS

⑥ Condor Slab . . . . 🔲🔳🔲 ⬜ **VS 4c**
4m. The centre of the slab is climbed passing a hole to a ledge
en a finish up the face above and slightly right. Good climbing
at is poorly-protected. A Friend 3.5 is useful near the top.

⑦ A.M. Anaesthetic . . . . 🔲🔳 ⬜ **HVS 4c**
4m. The right arete of the buttress is precarious, and once
gain, protection is somewhat lacking where most needed.
Gary Gibson 1978

⑧ Cracked Arete . . . . 🔳 ⬜ **HS 4b**
4m. Climb the well-travelled slab to a ledge then tackle the
ab on the left of the chimney on slopers to a final crack.

⑨ Condor Chimney . . . . ⬜ **VDiff**
m. The chimney at the back of the ledge is pleasant enough
nd is easiest if you don't get in too deep. Finish on the right.

⑩ Nosepicker . . . . ⬜ **E1 5a**
m. Climb the acute arete throughout, carefully following the
ft-hand side of the jutting nose of rock.
Jonny Woodward 1976

㉛ Time to be Had . . . . 🔲 ⬜ **HVD**
8m. The thin twisting cracks in the wall to the right are pleasant
and well-protected. There is a choice of finishes.
FA. Gary Gibson 1978

㉜ Tobacco Road . . . . 🔲 ⬜ **VS 4c**
8m. The nicely technical centre of the wall on improving holds.
The initial bulge (**5b** direct) might have you blowing a little.

㉝ Wheeze . . . . 🔲🔲 ⬜ **HVS 4c**
14m. Climb the easy lower rib then the poorly-protected upper
arete, stepping right above the bulge for maximum exposure.
FA. Jonny Woodward 1976

㉞ Bruno Flake . . . . 🔲🔲 ⬜ **VS 4b**
8m. The steep groove just round to the right is awkward; you
may arrive at the top 'ready rubbed'. Big gear helps.

㉟ Navy Cut . . . . ⬜ **VDiff**
8m. The twisting groove/niche in the slab to the right leads to a
position below the roof and has a tough exit right at the top.

㊱ Chicane . . . . ⬜ **S 4a**
6m. The blunt central rib from a block. Head right then left.
FA. Gary Gibson 1978

㊲ Lung Cancer . . . . ⬜ **S 3c**
6m. The right edge of the wall, zigzagging through the bulges.
Typically the climbing eases as soon as the runners arrive!
FA. Jonny Woodward 1977

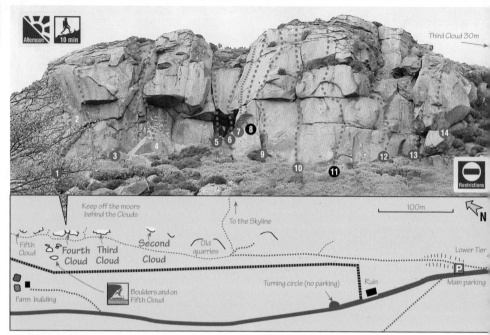

Staffordshire

Whaley Bridge

Kinder

Bleaklow

Chew

Lancashire

Cheshire

Newstones

Ramshaw

Hen Cloud

Roaches

Third Cloud 30m

Keep off the moors behind the Clouds

To the Skyline

100m

N

Fifth Cloud

Fourth Cloud

Third Cloud

Second Cloud

Old quarries

Lower Tier

P

Turning circle (no parking)

Ruin

Main parking

Farm building

Boulders and on Fifth Cloud

THE FIVE CLOUDS

The bumpy ridge to the south west of the Roaches has a small collection of quality climbs and is usually quieter then the other cliffs in the immediate area.

APPROACH - Park as for the Roaches. Go through the gate then turn left along a sunken track. Follow this towards The Clouds, passing under the old quarries.

THE FOURTH CLOUD

The Fourth Cloud is not as good as its bigger neighbour number Three but still has a few short problems of interest.

ACCESS - Birds have nested on the ledge above *Boysen's Delight* and access has been restricted in the past. If the birds return, signs will be posted.

❶ Meander . . . . **VDiff**
8m. The centre of the slab, trending left once past the overlap.

❷ Meander Variation . . . . . **HVS 5b**
10m. From *Meander*, meander right to climb the steep wall.
FA. Chris Hamper 1977

❸ Stranglehold **E1 5b**
10m. Undercut up the right edge of the wall then go!

❹ Smun . . . . **VS 4c**
8m. Smun indeed! Spring up the wall to a diagonal flake and follow this strenuously rightwards until the crack on the right can be reached for an easier finish.

❺ Left-hand Block Crack . . . . **S 4a**
6m. Climb the roof and take the left-hand groove in the recess.

❻ Right-hand Block Crack . . . . . **S 4a**
6m. The similar feature right again.

❼ Winter in Combat **E1 5c**
6m. The slab and arete on the side-wall are quite technical.

❽ The Shining Path **E7 6c**
10m. A hard pull over the roof leads to a horizontal break (Friends) then smear up the centre of the impossibly bald slab.
FA. Mark Katz 1996

❾ Private Display **E1 5b**
10m. Start from a boulder then climb the arete and thin crack.
FA. John Yates (in ripped trews) 1970

❿ Boysen's Delight . . . **E1 5c**
10m. A thin crack leads with difficulty (and good runners) into the easier twisting fissure above and often some bird plop!
FFA. Martin Boysen 1968

⓫ Mirror, Mirror **E4 6b**
10m. A little beauty. Climb the centre of the wall with difficult moves left and a tricky section past the curving overlap. A right hand exit is somewhat easier.
FA. Andrew Woodward 1977

⓬ Mantelshelf Route . . . . **Diff**
10m. Mantel-a-way up the ledges and finish up the groove.

⓭ Chockstone Corner . . . . **Diff**
6m. The groove with the expected jammed stone.

⓮ Roman Nose **E2 5b**
6m. Start on the right and stride out onto the beak which is followed delicately via sketchy finger flakes.
FA. Dave Jones 1977

Fourth Cloud 30m

Second Cloud 50m →

THE THIRD CLOUD

The juiciest climbing on the Clouds is on the third lump, *Rubberneck* and *Appaloosa Sunset* are the best but *Crabbie's Crack* and *Flower Power* are also worthwhile. If you are into gritstone at its most technical then the well-named *Who Needs Ready Brek?* should offer food for thought!

① Glass Back . . . . ☐ **VDiff**
6m. The awkward left-hand fissure in the main buttress.

② Elastic Arm . . . . ☐ **HVS 5b**
6m. The wide crack in the upper half of the face can be gained from the left (if you must) and is a nightmare of a thrash.
FA. Dave Salt 1960s

③ Sands of Time . . . . ☐ **E4 6a**
6m. Climb to the break (*Persistence* - **V3**). The blunt nose above the mid-height break gives a more serious continuation.
FA. (Sands of Time) Richard Pickford 1993

**④ Who Needs
Ready Brek?** . . . . ☐ **E4 7a**
8m. Start up *Persistence* and follow the unbelievably-thin break rightwards, desperate! Pull up to the main break then bale out.
FA. Simon Nadin 1986. Still unrepeated nearly 20 years later?

⑤ Cloudbusting . . . . . ☐ **E4 6b**
8m. Another technical test-piece, although less so than *Ready Brek*. Start left of *Rubberneck* and climb the wall diagonally leftwards with difficulty, passing a vague ramp. Escape off left.
FA. Simon Nadin 1986

⑥ Rubberneck . . . . ☐ **HVS 5a**
14m. Follow the superb central crack with good gear and fine sustained climbing. At the top of the crack, climb the wall up and right for the most fitting finale.
FA. Robin Barley 1967

⑦ Appaloosa Sunset . . . . ☐ **E3 5c**
16m. Quality face climbing, though with a bold central section. Climb the right arete of *Rubberneck* (a highish runner is permissible) then trend right by high-stepping and tricky mantelshelves before following holds straight up the wall, which eases gradually with height.
FA. Dave Jones 1977

⑧ Eclipsed Peach . . . ☐ **E4 6a**
16m. The direct start to *Appaloosa* is technical and bold until holds on the regular route are reached.
FA. Alan Williams 1983

⑨ Laguna Sunrise . . . ☐ **E4 6c**
14m. Climb to the right of the overlap then head up and left with great difficulty to join *Appaloosa*. Finish up this.
FA. Simon Nadin 1984

⑩ The Left-hand Variant . . ☐ **HVS 4**
16m. The flakes to the left of the fine crack are sustained and awkward to protect. A more direct start is *Bakewell Tart* - **E2 5c**
FA. John Yates 1968/John Hudson 1991

⑪ Crabbie's Crack . . . . . ☐ **HVS 4**
16m. A classic jamming crack. Follow the fissure to its end an finish up the exposed arete on the right - *Flaky Wall Finish*, or (more in keeping) the thin crack on the left.
FA. Bob Downes early 1950s

Third Cloud 50m

Approach from main parking

17 18 19 20 21 22 23 24 25 26

THE SECOND CLOUD
The first really significant rock reached from the parking is on the Second Cloud. The routes here are often considered as extended bouldering although there are also a few good cracks to have a go at using ropes and runners for those into that kind of thing!

12 Flower Power Arete . . . E2 5c
4m. Climb the arete then stretch right and continue up a tricky roove to ledges. An easier corner crack remains.
A. Martin Boysen 1968

13 Icarus Allsorts E4 6a
4m. From a boulder, balance out left then climb the slab to the base of a groove. Move out left again and carefully climb the arete. Not well-protected so care is required.
A. Al Simpson 1977

14 The Little Flake . . . . HVS 5a
4m. The little flake on the right is inclined to be luminous and is an awkward tussle - not one for your best clothes.
A. Dave Salt 1960s

15 Geordie Girl E3 5b
4m. The front face of *The Big Flake* is climbed by precarious laybacking and delicate smearing.
A. Geoff Hornby 1990s

16 The Big Flake . . . . VDiff
4m. The flake is really more of a groove-cum-chimney thing.

THE SECOND CLOUD

17 Jimmy Carter . . . . HVD
4m. The pleasant wall on the far left.

18 Stalin . . . . VDiff
4m. The crack is worthwhile at the grade.

19 Legends of Lost Leaders . . . E2 5c
4m. The centre of the wall has a tricky mantelshelf and layback flake finish, although you shouldn't get lost on it.
A. Gary Gibson 1979

20 Lenin . . . . VDiff
8m. The widening and right-trending crack has a tricky start but is still more reasonable than its namesake ever was!

21 Yankee Jam . . . . VS 5a
8m. Climb the awkward leaning fissure.

22 Finger of Fate E2 6a
8m. The left-hand side of the sharp arete is precarious, sustained and excellent.
FA. Simon Nadin 1983

23 KGB . . . . HVS 4c
6m. Start on the other side of the arete and finish on the crest.
FA. Ian Johnson 1977

24 The Outdoor Pursuits Cooperative E1 5a
8m. Climb to a small ledge then make fingery moves to pass the U-shaped crack.
FA. Peter Buswell 1998

25 Communist Crack . . E1 . . VS 5a
8m. The right-leaning crack is best climbed by awkward laybacking.

26 Marxist Undertones . . . . . VS 5b
8m. From just right of the crack, under-cling up and right via flakes to reach easy ground.

THE FIRST CLOUD *away to the right is a bit of a nonentity.*

Staffordshire Whaley Bridge Kinder Bleaklow Chew Lancashire Cheshire Newstones Ramshaw Hen Cloud Roaches

A quiet day on Hen Cloud.
The Arete (VDiff). Page 85

The superb castellated buttresses of Hen Cloud offer some of grit's finest crack climbs and also routes which are amongst the longest anywhere on grit, including some genuine multi-pitch climbs to savour. Perched above a steep bank, the positions are superb as is the outlook but, despite all these positives, the crag is rarely crowded. The climbs cover the grade spectrum and like the nearby crag of the Roaches, there is an excellent selection of lower grade climbs.

Basically the cliff is split in two by a diagonal grassy ramp which provides an easy descent. To the left of this are the longest routes on the cliff and, to the right, a fine wall gradually increasing in height from left to right, which swings round to face east. Both facets are split by a fine set of cracks and grooves. Over on the far left are some shorter walls and a trio of fine towers.

BIRD RESTRICTIONS - In recent years there have been occasional voluntary restrictions due to nesting birds. These are indicated by signs. As soon as it is clear that the birds (ring ouzels) are not going to nest, as has happened in recent years, the signs will be removed.

APPROACH Also see map on page 44

There is limited but free roadside parking on the main road to either side of the gravel road that loops round below the cliff, park sensibly here. Follow the track until it heads away to the right then tackle the steep slope direct keeping to either of the stone-flagged paths so as to avoid any further erosion.

CONDITIONS

Despite facing south the crag is inclined to be green and lichenous, especially on the left (because of the grass ledges) and as such is not a good destination after damp weather. Some routes, again particularly on the left-hand side, take seepage for the same reason. The right-hand part of the cliff tends to be cleaner and faster drying, and it also gets the sun earlier in the day, making it a viable venue on an 'improving' day.

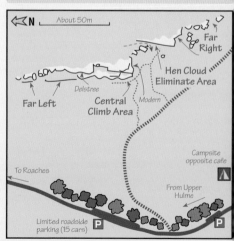

HEN CLOUD - FAR LEFT

The left-hand side of the cliff is dominated by three tall and impressive towers. To the right is a steep section of walls above a green lower tier which is split by a long horizontal roof. There are some worthwhile (and hard) routes here that are always quieter than the main section of the cliff away to the right. *Bulwark* is a particularly fine E1, bold and exhilarating and *Slowhand* is only marginally less magnificent. The steep walls above the lower tier have some worthwhile but neglected climbs in the upper grades but few real classics; bald aretes and bold faces are pretty much the name of the game here.

❶ Nutted by Reality E1 6a
8m. The middle of the pale wall on the far left of the crag is precarious and technical, especially in the lower section.
FA. Simon Horrox 1978

❷ Slipstreams .... HVS 5a
8m. Twinned shallow cracks lead to a flake on the left.
FA. Dave Jones 1979

❸ Little Pinnacle Climb ...... VDiff
8m. The stepped groove at the right edge of the terrace leads past ledges to a finish over the eponymous pinnacle.

❹ November Cracks ...... S 4a
12m. Climb the parallel cracks up the left-hand side of the first tower to a finish up the groove above.
FA. Arthur Burns 1927

❺ Bulwark E1 5b
12m. Bold and satisfying. From the ledge on the right traverse out left to reach the airy arete and balance up this to a juggy finish.
FA. Probably Joe Brown, late 1950s

❻ Slowhand E1 5b
12m. The right-hand side of the face past a crack and a pocket. The delicate finale is most easily overcome by a long stretch.
FA. Dave Jones 1978

❼ Mindbridge E7 6c
12m. The right wall of the chimney is fierce and bold with low gear for the crux but not for the finish on the slopy fluting. Bridging on the opposite wall is not allowed. Usually very dirty.
FA. Simon Nadin 1984

❽ Master of Reality E6 6c
12m. An overhanging gritstone 'tufa' provides one of the finest hard routes in Western Grit. Spaced gear on the lower wall protects the hard static moves to the break (though a dyno is easier). Superb and powerful moves lead up the vein and usefully the whole route doesn't get too green in winter.
FA. Simon Nadin 1983

❾ Master of Puppets E6 6b
12m. The right arete has a scary start to reach the break and a tough upper section on spaced monos and poor slopers.
FA. Mark Sharratt 2003

❿ The Notch .... VS 4c
12m. The tight groove between the right-hand towers. Start up the left-hand crack to a block then climb a shallow groove before moving out left to a crack near the arete.

⓫ Chicken E1 5a
12m. Climb the finger-crack in the third tower to its end then move right before stepping back left and teetering up the left-trending groove for a bold finish. **The Direct** is **E4 6b**.
FA. Tony Nicholls early 1960. FA. (Direct) Gary Gibson 1981

⓬ Pullet E1 5b
12m. Climb the wall to the ledge on *Chicken* and follow it to the base of its final scoop. From here, step right to climb the steep arete. A climb with the potential for many (poor?) word games and groan-worthy puns!
FA. Simon Horrox 1978

⓭ Piston Groove .... VS 5a
12m. The arduous groove that bounds the right-hand side of the tower. Bridging is the most elegant way of climbing it, at least on the blunt end!

⓮ The Mandrake E5 6a
10m. Climb the wall leftwards past an overhang to the arete and a bold finish. A side-runner in *Victory* protects the start but not the upper section. May never have had a 2nd ascent.
FA. Jonny Woodward 1979

⓯ Mandrill E5 6b
10m. The wall with a small roof to the right of *The Mandrake* has good but difficult-to-place micro-wires just over the lip, and the whole affair proves to be very exhausting.
FA. Andy Cave 2000

⓰ Victory .... VS 4c
10m. The angular groove which curves over leftwards at the top is an awkward thrash for most of its length.

⓱ Green Corner .... S 4a
8m. A luminous groove is one of the few lower-grade routes in the vicinity; pity it is often an unpleasant struggle.

⓲ Blood Blisters E4 6b
10m. Gain the thin crack right of the arete with difficulty then slap up the arete to a gruesome rounded exit.
FA. Gary Gibson 1981

⑲ Electric Chair ...... 🔲 **E2 5c**
10m. Climb direct to reach a narrow ledge in the centre of the wall. Then trend left to a crack before heading back right to finish up a precarious scoop.
FA. Jim Moran 1978

⑳ Bad Joke .... 🔲 **E4 5c**
8m. From the ledge of the previous route, climb the wall direct, Bald, bold and not really all that funny! Usually needs brushing.
FA. Gary Gibson 1979

㉑ Gallows .... 🔲 **E2 5b**
8m. Swing up the right-hand arete of the square wall, starting on the left and change sides to finish.
FA. Jim Moran 1978

㉒ Recess Chimney .... 🔲 **VDiff**
8m. Climb the wide chimney by climbing the left-hand side of the large block then choose an exit; the right-hand side is technically a little easier, the left is less of a physical struggle.

㉓ Dog Eye Rib ... 🔲 **E6 6b**
8m. A serious undertaking up the exposed rib. The crux involves a technical stretch for slopers and the finish is the stuff of nightmares. All the pockets are worse than they look, with one (just) taking a small camming device. Start from a block in the gully, or direct via a bouldery 6c move.
FA. Andy Popp 1987

㉔ The Sorcerer .... 🔲 **E3 6a**
8m. Climb the thin seam right of the arete with a taxing initial sequence then gradually improving holds.
FA. Jim Moran 1978

㉕ High Tensile Crack .... 🔲 **HVS 5b**
8m. The thin crack right again is tougher than it looks and proves to be a trying, tiring struggle for most.
FA. Colin Foord 1968

The final set of routes here are on the lower tier. The routes mostly follow cracks but sadly the wall is almost always very green, taking drainage from the grass slope above.

㉖ Buster the Cat .... 🔲 **HVS 5b**
8m. The crack and groove on the far left left give awkward and usually somewhat dirty jamming.
FA. Dave Jones 1979

㉗ Pug .... 🔲 **VS 4c**
8m. The better-defined jamming crack just right terminates in a grass-filled recess. Finish up this!

㉘ A Flabby Crack . 🔲 **E6 6c**
12m. Technical and excellent when dry, despite the grass on the ledge and the chimney finish. Tackle the thin crack-line with crucial final moves to gain the break and a much easier escape.
FA. Neil Travers 1992

㉙ The Stone Loach ..... 🔲 **E5 6b**
10m. An extended boulder problem leads up the thin crack past a niche to the break. Finish up the evil wide crack above (*Anthrax*) or, more pleasantly, wimp rapidly off rightwards.
FA. Gary Gibson 1982

㉚ Anthrax .... 🔲 **E3 5c**
14m. Multi-pitch 'pleasure'. The tasty thin (and usually green) crack in the arete of the chimney to the break (possible belay) then crawl left to finish up the 'evil wide crack'.
FA. Steve Bancroft, John Allen (alts) 1975

㉛ The Lum .... 🔲 **HVS 4c**
8m. The coffin-shaped chimney is grunted direct. Finish up the hanging flake on the left or just walk off right.

㉜ Bantam Crack ...... 🔲 **VS 4c**
8m. The diminutive hand-crack on the right is pleasant enough.

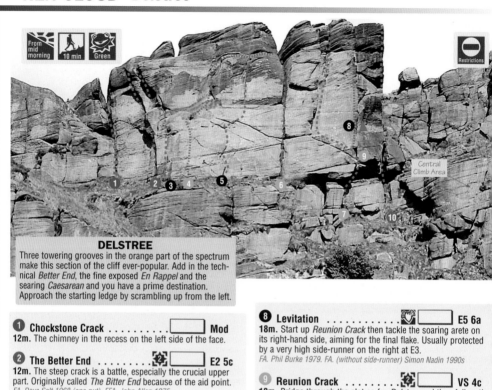

From mid morning · 10 min · Green · Restrictions

DELSTREE

Three towering grooves in the orange part of the spectrum make this section of the cliff ever-popular. Add in the technical *Better End*, the fine exposed *En Rappel* and the searing *Caesarean* and you have a prime destination. Approach the starting ledge by scrambling up from the left.

❶ Chockstone Crack . . . . Mod
12m. The chimney in the recess on the left side of the face.

❷ The Better End E2 5c
12m. The steep crack is a battle, especially the crucial upper part. Originally called *The Bitter End* because of the aid point.
FA. Dave Salt 1968 (one nut). FFA. John Allen 1975

❸ The Raid E4 6a
12m. Climb into the precarious groove in the arete to reach a ledge then take the hard crack to a finish up runnels.
FA. Jim Moran 1978

❹ En Rappel . . . . HVS 5a
16m. Mantel up the left-hand side of the front face, linking ledges, move right up to a slabby groove and climb this to more ledges. Escape up the chimney away on the right. A direct finish above the groove is better but harder, though still **5a**.
FA. Arthur Burns (Blizzard Buttress) 1927 Direct Finish, Joe Brown 1961

❺ Caesarean E4 6b
16m. A superb line cutting up the thin cracks in the steep face. Well-protected throughout but fingery, technical and sustained.
FA. Jonny Woodward 1980

❻ Main Crack . . . . VS 4c
16m. The left-hand of the trio of cracks is of an awkward width throughout and, to add to the fun, the exit is tricky too.
FA. Joe Brown 1950s

❼ Delstree . . . . HVS 5a
18m. The magnificent central crack set in a shallow groove is approached from a cave recess. It is delicate up the ramp and strenuous up the groove - hence the name. A rounded exit completes the fun, though according to an acquaintance who has been to Thailand it is nothing like an elephant's arse!
Photo page 31.
FA. Joe Brown late 1950s

❽ Levitation E5 6a
18m. Start up *Reunion Crack* then tackle the soaring arete on its right-hand side, aiming for the final flake. Usually protected by a very high side-runner on the right at E3.
FA. Phil Burke 1979. FA. (without side-runner) Simon Nadin 1990s

❾ Reunion Crack . . . . VS 4c
18m. Bridge through the slot as for *Delstree* and then follow the slab and the curving corner by mild laybacking to a juggy exit.
FA. Joe Brown late 1950s

❿ The Pinch E1 5c
20m. From a short way up the gully, climb the right-hand face of the tower to the last horizontal then step left and improvise those last couple of metres using a pinch-grip if you want!
FA. John Holt 1978

CENTRAL CLIMB AREA

⓫ Press on Regardless E2 5b
10m. The smart soaring arete on the right-hand side of the gully gives bold moves up the gully face, gained from the left along the first break. Wild positions make it worth the effort.
FA. Dave Jones 1978

⓬ Roof Climb . . . . VS 4b
The first route to climb both tiers.
1) 4b, 20m. A crack leads to a step right into a groove then move back left again up another groove leading to the terrace.
2) 3b, 10m. Finish up the deep crack and easy chimney above.

⓭ The Long and Short . . . E1 5b
1) 5b, 15m. Climb the luminous groove in the wall and, at its top, pull out left and climb up to the terrace.
2) 5b, 10m. The wide fissure above is hard work; at its closure exit right and finish up the wall.
FA. Tony Nicholls early 1960s

CENTRAL CLIMB AREA
The tallest part of the cliff, home to some great multi-pitch routes and the site of the only benightment on grit, *Central Climb*, where John Laycock was rescued by his climbing partner and their chauffeur.

5 routes - see next page

From mid morning | 10 min | Green | Multi-pitch

---

⑭ Anaconda .... 🏴 E4 6b
A devious climb which needs more attention.
1) 6a, 15m. Climb the shallow groove to an overlap and move leftwards. Then trend right to a small flake and tricky moves to the ledge and belay.
2) 6b, 10m. Climb the centre of the wall (hard but a good wire) then move left to the 'boot flake'. Pull up and left to join *The Long and Short* to finish.
FA. John Gosling 1976

⑮ Borstal Breakout .. 🏴 E4 6b
A better route than *Anaconda* but it can suffer from being dirty. Pitch 1 is an excellent E4 6a.
1) 6a, 20m. A short crack leads to a ledge (possible belay). Continue up the crack to its termination then head right up another thinner crack. Hard moves above gain a pocket and then the ledge - a brilliant pitch.
2) 6b, 10m. Climb straight up as for *Anaconda* but move right up a crack to easier ground.
FA. (Pitch 1) Jim Moran, (Pitch 2) Dave Jones (1 nut) 1978

⑯ Central Climb Direct ... 🏴 VS 5a
Not much more direct than the original.
1) 5a, 14m. Climb the wide crack that splits the face on the right awkwardly to a good stance on the regular route.
2) 4c, 14m. The flared groove, then the flake on the left, lead to a ledge. Originally the wall on the right was climbed, deviously.
3) 4a, 10m. Finish up the widening and easing crack just left.

⑰ B4, XS ..... 🏴 E7 6b
24m. The soaring arete is a fearsome challenge; a western *End of the Affair* perhaps? From the first stance on *Central Climb* move out to the arete and climb it firing on all cylinders. There is gear low down but a speedy belayer will still be needed.
FA. Simon Nadin 1986

⑱ Central Climb .... 🏴 VS 4c
An old classic finding a sneaky way up the crag's tallest face.
1) 4b, 14m. Shin up the wide crack with difficulty and hidden holds to a hard exit and a stance at the base of the main corner.
2) 4c, 14m. Climb the tough wide groove (OK it's 5a!) past a ledge (stance?) to a bigger picnic-style ledge on the left.
3) 3c, 10m. The groove rightwards, or the one out right (**4b**).
Photo page 81.
FA. John Laycock 1909

⑲ Encouragement ... 🏴 E1 5b
1) 5b, 14m. Climb the wall on crisp crimps (spaced gear) to the base of an elegant groove. Bridge up this to a good stance.
2) 5b, 14m. The solid jamming crack leads all too soon (unless pumped senseless - 5c) to easy ground. Exit boldly left up the wall or escape out right to easy ground.
FA. Tony Nicholls early 1960s

⑳ K2 .... 🏴 S 4b
A daunting Himalayan classic - then again perhaps not!
1) 4a, 12m. Climb the short steep groove to a stance.
2) 4b, 18m. The steep and slippery crack behind is the crux and leads to the easy upper ridge of *The Arete*.
FA. Arthur Burns 1927

㉑ The Arete .... 🏴 VDiff
A rambling classic up the ridge which has a mini-Alpine feel.
1) 6m. Climb to a belay on the ledge below a step.
2) 20m. Tricky and exposed moves above the ledge then relatively easy ground to the top. *Photo page 80.*

㉒ Arete Wall .... 🏴 VS 4b
16m. The short but steep crack in the shady north wall.

Change in viewing angle

Lots of sun | 10 min

The Arete

Restrictions

HEN CLOUD ELIMINATE AREA

⑧ Problem 1 . . . . 🔲 **V2 (5c)**
A magic little problem up the veins. There is a nice **V0 (5a)** problem up the ramp to the left as well.

⑨ Stokes' Line . . . . 🔲 **E1 6b**
6m. Perplexing initial moves gain the crack - sometimes.
FA. Mark Stokes 1977

⑩ This Poison . . . . . . 🔲 **E3 6b**
8m. The narrow wall also has a fiercely technical start. If successful, finish leftwards through the bulge above.
FA. Gary Gibson 1989

⑪ Slimline . . . . 🔲 **E1 5b**
8m. The slim seam that develops into a crack is precarious.

⑫ Peter and the Wolf . 🔲 **E6 6b**
10m. The blank wall gives a harrowing solo. Nice pocket work leads to the final hard move; undercutting to reach the break.
FA. Andy Popp 1990s

⑬ Fast Piping . . . . 🔲 **E4 6b**
10m. The wall just left of the first long fissure is technical and sustained until the beckoning crack above is reached.
FA. Gary Gibson 1981

⑭ Hedgehog Crack . . . . 🔲 **VS 4c**
10m. The crack widens gradually from finger locks to good hand-jams to plain awkward. The finish is wide and perplexing.

⑮ Comedian . . . . 🔲 **E3 5c**
12m. The bulging groove is approached via a steep wall and deep break (large Friends which get in the way of your hands). Lean left to gain the groove and follow it with sustained interest. High in the grade. Thought by some to be only worth a brace of stars - stingy sods!
FA. Steve Bancroft 1976

⑯ Frayed Nerve . . . . . 🔲 **E5 6b**
12m. Climb the scooped wall just right to the same break and then the steeper wall to enter a tiny but technical groove.
FA. Gary Gibson 1982

MODERN AREA
The next routes are arranged around the gully between Central Climb Area and Hen Cloud Eliminate Area. The first two are on the tower behind *The Arete* and provide popular lower-grade challenges.

① Modern . . . . 🔲 **S 4a**
20m. Climb the long curving flake to a good 'sit-down' ledge. Finish up the crack in the right arete.

② Ancient . . . . 🔲 **VDiff**
16m. The right arete of the face, passing a niche, to the ledge of *Modern*. Step left to the crack in the headwall.

③ Small Buttress . . . . 🔲 **HVS 5a**
6m. The short rounded arete at the top of the gully.
FA. Dave Jones 1979

④ Bitching . . . . 🔲 **E1 5b**
8m. The thin crack in the small buttress to the right.
FA. Gary Gibson 1978

⑤ Bow Buttress . . . . 🔲 **VDiff**
10m. Follow a diagonal crack out to the arete then climb the battered flake on the adjacent face.

⑥ The Driven Bow . . 🔲 **E7 6c**
8m. Direct up the scary rippled wall above the short crack.
FA. Jon Read 2002

⑦ Solid Geometry . . . . . . 🔲 **E1 5b**
8m. The smart arete has some delightful moves.
FA. Dave Jones 1980

Staffordshire | Whaley Bridge | Kinder | Bleaklow | Chew | Lancashire | Cheshire | Newstones | Ramshaw | Hen Cloud | Roaches

HEN CLOUD ELIMINATE AREA

The long tapering wall that forms the right-hand side of Hen Cloud has many superb routes across a spread of grades, and tends to be less green than the rock further left. The place is worth a day or two of your time. The right-hand end of the crag has more great routes from the ancient classic of *Great Chimney*, to the superb *Bachelor* routes and some stunning soaring aretes too.

⑰ Second's Retreat . . . . ☐ **HVS 4c**
14m. The groove is always an awkward battle and is often lurid.
FA. Joe Brown 1952

⑱ Second's Advance . . . . ⬚☐ **HVS 5b**
14m. The wall (with tricky mantelshelf) and the hanging crack above and right are altogether a pleasanter affair.
FA. Bob Hassall 1962

⑲ Corinthian . . . . ⬚⬚⬚☐ **E3 5c**
16m. The long bulging and technical crack is gained from the left, has a whole bunch of sloping holds, and is superb. An old peg remains (tut tut!) by the crux and should be backed-up.
FA. Steve Bancroft 1976

⑳ Hen Cloud Eliminate . . ⬚⬚☐ **E1 5b**
18m. The steep cracks in the wall give a steep and superb pitch. Layaways and jugs lead to a tricky entry into a shallow nipple-eroding groove which requires a bit of 'udgery'.
FA. Joe Brown, late 1950s

㉑ Cool Fool . . . . . . ⬚⬚⬚☐ **E5 6b**
18m. The long bulging arete. Climb to a block on the right then tackle the arete, sadly with a deviation at half-height to place runners in the crack on the right. Grade unconfirmed.
FA. Gary Gibson 1982

㉒ Rib Crack . . . . ⬚☐ **VS 4c**
18m. Climb into the chimney and then head up the hanging crack in its left wall by surprisingly pleasant moves.
FA. Bob Hassall 1962

㉓ Rib Chimney . . . . ⬚☐ **S 4a**
18m. The long chimney is approached by a crack to pass blocks and then gives classic bridging, as well as back and footing, if you don't get too involved with its dark depths.

㉔ Caricature . . . . ⬚⬚⬚☐ **E5 6b**
20m. The upper half of the face right of the chimney is classy and intense. Runners in the gully and a second belayer away to the right should reduce the danger on the nasty sequence to gain the front face. From a good flake (runners) make one hard move using a mono and you're almost there - then just go!
FA. John Allen 1976

㉕ Chiaroscuro . . . . . ⬚⬚⬚☐ **E6 6b**
24m. Follow *Bachelor's Left-hand* to the top of its crack then move left and teeter up the vague rib to good holds on *Caricature*. Climb the head-wall from right to to left (runner on the right) aiming for a final thin seam. Grade unconfirmed.
FA. Gary Gibson 1985

㉖ Bachelor's Left-hand . . ⬚⬚⬚☐ **HVS 5b**
24m. A major classic up the tallest buttress here and one of the best routes in Western Grit. Climb a tricky crack, a bulge then steeper cracks to a long move on a pocket to reach a huge flake (long tape runner). Reach the slab and ledges then step left and finish up the fine jamming crack to an awkward bulging exit.
Photos page 1 and 89.
FA. Don Whillans late 1950s

㉗ Parallel Lines . . . . ⬚⬚⬚☐ **E6 6c**
14m. The blank wall via a thin seam and tenuous moves to reach a left-trending ramp. Finish up or down *Bachelor's Climb*. A side-runner plus some unreliable gear at mid-height give little in the way of reassurance for the crucial crimpy moves.
FA. Simon Nadin 1985

㉘ Bachelor's Climb . . . . ⬚☐ **VS 4c**
28m. Another great route. Climb the steep bulging crack left of the arete on jams to a ledge, then continue by more jamming to a good stance on The Pulpit. Step back down, traverse left to the bulging crack and storm this by more glorious jamming.
FA. (pitch 2) Joe Brown 1952 (before this it finished up Great Chimney)

㉙ Space Probe . . . . ⬚⬚☐ **E4 6a**
The main arete of the Batchelor's wall.
1) 6a, 10m. Start on the left and make hard moves past poor gear until you can sprint up the arete to the pedestal.
2) 5c, 8m -The Helter Skelter Finish. Take the continuation arete until a couple of gripping moves left enter a short groove.
FA. Pitch 1 Jonny Woodward 1979. Pitch 2 Steve Bancroft 1977

HEN CLOUD - FAR RIGHT

The last section of wall, just around the corner from the tall Batchelor's Area, has the classics of *Great Chimney* and *Rainbow Crack* and a few top-notch hard routes like *Chameleon*. Further right the occasional worthwhile line is to be found scattered across the various buttresses, where seclusion is almost guaranteed.

Space Probe

1 Great Chimney . . . . **S 4a**

18m. The classical wide fissure is climbed by the left-hand corner with a step left onto The Pulpit if a rest is needed. Gain the right-hand crack a little higher. The right-hand crack can be followed throughout at HS but the gangly can bridge the whole affair. Well-protected throughout. *Photo page 6.*
FA. Siegfried Herford 1913

2 Rainbow Crack . . . . **VS 5a**

18m. The long crack and flake in the right-hand wall of the chimney give a fine jamming and laybacking pitch. It can be gained from the left (or direct which is nearer **HVS**).

3 Aretenaphobia **E6 6b**

18m. The stunning soaring blunt rib left of *Chameleon*, with much-needed runners placed in that route, whilst on the lead.
FA. Seb Grieve 1995

4 Chameleon **E4 6a**

12m. The beckoning flake in the front of the buttress is approached from the right by strenuous undercutting to good holds above the roof. Pass this with difficulty then get motoring up the layback flakes on the head-wall. Top end of the grade.
FA. Steve Bancroft 1977

5 Saria **E5 6a**

10m. The right-hand arete of the *Chameleon* face is climbed throughout and was formerly a fairly major sandbag at E3.
FA. Martin Boysen 1986

6 Left Twin Crack . . . . **HS 4a**

10m. The right-angle groove in the green recess is awkward.

7 Right Twin Crack . . . . **VS 4b**

10m. The opposite corner is similar but just a gnat's harder.

To the right is a massive tilted block and beyond this a pair of buttresses:

8 Thompson's Buttress Route 1 . . . **S 4a**

16m. Climb the central groove to a green exit onto a large ledge. The left side of the face behind gives a pleasant and well-protected continuation. The 'obvious' leftward descent isn't one!
FA. Archer Thompson c1910

9 Thompson's Buttress Route 2 . . . **HVD**

16m. Scale the awkward giant's-staircase to the right of the groove to reach the big ledge then follow the wide central crack above to a tricky exit.
FA. Archer Thompson c1910

10 Tree Chimney . . . . **VDiff**

14m. The tree has long gone but the imposing rift remains. It is tough where it is at its shallowest and is steep throughout.

11 Pinnacle Face . . . . **HVS 4c**

12m. The best route hereabouts. The left-hand side of the face is climbed starting up a short crack and tending slightly left on holds that are invariably a disappointment. Finish up the flake in the left arete. Escape from the top is problematical!

12 Pinnacle Rib . . . . **HVS 5a**

14m. The crack right of the arete of the block leads to its crest. The continuation arete is steeper and well positioned though at least there is some gear to be had.

The spectacular jutting prows that make up Ramshaw Rocks lean out towards the A53 Leek to Buxton road, the in-dipping strata being the exposed outer edge of the down-fold in the rocks here known as the Goldsitch Syncline. This geology makes for steep and exhilarating climbing, with many excellent juggy outings following steep and improbable lines. The place is also well-known for its ferocious wide cracks and some of grit's most rounded exits; a venue for the aficionado perhaps. Ramshaw is the least popular of the Staffordshire triptych, though this can only be a reflection of its easterly aspect and the quality of the other two cliffs.

APPROACH Also see map on page 44

There is parking on the minor road that runs round behind the rocks, reached from the A53, not to be confused with the two minor junctions just to the south that lead out to the Roaches. From here, tracks lead up to the ridge and over to the rocks, mostly just out of sight, five minutes away. To reach the

Mark Sharratt on *Dangerous Crocodile Snogging* (E7 6b) at Ramshaw. *Page 95* Photo: Sharratt Collection.

routes further along the cliff, the easiest option is to follow the cliff-top path then drop over at the appropriate point. The only difficulty with this is working out exactly where you are. A bit of trial and error might be needed, or careful reading of our map.

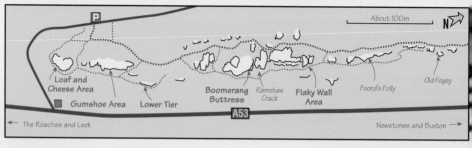

CONDITIONS

A series of east-facing (a real rarity) and south-east-facing prows and buttresses means tha early risers can enjoy the place in the sun, the rest of us tend to use it as a shady retreat on hot days. A couple of the buttresses protrude above the level of the ridge and get the sun for a more extended period, the Flaky Wall routes being the most notable of these.

OTHER GUIDEBOOKS - A more complete list of routes at Ramshaw is published in the BMC *Staffordshire* guidebook.

Colin Binks climbing *Flaky Wall Direct* (VS 4b) at Ramsahw.

Morning | 3 min | Green

The Loaf & Cheese

Descent

Descent

The Crank - 40m

THE LOAF AND CHEESE AREA

The section of Ramshaw Rocks nearest the road has a pleasant collection of lower grade routes, plus a mini-summit and a couple of rounded horrors. Not surprisingly the former are (much) more popular that the latter.

1 Assembled Techniques **E5 6a**
8m. The road-face of the lower wall leads with difficulty to the base of the upper tower. Finish up the left-hand arete of this.
FA. Richard Davies 1986

2 Loaf and Cheese . . . . **VS 4c**
10m. Climb a diagonal crack to ledges (crux) then easier work up the back of the Cheese, or the Loaf? Reverse back down.

3 Dream Fighter **E3 6a**
8m. Climb the arete to the break then shuffle leftwards and 'crawl' desperately up onto the final slab.
FA. Richard Davies 1984

4 Green Crack . . . . **VS 5a**
8m. The crack and widening green groove are classic Ramshaw terrain. One for digging out the bullet-proof clothing maybe?
FA. Pete Harrop 1972

5 National Acrobat **E5 6c**
10m. The water runnel that splits the large bulge is desperate. It is well-protected, but it requires a hideous mantel on a skin-ripping fist-jam and is only suitable for extreme masochists!
FA. Jonny Woodward 1978

6 Traveller in Time **E4 6a**
10m. Sprint up the flake then swing left and make a swift mantelshelf before climbing a precarious scoop to a desperately rounded exit. Large Friend protects the last move. Every move is supposed to be worth three stars!
FA. Andrew Woodward 1977

7 Body Popp **E4 6b**
10m. A right-hand finish to the previous route gives wild laybacking up the exposed and rounded arete.
FA. John Allen 1984

8 Wall and Groove . . . . **VDiff**
10m. Climb the slabby wall up and right to reach a ledge awkwardly then finish up the groove above. Gaining the ledge direct through the bulges is easier but a bit steeper.

9 The Arete . . . . **S 4a**
10m. Tackle the juggy bulges to the ledge then rapidly layback the short-lived arete above on its right-hand side.

10 Louie Groove **E1 5b**
8m. The shallow blank groove is a good test of footwork; small wires protect. Precarious but quite low in the grade.
FA. John Yates 1968

11 Leeds Slab . . . . **HS 4b**
8m. Pull through the central overlap and finish up the blunt rib

12 Leeds Crack . . . . **Diff**
6m. The pleasant jamming crack up the right side of the slab.

13 Honest Jonny . . . . **Diff**
6m. The right-facing groove just before the end of the wall.
FA. Jonny Woodward 1976

GUMSHOE AREA

The next section to the right consists of a thrusting buttress with a smooth wall to its right which is split by the short-lived but beautiful straight crack of The Crank.

14 Masochism . . . . **HVS 5b**
10m. The two-tiered crack is an almighty thrash - enjoy!

15 T'rival Traverse **E2 6a**
8m. Teeter leftwards along a scoop (runners up and right) passing a flake to a tricky mantelshelf finale.
FA. Graham Hoey 1987

16 Rock Trivia **E2 6c**
6m. The wall on the right is climbed desperately, though fortunately a high side runner is available, largely removing the risk.
FA. John Allen 1987

Dangerous Crocodiles 120m

Descent

The Lower Tier - 90m

GUMSHOE AREA

This is probably the most popular section of the cliff; close to the parking, a classic jamming crack and some lower-grade juggy fare just a little further to the right.

17 Trivial Traverse . . . . **HVS 5a**
10m. Skip along the high break. Trivial indeed, but still fun!
FA. Martin Boysen 1977

18 Sneeze **E1 5b**
8m. The left-hand arete of the next face leads to a thin crack.
FA. Nick Longland 1979

19 The Crank . . . . **VS 4c**
8m. Crank on those classic jams up the handle-shaped crack to a trickier finish. Short but oh so sweet, and 5a for wall-rats!
Photo page 5.
FA. Joe Brown 1950s

20 Ultimate Sculpture . . . **E8 7a**
8m. A solo up the arete right of *The Crank*. Has not been re-led since the demise of some pebbles a few years ago, though the moves are all possible. Basically two hard moves to reach a good pocket on the left of the arete. The route is 'safe-ish' with an attentive spotting team; just ensure to aim rightwards!
FA. Justin Critchlow mid 1990s

21 Chockstone Chimney . . . . **VDiff**
8m. The tricky rift has the expected eponymous feature.

22 Maximum Hype **E3 5c**
10m. The tilted rib that hangs over the chimney is approached from it and is taken right and left, usually at speed.
FA. John Allen 1987

23 Gumshoe **E2 5c**
14m. Excellent climbing up the middle of the face, being steep and stretchy although with plenty of buckets to swing about on. The finish feels a bit bolder and a long way off the ground.
FA. Martin Boysen 1977

24 Wine Gums **E4 6a**
14m. Follow *Gumshoe* to above its crux then climb rightwards up the leaning wall with considerable difficulty.

25 Tally Not . . . . **HVS 5c**
14m. Climb a series of steep grooves up the right-hand side of the steepest part of the face. Perhaps it should have been called *Tarry Not* because of the not inconsiderable angle of the rock.
FA. Martin Boysen 1972

26 Battle of the Bulge . . . . **VS 4b**
10m. The bulging crack is jammed, battled and bridged.

27 The Cannon . . . . **HVS 4c**
12m. A steep pushy start gains a groove and this leads to the projecting snout of 'the cannon' which is passed with difficulty.

28 Torture **E4 5c**
12m. Direct through the stacked roofs. Strenuous and reachy.
FA. Gary Gibson 1981

29 Whilly's Whopper . . . . **VS 4c**
12m. Enter a shallow groove from the right and trend left up the slab passing a bell-shaped flake near the top.

30 Phallic Crack . . . . **S 4a**
12m. Classic. The steep central crack line is climbed passing the phallus early on then continue up the widening crack.

31 Alcatraz **E1 5b**
12m. Climb the groove to a roof then make bold moves out right to enter and climb the crack on better holds.
FA. Dave Salt 1968

32 Juan Cur **E5 6a**
14m. The leaning prow is bold and strenuous although there is protection from Friends and a large Hex in the slot. Originally it traversed left to join *Alcatraz*, but it is better to swing into the finish of *The Untouchable*. The name is aimed at persons unknown who stole part of the belay whilst the route was being worked!
FA. Seb Grieve 1990s

33 The Untouchable **E1 5b**
12m. The steep crack in the left wall of the angular groove is reached via an 'expando-flake' and gives quality (though tough and painful) jamming. The route is always in the shade.
FA. Colin Foord 1968

34 Corner Crack . . . . **S 4a**
8m. The groove on the right is an awkward customer.

35 The Rippler . . . . **VS 5a**
8m. Teeter up the crinkly wall to a ledge and use a couple of chipadedoodahs to finish. A **Direct Start** is **6a**.

Staffordshire
Whaley Bridge
Kinder
Bleaklow
Chew
Lancashire
Cheshire
Newstones
Ramshaw
Hen Cloud
Roaches

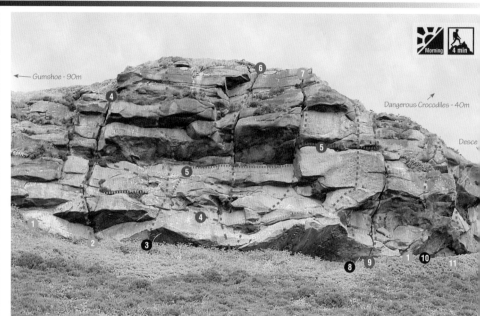

Morning | 4 min

←— Gumshoe - 90m

Dangerous Crocodiles - 40m

Desce

THE LOWER TIER

This section of rock has a trio of memorable roof cracks and some more modern desperates up the walls in between. It also features some excellent bouldering with superb soft grassy landings. Seldom busy, in a lovely situation, the verdant base can be very pleasant on a sunny morning, which is more than can be said for the roof cracks - at any time of the day or night.

1 Hem Line . . . . **V3 (6a)**
22m. An interesting boulder traverse along the lip of the lowest overhang, with crucial moves to pass the rib of *Tierdrop*, before eventually being forced back to the ground.

2 Crab Walk Direct . . . . **VS 5b**
10m. Pull powerfully over the roof at the crack and saunter up the grassy groove above to the top.

3 Sketching Wildly . . **E6 6c**
14m. Tackles the tiered roofs head on. Undercut past the first overhang, to where poor Friends just about protect hard moves rightwards over the next roof to better gear and, surprise surprise, a nasty sloping finish.
FA. Rob Mirfin 1994

4 Crab Walk . . . . **S 4a**
16m. Pull over the centre of the roof at a scoop then traverse crabwise leftwards between the overlaps to escape up the grassy groove at the left-hand end of the face.

5 Abdomen . . . . **S 4a**
18m. Another bizarre route. Start as for *Crab Walk* but climb to the roof then hand-traverse, and/or crawl rightwards along the break until thankfully upward escape becomes possible.

6 Brown's Crack **E2 5c**
14m. The central crack leads awkwardly to the capping overhang which provides the main meat of the route. An awkward accursed struggle for most, prepare to be mauled! *"Technically by far the most difficult route here"*, 1973 guide.
FA. Joe Brown 1950s

7 Prostration . . . . **HVS 5**
14m. Climb rightwards to the central roof crack, have a quick lie down in the slot, then pull smartly onto the wall to finish.
FA. Joe Brown 1950s

8 Colly Wobble **E4 6b**
12m. The pink hanging wall is gained via a pull over the overhang past four ancient drilled holes. A tri-cam or inverted wire in one of the holes just about protects the wobbly and massive stretch to reach easy ground above.
FA. Simon Nadin 1987

9 Don's Crack **E1 5b**
10m. Not unexpectedly, the right-hand crack is thuggish. Fortunately it is well-protected and the difficulties are soon ove Thought by many to be a harder proposition than Brown's!
FA. Don Whillans 1950s

10 Tierdrop **E5 6b**
8m. A classic micro-route which is short on length but big on impact. Just a bit too big to be considered a boulder problem, although it is usually climbed with mats and spotters. Climb u from the right and use the ancient carved runnels for holds.
FA. Nick Longland 1980

11 Tier's End . . . . **VS 5a**
8m. Pull over the right-hand end of the overlap to enter and climb the hanging groove which is over all too soon.

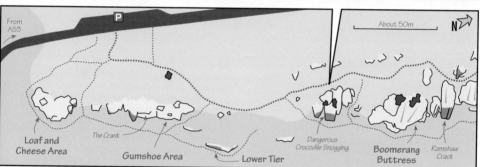

DANGEROUS CROCODILE SNOGGING
A pair of isolated buttresses, the right-hand of which
has some of the Peak's most popular hard grit routes.

Boomerang Buttress 20m

From A53

P

About 50m   N

Loaf and
Cheese Area

The Crank

Gumshoe Area

Lower Tier

Dangerous
Crocodile Snogging

Boomerang
Buttress

Ramshaw
Crack

---

① The Comedian .... HS 4b
10m. Climb the scooped front of the face until it is possible to crawl rightwards and then stretch for the top. Hilarious! A left-hand finish is easier but much less amusing!

② The Comedian Direct .... HVS 5a
8m. Climb the scoop and then the awkward juggy nose directly above. Also comical but less so than the original route!

③ Pat's Parched E1 5b
6m. The centre of the slab across the gully is unprotected.
FA. Pat Quinn 1991

④ Camelian Crack .... VDiff
6m. The pleasant flake that bounds the right side of the slab.

⑤ Blockbuster ... E5 6c
10m. Essentially an alternative start to *Dangerous Crocodile Snogging*. Start in *Camelian Crack* and break out right, making a few technical moves to gain the large hold in the middle of the wall. Finish direct. Better protected than the original line but a fall would still lead to a nasty clatter. Very height-dependent.
FA. Andy Turner 2001

⑥ Dangerous Crocodile
Snogging E7 6b
10m. A fine test-piece from the Nadin era of the mid 1980s. Roll into the slot below the fin of *Clippity Clop...* (very large Friend). Use the fin above to get established on the left-hand wall, from where a committing slap for the sloping top and some extreme scrabbling might just ensure victory. *Photo page 90.*
FA. Simon Nadin 1986

⑦ Clippity Clop, Clippity Clop,
Clippity Clop E7 6c
10m. The elegant arete of *Dangerous Crocodile Snogging* is technical and bold, and involves vertical 'a cheval' movements taken at a gallop, in an effort to gain height. Formerly soloed (at E8). A distant Friend 6 and possibly something even larger may protect .... well sort of!
FA. Seb Grieve Friday 13 September 1991. A typical choice of date for Seb to solo the first ascent.

⑧ Elastic Limit E2 6a
10m. Cross the roof by an immense span and some foot trickery. Then monkey past the lip to gain the ledge on the right and finish easily.
FA. Nick Longland 1977

95

Descent

BOOMERANG

A classic VDiff and some worthwhile routes in the 'orange zone' make this area worth a visit. Those who like their sport delicate and bold are also catered for with the memorable outings of *Wickslip* and *Handrail Direct*.

❶ Creep, Leap, Creep, Creep E4 6b
6m. The blunt arete is climbed on its right-hand side and has runners at two-thirds height. The final section can be leapt up or crept up depending on your style - or total lack of!
FA. Nick Dixon 2001

❷ The Wriggler .... HS 4b
6m. The twisting crack in the left-hand side of the buttress is as awkward as it looks - and the name tells a tale. A very 'traditional' Hard Severe from the days when men were men!

❸ Arete and Crack .... VDiff
12m. From the left edge of a recess, climb the arete above and the crack left again, to a leftward exit up the chimney.

❹ Handrail E2 5c
14m. Follow the previous route until the break on the right can be reached. Swing wildly along this below the overhang to a finish through the beckoning notch.
FA. Martin Boysen 1977

❺ Handrail Direct E4 6a
12m. A precarious and unprotected scoop leads to the start of the handrail. Scary stuff. Rumoured to be only E1 with a courageous spotter, but get that landing well-padded!
FA. Simon Nadin 1984

❻ Cedez le Passage E6 6b
12m. Climb the steepening slab to the right until forced left into the previous route. Apparently the much-needed direct finish is 'impossible'; now there's a challenge if ever there was one.
FA. Nik Jennings 2000

❼ Assegai .... VS 4c
12m. The groove gives awkward climbing especially at the overhang. Best enjoyed on the sharp end!

❽ Bowrosin .... VS 4c
16m. Reach the crack via the slab. The bulge just above is tricky and the crack beyond that, more pleasant.

❾ English Towns E3 5c
16m. A route that makes the most of the rock to the right of *Bowrosin*. For the harassed, side-runners can be placed from the route, lowering the grade a notch or two.
FA. Gary Gibson 1979

❿ Boomerang .... VDiff
16m. The elegant slanting groove is a classic with a steep start then a fine flake forming a mild uphill hand-traverse. The initial wide section is the crux (thread runner), after that get shimmying. A great place to start your comeback.

⓫ Wick Slip E5 6b
14m. The aesthetic curving arete above the start of Boomerang is precarious and bold. Side-runners in the crack on the left only reduce the grip factor a little.
FA. Nick Dixon 1987

⓬ Monty E4 6b
14m. Climb the slab on good pebbles to a crack. Traverse this to its end and finish up the arete. Could do with a direct finish.
FA. Mike Cluer (named after his dog) 1990s

RAMSHAW CRACK

This is real Ranshaw territory; short routes but savagely steep walls and cracks which will repel all but the most determined of attempts. The classic Ramshaw Crack is a real 'old-style' E4.

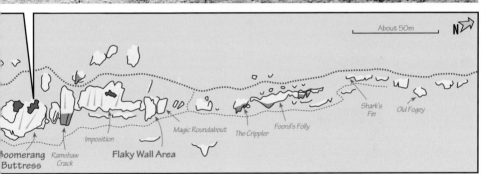

Staffordshire · Whaley Bridge · Kinder · Bleaklow · Chew · Lancashire · Cheshire · Newstones · Ramshaw · Hen Cloud · Roaches

---

③ Watercourse . . . . 　HS 4a
4m. The long groove is just about worthwhile when dry. Follow it past a grass field then take its leftward continuation before escaping out left and finishing up an exposed crack.

④ Dan's Dare . . . . 　VS 4c
9m. Climb a groove to ledges and then the arete on the right.
Pete Ruddle 1969

⑤ Gully Wall . . . . 　HVS 5a
9m. Climb the side-wall of the gully and the prow above.

⑥ Little Nasty . . . . 　E1 5b
9m. Pull into the nasty little crack and continue to a ledge. Finish up the wall to the left via a shallow groove (crux).

⑦ Electric Savage . . . 🎌🐚💣　E3 5c
12m. A short but impressive outing up the left edge of the giant roof. From above the initial bulge on *Little Nasty*, move right along a flange and pull over onto the terrace. Gain the beckoning flake and from its end make committing moves to finish.
Jonny Woodward (pitch 2) 1978 Nick Longland (pitch 1) 1979

⑱ Ramshaw Crack . . . 🔟💣🐚　E4 6a
12m. Climb a crack on the right then, from a lying-down position on the shelf, attack the awesome roof crack which widens from hands to useless in a very short distance. Holds out left help bridge the gap. Western roll into the final section and hoot for glory at having tamed the man-eater. A giant Friend slammed into the middle of the crux makes it more like E3.
FA. Joe Brown 1964 (one sling). FFA. Gabe Regan 1977

⑲ Never, Never Land . 🔟💣🐚　E7 6b
12m. The north-facing wall is arduous and bold. From the top of the crack leap out right to a crappy, creaking flake. Stuff some gear behind this if you want but it has been tested and it doesn't hold! When prepared, climb the centre of the wall direct to a finish guaranteed to focus the mind somewhat!
FA. Simon Nadin 1986

⑳ Green Corner . . . . 　S 4a
6m. The bounding groove gives pleasant climbing when it isn't too green, though sadly it often is.

FLAKY WALL

The steep juggy routes on the well-named Flaky Wall have always been popular. The lower walls to the left see less traffic, though there are worthwhile pitches here too.

❶ Zigzag Route . . . . **VDiff**
10m. Climb the disjointed cracks in the right wall of the groove, right then left to a final mantel. Steep cracks to the right give two variation starts at awkward **4c**.

❷ Roller Coaster . **E6 6c**
10m. The impressive prow has been climbed - but only a couple of times! Start in the centre, head left then ride it!
FA. Simon Nadin 1990s

❸ Boom Bip **E7 7a**
10m. The direct line up the buttress. The crux is a big dyno to the top of the crag. Gear at half-height protects - just about.
FA. Tom Briggs 2002

❹ Imposition **E1 5b**
8m. The leaning crack to the right of the prow is an uphill struggle all the way.

❺ Iron Horse Crack . . . . **Diff**
6m. Steam up the short curving, cracked groove in the wall.

❻ Scooped Surprise **E3 6a**
6m. A short diagonal crack gives access to the scoop. Interesting but barely independent.
FA. Simon Nadin 1984

❼ Tricouni Crack . . . . **HS 4b**
6m. The diagonal crack gives solid finger-jamming practice and must have been a complete sod in skidding, screeching nails.

❽ Rubber Crack . . . . **VS 4c**
6m. Pull into the flake system and finish up the groove above.
FA. Steve Dale 1973

❾ Darkness . . . . **S 4a**
12m. Climb the slab to the steep groove on the left. Bridge this then finish up the wide crack directly above the lower slab.

The next few routes finish on top of a tower. Belaying is a bit awkward and getting off the summit requires exposed down-climbing.

❿ Flake Gully . . . . **Mod**
6m. The gully on the left is a mild scramble. Continuing to the top of the tower increases the grade (**Diff**) and quality.

⓫ Flaky Wall Direct . . . . . **VS 4b**
14m. Take the right-hand edge of the south-facing side-wall or jugs to a rest then pull left past a rock tooth (which will come off one day - get your belayer to stand aside) into the final steep groove on solid finger jams. *Photo page 91.*

⓬ Flaky Wall Indirect . . . . **VS 4c**
16m. From the ledge on *Flaky Wall Direct*, follow flakes out right then swing round the arete and finish up the exposed face.

⓭ Cracked Gully . . . . **Diff**
12m. The right-trending break that splits the face right of centre is fairly straightforward.

⓮ Cracked Arete . . . . **VDiff**
12m. The juggy arete just right again is awkward to start.

⓯ Arete Wall . . . . **Diff**
10m. The groove bounding the buttress is obviously misnamed

MAGIC ROUNDABOUT

⓰ Crystal Tipps **E1 5c**
8m. Stride onto the slab from the left and climb to and up the elegant curving flake that hangs above its left edge.
FA. Andrew Woodward 1976

⓱ The Ultra Direct **E2 6b**
8m. Scratch a way onto the slab then climb rightwards to a finish over the narrowing overlap that caps the wall.
FA. John Allen 1984

⓲ Magic Roundabout Super Direct **E1 5c**
8m. Layback up the flake that splits the overhang then step right to climb the slab, finishing as for *Magic Roundabout*.
FA. Jonny Woodward 1975

Descent

Descent

Morning   7 min

Magic
Roundabout

Staffordshire · Whaley Bridge · Kinder · Bleaklow · Chew · Lancashire · Cheshire · Newstones · Ramshaw · Hen Cloud · Roaches

Morning · 7 min

Descent

The Crippler - 80m →

MAGIC ROUNDABOUT
A pleasant and popular slab and below it a short face with three neglected but worthwhile crack climbs. Always quiet.

Staffordshire · Whaley Bridge · Kinder · Bleaklow · Chew · Lancashire · Cheshire

19 Magic Roundabout Direct . . . . **HVS 4c**
m. Climb the delicate scoop then move right and follow the green streak boldly to reach easier ground.

20 Magic Roundabout . . . . **S 4a**
0m. Start at an alcove then 'walk' precariously up the thin amp to reach the black flake above the centre of the face.

21 The Delectable Deviation . . . . **VS 4c**
0m. Foot traverse the handholds of the regular *Magic Roundabout* to reach the same finish.

22 Perched Flake . . . . **Diff**
m. Climb onto the flake on the right and finish up the rib.

23 Be Calmed **E2 6c**
m. The highly technical scoop on the back of the tower.
A. Graham Hoey 1986

24 Force Nine **E4 6c**
8m. The pebbly slab direct is harrowing even on a calm day.
FA. Simon Nadin 1985

25 Port Crack . . . . **S 4a**
8m. Enter the crack by bridging an awkward groove, or by a traverse from the left, then follow it pleasantly.

26 Time Out **E2 5c**
8m. The central seam is hard where it fades. Stretch up and right to finish up a second shorter crack.
FA. Gary Gibson 1979

27 Starboard Crack **E1 5b**
8m. The right-hand crack is short, sharp and 'ard, with difficulties concentrated in passing the bulge at one third height.

Newstones · Ramshaw · Hen Cloud · Roaches

99

Morning | **10 min** | (14) on the roof 40m

FOORD'S FOLLY

The final few buttresses appear to offer little more than steep bouldering until you stand underneath them. *The Crippler* gives an excellent steep HVS while *Foord's Folly* is a classic thin finger-jamming exercise, and there are other quality outings. **APPROACH** - See map on page 95. Use the crag-top path and keep walking to just beyond the highest point of the ridge.

1 Big Richard .... S 4a
10m. Climb onto a tooth (sling runner) then continue up a wide crack and the juggy wall.

2 The Proboscid .... HVS 4c
10m. Follow *Big Richard* to the ledge then move right and layback the flying 'nose'.
FA. Nick Longland 1980

3 The Crippler .... HVS 5a
12m. Excellent juggy climbing. Follow the diagonal overlap leftward strenuously then pull over and sprint up a short flake.
FA. John Yates 1969

4 Escape E1 5b
10m. Swing onto the wall and climb it with difficulty. Avoiding the chimney just to the right also proves to be rather tricky.
FA. Martin Boysen 1977

5 Mantrap .... HVD
8m. The awkward chimney is hard work.

6 Great Scene Baby .... S 4a
10m. Traverse right to reach the crack (or do it direct at **5b**) which leads to a good steep finish over the nose.

7 Groovy Baby .... HS 4b
10m. The next groove is technical (for that read awkward) to access but much easier and more pleasant above.

8 Pile Driver .... VS 4c
16m. Start as for *Groovy Baby* but move right to climb a groove then move right again and scale the left-hand side of the prow via a good jamming crack. A bouldery **Direct Start - V4 (6b)** is also possible for the suitably talented.

9 The Press E1 5b
16m. Climb *Pile Driver* but stay low until it is possible to enter the steep crack that runs up the right-hand side of the prow. Press on up this rapidly before you get too pumped.
FA. Bob Hassall 1971

10 Night of Lust E4 6b
14m. Climb the bulge (great boulder problem - **V5**) then continue up the wall to the right of the final arete.
FA. John Allen 1984

11 Curfew .... HVS 5
12m. The leaning groove is best entered by a swift 'barn-door layback. Once established, it eases with height.

12 Foord's Folly E1 6a
10m. The superb crack and groove are usually soloed as stopping to place gear is such hard work and may make it E2.
FA. Colin Foord late 1960s. FFA. John Allen 1973. Originally it was climbed on a wet day using nuts to an in-situ peg and called The Big Frig (VS and A1). The name was changed just before the 1973 guide went to print. Chris Craggs took the peg out in the late 70s.

13 The Swinger .... VS 4c
12m. Swing up and left using the diagonal breaks to a good rest before finishing up the steep and exposed arete.
FA. Martin Boysen 1972

Back on the crag top, about 40m right of the last routes, is a leaning roof.

14 Shark's Fin .... HS 5a
6m. The flake that crosses the overhang is great training for th bigger Ramshaw routes, and one or two at the Roaches! The shortest three star route in the guide? From its top, try and spe the huge frog!

OLD FOGEY

15 Early Retirement .... Diff
6m. The scrawny groove and crack on the left is over-rated.

16 Rash Challenge E1 5a
8m. The leaning front of the buttress is climbed right then left.
FA. Jonny Woodward 1976

17 Honking Bank Worker E2 5c
8m. The arete and wall above have one of the strangest names
FA. Allen Williams 1984

18 Extended Credit ...... HVS 5
8m. The right-hand side of the buttress using the diagonal breaks to a finish up a scoop that 'leads you along'.
FA. Dave Salt 1973

Pocket Wall and Old Fogey 30m

OLD FOGEY

he final small buttresses are 20m from *Shark's Fin* and 60m ⸱om *The Swinger*. There is one more buttress at Ramshaw but ⸱ is on private land and rather undistinguished; hence it is not ⸱escribed here.

19 Caramta . . . . **S 4a**
2m. The pleasant jamming-crack to a finish over the bulges.

20 The Prism . . . . **VDiff**
0m. Bridge the central crack system to a choice of finishes.

21 Approaching Dark **E1 6a**
⸱m. The bulges lead rapidly (or not at all) to easy ground.
A. Richard Davies 1984

22 Lechery . . . . **HS 4a**
⸱m. The right arete is pleasantly varied; strenuous, and then ⸱elicate, and finally strenuous again.

23 Ceiling Zero . . . . **HVS 4c**
⸱m. Climb through the centre of the bulges via a 'jug-fest'.
⸱A. Gary Gibson 1980*

24 Pocket Wall . . . . **HS 4a**
⸱m. Climb the steep pocketed wall behind the lower buttress.

25 Curver . . . . **HVD**
8m. The curving line below the bulges, just down the slope, finishing up a flake crack on the right-hand wall.

26 Old Fogey **E3 5c**
12m. From the gully on the left cross a ramp to the arete, move round this and follow the steep, flaky crack. Good sport, though inclined to be dirty early in the year.
FA. Martin Boysen 1977

27 Old Fogey Direct **E5 6b**
16m. The steep wall used to have some pebbles on its left-hand side. These have fallen off but you can still climb the slab on its right at about the same grade. The flake crack above gives sanctuary. Short-lived but both absorbing and gripping.
FA. Jonny Woodward 1980

28 King Harold . . . . **S 4a**
10m. The wide rift on the right-hand side of the buttress.

29 Little Giraffe Man . . . . . . **HS 4a**
16m. Climb the rib until it is possible to cross the chimney and climb the thin crack that splits the roof. Shouldn't really require all that long a neck!
FA. John Yates 1969

NEWSTONES and BALDSTONES

Staffordshire
Whaley Bridge
Kinder
Bleaklow
Chew
Lancashire
Cheshire

Graham Parkes on *Incognito* (VS 4c) at the Baldstones. Page 106

A pair of secluded and quiet outcrops that can easily be combined in a single visit. Although well-known as a bouldering venue, there are also some worthwhile 'proper' climbs here, with the added attraction of a mini-summit or two, so it is worth bringing the rope and runners along. The most famous climb here is the hanging off-width crack of *Ray's Roof* (E7 6c), first climbed by Ray Jardine, the inventor of Friends, (the first true camming devices), way back in 1977. Despite the advances in climbing standards in the intervening 25 years, the route still sees few successful attempts.

APPROACH Also see map on page 44

There is parking for half a dozen plus cars on the roadside by the cottage. Take the track to the right of the cottages to arrive at the obvious nose of Charlie's Overhang, the first buttress of the Newstones, in about five minutes. To reach the Baldstones continue along the base of the crag to its end and a stile. Cross this then follow the ridge downhill along the line of the collapsed drystone wall to reach the cliff which remains hidden until one is quite close.

CONDITIONS

The cliffs take the form of a small series of rounded buttresses separated by 800m of grassland. The cliffs generally face east and so are in the sun in the morning, like nearby Ramshaw. On hot summer days, the cliffs make an ideal venue, with the rock in the shade but the sun easily available just around the corner. The cliffs are the most tranquil in the area, a great place to chill, and maybe do the odd route!

 BOULDERING - There is plenty of bouldering, especially at the Newstones . Some areas are indicated on the topos. Full coverage is given in the 1998 Peak Bouldering ROCKFAX.

OTHER GUIDEBOOKS - A more complete list of routes at the Newstones/Baldstones is published in the BMC *Staffordshire* guidebook.

Staffordshire · Whaley Bridge · Kinder · Bleaklow · Chew · Lancashire · Cheshire

CHARLIE'S OVERHANG AREA

The first buttress encountered presents an impressive nose which sets the heart racing of many a boulderer. The routes here tend to be a little high to be given 'V' grades but they are usually soloed. Further right is the jutting Ripple Buttress and Hazel Barn to the right again.

 BOULDERING - The short wall behind Hazel Barn has some of the best micro-problems hereabouts.

Hazel Barn Bouldering

Hazel Barn Area 30m

1 **Leather Joy Boys** . . . . . 🗺🗺 ▢ **V7 (6c)**
Climb steeply to the break then traverse along it rightwards on knuckle-grinding jams. Probably nearer E4 than V7!
FA. Mark Stokes 1984

2 **Charlie's Overhang** . . .▨🗺 ▢ **E2 5c**
6m. A brilliant little mini-route. Climb to the lip and contemplate the next move; then reverse to the ground ... or push on! V3ish.
FA. Tony Barley 1970s

3 **Newstones Chimney** . . . . ▢ **Diff**
6m. The awkward chimney. Starting up the crack on the left is worth **VDiff**.

4 **Moonshine** . . . . ▨▨ ▢ **HVS 5c**
6m. The middle of the wall through a bevy of bulges.

5 **Praying Mantle** . . . . ▢ **HVS 5b**
6m. Swarm on to the nose and finish warily through the shelving scoop above. Used to be good value at 4c!

Past some small buttresses with good bouldering is a fine wall with a seductive line of diagonal ripples.

6 **Ripple** . . . . ▨🗺🗺 ▢ **V4 (6a)**
The super line of finger-holds is longer and harder than it looks.
Photo page 103.

7 **Martin's Traverse** . . . . . .▨ ▢ **V1 (5b)**
The lower line is quite a bit easier.

8 **Hazel Brow Crack** . . . . . . ▨ ▢ **S 4a**
8m. Climb the juggy groove to bulges which are passed by moving leftwards.

9 **Hazel Barn** . . . . ▨ ▢ **VDiff**
8m. The shallow groove (quality holds) leads to a steeper exit.

10 **Hazel Groove** . . . . . ▨🗺 ▢ **V4 (6a)**
8m. Gain the short groove in the side-wall via an eliminate problem start.

11 **Nutmeg** . . . . ▢ **HS 4b**
8m. Climb past the solid flake onto the wall above.

Morning · 5 min

Change in viewing angle

Hazel Barn Bouldering

Sly Buttress 20m

Newstones · Ramshaw · Hen Cloud · Roaches

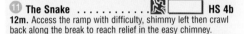

Sly Buttress 5m →

Change in viewing angle

Staffordshire
Whaley Bridge
Kinder
Bleaklow
Chew
Lancashire
Cheshire

SLY BUTTRESS AREA

The final buttresses at the Newstones are very pleasantly situated. They offer less for the boulderer but there is still plenty there; just follow the chalk and your imagination (or check the ROCKFAX Bouldering guide). For roped teams, the cracks on Sly Buttress are of considerable interest.

① Scratch Crack . . . . . . **HS 5b**
m. The undercut crack requires determined jamming to enter.

② Itchy Fingers . . . . **V3 (6a)**
limb the small wall on crimpy edges.

③ Bridget . . . . **V0 (4c)**
he slabby corner is pleasant, try bridge-ting it.

④ Rhynose . . . . **VS 4c**
m. Climb the easy crack in the side wall then make exposed nd awkward moves in to the final groove that cuts the roof.

⑤ Hippo . . . . **VDiff**
m. Follow the groove and the shallow chimney through the ulges and wallow on up the front face.

⑥ Rosehip . . . . **S 4a**
m. Climb rightwards through the lower bulges then continue p the easier flaky wall above.

⑦ The Witch . . . . **Diff**
m. Climb the groove left of the flakes then step left and vander up the mild face watching for crusty rock.

⑧ Candy Man . . . . **S 4a**
m. Climb rightwards up the front of the buttress over a series f bulges on the large perched flakes.

⑨ Trepidation **E4 6a**
0m. Start on the left and climb to the left-to-right break. Take his into the centre of the wall and finish with ... well you guess!

⑩ Sly Stallone . . . . **V4 (6?)**
rom a small edge, leap for the lip. The arete just to the left is a ery rounded **V6 (6b)**.

⑪ The Snake . . . . **HS 4b**
12m. Access the ramp with difficulty, shimmy left then crawl back along the break to reach relief in the easy chimney.

⑫ The Fox **E2 5b**
10m. Use cunning to tackle the wide left-hand crack. Reach the loose chockstone and wrestle with this then finish more easily. At least a grade harder for shorties. It was great value at HVS!

⑬ The Vixen . . . . **VS 4c**
10m. The right-hand crack gives excellent though short-lived jamming. Passing the initial overhang is the crux. Step left into the easy chimney to finish.

⑭ The Sly Mantelshelf . . . . . . **HVS 5b**
10m. Pull and push a way onto the left-hand edge of the elegant vein. Mantel up at its centre and finish more easily.

⑮ Sly Super Direct . . . . **V2 (5c)**
Gain the centre of the vein from directly below.

⑯ Sly Corner . . . . **VS 4c**
Start around to the right and rock up onto the arete. Tiptoe along to the centre of the vein then up. Using the vein for your fingers from the left is *Sly Direct* **4c**.

Angle Iron belay

Early morning 12 min

on side wall

Gold Rush 10m →

The first routes are around the arete on the slabby side-wall.

❶ Perambulator Parade . . . . . 🖼️ ⬜ **VDiff**
12m. Pull onto a ramp and follow it left then back right to the shady side of the tower. Climb this rightwards to a restricted stance and angle-iron belay. Abseil off carefully.

❷ Incognito . . . . 🖼️ ⬜ **VS 4c**
10m. Climb the centre of the slab (hard start) to a shallow groove (small wires) and an awkward leftward exit to the top. *Photo page 102.*

❸ Baldstones Face . . . . 🖼️ ⬜ **VS 4b**
12m. 'Walk' up the diagonal break rightwards to access the arete and finish up this in a fine position.

❹ Original Route . . . . 🖼️ 🖼️ 🖼️ ⬜ **E2 6a**
12m. The central groove is problematical until the first decent finger-jam is reached (a V2 problem). Teeter up the scoop above (no gear after the start) to an easier finish.
FA. Martin Boysen 1960s

❺ Baldstones Arete . . . . . 🖼️ 🖼️ ⬜ **HVS 4**
12m. Climb the leaning wall on the right to ledges then balance out to the arete and climb this, first right then left. Superb.

To the right is a wide bulging wall with some 'interesting' line

❻ Gold Rush . . . . 🖼️ 🖼️ ⬜ **E4 5c**
10m. An impressive line but usually dirty and seldom climbed. Traverse out right to enter the inverted scoop in the overhang and exit rapidly up a short crack. Unprotected and harrowing.
FA. Jim Campbell 1976

❼ Goldsitch Crack . . . . . 🖼️ 🖼️ ⬜ **HVS 4**
12m. The compelling 'arse' is approached steeply from the right and squirmed up with some trepidation.

❽ Baldstones Traverse . . . 🖼️ 🪓 ⬜ **V7 (6**
The line of sloping holds gives a pumpy traverse.

❾ Blackbank Crack . . . . ⬜ **VDiff**
12m. Climb the zigzag crack in the right-hand side of the face

❿ Forking Chimney . . . . 🖼️ ⬜ **Diff**
10m. The chimney is a forking struggle, though worthwhile.

⓫ Bareleg Wall . . . . ⬜ **VS 4b**
10m. Climb the groove then make an awkward move rightwar towards a better finish up the wide crack.

⓬ Morridge Top . . . . 🖼️ ⬜ **VS 5a**
8m. The pleasantly technical wall on the far right.

Ray's Roof Buttress

Early morning 12 min Green

Elephant's Wall

On side wall

Staffordshire

Whaley Bridge

Kinder

Bleaklow

Chew

Lancashire

Cheshire

AY'S ROOF AREA

▪e last buttress is home
▪ one of the most
▪amous routes anywhere
▪ grit - *Ray's Roof* - a
▪gendary ascent from the
▪0s by visiting American
▪ay Jardine. It has only
▪en handful of repeats
▪nce despite many
▪tempts. Apart from this
▪ere is little to excite here
▪ the roped climbing
▪ont, but there is a superb
▪le wall for boulderers.

● **Minipin Crack** . . . . ☐ **VDiff**
▪n. The kinked fissure gives a couple of awkward moves.

● **All-star's Wall** . . . . 🔲☐ **HVS 5a**
▪n. The right-hand side of the wall utilises a useful pocket and
▪horizontal break though it is all over far too soon.
▪. *Martin Boysen 1970s*

● **Ray's Roof** . . . . 🔲🔲☐ **E7 6c**
▪n. The widening hanging fissure is the hardest of its sort in
▪e Peak. Getting a foot jammed near the lip is just the start of
▪ur difficulties! A couple of big Friends are a good idea - to
▪lp carry your mauled body back to the car!
▪. *Ray Jardine 1977*

● **Johnny's Indirect Rear Entry** 🔲☐ **E5 6b**
▪n. The technical three dimensional 'slug-trail' on the wall.
▪. *The Johnnys (Woodward and Dawes), 'one summer'*

▪bove and right of Ray's Roof is a small wall with some near-
▪erfect bouldering and excellent landings

● **Ganderhole Crack** . . . . ☐ **S 4a**
▪n. The crack starting behind a block.

⑥ **Fielder's Indirect** . . . . ☐ **V1 (5b)**
Spiral round the rib from left to right, then climb the slab.

⑦ **Fielder's Corner** . . . 🔲🔲🔲☐ **V5 (6b)**
Accessing the beckoning hanging groove requires the strenuous use of a mono - all very ungritstone-like.

⑧ **Fielder's Wall** . . . . 🔲🔲🔲☐ **V9 (6c)**
On the face to the right there is just the one sloping pocket -
somehow use it to climb the wall.

⑨ **Elephant's Eye** . . . . . . 🔲🔲☐ **V4 (6a)**
From the flake, span left to a pocket, and then go!

⑩ **Elephant's Ear** . . . . 🔲☐ **V0 (5a)**
The elegant curving flake gives quality laybacking moves.

⑪ **Clever Skin** . . . . 🔲🔲☐ **V7 (6b)**
The tiny arete provides this skin-trashing gem.

GIBB TOR BOULDERING -
There is bouldering on Gibb
Tor, which can be clearly
▪een from this end of the Baldstones.
▪owever please note that you must
▪ot try to get to Gibb Tor from here
▪ince the area between the two crags
▪ an SSSI.

Newstones

Ramshaw

Hen Cloud

Roaches

WHALEY BRIDGE AREA

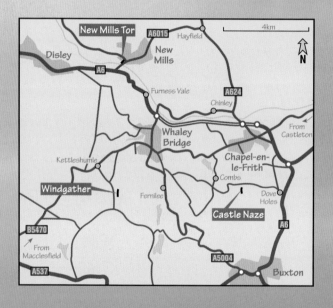

New Mills Tor
A6015
Hayfield
Disley
New
Mills
A6
Furness Vale
A624
Chinley
Whaley
Bridge
From
Castleton
Kettleshulme
Chapel-en-
le-Frith
Combs
Windgather
Fernilee
Dove
Holes
Castle Naze
B5470
A6
From
Macclesfield
A5004
A537
Buxton
4km
N

Staffordshire
Whaley bridge
Kinder
Bleaklow
Chew
Lancashire
Cheshire

New Mills Tor
Castle Naze
Windgather

The little twin sister of Castle Naze, here the climbs are generally short but well worth doing. The cliff faces west and gets both the afternoon sun and the wind. Finding belays at the top of the cliff sometimes requires a bit of cunning, an extra length of rope might be found useful to extend those that lie a long way back. Some belay stakes may be added in the near future, whether these are to help climbers belay at the top of the cliff, or to facilitat the fixing of top ropes for instructional groups remains open to question.

The strata of the rock dips into the hillside and this tends to lead to good juggy holds. The routes that follow cracks are generally very well-protected though some of the more-open face climbs need a wary approach, especially from teams new to the wonderful world of outdoor climbing. Skills learned here should serve you well.

Considering that the cliff has been popular for a hundred years, it is in remarkable condition please do your bit and see if we can get another hundred years out of the place.

APPROACH Also see map on page 108

There is parking by the road below the cliff for a dozen or so cars, and from here access takes a couple of minutes via the fenced track. The more remote buttresses may require double this approach time! If the parking is full, park back up the road by the old quarry or consider a visit to Castle Naze.

CONDITIONS

Looking out toward the west the cliff is inclined to catch any 'weather' that is going, though this exposed aspect keeps the cliff free from lichen, and also helps it to dry immediately after rain. The cliff is extremely popular with outdoor centres, though fortunately the place is extensive enough that you can usually find a buttress to go at. Windgather is at its most delightful on warm summer evenings whe the setting can be enjoyed to the full.

BELAYING

There have been a couple of recent attempts to legitimise the fixing of belay stakes (or bits of piping sunken into the ground) along parts of the cliff where belays are a little tricky to organise. This initiative has been taken by several Outdoor Centres. For everyone else who climbs here, expect to have to work a little at sorting cliff-top stances and take this chance to learn a skill that will stand you in good stead as you move on to bigger things.

Hard Diffs or VDiffs

Windgather is one of the few cliffs in this guide with a preponderance of routes in the lower grades. Because of technical issues with the ROCKFAX online Route Database we have upgraded all the Hard Difficult (HDiff) climbs to Very Difficult (VDiff) - we hope this will not upset too many people - at least there should be a few soft touches here now!

OTHER GUIDEBOOKS - A

more complete list of routes at Windgather is published in the 1991 BMC *Kinder* guidebook.

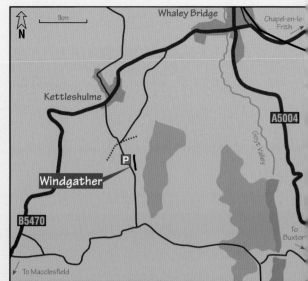

Staffordshire

Whaley bridge

Kinder

Bleaklow

Chew

Lancashire

Cheshire

Descent

NORTH BUTTRESS

The tall blocky buttress 120m left of the gate can be recognised by the widening upper section of *Green Crack* splitting its steepest and tallest section. There are several good climbs here that tend to be less busy than those nearer the car park - the approach only takes minutes longer!

❶ The Rib .... **VS 5a**
8m. From a block climb the centre of the protruding rib, passing just to the left of the nose by a couple of strenuous pulls on 'crimpy' holds.

❷ The Rib Right-hand .... **VS 4c**
8m. From the block a short flake gives access to the rib and this is followed on its right-hand side apart from the last couple of moves. Easier and better protected than *The Rib*.

❸ The Staircase .... **Mod**
8m. The pleasant stepped groove is as good a beginner's climb as any of the cliff, and is less polished than most hereabouts.

❹ Green Slab .... **S 4b**
8m. Climb the flake or the slab just left and make a tricky move to pass the overhang and gain the wall above. Finish more easily up the face. The gear is rather spaced - care required.

❺ Black Slab .... **HVD**
8m. Pull through an awkward bulge and then climb the flake above before finishing up the steep final wall. The upper section is quite awkward to protect.

❻ Green Crack .... **S 4a**
10m. Climb the groove and a polished scoop then bridge up to enter the steep tricky crack that splits the final wall. The wide upper section is awkward to protect, so make a point of getting a good safety net before you 'go for it'.

❼ North Buttress Arete Direct . **VS 5a**
10m. A great route though with a bold start. Pull onto the arete and climb its bulging left-hand side throughout. Not well-protected in its lower section.

❽ North Buttress Arete .... **HVD 4a**
10m. Climb an awkward groove and crack on the right side of the face to a ledge then move left via a niche to the arete and continue on its pleasantly exposed left-hand side.

❾ Chimney and Crack .... **VDiff**
10m. Climb onto the recessed edge then step left into the chimney and follow this and then the crack above to a taxing finish - which fortunately can be well-protected.

10m to the right of North Buttress is an isolated and wrinkled rib protruding from the heather slope.

❿ Heather Buttress .... **Diff**
8m. The crinkly arete is climbed to a to a ledge below the roof. Make an awkward pull through then tackle the short steep wall above. Not too well-protected but generally well in balance.

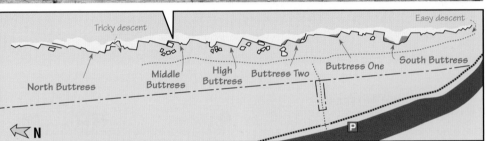

MIDDLE BUTTRESS

An attractive buttress towards the middle of the cliff and split by a series of cracks and with a fine jutting right–hand arete. The classic mini-desperate of *Portfolio* is found here along with some much pleasanter and much easier routes.

① Taller Overhang .... **VS 5a**
8m. The low roof is a short-lived struggle; a beefy pull gains a rest then more of the same - or scuttle off left.

② Small Wall .... **S 4b**
6m. After the short technical wall is a ledge and easy ground. Quite polished and substantially harder for the short.

③ The Corner .... **Mod**
8m. The corner groove is polished as its lower part is much used as a descent route. Climb it direct.

④ Portfolio .... **HVS 5b**
8m. Still one of the hardest routes on the cliff, rumoured to be a Joe Brown offering. Climb to the bulges and pull fiercely through these (well-protected) onto the short headwall.

⑤ Wall Climb .... **HVD**
10m. The parallel cracks and short chimney above would appear to be misnamed though are well worth doing anyway.

⑥ Centre Route .... **S 4a**
10m. Climb the awkward wall past an overlap to a finish up a thin crack. Not well-protected until the upper section.

⑦ The Slant Start .... **HVD**
10m. From the chimney on the right trend left to the upper section of *Centre Route* using polished holds.

⑧ Chockstone Chimney .... **Diff**
10m. Tackle the widening crack that never gets wide enough to be really worthy of the title 'chimney' The upper section is awkward but safe and as expected - well-glossed.

⑨ Mississippi Crack .... **S 4a**
10m. Climb into the good hanging crack in the face to the right and finish up the short groove above. Quite hard for the grade but at least the gear is good throughout.

⑩ The Medicine .... **HS 4a**
10m. Scale the stacked overhangs to the left of the arete to a tricky mantelshelf. If you start to struggle always remember it's doing you a power of good!

⑪ Middle Buttress Arete .... **VDiff**
10m. Start just left of the arete and climb up to and into a groove which leads to a ledge. Move left and follow the well-positioned arete to finish.

Tricky descent

HIGH BUTTRESS

The most popular buttress on the cliff and with good reasons; it is the tallest piece of rock here and the majority of the climbs are well worth doing. *High Buttress Arete* is one of the Peak's better Diffs and a great introduction to the cliff on whichever end of the rope.

① Bulging Arete .... **S 4a**
10m. Tackle the small overhang by its right-hand edge. Short and just a bit sharp, at least until you find the hidden hold.

② The Corner .... **Diff**
10m. The pleasant groove is followed throughout and makes a great first lead with solid gear placements throughout.

To the right and roughly halfway up the face is an orange sandy depression that has a passing resemblance to an oversized footprint, that of a passing dinosaur perhaps?

③ Toe Nail .... **VDiff**
10m. Climb straight up the wall to reach 'the toe' then continue in the same line to finish. Good climbing but the protection is somewhat lacking where most needed.

④ Zigzag .... **Diff**
14m. A pleasant (and misnamed) diagonal on which the protection is rather spaced. Best avoided on busy days! Start as for *Toe Nail* and trend right to finish above the ledge on *Footprint* or better still continue all the way out to the arete.

⑤ Footprint .... **VDiff**
10m. Start just to the right of 'the heel' and climb directly up the face passing a bevy of small overhangs. Good climbing but with only mediocre protection.

⑥ Nose Direct .... **HVD**
12m. Begin left of the arete at a niche and climb to 'The Nose'. Pass this by moving left before finishing direct. well-protected though with a steep and perplexing crux.

⑦ Director .... **VS 4c**
12m. The wall and bulges just to the left of the arete are tackled super-direct. If you get involved with any weaving about you don't really earn the tick!

⑧ High Buttress Arete .... **Diff**
12m. Follow the crack up the pleasant right-hand side of the arete to a ledge then finish direct or step left, both are nicely exposed. Good gear and great positions make this one of the best climbs on the cliff - a little more length and it would get the ultimate accolade of three stars. *Photo page 111.*

⑨ Heather Face .... **HVD**
10m. The south-facing wall direct via a variety of useful cracks and not too much in the way of greenery. The start is on rounded holds and not well-protected, though at least the sting in the tail has good runners.

Staffordshire | Whaley bridge | Kinder | Bleaklow | Chew | Lancashire | Cheshire

New Mills Tor | Castle Naze | Windgather

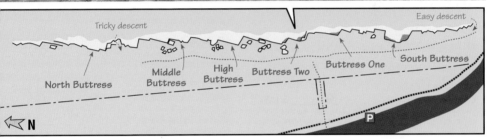

BUTTRESS TWO
A close-packed set of worthwhile routes ensures the popularity of this buttress, as does the fact that it is the nearest bit of rock to the road!

❶ Rib and Slab .... ☐ **Mod**
8m. The clean, narrow rib on the left side of the buttress is climbed via a perched flake. Pleasantly mild.

❷ Buttress Two Gully .... ☐ **Mod**
8m. The open gully on the left-hand side of the buttress gives pleasant bridging, another great first lead.

❸ Leg Stump .... ☐ **Diff**
8m. The slab to the right of the gully is climbed via a shallow groove or the bubbly rib to its left and then finished direct. Good moves but rather sparse gear.

❹ Middle and Leg .... ☐ **Diff**
8m. The fissure on the right-hand side of the slab has a wide middle section and a steep juggy finish.

❺ Centre .... ☐ **HVD 3c**
8m. The narrow slab just right pulling over a nose to start and passing an overlap. There is not much gear until just below the top, so some care is required.

❻ Squashed Finger .... ☐ **HVD**
8m. Hopefully the awkward leaning crack is misnamed. Quite hard work but well-protected where it matters.

❼ Struggle .... ☐ **VS 4c**
8m. It does just what it says on the tin! Battle up the well-protected crack splitting the overhanging nose.

❽ Corner Crack .... ☐ **VDiff**
8m. The leaning groove with a crack in the back is pleasant and has good gear throughout.

❾ Aged Crack .... ☐ **S 4a**
8m. From a boulder climb the bulges into the crack on the left (awkward to protect) and follow it more easily.

❿ Traditional .... ☐ **HS 4a**
8m. From the boulder swing right and climb straight up the face passing a flake. Good climbing upon which small Friends could well be found useful.

⓫ Broken Groove .... ☐ **Diff**
8m. The short left-slanting groove in the right-hand arete of the cliff is pleasant enough and is well-protected.

⓬ Cheek .... ☐ **VS 5a**
8m. Climb leftwards to the arete from a block on the right (opposite the path to the cliff). A steep little number with good but rather fiddly protection.

BUTTRESS ONE
There are only a small set of worthwhile routes on Buttress One but that means it tends to be quieter than elsewhere.

① Face Route 2 . . . . **Diff**
8m. The cracks on the left are followed slightly rightwards to a shallow groove and a finish passing the left-hand side of a small overhang.

② Face Route 1 . . . . **HVD**
8m. Pull over a bulge in the centre of the buttress then plod on up the striated face to a ledge and an interesting finish in the same direct line. Poorly-proected.

③ First's Arete . . . . **VDiff**
8m. Climb into a grassy niche then exit right from this and take the crack on the right-hand side of the arete before moving back around to the left for a pleasant finish.

④ Side Face . . . . **S 4a**
8m. The centre of the south-facing wall is climbed using a set of unhelpful shelving holds to a finish via a small niche.

SOUTH BUTTRESS

⑤ Overhanging Arete . . . . **VDiff**
10m. From the gully, trend right across the wall to the arete.

⑥ Leg Up . . . . **VS 4b**
10m. From a block under the roof pull onto the undercut arete with difficulty then finish easily.

⑦ Route 2 . . . . **VS 4b**
10m. From the same block move right to pass the bulge then follow the good crack to a finish on the right.

⑧ Route 1.5 . . . . **HVS 4c**
10m. The centre of the face is steep and strenuous.

⑨ Editor's Note . . . . **VS 5a**
10m. From the recess pull left and climb the right-hand side of the face. Another pumpy little number.

⑩ South Buttress Arete Direct . . **E1 5b**
10m. From the recess pull right onto the steep arete and sprint smartly up this. The grade is for lanky gymnasts who can actually reach the holds and manage the initial moves!

⑪ Route 1 . . . . **HS 4a**
12m. Start up the groove on the right then make a tricky traverse past the arete to a ledge. Finish up and left past blocks.

⑫ South Buttress Crack . . . . . **Mod**
10m. The groove that bounds the buttress on its right.

⑬ Left Triplet Crack . . . . **Mod**
6m. The baby of the trio.

⑭ Middle Triplet Crack . . . . **S 4a**
6m. Steep but with a choice of biffos and good runners.

⑮ Right Triplet Crack . . . . **S 4a**
6m. Quite strenuous but can be well-protected

⑯ Overlapping Wall . . . . **S 4a**
6m. The short steep face that is almost the cliff's last gasp.

SOUTH BUTTRESS
The most southerly buttress here takes the form of a large square block of rock with a cave/recess at its bottom right-hand corner. The routes here tend to be harder than elsewhere on the cliff so if you think you are tough enough - then step this way.

CASTLE NAZE

An excellent though not very extensive outcrop which can be considered as Wingather's bigger brother, with taller, steeper routes and more climbs in the 'orange zone'. Many of the routes follow steep cracks and grooves and on most climbs the protection is excellent.

Castle Naze has seen the attention of climbers for a century or so now. It is not as popular as nearby Windgather, the lack of really easy routes and the fact that fixing belays above the cliff is awkward tends to reduce the number of teams interested in top-roping. Also the style of climbing, often involving steep jamming, requires a bit of technique and gritstone 'savvy'. If you have learnt the basics indoors or at Windgather, a session or two here should hone your technique before moving on to even bigger things.

Colin Binks on *Nozag* (VS 4c) at Castle Naze. *Page 122*

APPROACH Also see map on page 108

The crag is situated high above the tiny village of Coombs, to the south of Chapel-en-le-Frith. There is parking for 3 cars in a muddy layby on the minor road that runs between Dove Holes and Combs. Walk up the road for 30m and then follow the steep track that slants rightwards up the cliff passing a steep wooden fence (4b?) to the left-hand end of the cliff.

CLIFF-TOP BELAYS

Above much of the cliff is a steep bank where belays are awkward to find; some care and ingenuity is required. There are a few spikes in place but long slings for lassoing blocks may come in handy.

CONDITIONS

The cliff faces west into the afternoon sun but is exposed to the west wind because of its situation close to the ridge of the hill - great for keeping the mosquitoes away in high summer but too bracing for most on drafty spring and autumn days. The crag dries quickly except for the north-facing area of rock to the left of *The Crack*.

OTHER GUIDEBOOKS - A more complete list of routes at Castle Naze is published in the 1991 BMC *Kinder* guidebook.

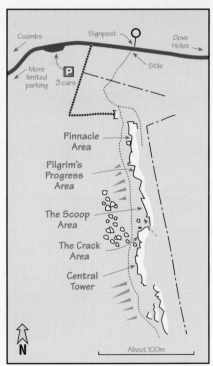

Staffordshire

Whaley Bridge

Kinder

Bleaklow

Chew

Lancashire

Cheshire

PINNACLE AREA

The left-hand side of the cliff has an excellent collection of lower-grade climbs on quality rock. There is the occasional loose block and belaying at the top of the cliff requires care.

❶ Double Crack . . . . **VDiff**
4m. The wide fissure becomes parallel cracks and has interesting moves passing the small beak.
FA. Jim Rubery 1984

❷ The Arete . . . . **HS 4b**
4m. The slabby arete is short and sweet. A side-runner may help the timid and a small Friend is useful just below the top.
FA. Jim Rubery 1984

The bay and wall to the right have four short and unrecorded routes following the obvious cracks - Diff to HVD.

❸ Pinnacle Crack . . . . **VDiff**
6m. Climb the left-hand wall and the wide crack (awkward to reach) then step left to the crack in the wall.

❹ Pinnacle Arete . . . . **VDiff**
6m. The outside edge of the pinnacle has a bold-feeling start. Be warned, the top block moves. Step left or right to finish.

❺ Sheltered Crack . . . . **VDiff**
6m. Surprisingly the crack behind the pinnacle is not sheltered from the west wind, though it is steep and well-protected.

❻ Bow Crack . . . . **HVD 3c**
6m. Take the thin right-hand branch to gain a block (crux) and a steep finish. Avoiding the bridging start (and perhaps wearing blinkers) gives a more consistent pitch.
FA. Jim Rubery 1984

❼ Slanting Crack . . . . **S 4a**
6m. Climb the crack to a groove with tricky moves to get past the big triangular chockstone and up the final corner.

**❽ Overhanging
Chockstone Crack** . . . . **VDiff**
8m. Climb past the right-hand side of the huge chockstone using holds on the right to gain the upper crack. Easier than it looks. A dirty through route avoids all the good climbing!!

❾ The Fifth Horseman . . . . . . **HVS 5a**
8m. Gallop up the narrow wall just right.
FA. Jim Rubery 1984

To the right is a ledge accessed by several short cracks. There are two interchangeable finishes up the wider cracks above; the left is a poorly protected HS 4b, and the right is S 4a.

❿ V-Corner . . . . **S 4b**
8m. An awkward thrutch or left-facing layback leads to the ledge and a finish up the easier right-hand crack.

⓫ Thin Cracks . . . . **VS 5a**
8m. The thin crack to the ledge (hard until the footholds start to arrive) and then select a way on to the cliff top - see above.

⓬ Muscle Crack . . . . **VDiff**
8m. The wider central crack to a choice of (harder) finishes.

⓭ Bloody/Block Cracks . . . . **S 4a**
8m. Either fissure to the recess and the flake crack above.

⓮ The Nose . . . . **VS 4b**
12m. Climb leftwards out of the recess (wide bridging?) to a slot then step back right onto the top of the overhang and climb the crucial upper arete which is not well-protected.

118

Descent - - - - ➤

Staffordshire

Whaley Bridge

Kinder

Bleaklow

Chew

Lancashire

Cheshire

PILGRIM'S PROGRESS AREA

A fine set of climbs in the S and HS categories which mostly follow good crack systems. Some of the routes are quite technical for their grade but protection is usually plentiful and easy to place, a good venue for learning the art.

15 **The Nithin** . . . . **S 4a**
12m. The right-hand crack in the recess (awkward) to a ledge and the wide crack on the left. The arete direct is **HS 4a**.

16 **Flake Crack** . . . . **HS 4b**
12m. Climb a flaky crack in the gully wall to the ledge on the left and continue up the flake with care to a tricky exit.

17 **The Flywalk** . . . . **S 4a**
10m. The battered cracks in the right wall are worth doing to ledges (not bridging to the opposite wall of the groove is probably worth **VS 4b**), then finish out right.
The groove direct is **Main Corner - S 4a** but sadly avoiding the cracks of *The Flywalk* is practically impossible.

18 **The Niche** . . . . **S 4a**
12m. The niched-crack gives good steep climbing on solid jams. Passing the niche is a little awkward but the gear is good.

19 **Niche Arete** . . . . . . **VS 5a**
12m. Climb the delicate arete with stretchy moves. Protection at the level of the niche is below the crux! Serious for the short.

20 **Orm and Cheep** **E1 6a**
12m. The shallow slanting groove in the side-wall leads to the pocketed face (side-runner) and sprint. No deviations allowed!
FA. Al Evans 1989

21 **Studio** . . . . **HS 4b**
12m. Climb the good crack then mantelshelf rightwards (hard but safe) or layback (easier but bolder) then follow the cracks only. Following the left-hand crack is harder. *Photo page 108.*

22 **A.P. Chimney** . . . . **HS 4a**
12m. The wide crack in the groove is 'absolutely perpendicular' and also quite steep. Classic bridging or technical thrutching are the usual forms of progress. The upper part is easier.

23 **Pod Crack** . . . . **HVS 5b**
10m. Climb the thin cracks past the pod to a final groove.
FA. Jim Rubery 1984

24 **Pitoned Crack** . . . . **HVS 5b**
12m. The thin crack is gained from the next route. Once aided and still manages to be a little artificial.

25 **Pilgrim's Progress** . . . . **HS 4b**
12m. The steep crack with the odd holds on the arete will test your jamming technique. The groove above has a tricky exit.

26 **Little Pillar** . . . . **VS 4b**
12m. A tough start up twin cracks and an awkward finish.

27 **Ledgeway** . . . . **HVS 5a**
12m. Climb the curving crack to a good ledge then climb the wall on the right passing a slanting crack. The arete to the left of the start is **Short and Sweet - 6a**.

28 **No Name** . . . . **S 4b**
12m. Climb the tough groove to the right end of the ledge and the easier continuation directly above.

29 **Keep Buttress** . . . . **HVS 5a**
12m. Climb thin parallel cracks to the protruding square arete and tackle this by the steep groove on the right.

30 **Keep Corner** . . . . **S 4a**
12m. The groove left of the jutting buttress was popular in antiquity, hence the polish. Awkward but well-protected and a nice pitch. The last section is easier than it looks from below.

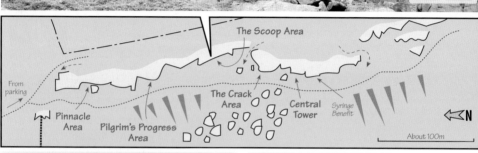

THE SCOOP AREA

The central part of the cliff has its best known feature climbed by its most famous route; *Scoop Face*. This was a test-piece in years gone by and the eroding ground and polished holds mean that it is still no push-over 90 years on.

① Keep Arete .... **VS 4b**
12m. The steep left arete of the buttress is climbed passing a small thread at half-height. Delicate and quite bold.

② Scoop Direct .... **HVS 5b**
12m. Climb steeply into the scoop then balance up its left edge using a thin crack before finishing straight up or rightwards into the wide crack which is a touch easier.

③ Scoop Face ..... **HVS 5a**
12m. The classic of the crag. Using glassy slopers reach a good hold (5b for the short) and attain a standing position precariously. Pad across the scoop and go up a thin crack to a pocket (big nut) and a tricky (crucial if you are pumped?) finish on the left. Barefoot ascents have long been traditional though the modern alternative of sticky rubber is a much better idea! For those who can't manage the start, the scoop can be accessed from *Keep Arete* at **VS 4c**. *Photo opposite.*
FA. Stanley Jeffcoat 1914

④ Scoop Face Direct .... **HVS 5c**
10m. Climb left from the block with difficulty (5b for the tall), up the wall and into the centre of *The Scoop* via a good pocket and hard mantelshelf. Finish as for the regular route.

⑤ Scoop Wall **E1 5b**
10m. Climb the steep wall on spaced holds to reach the right–hand edge of *The Scoop*. Jig left then right to finish, neatly outflanking the capping overlap.

⑥ Footstool Left .... **S 4a**
8m. The wide crack that passes to the left of the tall tooth is a bit of a struggle at the bottom and manages to feel rather committing at the top when passing the overhang.

⑦ Piano Stool .... **HVS 5b**
10m. Laying away up the steep front face of the tooth is a bit artificial; if successful continue up the arete above.
FA. Malc Baxter 1988

⑧ Footstool Right .... **HVD 4a**
8m. The oft-green groove to the right of the tooth has good holds and good protection and is worth doing when dry.
FA. Dave Gregory 1984

⑨ Layback .... **VDiff**
8m. The pleasant flake and groove above require a slightly blinkered approach, though the moves are good enough.

⑩ Combs Climb .... **S 4a**
8m. The thin crack throughout. A good sustained micro-route though avoiding a foot in the previous climb might be difficult.
FA. Dave Gregory 1984

⑪ Staircase .... **HVD**
8m. The obviously-named feature leads left then right to a finish up the groove just to the right of the previous route.

Colin Binks climbing the left-hand start to *Scoop Face* (VS 4c) at Castle Naze. *Opposite*

Descent

THE CRACK AREA
The tallest buttress on the cliff and home to some of the very best outings here. Routes such as *The Crack* and *Nozag* would be immensely popular were they on one of the Eastern Edges. Here they don't see much traffic at all.

The first route is mentioned for its historical significance.

Herford's Girdle Traverse
VS 4b
90m. Seigfried Herford invented the genre here, the route that spawned a thousand imitations from Scafell to El Cap. Left to right is usual from the start of the cliff to *Deep Chimney* and an hour was thought a good time in the 1920s. Reaching and descending *Keep Corner* is generally regarded as the crux, especially for the second man. The precise line and the stances are left for the adventurer to rediscover.
FA. Seigfried Herford c.1910

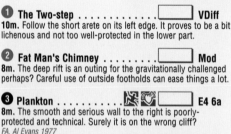

1 The Two-step . . . . **VDiff**
10m. Follow the short arete on its left edge. It proves to be a bit lichenous and not too well-protected in the lower part.

2 Fat Man's Chimney . . . . **Mod**
8m. The deep rift is an outing for the gravitationally challenged perhaps? Careful use of outside footholds can ease things a lot.

3 Plankton **E4 6a**
8m. The smooth and serious wall to the right is poorly-protected and technical. Surely it is on the wrong cliff?
FA. Al Evans 1977

4 Deep Crack . . . . **VDiff**
8m. Obvious from the name. Pleasant moves lead up the crack, starting from the base of the chimney and keeping left.
FA. Dave Gregory 1984

5 Deep Chimney . . . . **VDiff**
8m. The dark fissure cuts deep behind the buttress, severing it from the hillside behind. Get stuck into this one for maximum pleasure. A 'classic' of its genre if you know what I mean!

6 Birthday Climb . . . . . . **HVS 5b**
14m. A crack leads to a recess, trend left from this to reach a hidden flake set in the left arete and follow this strenuously to the top. Fine exposed climbing.

7 The Crack . . . . **VS 4b**
14m. Start as for *Birthday Climb* (a bit of a boulder problem) but follow the excellent steep fissure through the overhang and up the face above, on solid jams throughout.

8 Nozag . . . . **VS 4c**
14m. Follow the right-hand crack to the arete of the buttress until it starts to slant away right. Pull onto the face and follow thin crack directly and with some difficulty in the upper part (big Friend). Superb climbing with a perfectly-positioned crux and high in the grade. *Photo page 117.*

9 Zigzag Crack . . . . **HS 4b**
12m. Follow the previous route but stay with the diagonal crack all the way to reach the wide fissure and an easy finish.

10 Zig-a-Zag-a . . . . **VDiff**
12m. Climb the groove to a ledge then the wall immediately right of the chimney. Beware of an unexpected loose block that lurks a short distance below the top.
FA. Dave Gregory 1984

11 Long Climb . . . . **VDiff**
14m. Climb the blocky groove to a ledge then select a finish. The main angle is the easiest and there are trickier options to either side though trying to stay independent spoils the route.

CENTRAL TOWER

The second most impressive part of the cliff has a small selection of worthwhile climbs in a setting that is far from central. Down and right of the Central Tower is a quarry with a trio of unremarkable routes, refugees from the one of the grottier bays at Millstone perhaps?

❶ Central Tower . . . . 🔲 **VDiff**

12m. A green groove leads to a ledge on the right, step out left to another ledge and finish by the groove on the right. A bit vegetated, but still worth the effort and excitingly exposed towards the top!

❷ Atropine . . . . 🔲 **VS 4b**

14m. Excellent and exposed. Climb over a flake to a ledge (awkward) then take the slabby ramp and thin crack (crux) on the left to ledges. Tackle the strenuous layaway flake-crack to more ledges then choose a finishing crack, the right-hand one being both a little harder and also a little better.
FA. Lew Hardy 1977

❸ The Ugly Bloke . . . . . . 🔲 **E3 6a**

12m. Fierce and serious with only so-so gear. Climb to the top of the slabby ramp then step left and power up the wall on tiny holds to a poor pocket. From here finish with care. Said to be E5 if the runners rip!!
FA. Joe Bawden 1997

❹ Primadonna . . . . 🔲 **E4 6a**

12m. From the top of the ramp climb the arete on its right-hand side throughout. The crux is short but serious and very much height dependent, prepare for a torrid time if you are short.
FA. Joe Bawden 1997

❺ Belladonna . . . . 🔲 **E1 5c**

12m. Devious though with some good moves and a certain logic to the line. Follow *Primadonna* up the right-hand side of the arete until forced out right below an overlap. Pull over this to reach a second overlap then trend back left (beware of a loose hold) to the upper arete and an exposed finish.
FA. Al Evans 1977

❻ Green Crack . . . . 🔲 **S 4a**

14m. From the ledge at the start of the previous three routes follow the groove trending right to a steep final section. It is best to belay just below the top to avoid getting too involved with the loose slope above.

To the right the cliff has been quarried in the past and the rock is still unreliable to a greater or lesser extent. Half a dozen routes have been claimed here in the past though several of them, especially the easier offerings, are not very edifying experiences. The rest are just about worth doing!

❼ Morocc'n Roll . . . . . . 🔲 **E1 5c**

16m. The thin crack slanting up the steep slab leads to a groove and higher, a ledge (possible stance - an old peg may be in place). Finish up the totty arete on the right.
FA. Jim Rubery 1986

❽ Syringe Benefit . . . . . 🔲 **E1 5c**

16m. The right-hand crack is tricky to start, then continue in the same line to a finish as for *Morocc'n Roll*.
FA. Jim Rubery 1986

❾ Peg Crack . . . . 🔲 **E1 5c**

16m. The thin once-pegged crack gives good moves although the tottering grot above rather spoils things.

NEW MILLS TOR

The secret crag of Western Grit, set in a deep gloomy gorge right bang in the centre of New Mills. The cliff is witheringly steep, and surprisingly tall for grit. The rock is a rather soft and sandy gritstone, not the well-weathered stone you might be used to. These various factors all add up make the routes here intimidating and pumpy propositions. Although some of the routes are esoteric the best of the climbs here are very good and the oddness of the setting adds to the whole experience of the place - if you are passing by, call in and sample the unique experience that is New Mills Tor.

APPROACH Also see map on page 108

There is limited (pay and display - time limits apply) parking on the small loop road behind the bus turning-circle in the centre of New Mills. If this is full, or you fancy climbing for longer than an hour or two, there are various quiet side-streets nearby where parking is possible. From behind the bus turning-circle a steep path leads down through classic 'Summer Wine' scenery to the left-hand end of the cliff, five minutes away. If you have come for a big session it is worth saving enough strength for the steep walk back out!

> **OTHER GUIDEBOOKS -** A more complete list of routes at New Mills Tor is published in the 1991 BMC *Kinder* guidebook.

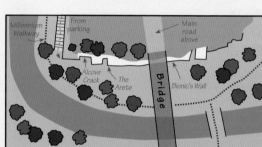

CONDITIONS

The crag is steep enough to stay dry in light rain and the tree canopy in summer adds to this shelter. The steepest part of the cliff is right under the viaduct, and this stays dry even in monsoon conditions, so next time the summer weather is poor it might be worth considering trying a session here - its cheaper than the wall and it will doubtless do you more good!

BOULDERING - The angle of the rock, the tree canopy and the easy access make the crag a viable venue for a work-out.
The girdle of the viaduct pillar gives a good pump. The traverse from *Overlooked Groove* to *Deception* is **V3 (5c)** and the extension is **V5 (6b)**.
The low crossing of the *Electric Circus* wall is also **V5 (6b)**.
The *Honcho* start is a good **V4 (6b)** and there are worthwhile problems just left.
The area under the ramp (*Bionics Wall*) has problems from **V1 (5b)** upwards.
Photo page 30.

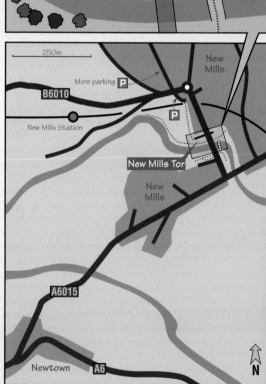

8 **Electric Circus** . . . . 🔲🔲🔲🔲 **E3 5c**
26m. A big scary pitch weaving its way up the wall. Climb to the top of the flake then traverse right (old peg) to a crack which leads to a rattly traverse back left to reach the upper crack. The direct link is **Short Circuit - E4 5c** and it is terrifying
FA. Dennis Carr 1977 FA. (Short Circuit) Al Evans 1977

9 **Oak Tree Wall** . . . . 🔲🔲 **E3 5c**
22m. The gap in the centre of the wall. Climb *Electric Circus* to 5m then traverse right and climb to, and through, the overhang passing 2 peg runners. Finish up the steep right-hand of the cracks in the final wall.
FA. Al Evans (1 rest) 1979 FFA. Nick Colton 1979

10 **The Grim Reaper** 🔲🔲🔲🔲🔲 **E5 6b**
22m. An arduous outing up the right-hand side of the wall - bold and fierce. Climb the wall (technical crux) to a peg then head right to a flake under the overhang. Pull leftwards over this (peg) and head left to a resting ledge. Finish steeply on better holds.
FA. Nick Colton 1979

The central section of the cliff is rather overgrown and although it has the odd decent route, the best plan is to make for the rock under the impressive arch of the road bridge away to the right where things improve somewhat.

ALCOVE CRACK and THE ARETE
From the foot of the steps the first rock encountered on the right is a shady bay with the central classic line of *Alcove Crack*. Just beyond this is the soaring jutting edge of *The Arete*. The angle of the rock and the tree canopy means that routes here often stay dry during light summer rain.

1 **Alcove Crack** . . . . 🔲🔲🔲 **HVS 5a**
20m. The dramatic fissure in the back wall of The Alcove gives a steep and well-protected tussle. *Photo page 125.*
FA. Dennis Carr 1977

2 **Porky's Wall** . . . . 🔲🔲🔲 **HVS 5c**
8m. Fat boys might enjoy the fingery centre of the wall on the jutting buttress on the right-hand side of the alcove.
FA. Jim Burton 1979

3 **Piggy's Crack** . . . . 🔲🔲 **VS 4c**
8m. The short crack in the wall. Beware - bees in the summer.
FA. Al Evans 1977

4 **The Steeple** . . . . 🔲 **HVS 5a**
8m. The steep arete on the right of The Alcove. Try to avoid the tree - possibly impossible.
FA. Loz Francomb 1977

5 **Clotted Cream** . . . . 🔲 **VS 4c**
8m. The short right arete of the squat buttress (not marked on topo) is pleasant enough.
FA. Al Evans 1977

6 **The Arete** . . . . . . 🔲🔲🔲🔲 **E3 5b**
22m. The long and impressive arete is steep and intimidating, sadly some of the rock is a bit soft. Avoid the initial bulge on the left then pull back right to a resting ledge. Continue up the scary upper section (runners to the right) to an easier finish.
FA. (in two bits) Al Evans 1976 Jim Burton (in one push) 1977

7 **Mather Crack** . . . . . . 🔲🔲🔲 **E2 5b**
22m. The long and steep crack gives a good pumpy pitch. The quality of the runners makes up just a little for the angle and the occasional disposable holds.
FA. Terry Wyatt 1971. FFA. Dennis Cars 1977

DESCENTS
Most of the routes finish in the trees at the top of the crag where there are plenty of places to fix up a safe abseil.

Staffordshire

Whaley bridge

Kinder

Bleaklow

Chew

Lancashire

Cheshire

⑯ Honcho E4 6b
14m. Begin 2m left of *Deception's* twin cracks and pass a peg runner with difficulty. Continue direct passing a break to ledges and an escape. Apparently it was originally graded HVS!
FA. Nick Colton 1979

⑰ Deception .... HVS 5a
14m. The twin bending cracks are crusty and currently have an ivy cornice to deal with. A bit of traffic might improve things!
FA. Al Evans 1977

**⑱ The Redemption of a
Grit Pegging Antichrist** E3 5c
16m. Climb to the tip of the ramp then head directly up the wall by sustained strenuous moves to a finish up a shallow corner.
FA. John Gosling 1985

⑲ Bionic's Wall E4 6a
16m. Sustained and strenuous but good honest fun! From the middle of the ramp blast straight up the wall on flat holds and the odd jam, passing 2 peg runners. Trend right to finish.
FA. Dave Beaver 1979

⑳ Hallelujah Chorus E5 6b
16m. From the tip of the ramp attack the wall to reach a juggy break, then take the continuation leftwards to a hard exit.
A **Direct Start** is possible at the same grade,
FA. Mike Warwick 1985 FA. Direct Start Al Evans 1986

㉑ Heavy Duty E2 5b
16m. Climb into the hanging groove (peg). At its top swing up and right before trending back left by sustained climbing.
FA. Al Evans 1977

㉒ King of the Swingers .. E1 5b
26m. A pumpy diagonal that is not too hard but keeps on coming. Climb *Heavy Duty* to the peg then follow the break diagonally across the wall all the way to a finish up the final shallow corner of *Redemption*.
FA. Al Evans 1989

THE BRIDGE and BIONIC'S WALL
The right-hand side of the cliff has a fair collection of steep routes on reasonable rock. The arch of the road bridge far above makes this the Peak's best wet-weather grit venue, and the angle of the routes ensures a good workout session. The easier routes here suffer from a lack of traffic.

⑪ The Overlooked Groove ..... HS 4b
14m. From the strange reddish-brown orifice climb the stepped right-facing groove throughout. The crucial entry into the upper groove is well-protected. Care required with the exit.
FA. Al Evans 1976

⑫ Original Route .... VD 3c
16m. Follow the 'giant's staircase' up and left to a mighty tree by awkward moves between good resting ledges. Never quite as easy as it looks, but always on good holds.
FA. Terry Wyatt early 1970s

⑬ Cracked Corner .... HS 4b
14m. Start up *Original Route* but continue in a direct line up the steep crack to the continuation groove above. The crux is leaving the good ledge and requires a bit of a stretch.
FA. Al Evans 1977

⑭ Viaduct Crack ...... HVS 5b
14m. Start at a ledge (or more easily from the left) and climb the steep vague crack-line until it is possible to trend right to resting ledges. Escape off left, or better, continue up the short, steep and pumpy wall above.
FA. Dennis Carr 1977 Direct Finish Al Evans 1989

⑮ Viaduct Wall .. E2 5b
14m. The ever-dry wall under the arches gives a steep and pumpy pitch (aren't they all) with a couple of reachy moves and precarious mantelshelf to reach easier ground.
FA. Al Evans 1977

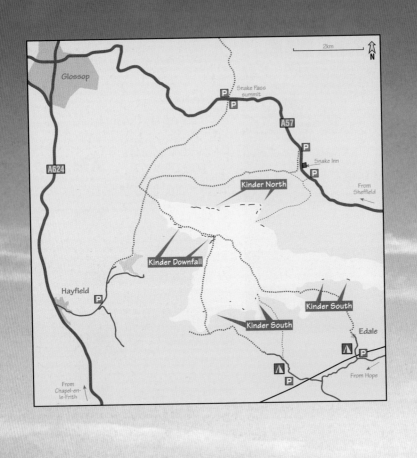

KINDER

Dave Spencer climbing *Eureka* (VS 4c)
Kinder North. *Page 144*

KINDER SOUTH

Staffordshire
Whaley Bridge
Kinder
Bleaklow
Chew
Lancashire
Cheshire

Kinder Downfall
Kinder North
Kinder South

A scattering of cliffs that overlook the tranquil Edale valley, and reflect the kinder side of Kinder - big bulbous outcrops of coarse but clean rock that get all the sun that is going. If you have never climbed on Kinder and want to escape the crowds of the Eastern Edges - then this is probably the best place to start. The fact that the individual outcrops are aligned along the rim of the moor means it is possible to do routes on several cliffs getting between them by the high level footpath that runs along the edge of the moor. Fine views, easily linked crags and good routes all add up to classic ingredients for a great mountain day out.

Jim Rubery on *Upper Tor Wall* (HS 4b) on Upper Tor. *Page 136*

APPROACH See map on pages 128 and 133

There is an extensive Pay and Display car park at the entrance to Edale village, (note the position of The Nag's Head for an encounter on the return journey). This car park is ideal for the steep ascents to Upper Tor and Nether Tor either directly up Grindsbook or the path leading out right onto The Nab and up towards Ringing Roger, then back left to the cliffs.

A little further up the dead-end road, running up the main valley, is parking on the left in a large lay-by, or just before this under the railway viaduct, room in total for about 20 cars. From here a good track leads to and through Upper Booth and then on up the steep path of Jacob's Ladder on the ancient packhorse route over to Hayfield. A right turn at the top of the steepest section leads to the small but high quality outcrop of Upper Edale Rocks and from here the rim-path runs right past The Pagoda and then Crowden Towers which are reached by a detour out to the south. The path continues eastwards onto Crowden Clough Face then beyond this is Upper Tor and finally Nether Tor, from which point the path descends rapidly back to Edale and that prebooked appointment! It is worth noting that, on some maps, Crowden Clough face is marked incorrectly as Crowden Tower.

CONDITIONS

A set of sunny cliffs that are in condition a lot more often than might be expected from their lofty situation. The cliffs take little drainage and are rapid drying. The altitude here is a little higher than the classic Eastern Edges, and so the temperature up here is likely to be a couple of notches lower, though on the plus side there is a good chance you will have your chosen cliff to yourself.

OTHER GUIDEBOOKS - A more complete list of routes on Kinder is published in the 1991 BMC *Kinder* guidebook.

UPPER EDALE ROCKS

A delightful but small outcrop of quality rock that would be very popular were it a little (or a lot) nearer the road. There is now an impressive collection of hard (and bold) routes here; a suitable destination for grit gurus with big legs!
APPROACH - Slog up Jacob's Ladder and follow the Pennine Way northwards. Upper Edale Rocks is on the left, before Kinder Low summit, just below the plateau.

1 Gather Ye Gritbudds . . .   **E1 5c**
8m. The roof at the left-hand end of the cliff is short but technical, and also has a hard exit.
FA. Paul Mitchell 1990s

2 Outlook . . . .   **Diff**
10m. The open twisting groove on the left-hand side of the cliff is climbed over shelving rock.

3 Rock Bottom . . . .   **VS 4c**
10m. Follow cracks in the wall.
FA. Dave Banks 1977 Always misplaced in earlier guides.

4 Pencil Slim . . . .   **VS 4c**
10m. Climb the steep awkward crack to a hard exit.

5 Avatar **E1 5b**
10m. The precarious wall right again to a tricky sloping exit.
FA. Jonny Woodward 1980

6 Traverse and Crack . . . . .   **VDiff**
10m. Mantel onto the collapsed block (I bet that went with a real bang) to reach the pleasant hanging corner crack that rises above its right edge.

7 Well Suited **E3 5c**
10m. The steep face past a pocket to a hard exit.
FA. Steve Bancroft 1987

8 Bending Crack . . . .   **VDiff**
8m. The curving crack leads around onto the east face then into the easy finishing groove.

9 Straight Crack . . . .   **Diff**
8m. Climb the angular groove past a niche.

10 Winter's Block **E2 5b**
10m. The steep arete on the right reached from the groove that *Bending Crack* finishes up. The more direct start is **5c**.
FA. Mark Clark 1987

11 Kinder Surprise **E4 6a**
6m. The first of the really hard routes here follows the blunt arete on its right-hand side. Short but sharp.
FA. Dan Honneyman 2000

12 Creme Eggs **E5 6c**
6m. Highly technical climbing up the east-facing wall using a ladder of curly crimps.
FA. Tom de Gay 2000

13 Layback Crack . . . .   **S 4a**
6m. The flake-crack to the left of the giant overhang.

14 Our Doorstep . . . .   **VS 4c**
6m. The groove on the immediate left of the big roof is more awkward than it looks.
FA. B Barrett 1977

15 Trivial Pursuits . . . . .   **VS 4c**
16m. From the top of *Our Doorstep* move around the arete, descend a little then traverse above the great overhang all the way to a short crack just before the far arete.
FA. Chris Hardy 1986

16 Stigmata **E6 6c**
6m. The fine left arete of the roof is reached by some wild jumping and slapping, then gibber up it. Rumoured to have been soloed in trainers on more than one occasion!
FA. Andy Barker 1994

17 The Mentalist's Cupboard **E7 6c**
8m. The enticing crack that splits the lip of the roof is gained from the right by a huge swing and gives a titanic struggle.
FA. Tom de Gay 2001

18 Help Meeee! **E5 6b**
6m. The right-hand arete of the overhanging block and the bold wall above the useful slot. Alternatively finish out left; said by some to be easier and better.
FA. Andy Barker (Direct) 1994 FA. (left-hand) Martin Veale 1994

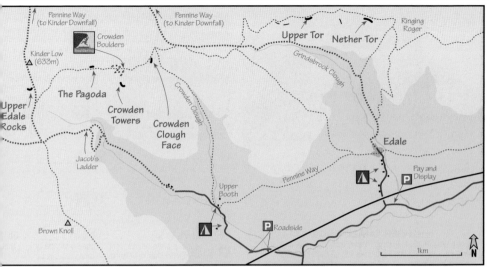

Staffordshire

Whaley Bridge

Kinder

Bleaklow

Chew

Lancashire

Cheshire

THE PAGODA

A huge cowpat-like blob of gritstone which has four routes all named after their pioneers. The routes are well-rounded, difficult to protect and traditional sandbags. Maybe the old guys were good at poorly protected squirming up flared cracks and sloping ledges; obviously it's pretty much a lost art. The routes are hard enough in sticky rubber, they must have been Hell in nailed boots!

APPROACH - It can be approached from either Crowden Clough or Jacob's Ladder. The latter is probably preferable if only because you can see the crag on your approach. There is little to choose between them distance-wise.

① **Morrison's Route** . . . . . **S 4a**
18m. Start in the groove on the left and climb right to a large shelving ledge. Bridge the groove above then finish up the short wall behind on slopers
FA. Don Morrison 1956

② **Hartley's Route** **E1 5b**
20m. A steep bulging crack is awkward then move out right to a projecting flange and pull onto a shelf with difficulty. The wall and groove lead to another hard rightward exit to a bigger ledge and possible belay. Finish out left.
FA. Herbert Hartley 1949

③ **Herford's Route** . . . . . **HVS 5a**
18m. Climb the centre of the face (nail-scratched!) passing a slot to reach a difficult mantel onto a ledge. Follow the rounded cracks above to another awkward grasping exit. After completing the route double check the first ascent date!
FA. Siegfried Herford 1910

④ **Dewsbury's Route** **E1 5b**
20m. Climb the chimney on the right which leads to a groove and a difficult finale on slopers.
FA. Mick Dewsbury 1977

Eastern Tower 100m

CROWDEN BOULDERING (WHIPSNADE) - The moors above Crowden Towers contain one of the best boulder fields in The Peak. If it was situated anywhere near a road it would be popular and well developed but its setting at the top of a steep 1 hour slog means that you are unlikely to have to queue for the problems. Don't forget the mat!
WARNING - Be aware of bouldering alone in remote locations!

CROWDEN TOWERS

Two isolated and contrasting crags. Recent additions make the East Tower a suitable destination for the hard-core whereas the West is perhaps more suited to the tweed brigade. The leap between the towers is purported to have been done in 1952 by one of the Pigott clan, but as they are c.100m apart this appears unlikely!
APPROACH (See map on previous page) - Take the Crowden Clough approach from Upper Booth all the way to the moor edge - or nip up a route on Crowden Clough Face. Follow the vague summit path south west, towards the extensive boulder field. The towers are just below the rim.

❶ Five o'clock Shadows .... ▚▢ **E1 5b**
8m. The rounded left-hand arete of the buttress.
FA. Keith Ashton 1999

❷ Bristly Chimney .... ▢ **S 4b**
8m. The rough, tough chimney on the left-hand side of the face.

❸ Flake and Chimney ...... 🗿▢ **VS 5a**
12m. Reach and pass the flake in the wall with difficulty then romp up the widening rift above.
FA. Keith Ashton 1989

❹ Short Chimney .... ▢ **S 4a**
10m. The central chimney is the same height as the other two!!

❺ Pear Chimney .... ▢ **VS 4c**
10m. The right-hand rift has a useful 'pear-drop' chockstone just before the angle eases. Finish to the left or add a direct.
FA. Eric Byne 1933

❻ Kensington Left Crack .... ▚▢ **VS 4a**
12m. Climb the wide crack to its end then squirm left to the tricky finishing fissure, precarious and gripping!

❼ Suture .... 🔷▚🔵▢ **E2 5b**
10m. Escape the clutches of the crack for the bold wall above.
FA. Greg Cunningham 2001

❽ Violent Outburst .... 🔷▮▢ **E2 5b**
12m. The narrow face leads to a deep break and tricky pocketed wall above. Finish with a longer than average stretch.
FA. Keith Ashton 1989

❾ Kensington Right Crack ...... ▢ **VDiff**
12m. The wider right-hand crack to an awkward finish.

❿ Alpine Sports .... 🔷▢ **S 4a**
18m. Climb the groove to the roof then move right round the arete and trend right to a good ledge. Finish up the final corner.
FA. Dave Banks 1976

⓫ Kensington High Street ...... ▢ **VDiff**
12m. The left-hand chimney in the alcove is a stroll for most.
FA. Dave Banks 1976

⓬ Snow + Rock .... ▢ **VDiff**
12m. The crack leads to a move right to enter the ever-widening right-hand chimney. Saunter up this in casual style.
FA. Dave Banks 1976

⓭ Fashion Statement .... 🔷▚▢ **E3 5c**
14m. Start just left of the roof and climb a runnel to the break and then the wall on big pockets to another break (large Friends) and then the final tier on smaller pockets.
FA. Dave Turnbull 1990s

⓮ Bethan .... 🔷🗿▢ **E5 6c**
14m. Take the thin crack to a break then tackle the roof and technical groove left of the arete with extreme difficulty.
FA. Simon Nadin 2000

Afternoon   70 min

Staffordshire

Whaley Bridge

Kinder

Bleaklow

Chew

Lancashire

Cheshire

CROWDEN CLOUGH FACE

A fine piece of rock, with a good set of routes, overlooking the upper section of Crowden Clough.
APPROACH (See map on previous page) - Use the Crowden Clough approach from Upper Booth. Crowden Clough Face is the significant buttress at the top of the clough on the left.

⑮ Privilege and Pleasure **E3 5b**
2m. Climb into a recess then extend-a-way up and onto the hanging flake in the wall above. Climb this to its apex and then finish rightwards across the final wall.
A. Keith Ashton 1989

⑯ Club Class **E5 6b**
2m. The thin crack and imposing pocketed wall up the right-and side of the face give a sustained and powerful pitch.
A. Andy Cave 1999

⑰ Kindergarten **E1 5b**
2m. The left-hand side of the buttress is climbed with increasing difficulty; it is more of a challenge than expected.
A. Con Carey (in bare feet!) 1988

⑱ Piggy and the Duke . . . . **VS 4c**
2m. John Wayne's only new route on Kinder - perhaps? Climb the crack then move right on to the arete and a rounded finish.
A. Dave Banks 1976

⑲ Bags That . . . . **HS 4b**
0m. The short north-facing wall passing a good ledge.
A. Keith Ashton 1989

CROWDEN CLOUGH FACE
The next buttress is about 500m over the moors to the east.

⑳ Nightflight **E4 6b**
2m. The arduous bulges at the left-hand side of the cliff.
A. Neil McAdie 2000

㉑ Olympus Explorer **E1 5b**
4m. The left arete of the slab is reached by an overhanging rack and has the crux right at the top.
A. Con Carey 1988

㉒ Indianapolis Slab . . . . **VS 4c**
6m. Broken ground leads to the centre of the slab which is climbed rightwards on a useful array of pockets.
A. Dave Banks 1988

㉓ Sons of the Desert **E7 6b**
0m. Layback the the impressive left-hand side of the arete to the upper breaks and a choice of finishes. An even harder alter-ative is to climb the arete initially á cheval and then on its right **Grooverider, E7 6c)**.
A. Andy Popp 1990s. FA. (Grooverider) Neil Gresham 1998

㉔ Arabia **E3 5c**
20m. The imposing rounded arete is low in the grade and quite superb - a moorland classic. A crack and groove leads out to the arete at half-height. This gives sustained climbing (big Friends) to an exciting finish up the pocketed headwall that might leave you gasping and grasping. *Photo page 131.*
FA. Mark Clark 1989

㉕ Central Route . . . . **VS 4c**
20m. The steep crack splitting the face has hard finger-jamming moves around the overhang and may have in-situ jackdaws.
FA. Eric Byne 1933

㉖ Asparagus **E1 5b**
24m. A wandering trip with some good climbing. Climb the leaning crack to a junction with *Central Route*. Pull through the bulge then head left round the arete on poor jams to a crack (possible stance) and then a steep finish **(5a)**.
FA. Don Morrison 1956

㉗ Andromeda **E4 6b**
14m. The blunt arete. Climb to the first break with difficulty, then continue in the same line by bold and balancy climbing.
FA. Harry Venables 1989

㉘ Middle Chimney . . . . **Diff**
14m. The deepening groove starting over a block is worthwhile.
FA. Arthur Birtwhistle 1936

㉙ Windy Miller **E5 6a**
14m. Start on the right and traverse the first break then follow the narrow buttress direct to a bulging upper section tackled via a vague groove line.
FA. Airlie Anderson 1990s

㉚ Chimney and Slab Variations . . . **VDiff**
14m. Climb a crack into the deepening groove and follow this to easier ground and the expected choice of finishes.
FA. Arthur Birtwhistle, Geoff Pigott (alts) 1936

Lots of sun | 60 min

Descent

Staffordshire

Whaley Bridge

Kinder

Bleaklow

Chew

Lancashire

Cheshire

Kinder Downfall

Kinder North

Kinder South

UPPER TOR

A fine south-facing outcrop overlooking Edale. The rock is clean and rough and there are many excellent climbs. If you have never climbed on Kinder you could do worse than start your apprenticeship here. The walk-in is marginally less crippling than that to many of the other crags on the moor.
APPROACH - Use the Edale approach up Grindsbrook Clough. Upper Tor overlooks the upper section of the Clough and can be reached by a steep grind from directly below.

❶ Diamond Arete ...   **E2 5c**
12m. On the far left side of the cliff take the wall and arete to the left of *Chockstone Chimney* to a reachy and rounded finish.
FA. Chris Hardy 1989

❷ Chockstone Chimney ....   **Diff**
12m. The obvious chimney is bridged past the large jammed boulder that provides its name.

❸ Plumbertime **E4 6b**
18m. The steep wall at the left-hand side of the main face to the tricky bulge then tackle the imposing final tower on pockets.
FA. Sam Whittaker 1998

❹ Half a Friend/High Life .   **E2 5c**
16m. Take the obvious direct start to *Upper Tor Wall* up the face left of its groove (**HVS 5a**) joining it at half height. From here tackle the well-positioned bulging upper arete out on the right.
FA. Michael Howlett 1997. FA. (High Life) Dave Simmonite 1998

❺ Upper Tor Wall ....   **HS 4b**
18m. A classic moorland jug-fest, photogenic and excellent. Climb the groove on the right then step out left and tackle the superb flaky wall to ledges and a possible stance. From the ledge step out right to a glorious finish up the widening crack.
Photo page 34 and 130.
FA. Arthur Birtwhistle 1936

❻ Hiker's Chimney ....   **HS 4b**
16m. Follow *Upper Tor Wall* to the first roof then step right and climb the crack as it widens to a hard exit over the chockstone.
FA. Arthur Birtwhistle 1936

❼ Hitching a Ride **E1 5c**
16m. The crack, passing an arse-shaped overhang with difficulty.
FA. Keith Ashton 1989

❽ Hiker's Crack ....   **S 4a**
16m. Climb left of a slumped pinnacle and follow cracks up and then leftwards to an exit as for *Hiker's Chimney*.

❾ Hiker's Gully Left ....   **HVD**
12m. Follow *Hiker's Crack* until it heads left, then climb the crack in the continuation wall into the wide upper gully.
FA. Geoff Pigott 1936

❿ Hiker's Gully Right ....   **S 4a**
12m. To the right of the tilted pinnacle follow the gully direct.
FA. Geoff Pigott 1936

⓫ Hitch Hiker ....   **VS 4b**
14m. From *Hiker's Gully Right* follow the awkward slanting flaky crack and ramp up the buttress just to the right.
FA. Alan Austin 1958

⓬ Three Flakes of Man ..   **E1 5c**
14m. Climb the wall right of the arete using a series of three flakes, each bigger than the last, from finger-tip to full body.
FA. Malc Baxter 1988

⓭ Grunter ....   **VS 4b**
16m. Climb the right-hand crack (left of a free-standing tower) then trend left to the final grunty section of the previous route.
FA. Don Morrison 1965/Andy Bailey 1986

⓮ The Punter **E1 5b**
14m. From the converging cracks on *Grunter* climb the delightful but short-lived pocketed wall directly above.
FA. Pete Robins 2000

Lots of sun | 60 min

Descent

Staffordshire · Whaley Bridge · Kinder · Bleaklow · Chew · Lancashire · Cheshire · Kinder Downfall · Kinder North · Kinder South

⑮ Snorter . . . . `VS 4c`
2m. The crack left of the tower is reached by bridging, then ackle its extension directly above.
A. John Loy 1965

⑯ Pinnacle Gully . . . . `Diff`
4m. Start up *Snorter* but take the narrow gully behind.

⑰ Scalped Flat Top . . . . `E2 5c`
0m. Sprint up the right-hand face of the tower until the crack n its front face can be gained by a harrowing swing left.
A. Mark Clark 1987

⑱ Brain Drain . . . . . . `HVS 5b`
0m. Bridge up into the gully to pass the narrowing then hop nto the right wall and climb this on rounded holds to the top.
A. Malc Baxter 1989

⑲ The Ivory Tower . . . . . `HVS 5b`
2m. Another moorland classic. Climb the steep wall to a ledge hen the crack and bulges above. Step left to a thin crack, climb his and finish up the scooped wall above on sloping holds.
A. John Loy 1966

⑳ Artillery Chimney . . . . . . `HS 4b`
2m. Tackle the crack to the projecting spike of 'the gun'. Climb he right-hand side of this and the overhangs above.

㉑ Promontory Groove . . . . `VDiff`
2m. Climb the groove and pass to the right of the large jutting ose of the Promontory to reach easier ground.
A. JW Puttrell 1890

㉒ Cave Rib . . . . `HVS 5a`
2m. The technical left arete of the recess leads to a finish up he milder layback flake directly above.
A. Keith Ashton 1989

㉓ Cave Gully . . . . `S 4a`
2m. Head up to the roof of the cave then traverse out left and limb the arete and crack above as for *Cave Rib*.

㉔ Brutality . . . . `E1 5b`
16m. Climb the steep cracks to the bulges then move out right and reach the roof before traversing left and battling a way into the final widening fissure - a beautifully brutal beast.
FA. John Loy 1965

㉕ Greenfinger . . . . `VS 4c`
12m. The slabby groove to enter a green crack, then graze away up this. Almost always a little grungy.
FA. Don Morrison 1966

㉖ Robot . . . . `E2 5c`
12m. Climb the slab then step right and climb the hollow-sounding flake through the bulges trending right.
FA. Steve Bancroft 1987

㉗ Do the Rocksteady . . . . `E7 6c`
14m. The roof and wall left of *Robert*. From gear at the back of the roof reach round the lip to a poor pocket. Move left along lip to large slopy pocket, then to better holds above.
FA. Sam Whittaker 2001

㉘ Robert . . . . `E2 5c`
16m. The beckoning roof crack is a bobby dazzler of gritstone jamming and is reached by the easy groove on the right, or better, the front of the rib to its left. Slam in the lockers and go!
FA. Don Morrison (1 sling) 1966. FFA. Graham Hoey 1976

㉙ Young Turks . . . . `E4 6b`
16m. The leaning ramp/groove above the roof is technical and strenuous. Follow it until an easy escape out right is reached.
FA. Andy Bailey 1984

㉚ The Cheesemonger . . . `E6 6b`
12m. The roof above the ramp of *Young Turks* has hard moves on poor pockets to reach a rounded flake and a hard exit.
FA. Ben Bransby 2000

㉛ Pedestal Wall . . . . `HVD`
16m. Take the initial groove of the original start to *Robert* then climb the groove rightwards below the overhangs. Pass the pedestal and climb the final wall trending right, on good holds.
FA. Arthur Birtwhistle 1948

Staffordshire

Whaley Bridge

Kinder

Bleaklow

Chew

Lancashire

Cheshire

Kinder Downfall

Kinder North

Kinder South

NETHER TOR - LEFT

The impressive face at the eastern end of the moor was formed by a landslip in the relatively recent past, hence the angular, unweathered and quarry-like nature of much of the cliff. Although quite extensive there are only two main areas of real interest to the visiting climber. On the far left is a tall natural buttress split by the jagged wide crack of *Moneylender's*.

APPROACH (see map on page 133) - Use the Edale approach and walk up Grindsbrook Clough to the second wooden bridge. Turn right then follow a path directly up the hillside to Nether Tor. The routes described first are on the fine buttress at the left of the crag.

❶ Loan Arranger . . . . ⬜ **VS 4c**
18m. Climb the chimney crack to a ledge, follow a flake on the left to a second ledge and an easy finish up an open groove.
FA. Al Parker (the masked stranger?) 1976

❷ Beautiful Losers . . . 🔲🔲🔲⬜ **E3 6a**
22m. Climb to the first ledge on *Loan Arranger* then swing right to a flake and climb this to a roof, which is passed with difficulty to a taxing mantelshelf. Finish out left more easily.
FA. Con Carey 1978

❸ Moneylender's Crack . . 🔲🔲⬜ **VS 5a**
18m. The wide and steep zigzag fissure is much better than it looks. Climb direct or cop out and swing into the crack from the right and climb it steeply, usually passing an in-situ nest. Leaving the cave is the crux.
FA. Arthur Birtwhistle 1950

❹ Mortgage Wall . . . . . 🔲🔲⬜ **HVS 5**
20m. Climb the cracks on the right to a heathery ledge then head across the steep wall on the left for a pumpy finish.
FA. John Gosling 1976

❺ Usurer . . . . ⬜ **HS 4b**
14m. The chimney and shallow groove that bound the buttress on the right are OK with a confident approach.

NETHER TOR - RIGHT

Well to the right is the other good piece of rock hereabouts; a rather flash-looking wall which is worth a bit of your time.

❻ Broken Chimney . . . . ⬜ **VDiff**
12m. The flake is climbed leftwards to a block-filled cleft which leads to an awkward exit

❼ Edale Bobby . . . . . 🔲🔲🔲⬜ **E5 6a**
16m. It's a fair cop! The imposing arete is approached via a block and climbed on an array of pockets to the difficult leaning upper section which gives technical and bold laybacking.
FA. Steve Bancroft 1987

❽ Square Cut . . . . ⬜ **VDiff**
16m. The obviously named and turfy rift is tricky just before it fades. Climb the short face above or escape off left.

❾ Kelvin's Corner . . . . ⬜ **HS 4b**
14m. The crack leads to a hanging groove in the upper part of the wall. Finish up this or escape left across ledges.
FA. Kelvin 19 bow and arrow

Descent

Staffordshire
Whaley Bridge
Kinder
Bleaklow
Chew
Lancashire
Cheshire
Kinder Downfall
Kinder North
Kinder South

Lots of sun   60 min

NETHER TOR - RIGHT

The tallest buttress on the cliff has some worthwhile routes most notably the jagged cracks up the smooth wall formed by the ancient landslip.

⓪ The Incarcerated Sock Juggler

s The Mushroom Kid . . . . . . 🖾 ☐ **E4 6a**
2m. Start right of the tree and climb the wall by hard undercut moves (Friend 1.5) and slopers to a boss and make crucial mantelshelf moves to pass this. Finish on pockets and a hidden rack round to the left.
1. Dan Honneyman 2001

❶ Black Seven . . . . 🔲🖾 ☐ E1 5c

2m. From a groove climb rightwards across the wall and enter a short corner with difficulty. From the top of the corner averse left to ledges and finish directly over the narrow roof.

❷ Crimson Wall . . . . . . 🔲🖾 ☐ E2 5c

4m. An attempt at a more direct finish. Follow *Black Seven* to e end of its traverse then reach the next break and follow it ack right to another ledge. Pass the detached block to a taxing nish up a thin crack.
1. Jonny Woodward 1980

❸ Snooker Route . . . . . 🔲🖾 ☐ VS 5a

8m. The well-pocketed wall leads to a substantial holly that is bloody nuisance. Skirt this to reach a ledge then a detached ock before moving way out left to a finish up a groove. The ute is rather spoilt by the holly, and also the long traverse left • finish. Using the finish of *Black Seven* improves the climb onsiderably but ups the grade a notch.
1. Arthur Birtwhistle 1950

❹ Hot Flush Crack . . . 🔲🖾🔲 ☐ HVS 5c

6m. Start left of the arete and climb a technical scoop and a rack to the holly bush, or the wall to the right (the original ay). Step right and climb the wider crack (thread) through the apping overhang to a testing finish.

⓯ Flash Wall . . . . . 🔲🖾🖋☐ VS 5a

22m. Climb a slippery crack in the orange-tinted side-wall then its right-trending continuation to the final wide section. A photogenic and well-protected classic.
FA. Arthur Birtwhistle 1950

⓰ Bertie Meets Flash Gordon on his Way to Nether Edge . . . 🔲🖋☐ E1 5b

22m. Climb the crack in the right side of the wall on finger breaks until it is possible to traverse left to the finish of *Flash Wall*, or head up and right at a pumpy **E2 5c**.
FA. Jon Blenkharn 1990s

⓱ Recoil Rib . . . . 🔲🖾 ☐ E2 5c

20m. Climb the arete on the right to a possible stance then the bolder upper continuation that is sustained and precarious.
FA. Al Parker 1974

⓲ Edale Flyer . . . . 🔲 ☐ VS 4c

8m. The groove on the left-hand side of the upper buttress.
FA. Dave Banks 1989

⓳ T' Big Surrey . . . . . 🔲🖾🖾 ☐ E5 6b

10m. Approach the impressive arete from the left with some difficulty and climb it with sustained 'interest'. Named after a pub, this is a pitch that is short on length but big on impact! Needs a direct start.
FA. Gabe Regan 1989

⓴ Rejoyce . . . . ☐ HS 4b

8m. The crack just right of the arete of T' Big Surrey has a tricky overhang before it eases.
FA. Keith Ashton 1989

㉑ The Steamer . . . . 🔲🖾 ☐ E1 5c

8m. The wall on the right with hard moves to enter the thin groove and then easier climbing above.
FA. Harry Venables 1989

KINDER NORTH

There is much good climbing on the high and wild edges that ring the Kinder and Bleaklow plateaux, and the very best of this is to be found along the north-facing escarpment of Ashop Edge. It is perhaps to be expected that the climbing along this line of cliffs is both difficult of access and out of condition for much of the year, though this adds a certain cachet to days up here - the harder won, all the more memorable. The best area for a first visit is the Brothers' Buttress, though there is enough up here to keep most climbers busy for years - and then there are all those new routes to go at!

The cliffs are not the crisp and clean Eastern Edges, but a sterner set of venues. Come prepared for a bit a battle, wearing your old clothes and be prepared to go home grubby, battered and tired but hopefully well-satisfied.

Sheri Davy climbing *Misty Wall* (VS 4b) on Kinder North. *Page142*

APPROACH See map on pages 128 and 145

There is roadside parking for about 30 vehicles below the Snake Inn (and more further uphill from the pub) and from here paths leads down through the trees, over the footbridge. A left turn followed shortly by a right leads to a steady climb up the Fair Brook Valley all the way to the plateau (about 50 mins). Here, a left turn leads to Chinese Wall (not described) and a right out to Misty Wall and the jutting beak of Fairbrook Naze and the main section of Ashop Edge. A shorter approach (though with a slog of a final section) turns right over the footbridge, then follows a narrow path (wet in places) up onto the moor by the ruins of an old shooting cabin. From here you can select your buttress and attack the final slopes! Far and away the easiest approach is to walk in from roadside parking by the summit of the Snake Pass and follow the flagged path to Mill Hill from where the rest of the route is obvious. With a willing co-driver it is possible to be dropped off here and picked up back at the Snake Inn in good time for last orders - how very civilised!

CONDITIONS

The northern edges of Kinder are not a viable venue in any other than fine conditions; the cliffs are set as high as any in the Peak, face due north and are a respectable distance from the road. Some of the buttresses are slow to dry and become green and gritty after rain, though many jut proudly away from the moor and come into condition as soon as the weather starts to improve. It is always worth remembering, if you trek up here and things are not in prime condition, it is only 20 minutes around the rim to Upper Western Buttress or a forty minutes bog-trotting through the heart of the moor to the Southern Edges!

OTHER ROCK

Described here are almost 90 of the 250+ climbs available on the northern edges of Kinder Scout. If you enjoy these there are plenty of other good routes up here to go at. On the left when using the Fair Brook approach are the varied routes on the Chinese Wall. The first rock beyond Fairbrook Naze are the long cliffs of Cabin Buttress and then further on the extensive Black Overhangs, though both of these tend to be dirtier than the cliffs described. On the far right (first rock reached on the Snake Summit route) are Dead Chimney Buttress and then The Quadrinnacle, again home to a good set of climbs - consult the *1991 BMC Kinder Guidebook* for full details.

Ed Brown soloing *Jester Cracks* (HVS 5a) Kinder North. *Page 149* Photo: Tom Briggs

Staffordshire Whaley Bridge Kinder Bleaklow Chew Lancashire Cheshire

MISTY WALL
The rocks overlooking the upper section of Fair Brook have a good collection of climbs in a superb sunny setting. *Misty Wall* is the classic VS although the buttresses further right are also worth a look. The less popular routes are inclined to be gritty; a little regular traffic would help keep them clean.
APPROACH - From the roadside below the Snake Inn use the Fair Brook approach. As you near the top of the valley, Misty Walls are above and right of the main path in the base of the clough. Continuing to the plateau then turning right is far and away the easiest approach, though those looking for alpine training can attack the lung-busting slopes direct.

1 Pieces of Eight . . . . **S 4a**
12m. Climb the left-hand side of the jutting rib steeply to a big ledge (possible belay). Pull over the awkward overhang behind, starting on the right and finishing on the left, up a groove.
FA. Malc Baxter 1960

2 Doubloon . . . . **VS 4b**
12m. Climb the steep rib on its right-hand side to the large ledge where *Pieces of Eight* is joined. Finish as for this.
FA. Malc Baxter 1960

3 Stampede **E2 5b**
14m. Climb the left-hand side of the steep wall through a couple of bulges then shuffle right to finish up a short crack.
FA. Chris Craggs 1992

4 Round Up **E1 5b**
14m. Take the centre of the wall passing the bulges using rounded holds to finish up the blind crack of *Stampede*.
FA. Colin Binks 1982

5 Misty Wall . . . . **VS 4b**
14m. A Kinder classic up the rough and rugged crack just left of the arete and the wider fissures above. Gain the crack steeply from the right and follow it through bulges until it is possible to escape out right in an exposed position. *Photo page 140.*
FA. Alf Bridge 1929

6 Wind Wall . . . . **VS 4c**
14m. Follow *Misty Wall* for 5m then swing round onto the north wall and climb the centre of this passing a deep horizontal slot.
FA. Al Parker 1977

7 Zyphyr **E2 6a**
14m. Breeze up the thin flake in the side-wall to join *Wind Wall*
FA. Jonny Woodward 1981

8 Deviation . . . . **HVD**
14m. Climb the front of the separate squat buttress right of the gully. At its top step left to a deeply recessed chimney which has a tricky exit past a crusty chockstone.
FA. Malc Baxter 1964

9 Fixation . . . . **Diff**
14m. Climb the chimney on the right to ledges and a finish up the awkward restricted groove at the back of the bay.
FA. Malc Baxter 1961

10 Cassandra **E2 5c**
16m. Launch up the wall to the left edge of the great roof. Pass this moving left up the wall with difficulty to a deep break and a steep finish still trending slightly leftwards.
FA. Nick Colton 1979

11 Trojan **E1 5b**
16m. The imposing roof crack is just the battle the name suggests. Approach via a huge perched block and an awkward rest then set about the chockstoned-crack with conviction.
FA. Paul Nunn early 1960s

12 Meander Arete . . . . . **VS 5a.**
16m. A hard groove leads to the ledge atop the prominent block. From here meander out to the well-positioned arete on the left and finish up this. Sadly it is often rather dirty.
FA. Con Carey 1979

13 Meander . . . . **HS 5a**
16m. Follow *Meander Arete* to the platform then move right to another ledge and finish up the crack splitting the left wall.
FA. Malc Baxter 1961

14 Dependence Wall . . . . **S 4a**
10m. Climb the centre of the wall then outflank the roof on the left using some creaky flakes before heading back right up easier ground to finish.
FA. Malc Baxter 1960

15 Dependence Arete . . . . . . **VS 4c**
10m. Climb out to the arete from the left then follow it on the left-hand side passing a couple of overhangs with difficulty.
FA. Malc Baxter 1960

Kinder Downfall Kinder North Kinder South

FAIRBROOK NAZE AREA

A set of neglected buttresses unning out towards the jutting romontory of Fairbrook Naze. The climbing is not the best on he moor but the aspect is a unny one and the chances are hat you will have the place to ourself! Expect things to be ritty early in the season or fter rain; please remove any rass you find on the routes!

APPROACH - As for Misty Wall. erseverance Wall is situated elow the top of the moor bout 120m right of Misty Wall. ext and First Buttresses are he last decent bits of rock efore the jutting Naze itself.

1 Jogroans . . . . **S 4a**
m. The left arete then move right to a bold-feeling finish.
A. Ernie Jones 1964

2 Jubilation . . . . **HS 4b**
m. Climb the wall and finish left of the capstone.
A. Ernie Jones 1964

3 Mob Rule . . . . **VS 5a**
2m. Balance up the steep wall, on poor holds, to an easier nish up the slanting groove above.
A. Ernie Jones 1964

4 GP Arete . . . . **S 4a**
2m. The pleasant arete on the right of the initial wall, with a elicate central section.
A. Njal Parker 1964

5 Sweet William . . . . **S 4a**
m. From the large grassy ledge, climb the crack to the over-angs then escape out left and finish up a short slab.
A. Malc Baxter 1964

6 Lamb Chop . . . . **VS 4c**
0m. Follow *Sweet William* to the roof then traverse strenu-usly rightwards before climbing into and up the right-hand of a air of cracks that split the overhang.
A. Malc Baxter 1964

7 Hosanna . . . . **HVS 5a**
2m. Climb the face with difficulty to the break then finish up he awkward hanging groove splitting the roof just left.
A. Con Carey 1979

8 Pork Chop . . . . **HVS 5a**
2m. The right arete of the wall is delicate at mid-height.
A. Malc Baxter 1964

ast a few scrappy bits of rock are two more buttresses.

9 Bag End . . . . **HS 4b**
2m. Climb a short flake crack then the wall above on sloping olds to a finish on the left.
A. Njal Parker 1964

10 Bombadillo . . . . **HS 4b**
12m. Climb the steep arete of the buttress to a finish over the triangular nose on smaller holds.
FA. Malc Baxter 1964

11 Hobbit's Walk . . . . **VDiff**
18m. Start on the right then traverse left past the arete and across the face to a ledge. Finish up the easy groove behind.
FA. Njal Parker 1964

12 Black Widow . . . . **HS 4a**
12m. Pull over the edge of the roof and climb the wall right-wards to ledges. Finish out right.
FA. Eric Byne early 1930s

13 Tarantula Crack . . . . . **VS 4c**
12m. Climb the jagged crack to its end then shuffle right to the arete and an easier finish. The direct finish is a grade harder.
FA. Malc Baxter 1960 Nick Colton (Direct Finish) 1979

14 Flycatcher . . . . **HVS 4c**
12m. Pull round the left edge of the roof then sprint up the arete above which eases with height.
FA. Nick Colton 1979

Staffordshire | Whaley Bridge | Kinder | Breakow | Chew | Lancashire | Cheshire

EUREKA BUTTRESS
Named by Archimedes who was overjoyed at discovering this gritstone classic. A couple of excellent cracks and the eponymous route around the edge of the great roof make the buttress well worth a visit by climbers operating in the VS grade - when the conditions are right.

APPROACH (Map opposite) - Use the Fair Brook approach and follow the cliff-top path around until you are above the wall. Alternatively the shorter Ashop Clough approach can be used but be prepared for the tough final slog up the hill. Approach is also possible from the Snake Summit parking roadside spot - long but flat-ish and flagstoned for the most part: The path loops right to Mill Hill, drops down to Ashop Head before climbing steeply to the plateau. Hang a left here to reach the climbing.

① Ashop Corner Climb . . . . HS 4b
12m. The impressive-but-scruffy groove is initially climbed direct. Move out to its right wall to finish up the flakes with a crucial final section in a great position.
FA. Geoff Pigott 1948

② Roman Roads . . . . VS 4c
14m. Climb the corner then cross the right wall above the huge overhang to reach the front face. Tackle this just right of the arete to an exposed finish on a useful batch of pockets.
FA. Nick Colton 1982 Malc Baxter 1987

③ Ashop Crack . . . . VS 4c
18m. Climb the crack (or the flaky wall to its left, which is more in keeping but a less logical line) and the wide awkward continuation that splits the overhangs above. Kinder's version of *Robin Hood's Right-hand Buttress Direct* and not a bad attempt in this wild and windy setting.
FA. Eric Byne 1932

④ Ashop Climb . . . . HVD
18m. Start up the wide lower fissure of *Ashop Crack* but move right and awkwardly enter the wide right-hand fissure which gives classical squirming, then gradually eases to a sudden cliff-top exit.
FA. James Puttrell 1901

⑤ Orgasmo E1 5a
18m. Climb the face just to the right to reach ledges, pull through the roof then step left and climb the delicate face to a bold finale a long way above everything.
FA. Rich Thomas 1984

⑥ Eureka . . . . VS 4c
18m. The classic of the wall and spectacular with it! Climb the wall and groove to the huge overhang then traverse left in an exposed position to outflank it. Take the short crack and weave through the bulges above to finish. *Photo page 128.*
FA. Malc Baxter 1960

⑦ Ure . . . . VS 4b
12m. Scramble to the short slanting crack, and climb it! Normally over in a flash - or two.
FA. Nick Colton 1982

Kinder Downfall | Kinder North | Kinder South

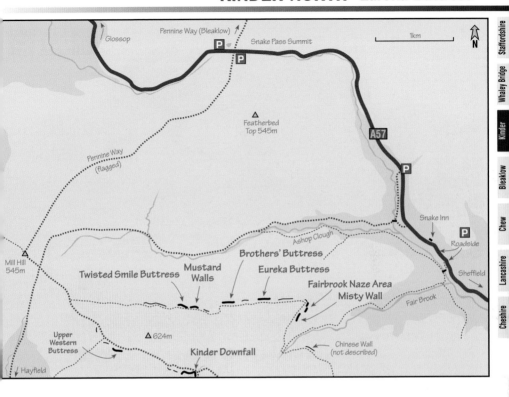

Staffordshire
Whaley Bridge
Kinder
Bleaklow
Chew
Lancashire
Cheshire

Up and right is another buttress, with big juggy bulges, most easily reached by a short scramble up a ramp, or by a short descent from the cliff top.

8 Twister . . . . **HVD**
10m. Climb the crack that twists away to pass the left edge of the overhangs; short-lived but in a fine position.
FA. Ernie Jones 1961

9 Britt's Cleavage . . . **E1 5b**
12m. Climb steep rock to a ledge then take the obvious break in the roof to a hairy finish out on the left.
FA. Jonny Woodward 1982

10 Trial Balance . . . . . **HVS 5b**
12m. The original attempt at the overhangs, Follow *Britt* to the ledge then avoid the roof on the right by a thin crack that leads to a tough sloping exit.
FA. Malc Baxter (some tension) 1965. FFA. Jonny Woodward 1982

Eureka Buttress

Not much sun

50 min

BIG BROTHER BUTTRESS

These are probably the best bits of rock on Kinder North. On the left is Big Brother Buttress; a fine steep wall riven by cracks and home to an excellent set of routes. Almost all the climbs here are well worth doing, so do 'em all!

APPROACH (See map on page 145) - All the main Kinder North approaches are possible and all have their merits (and drawbacks). The Fair Brook approach is long and takes you to the crag top. The Ashop Clough approach is short but hard work on the final slope. The Snake Summit approach is the easiest, long and undulating but flagged for the most part.

① Tin Tin Wall . . . . ▯ **HS 4b**
12m. Start up the chimney then climb the flakes on the right.
FA. Njal Parker 1961

② Barbara . . . . 🔲 ▯ **VDiff**
10m. A worthwhile flaky crack started from the grubby groove.
FA. Ernie Jones 1961

③ Jelly Baby Slab . . . . . 🔲🔲 ▯ **VS 4c**
12m. Wobble-a-way up the pleasantly precarious slab.
FA. Malc Baxter 1961

④ Sliding Chimney . . . . ▯ **S 4a**
12m. Slide up (or down) the chockstoned rift.
FA. Barry Roberts 1961

⑤ Legacy . . . . 🔲 ▯ **HVS 5a**
20m. The long rising diagonal gives a fine pitch. Well-protected (Friends) and with excellent positions. Superb and low in the grade, with an early crux then romping.
FA. Paul Nunn 1962

⑥ Spacerunner . . . . . 🔲🔲🔲 ▯ **E4 6a**
18m. The left-hand side of the main face is difficult in its lower section with hard climbing on tiny holds. It eases above.
FA. Andy Bailey 1984

⑦ Intestate . . . . 🔲▯ ▯ **E1 5b**
18m. Excellent and reachy. Follow *Legacy* (or *Big Brother*) to the middle of its traverse then climb the centre of the wall to a finish up a short crack. The obvious **Direct Start** is a stretchy **E1 6a** protected by small opposition wires.
FA. Paul Nunn (1 sling) 1967. FA. (Direct Start) Chris Craggs 1992

⑧ Big Brother . . . . 🔲▯ ▯ **E2 5c**
18m. Another reachy number that is as height dependant as the name suggests. Climb the steep left-hand edge of the recess and the short crack above to *Legacy*. Continue up the wall (long stretch and small holds) to the final easy section; superb.
FA. Jonny Woodward 1981

⑨ Brother's Eliminate . . . 🔲🔲 ▯ **HVS 5a**
18m. Climb out of the cave via the slanting crack and follow it right to a niche. Step out left and climb the wall and crack.
FA. Graham West 1960

⑩ Kinsman . . . . 🔲🔲 ▯ **E4 6b**
18m. Start up *Big Brother* but swing right and climb the difficult blunt arete to the easier upper section of *Legacy*.
FA. Al Rouse 1984

⑪ Squatter's Rights/Blue Jade 🔲 ▯ **E4 6b**
16m. The wall on the right is climbed desperately to the break. Recover then attack the marginally easier wall above.
FA. Paul Mitchell 1991

⑫ Little Boy Blue . . . . 🔲🔲🔲 ▯ **E1 6a**
16m. Climb left of the blunt arete to reach a ledge with difficulty. Move left to the diagonal crack and once past this, finish up the wall on the left, via a perched block.
FA. Graham West 1960

⑬ The Big Traverse . . . . 🔲🔲 ▯ **VS 4b**
34m. Excellent but best avoided on the rare days that the crag is busy. Climb the short wall to ledges then traverse left round the rib of *Legacy* and along the upper break to the far arete.
FA. Jonny Woodward 1982

⑭ Dirty Trick . . . . ▯ **S 4b**
10m. Approach the steep crux groove via a wall and shelf.
FA. Malc Baxter 1961

LITTLE BROTHER BUTTRESS

Overshadowed by its larger sibling and often neglected, the right-hand buttress has some excellent climbs. *Dunsinane* in particular is worth a look and lovers of sloping holds should enjoy palming a way up the wrinkled bulges of *Pot Belly*. **APPROACH** - As for Big Brother Buttress.

❶ Round Chimney .... ☐ **VDiff**
12m. The chimney on the left of the buttress is typical of its sort, naughty but nice, if you like that kind of thing.
FA. Graham West 1960

❷ Razor Crack .... 🔲☐ **S 4a**
12m. The narrow straight slash in the right-hand wall of the chimney is worth the effort when dry. At the top of the crack trend right across the wall to finish.
FA. Graham West 1960

❸ The Les Dawson Show .🔲🔲☐ **E4 6a**
12m. Ribald though escapable fun up the right-hand side of the rounded arete, with good runners at half-height and less good ones in between. Low in the grade when clean.
FA. Steve Bancroft 1989

❹ Growth Centre ....🔲🔲🔲☐ **E4 6b**
12m. The steep wall leads with difficulty to a desperate finale.
FA. Al Rouse 1984

❺ Dunsinane .... 🔲🔲☐ **VS 4c**
16m. Take the crack to its end then move right a couple of metres to a flake. At its top trend right again to a well-positioned finish on the arete. Almost a three star outing, but sadly not quite as good as the classics just over the way!
FA. Malc Baxter 1964

❻ The Savage Breast .🔲🔲🔲☐ **E1 5b**
14m. Climb the wall right of the crack to the break and runners then take the upper wall to a tricky finale up a shallow groove and blind crack to a rounded exit. The upper part is the old Direct Finish to *Dunsinane*.
FA. Gary Gibson 1983

❼ Motherless Children ...🔲🔲🔲☐ **E1 5c**
14m. Climb the central arete of the face on its left-hand side, passing the bulges with difficulty to reach the easier upper part of *Dunsinane*. Worthwhile and not quite as lonely a trip as the name might lead you to expect.
FA. Chris Hardy 1988

❽ Pot Belly .....🔲🔲🔲🔲☐ **E2 5c**
14m. Climb right of the arete to a jammed block below the bulging gut (thread under the roof) and pull over it with difficulty using a shallow crack and a poor set of slopers. Once established, finish much more easily.
FA. Graham West 1960

❾ Tum Tum .... 🔲🔲☐ **HVS 5b**
10m. The wide fissure is approached direct or from the previous climb. Entering it is difficult; gravelly jams enable a 'boss' to be reached then an awkward move reaches easier ground. Not one for the gravitationally-challenged, and especially hard for those with a beer belly.
FA. Malc Baxter 1960

Staffordshire

Whaley Bridge

Kinder

Bleaklow

Chew

Lancashire

Cheshire

MUSTARD WALLS

Kinder North saves one of its finest sections of rock until last; a great set of routes in as remote a setting as you could wish for. Despite this, the relatively easy walk in makes this a viable venue for long summer evenings.
APPROACH (See map on page 145) - It is possible to use any of the three main approaches to Kinder North although by far the easiest and quickest is from the Snake Summit via Mill Hill or straight across the moor (steep final approach) if it has been dry.

Not much sun | 50 min | Green

Descent

---

❶ Banjo Crack . . . . S 4a
6m. The flake crack left of the main bulk of the buttress.
FA. Graham West 1960

❷ Daddy Crack . . . . VS 4c
8m. The steep central crack is climbed on solid jams.
FA. Graham West 1960

❸ Mummy Crack E1 5b
8m. The right-hand crack is difficult to enter, then smack in the jams. You might need bandaging after a tussle with this one!
FA. Malc Baxter 1964

❹ Wicked Uncle Ernie E4 6a
10m. The left-hand side of the square arete across the gully saves its fun for the final tough section.
FA. Chris Hardy 1987

❺ Campus Chimney . . . . VDiff
14m. The lower crack leads to a deep and wider chimney.
FA. Peter Bamfield 1959

❻ Mustard Walls E2 5c
16m. Climb to the right edge of the roof and gain a ledge up and left with difficulty. Finish up the precarious steep slab.
FA. Malc Baxter 1964

❼ Machine Gun . . . . VDiff
8m. The twisting groove up the left-hand side of the buttress.
FA. Graham West 1960

❽ Glock Over E4 6c
12m. Climb the bulge then move left where a desperate move allows a standing position on a jug to be gained. Finish more easily. Sadly using the left arete lowers the crux to **5c**!
FA. Andy Barker 1994

❾ The Scratcher . . . . VS 4c
8m. Scratch and scrawm up the awkward wide crack.
FA. Jim Campbell 1976

❿ Two Twist Chimney . . . . . . S 4b
8m. The wider fissure to the right requires some contortions.
FA. Jim Campbell 1976

Not much sun | 50 min

Descent

Kinder Downfall

Kinder North

Kinder South

TWISTED SMILE BUTTRESS

The final buttress described is just right of Mustard Walls and features a prominent jutting prow, the jaunty jester's cap. The classics here are *Jester Cracks* and *Twisted Smile*, with *Monkey Madness* and *Candle in the Wind* appealing more to the hard core.

APPROACH - As for Mustard Walls.

⑪ Wire Brush Slab **E2 5b**
12m. Climb the lower arete to gain the hanging slab at a prominent pocket. Shuffle left and sprint up the excellent hanging upper arete. As wire brushes are taboo nowadays, you might want to try a toothbrush to clean the holds!
FA. Jim Campbell 1976

⑫ Tweeter and the Monkey Man **E4 6a**
12m. Trend right up the lower wall (possible stance) then step back left, above the overlap, and climb the precarious and bold upper slab on pebbles and scary friction.
FA. Harry Venables 1989

⑬ Knapp Hand .... **HS 4b**
18m. A long rambling pitch with a good finale up the scoop high on the right-hand side of the buttress.
FA. Peter Knapp 1954

⑭ Penniless Crack .... **S 4b**
8m. The steepening-crack to the left of the grassy gully.
FA. Malc Baxter 1962

⑮ The Slice .... **HS 4b**
12m. Climb the wall to the clean-cut diagonal crack.
FA. Malc Baxter 1962

⑯ Exodus .... **VS 4c**
18m. Trend left to pass the large overhang and gain the hanging arete. Climb the crack splitting the left edge of the second roof and finish up the slab.
FA. Peter Bamfield (2 points) 1959. FFA. Malc Baxter 1960

Just further right is the jutting prow of Twisted Smile Buttress.

⑰ Jester Cracks .... **HVS 5a**
16m. Climb the side-wall and then the slab on the right to a rest (poor thread) below the big roof. Swing left with difficulty then storm the superb jamming-crack that splits the peaked cap.
Photo page 141.
FA. Richard McHardy 1959

⑱ Monkey Madness .. **E6 6c**
16m. Wild. The front of the buttress between *Jester* and *Lobster Cracks*. Pull over the bulge then stretch upwards in a position of some danger. Continue over the next bulge then attack the steep final prow. It has big holds but limited gear.
FA. Andy Barker 1995

⑲ Lobster Crack .... **VS 5a**
14m. The left-hand parallel fissure is a steep struggle.
FA. Malc Baxter 1961

⑳ Crab Crack .... **HVS 5b**
14m. The right-hand fissure is hard to enter. If all else fails try sideways shuffling.
FA. Graham West 1961

㉑ Candle in the Wind ... **E3 5c**
16m. The fine soaring arete is approached from the right. Slant right to pass the initial overhang, shuffle left then pull up the arete itself. This is taken by easier climbing but the gear is poor.
FA. Chris Hardy 1988

㉒ Twisted Smile ...... **HVS 5a**
16m. One of the very best HVS routes in the Peak, its remoteness adding to its cachet. Climb the centre of the front of the buttress passing a vertical crack to a fine and lonely finish.
FA. John Gosling 1972

㉓ Count Dracula **E1 5b**
16m. Climb the slab to a position below the roof, traverse out left (exposed) and gain the upper wall awkwardly. Finish direct.
FA. Andy Bailey 1984

㉔ Harlequin **E3 6a**
14m. Steep and wild. Climb *Woe is Me* then traverse out left above the big overhang and take the right-hand side of the arete via a final bulge. The grade might need treating with respect!
FA. Johnny Dawes 1985

㉕ Woe is Me **S 4a**
12m. The crack past an awkward narrowing.
FA. Eric Byne 1954

Staffordshire / Whaley Bridge / Kinder / Bleaklow / Chew / Lancashire / Cheshire / Kinder Downfall / Kinder North / Kinder South

KINDER DOWNFALL

Staffordshire Whaley Bridge Kinder Bleaklow Chew Lancashire Cheshire

The cliffs around the famous cascade of the Kinder Downfall are amongst the most popular on the moor, mainly because of the dramatic setting but also because it is the location of a fine set of routes across a spread of grades with many good offerings across the lower end of the grade spectrum. The outcrops here tend to face between south and west and so get plenty of afternoon and evening sunshine. The shape of the valley tends to funnel westerly winds up towards the rim of the moor making climbing here a wild experience under these conditions and also turning the Kinder Downfall into the Kinder Upflow and showering unsuspecting passers-by on the moor behind. Also worth pointing out is the fact that the Downfall offers the Peak's best ice climbing venue in our increasingly infrequent harsh winters, though get here early if you don't want to find you are left with just a big pile of ice-cubes! A harsh frost with several days of sub-zero temperatures and full moon are the best conditions to aim for.

Falco Reche on *Downfall Direct* (III/IV) Kinder Downfall. *Page 156*

APPROACH See maps on pages 128 and 157

Access from any direction is a little arduous! From parking below the Snake Inn follow the path up Fair Brook then take 'the short crossing' (260 degrees, 0.9 km) which will pick up the sandy bed of the Kinder River and lead you down to the top of the Downfall. Alternatively from the top of the Snake Pass take the flagged path to the top of William Clough via Mill Hill then continue up onto the plateau to reach the top of Upper Western Buttress. Follow the plateau edge to the Downfall. If approaching from the west, park below the Kinder Reservoir, 1km east of Hayfield, which is 8km south of Glossop. Before starting the approach check out the plaque celebrating the 1926 mass trespass and thank your lucky stars. Walk up the side of the reservoir towards William Clough then the poor track beside the River Kinder direct (marshy and not really recommended) to the Downfall or, better and drier, hang a left up William Clough. Either follow it all the way to Ashop Head and join the Snake Summit route along the moor crest, or turn right just after the bridge across the stream and attack the slope direct - shorter but harder work.

CONDITIONS

> **OTHER GUIDEBOOKS -** A more complete list of routes on Kinder is published in the 1991 BMC *Kinder* guidebook.

The cliffs are arranged along the rim to the west of the cascade of the Downfall and look out south and west, so get plenty of afternoon and evening sun. As mentioned above, conditions here can be windy. Some of the rock is inclined to be gritty after rain though many of the better climbs stay clean enough throughout the year. In poor conditions some of the easier routes from 100 years ago make for a good challenging day out - all very 'traditional'!

Kinder Downfall Kinder North Kinder South

Dave Spencer high on Puttrell's 1900 classic *Zig-zag* (VDiff) at Kinder Downfall. *Page 155*

UPPER WESTERN BUTTRESS
The western-most decent cliff hereabouts has a fine sunny aspect and some good routes on the Upper Tier. The Lower Tier is dirty and best avoided and the left-hand side of the upper face is a bit crusty. Despite this, the upper right-hand area has some good routes in as fine a setting as anywhere on the moor.
APPROACH - See opposite.

1 Spike Chimney . . . . 🗝 ☐ **Diff**
16m. The deep rift on the left is worth seeking out and is climbed, passing the huge ringing flake of the spike, en route.
FA. Geoff Pigott 1950

2 Once in a Blue Moon 🗝 ☐ **E3 6a**
22m. The left arete of the buttress has taxing and reachy moves at mid-height with 'interesting' gear. Above this things ease.
FA. Graham Parkes 1999

3 The Dark Side of the Moon . 🗝 ☐ **E3 5c**
18m. The right arete of the buttress is approached through bulges (big thread) and climbed with a brief excursion onto its right-hand side and a finish up the front. Easier for the tall.
FA. Dennis Carr 1976

4 Extinguisher Chimney . . . . 🗝 ☐ **VS 4c**
18m. A classic narrowing-chimney which is less of a battle than it looks. Face right and squirm into the narrows to reach a ledge then finish with a restricted exit amongst the symbols. Don't disturb the symbols.
FA. Vin Dillon 1949

5 Candle Buttress . . . . . . 🗝 ☐ **HVS 5a**
18m. The buttress right of *Extinguisher Chimney* is gained awkwardly from the right and climbed delicately (useful flake round left) to easier ground.
FA. R Williams 1957

6 The Atrocity Exhibition . . . . 🗝 ☐ **E1 5b**
18m. A direct variation on *Candle Buttress*.
FA. Martin Kocsis 1997

7 Intermediate Route . . . . . . ☐ **HS 4b**
12m. Climb the striated wall slightly leftwards then finish back right up the rib that forms the edge of the previous route

8 South Wall . . . . 🗝 ☐ **VDiff**
12m. A little gem of a layback up the left-trending flakes. Western Grit's excellent answer to *Heaven Crack*.
FA. Eric Byne 1932

9 Pedestal Climb . . . . 🗝 ☐ **Diff**
8m. The front face of the squat pedestal leads to a groove.
FA. Eric Byne 1932

10 45 Degrees . . . . ☐ **HVS 5b**
6m. The short and sketchy slab is a good test of technique and is much steeper than the name suggests.
FA. Malc Baxter 1986

11 Curving Crack . . . . ☐ **S 4b**
6m. The obviously-named groove is tricky to enter then eases.
FA. Geoff Pigott 1948

12 Rock Reptile . . . . ☐ **HVS 5b**
6m. Slink up the right wall of the open recess using a fingery flake to make progress.
FA. Con Carey 1987

13 Singer Corner . . . . ☐ **S 4b**
8m. Enter the hanging layback with difficulty though on 'biffos'.

14 M.G. Route . . . . ☐ **HS 4a**
8m. The steep and juggy arete is quite a gripper.

15 Monkey Magic . . . . . 🗝 ☐ **HVS 5b**
8m. The steep wall to the right of the arete has a useful flake hold and provides good technical moves.
FA. Harry Venables 1986

16 The Funnel . . . . ☐ **HS 4b**
6m. The obviously named feature is fine for double jointed dwarfs, and a battle for the rest of us.

17 Eastern Promise . . . . ☐ **HVS 5b**
8m. Climb the wall, starting on the right up a thin crack, and continuing with care.
FA. Con Carey 1987

18 Eastern Crack . . . . ☐ **S 4a**
8m. The short-lived crack on glorious jams.
FA. Geoff Pigott 1948

19 Eastern Arete . . . . ☐ **HVS 5b**
8m. Pull leftwards onto the hanging arete and then sprint.
FA. Con Carey 1986

20 End Wall . . . . ☐ **VS 4c**
8m. The final short but unprotected wall on sloping holds.
FA. Geoff Pigott 1948

Staffordshire

Whaley Bridge

Kinder

Bleaklow

Chew

Lancashire

Cheshire

UPPER WESTERN BUTTRESS APPROACH -
(See map on page 157)
Either walk in from the Snake Summit or take the Hayfield approach past Kinder Reservoir. Cross a footbridge over William Clough and continue up to the col or attack the slope direct. Follow the moor crest path rightwards (SE) for about 200m until you are above the crag. The Upper Tier is best approached from the right looking at the photo on the opposite page.

KINDER BUTTRESS
A fine and remote gritstone buttress with one of Kinder's most famous outings. The *Left* and *Right Twin Chimneys* are 'classics' of another era whereas *Foreigner* and *Final Judgment* have a much more modern feel about them.
APPROACH - (See map on page 157)
As for Upper Western Buttress until the slog up the ridge. Either: continue along the path to reach Kinder Brook. Make your way up the side of the brook until the characteristic Kinder Buttress appears above you - usually damp. Or: follow the route to Upper Western Buttress and continue along the crest past the crag until Kinder Buttress can be seen down and right.

❶ **Foreigner** . . . . 🔲🔲 ⬜ **E3 5c**
16m. The steep wall high on the left-hand side of the cliff gives a bold pitch (around to the left on the topo). Climb the wall to the break (gear) then continue up above making an excursion out left into a shallow scoop below an overhang before heading back out right to finish.
FA. Con Carey 1986

❷ **The Mermaid's Ridge** . . 🔲🔲 ⬜ **VS 4c**
A Kinder classic; a fine climb, two varied and interesting pitches and of considerable historical interest.
1) 4b, 12m. Climb the bubbly ridge over a bulge (thread) to a stance on a good ledge.
2) 4c, 18m. Start around on the left of the ledge (move the belay?) and traverse right delicately onto the ridge. From here move right into a groove and climb this to the top.
FA. Siegfried Herford 1910

❸ **Glory Boys** . . . . ⬜ **VS 4c**
12m. The obvious narrowing-crack in the right wall is pleasant enough if a little short-lived.
FA. Keith Ashton 1986

❹ **Left Twin Chimney** . . . . 🔲🔲 ⬜ **VS 4c**
30m. The right-hand corner of the recess leads with increasing difficulty to the midway ledge and a stance. Use *The Mermaid's Ridge* approach to the groove above the roof but continue rightwards to a crack in a steep groove for an exciting finish.
FA. Siegfried Herford 1910

❺ **Pumping Irony** . . . . . 🔲🔲 ⬜ **E3 5c**
12m. The obvious evil wide grovel of what is really *Left Twin Chimney Direct*. Described in the 'old' Kinder guide as VS!
FA. Con Carey 1987

❻ **Right Twin Chimney** . . . 🔲🔲 ⬜ **HVS 5a**
30m. Follow the right-hand corner of the recess easily to an awkward shallow chimney. Squirm up this to the terrace (**4c** - possible belay). The leaning fissure above is hard to enter, and leads to a good grass ledge. Finish up the groove behind.
FA. Siegfried Herford 1910

❼ **Final Judgement** . . 🔲🔲🔲 ⬜ **E3 5c**
20m. Disjointed but exciting and exposed. Climb the square-cut right arete of the buttress by committing laying away to reach the security of the grass ledge. Move out left above a lot of space then swarm up the rounded arete to a harassing finish.
FA. Con Carey 1987

❽ **Boulevard Traverse** . . . . ⬜ **HS 4a**
12m. Climb the banana-shaped flake to its tip then traverse left into an awkward crack that leads to the grassy ledge. Finish up the wide crack behind.

❾ **Atone** . . . . ⬜ **E1 5b**
10m. Get up onto the tip of the flake as for the previous route then pull over the roof directly above and climb the awkward, wide and steep crack to a tricky exit.
FA. Paul Nunn 1964

Staffordshire

Whaley Bridge

Kinder

Bleaklow

Chew

Lancashire

Cheshire

① Domino Wall E1 5b
16m. Start left of the crusty rock and climb a bulge before shuffling right to a ledge. Continue carefully up the wall to the big shelf (stance) then finish rightwards up the short wall behind.
FA. R.Williams 1957

② The Ledge Shufflers E6 6c
14m. Used to be one of Kinder's more obvious 'last great problems'! Climb crusty rock to the bulges then head left through these, then up the arete aiming for the big flake in the roof. Finish phlegmatically. 'Several ropes were used on the first ascent to protect the start and the moves left. Gear included RPs and huge cams!
FA. Dave Turnbull 1999

③ Raggald's Wall ... E1 5a
18m. Start up the groove in the right edge of the wall to its apex then move left around the arete (care with the rope work!) and climb the delicate groove to a reachy move for the ledge. Finish up the wall behind.
FA. Paul Nunn 1964

④ Great Chimney Left-hand .. VS 4c
18m. Climb the groove as for *Raggald's Wall* but continue steeply in a direct line to a good ledge (possible stance). Finish up the arete on the left.

⑤ The Great Chimney ...... HS 4b
18m. Classic. The deep rift is approached via wide bridging to reach a scratched slab. From the small ledge above the left end of this slab, mantel into the chimney and follow it throughout. The exit is tricky. Originally split at a belay on the 'small ledge'.
FA. J.W.Puttrell 1903

⑥ The Ensemble Exit .... HVS 5a
18m. From the small stance part-way up *Great Chimney*, climb the groove on the right then take a steep crack to an undercut ledge out right. Pull over the capping block to a tricky mantelshelf finish, or escape out right.
FA. Paul Nunn 1964

The prow is an impressive 'Last Great Problem' which has been top-roped by many but awaits a lead.

⑦ Professor's Chimney ..... Diff
14m. Weaves up the wide, shallow, chimney. Start on the right and cross over to finish up the left-hand groove.
FA. JW Puttrell 1903

⑧ Professor's Chimney Direct . VDiff
14m. Follow the right-hand branch direct by interesting moves.

⑨ Pegasus Left-hand E1 5b
14m. A short awkward crack splits a small overhang. Climb through this then continue up the crack above until forced left.
FA. R. Williams (one peg) 1957 FFA. Con Carey 1987

⑩ Pegasus Right-hand ... VS 4c
16m. A thin slanting crack and its continuation.
FA. Al Parker - in mistake for the Left-hand, 1962

⑪ Left Fork Chimney ...... Diff
16m. Climb into the chimney then follow the left-branch,
FA. JW Puttrell early 1900s

⑫ Right Fork Chimney ...... S 4a
16m. The right-hand branch is better and harder than its neighbour and is accessed across a short glacis (a kind of easy slab) from the previous climb. Finish more steeply.
FA. JW Puttrell early 1900s

Kinder Downfall

Kinder North

Kinder South

Descent

Staffordshire
Whaley Bridge
Kinder
Bleaklow
Chew
Lancashire
Cheshire

THE AMPHITHEATRE

A fine set of routes in a particularly wild setting and including several classics from way back when. The whole area tends to funnel westerly winds and so can be a blowy place to climb. The Amphitheatre has such classics as *Great Chimney* whilst the steep cracks and walls facing the waterfall are home to some good traditional battles and the superb historical *Zigzag Climb*.

APPROACH (See map on page 157) - From the east (Snake Inn parking) take the Fair Brook path to the plateau then the 'short crossing' - (260 degrees, 1.9km) arriving above the Downfall. From here the easiest descent is down a gully just to the left (looking in) of the Amphitheatre - see topo. From the west follow either of the approaches as used to reach Kinder Buttress then continue to the Downfall. The moor edge path is quicker and drier than that in the valley bottom.

Morning | 70 min | Green

---

⑬ Embarkation Parade ..... VS 4c
12m. This one-time classic needs a spruce up. Climb right then left to gain the steep groove which gives sustained climbing. From the big grassy ledge finish up the corner at the back.
FA. Arthur Birtwhislte 1939

⑭ Crooked Overhang .... VS 4c
8m. Climb rightwards and then up into a cave (possible stance). Pull through the juggy roof to reach a ledge and corner which leads to the top.

⑮ Rodeo .... VS 4c
14m. A direct route up the right-hand side of the arete which superseds the old wandering line of *Crooked Arete*.
FA. Rebekah Smith 1998

⑯ Zig-zag .... VDiff
18m. A fine climb in a dramatic setting. Trend left up the face to a position on the tip of a flake. Step up and right delicately on a small polished foothold to the final widening crack.
Photo page 151.
FA. JW Puttrell c1900

⑰ Zig-zag Crack .... HVD
12m. The long narrowing-crack to the right of *Zigzag* leads via a steepening groove to a tough exit round a bulge.
FA. Eric Byne 1929

⑱ Spin-up .... HVS 5b
12m. Climb into the shallow left-facing groove in the steep wall then make fingery moves to easier ground and a crack.
FA. Con Carey 1987

⑲ Toss up .... HVS 5a
12m. Climb steeply into, and up, the right-hand groove. At its top, step left to join the *Spin-up*.
FA. Con Carey 1987

⑳ Chockstone Chimney ..... VDiff
12m. The steep rift has a series of (well?) jammed blocks. A well-protected tussle with an awkward finish.
FA. WJ Watson c1900

㉑ The Last Fling E2 5b
12m. Take the steep wall to the central roof then gain the ledge above this precariously. More balancy climbing gains the top.
FA. Con Carey 1987

㉒ Amphitheatre Crack ..... S 4b
10m. Bridge the wide crack to where it narrows then try to get established above the overhang - hard work!
FA. possibly J.W.Puttrell c1910

㉓ Amphitheatre Face Climb .. HS 4b
12m. Oddly named! Climb the groove to the roof then shuffle out left to a rest on the arete (thread). Finish awkwardly
FA. possibly J.W.Puttrell c1910

㉔ Five Ten .... HS 4a
10m. Climb the slotted face to a ledge, then continue up the tricky wall above.
FA. John Porter 1956

Descend Downfall Climb or down the gully beyond the Amphitheatre

Afternoon | 70 min | Green | Seepage

KINDER DOWNFALL

The rock climbing here is not the best but the setting is special and the best of the routes are well worth doing. Under the right (rare!) conditions the Downfall forms the Peak's premier ice-climbing venue. Apart from odd bits of ice bouldering all round the cirque there is the diagonal expedition of *Downfall Climb* (I/II) and the hanging icicle of *The Direct* (III/IV). Arrive early or be prepared to queue! *See photo on page 150.*

APPROACH - (See map on page opposite) - From the east (Snake Inn parking) take the Fair Brook path to the plateau then the 'short crossing' - (260 degrees, 0.9km) arriving above the Downfall.

From the west follow either of the approaches as used to reach Kinder Buttress. The moor-edge path is quicker and drier than that in the valley bottom. If you are approaching from above (via Fair Brook or Upper Western Buttress) the scramble descent is down a gully just to the left (looking in) of the Amphitheatre a couple of hundred metres beyond the Downfall, or make your way carefully down *Downfall Climb*.

❶ North Tier Climb .... VS 4c
1) 4c, 8m. Climb the strenuous jamming crack awkwardly to the wide grassy ledge that crosses the face.
2) 4b, 10m. Tackle the short-lived juggy wall above and then finish up a short groove.
FA. Paul Nunn 1964

❷ Dud Chimney E1 5a
14m. The shallow groove gives steep moves on rather unfriendly rock to a final difficult move.
FA. R Williams 1957

❸ Slip Sliding Away E3 5c
6m. A well-named route giving spooky and exposed climbing up the hanging slab (just an immense detached block) above a big drop. Short on length but more than big enough on impact
FA. Con Carey 1987

❹ The Glorious Twelfth .. E2 5b
22m. Climb the juggy leaning groove (creak, creak) to a good breather on a ledge on the right. Step back left and finish up the wide crack with difficulty.
FA. Alan McHardy 1973

❺ The Hunter E3 5b
22m. Steep and serious. Climb the wall to a big flake then traverse left to a second crusty horror of a flake. Layback (!) up this and press on through the bulges above to ledge. Climb the short bulging wall on the left (technical crux) to finish.
FA. Dennis Carr 1976

❻ The Beast E2 5b
24m. Devious. Start as for *The Hunter* but continue straight up to the roof then traverse right to the 'Dovecote Cave', Belay here or on the higher ledge. Move out left to finish easily.
FA. Dennis Carr 1966

❼ The Bloody Thirteenth E1 5b
24m. Climb the left-hand side of the sharp arete starting up a flake on the left then taking the groove directly to the cave. Finish as for the previous climb, or more easily out right.
FA. Paul Nunn 1973

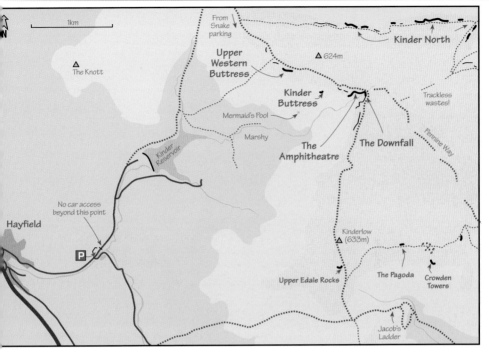

8 Shotgun Grooves . . . . . HVS 5b
'4m. The shallow grooves running up the right-hand side of the rete give a worthwhile and awkward pitch. There is a choice of nishes the same as for the previous climbs.
A. Al Parker 1976

9 Poacher's Crack . . . . . HVS 5a
2m. The sustained and steep cracks in the right-hand side of he wall give well-protected and steep climbing.
A. Ted Rodgers 1976

10 Downfall Groove . . . . . HVS 5a
8m. The crack in the back of the big angular corner is hard vork. The lower section can be bridged but the upper part is est jammed and proves sustained and awkward. The corner is ust a shadow of one of Puttrell's earlier exploits which ollapsed some years back. It now rests in pieces.
A. J.W.Puttrell (of the original route) c1900

11 Independence Crack . . . E2 5c
8m. The fierce finger crack a couple of metres right of the orner gives a sustained pitch with good but hard-won gear.
A. Dennis Carr (1 point of aid) 1976. FFA. Con Carey 1987

12 Hard Times E2 5c
'4m. Awkwardly cross the narrow ramp rightwards then climb he leaning shallow groove past a couple of unhelpful sloping edges to reach easier ground. Finish up the buttress on the left.
A. Al Parker 1979

13 Downfall Climb . . . . Mod
60m. An aquatic trip across the series of sloping ledges, OK in the dry but way too exciting if there has been much rain. Start on the right and climb up the groove or the ledges just to its left. Then follow the ramps up and left, passing the main flow, to a choice of finishing grooves. If already well-soaked, it is probably worth exiting easily rightwards.

14 Harvest . . . . HVS 5a
22m. Start from the sandy ledge part way up *Downfall South Corner* and trend left up the steep rock into a crack and onto a cave recess. Exit rightwards from this and continue steeply.
FA. Mick Dewsbury 1977

15 Downfall South Corner . . . . VDiff
40m. Grubby but well-worth doing. Start as for *Downfall Climb* but continue to a good stance in a sandy cave on the right. Pull out of the cave and take the shallow chimney to ledges then pass another bulge to a wider crack which leads (choice of exits) to the top.
FA. J.W.Puttrell 1900

To the right is the daunting bastion of Great Buttress, home to several worthwhile climbs, though sadly the cliff has become increasingly green, gritty and turf-ridden over the years and now sees little traffic. The routes are not described here.

BLEAKLOW and LONGDENDALE

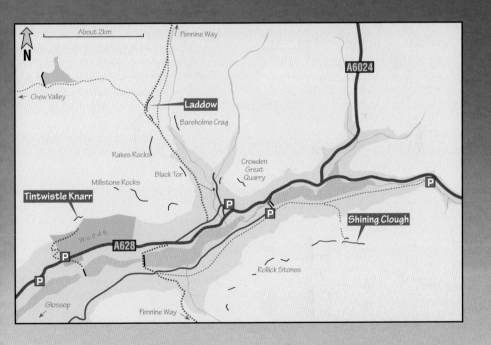

Dave Vincent on *Phoenix Climb* (VS 4c) Shining Clough. *Page 162*

Shining Clough is the best of the cliffs that fall under the banner of the Bleaklow area; it is a tall, sombre and very remote edge that is at its best on warm summer days when the cotton (grass) is high, the curlews mew over the plateau and the moors shimmer in the heat haze. Many of the climbs follow steep cracks, and therefore require a fair degree of proficiency in jamming. They tend to be green and gritty at the start of the season or after wet weather; in such conditions there are many better destinations in this guide.

On the far left are some short routes and then there is the collapsed buttress that was once home to the classics of *Orestes* and *Chalkman*, which fell down in the early 1980s. This is a sure-fire pointer to the fact that the whole cliff is the site of an ancient landslip and the other classics may one day head the same way. On the left-hand side of the main part of the cliff is the fine jutting arete of *East Rib* (HVS 5a) that gets the morning sun and is very photogenic.

Historically there are few details from before the 1950s, though many of the climbs put up before this date were the work of The Manchester University Mountaineering Club (Arthur Birtwistle and Co.) and later, members of the Karabiner Club along with the three Lowe Brothers.

OTHER GUIDEBOOKS - A more complete list of routes at Shining Clough is published in the 1991 BMC *Kinder* guidebook.

APPROACH Also see map on page 158

There is ample parking by the southern end of the dam across the Longdendale reservoir. Go through the gate and follow the undulating track eastwards for a couple of kilometres to a sign on the right pointing to Open Country just short of the keeper's lodge. Head up and left to the end of the wall then cross the stream and follow its steep left-hand (looking up) bank until it is possible to break out onto the moor and follow a variety of narrow tracks over to the cliff; about an hour from the parking. Alternatively walk from the parking at the eastern end of the Longdendale Trail, this takes about the same time - see map.

CONDITIONS

Shining Clough is a great venue but it is not recommended after poor weather as it is slow to dry and sees little in the way of sun. Ideal conditions are warm summer days after a dry

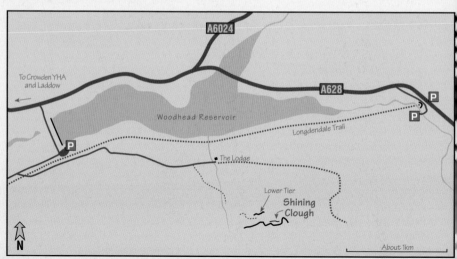

Staffordshire · Whaley Bridge · Kinder · Bleaklow · Chew · Lancashire · Cheshire · Hobson Moor · Tintwistle Narr · Laddow · Shining Clough

PHOENIX BUTTRESS

One of natural grit's more impressive buttresses and home to several worthwhile climbs including the superb *Phoenix* - one of Harding's very best. At a slightly lower grade *Via Principia* and *Atherton Brothers* are excellent and, a notch higher, the short but exposed *East Rib* is a 'must do'.

① Orang Arete . . . . 〔 〕 **VS 4b**
10m. Take the crack in the centre of the south-facing side wall to the deep break then move left and climb the short arete.
FA. Martin Whittaker 1986

② Grape Escape . . . . 🏔️🪨 〔 〕 **E3 6a**
10m. Follow *Orang Arete* to where it heads left then climb the thin crack in the wall above and finish with difficulty and a stretch (or cop out right at a lower grade). Small wires needed.
FA. Ivan Green 1995

③ Monkey Puzzle . . . . 🏔️🪨 〔 〕 **VS 4c**
10m. Follow the previous routes to the break but then move right (thread) to a block and a second wide crack. Finish steeply up this. A pumpy little number at the grade.
FA. Don Whillans late 1940s - the great man's first new route

④ East Rib . . . . 〔3〕 **HVS 5a**
14m. Good climbing in a superb setting with good rests and protection. From the base of the crack of *Monkey Puzzle* trend right to climb a flat overhang on the right (juggy but steep) and then the airy arete above. *Photo on front cover.*
FA. John Gosling 1960s

⑤ East Rib Direct . 🏔️🪨🌀 〔 〕 **E5 6a**
16m. Climb the steep lower section of the arete to join the regular route. A poorly-protected lead that can be dirty early in the season and is bold at any time of the year!
FA. Loz Francomb 1979

⑥ Icon . . . . 🏔️🪨 〔 〕 **HVS 5a**
16m. Climb the wide crack that splits the wall (big gear useful) to its end, then climb the final steep wall centrally.
FA. Tom Stevenson 1979

⑦ Green Crack . . . . 〔1〕 **S 4a**
14m. A poor start leads to a better finale. Climb the crack in the left wall of the deep gloomy chimney (reached by a grotty, grassy scramble) then bridge the exposed groove above.

To the right is the enclosed and unsavoury rift of East Chimney then the finest buttress on the cliff, home to Phoenix.

⑧ Atherton Brothers . . . . . . 〔2〕 **S 4a**
20m. Climb up the left-trending cracks (or more easily up the block on the left) then tackle the steep flake (not easy to protect) by sustained climbing until it is possible to mantelshelf onto a good ledge. Finish up the groove behind and wonder where the left wall of the one -time chimney went to!
FA. Arthur Birtwistle 1940s

⑨ Phoenix Climb . . . . . . 🏔️🪨 〔 〕 **VS 4c**
26m. Vintage Harding and well-worth the walk up! The superb straight crack gives classic jamming past a useful hole to reach easier but still-steep ground. A wider section of crack gains a ledge; climb the groove on the left then finish direct or move out right for a superb and airy exit. *Photo page 158.*
FA. Peter Harding 1947

Descent

Early morning · 60 min

⑩ Via Principia . . . . 〔3〕 **S 4a**
24m. The wide chimney crack in the nose of the buttress leads past a bulge to a gritty ledge (possible stance). Step left into the jamming crack in the exposed arete and climb this until the crack on the right can be reached. Continue up this then finish up the wall on the left. An excellent route at the grade.

⑪ Subsidiary Chimney . . . . . 🏔️ 〔 〕 **S 4a**
24m. From the ledge of *Via Principia* squirm up the narrow chimney with some difficulty especially at the narrows.

⑫ Ave . . . . 🏔️🌀 〔 〕 **VS 4c**
24m. From the ledge of *Via Principia* climb the steep flake just right of the chimney by committing laybacking to reach the wider continuation and finish awkwardly up this. Big gear.

⑬ Powerplay . . . . 🏔️🌀 〔 〕 **E2 6a**
8m. The centre of the flat face gives a fingery pitch. Climb the face left then right to ledges and an escape.
FA. Con Carey 1988

⑭ Little Red Pig . . . . . . 🏔️🌀 〔 〕 **HVS 5**
18m. Climb the crack and groove to reach the pillar above then tackle the steep slab right then left to a series of thin cracks linked by a big shallow pocket.
FA. Chris Wright 1986

⑮ Vanishing Groove . . . . 〔 〕 **S 4a**
18m. Follow the previous climb but step right to tackle the continuation of the lower groove. Grubby with a grass cornice.
FA. Keith Ashton 1988

Not much sun 60 min

Staffordshire

Whaley Bridge

Kinder

Bleaklow

Chew

Lancashire

Cheshire

THE RAINBOW FLAKE

To the right the cliff is split into two tiers, with a grassy terrace between them. The lower tier is scrappy though the upper one is better where three short buttresses each have a single climb. They are most easily reached by a zigzagging scramble from below. Right again is the striking fin of rock known as The Rainbow Flake, whose narrow front face is tackled by the astounding *Bloodrush*. Beyond this the deep groove of *Nagger's Delight* and the jutting rib of *Yerth*.

⑯ Birthday Chimney .... ⬜ VDiff
?0m. Scramble up the gully and climb the groove on the left throughout. Another route in need of a wash and brush-up!
FA. J. Warmsley 1949

THE RAINBOW FLAKE

⑰ Short Crack .... ⬜ VS 4c
0m. The obviously-named feature in the left-hand buttress.
FA. Al Parker 1974

⑱ Satyr .... 🔲🔳 ⬜ E4 5c
0m. The shallow ramp on the central buttress provides a delicate and harrowing lead, on which protection is lacking.
FA. Al Parker 1974

⑲ Solstice .... 🔳 ⬜ HVS 5a
3m. The zigzag crack and arete of the right-hand buttress.
FA. Al Parker 1974

⑳ Some Product ...... 🔲🔳 ⬜ E2 5c
3m. The thin crack in the north face of the fin leads out to the arete and a rapid sprint for the top.
FA. Loz Francomb 1979

㉑ Bloodrush .... ③🔲🔳🔳 ⬜ E6 6b
6m. Climb the mighty-bold frontal face of the fin by an increasingly harrowing series of 'monkey-up-a-stick' moves. A great and gripping outing which is well-named.
FA. Andy Cave 1990s

㉒ Saucius Digitalis .... 🔲🔳 ⬜ E4 6a
12m. The thin crack in the south face is a bit of a finger wrecker though protection is good. At its end, improvise a way left out to the arete, and finish more boldly up this.
FA. Loz Francomb 1979

㉓ Nagger's Delight .... 🔲🔳 ⬜ HVS 5a
12m. The steep groove gives good bridging and laybacking to a tricky exit out left. The final moves are often gritty.
FA. Pete Crew 1959

㉔ Naaden ..... 🔲🔳🔳🔳 ⬜ E1 5b
12m. Jam the fine crack in the right wall of the groove until it ends then climb the wall with a fierce fingery pull to start (5c for the short) and a stretchy final move rightwards at the top.
FA. Mike Simpkins late 1960s

㉕ Yerth .... 🔲🔳🔳 ⬜ E2 5c
14m. Climb through the stacked roof and follow cracks left of the arete until they end on a huge flake. Traverse round the arete, climb a short crack and make a crucial and scary mantelshelf to reach an easier finish.
FA. Mike Simpkins late 1960s

㉖ Cistern Groove .... ⬜ VDiff
12m. The steep groove is approached over broken ground.

Staffordshire

Whaley Bridge

Kinder

Bleaklow

Chew

Lancashire

Cheshire

Hobson Moor

Tintwistle Narr

Laddow

Shining Clough

PISA BUTTRESS

Shining Clough is blessed not with one especially fine buttress but with two. The squat barrel-shaped mass of Pisa Buttress is a superb clean piece of rock with a quartet of excellent routes that are amongst the first on the cliff to come into condition. Tick all the starred routes on this bit of rock and the walk up will have been well worth it.

❶ Galileo . . . . 🔲🔳🔲🔳 **E1 5b**
18m. A strenuous and sustained pitch though with good protection throughout. Climb the steep finger-crack to eventually arrive at a small ledge. Finish up the easier cracks above. The crux is the lower crack for the strong and the upper crack for the weak.
Photo page 161.
FA. John Gosling late 1960s

❷ Pisa Direct . . . . 🔲🔳 **VS 4c**
24m. From the lowest point of the buttress climb the crack just left of the arete, then the excellent right-slanting crack to just below the Leaning Tower. Head left for 4m to a ledge then climb the arete to a better ledge on the right. The leaning crack above leads to easier ground. Care with the rope work needed.
FA. Arthur Birtwhistle 1949

❸ Pisa Super Direct . . . . 🔲🔳🔳 **HVS 5a**
20m. Super direct and a super route. Start direct up thin cracks in the slab just right of the arete to join the parent route which is then followed to the Leaning Tower. Then climb the bulging crack and well-positioned crest of the buttress. One of the very best routes on Bleaklow.
FA. John Gosling late 1960s

❹ Stable Cracks . . . . 🔲🔳 **VS 4b**
20m. The continuous crack-line up the right-hand side of the face is just a touch wide for comfort. It gives a well-protected pitch (with enough large gear) and would improve with traffic.
FA. Peter Harding 1947

❺ Plastic Saddle . . . . 🔲 **E1 5c**
18m. The narrow slab just to the right is climbed centrally and gives a bit of a rough ride. Some gardening might be needed.
FA. Tom Valentine 1988

❻ Typists' Chimney . . . . 🔲 **Diff**
16m. The deep chimney groove that bounds the right-hand side of the slab. A grubby and gloomy affair.

❼ Unicorn Cracks . . . . 🔲 **HS 4b**
16m. Climb the diagonal crack in the right wall of the groove to its end then the cracks and a groove up and right to the top. Another route that sees no sun and few ascents.

❽ Trungel Crack . . . . 🔲🔳 **HVS 5a**
18m. Climb the crack just left of the arete, passing a recess, to a sloping shelf on the right. A continuation crack leads through an overhang to a finish up the crack in the left wall of *Unicorn Cracks'* final groove.
FA. Eddie Birch 1960s

Descent

the Leaning Tower

Not much sun

60 min

THE BIG WALL

❾ The Big Wall . . . . 🔲🔳🔳 **E3 6a**
20m. A classic with hard climbing, good runners and some lo-o-ong reaches. Climb a crack to a flat roof then stretch left to a thin crack and climb this to a ledge on the arete. Make difficult moves into a cave (often dirty) and harder moves out of it. A Friend 4 is essential to protect the final wall, although the short may have to avoid this last section on the left.
FA. Mike Simpkins 1960s. FFA. John Allen 1975

❿ Holme Moss . . . . 🔲🔳 **E1 5b**
16m. Climb the cracks in the right-hand side of the face through a bulge and head up the final tricky wall.
FA. John Hart 1979

⓫ Gremlin Groove . . . . 🔲🔳 **VS 4c**
14m. The long groove up the right-hand side of the smooth wall gives a good pitch. The crux is a stubborn overhang just below the final groove.
FA. Peter Harding 1947

⓬ Gremlin Wall . . . . 🔲 **HVS 5a**
14m. Climb the steep wall to a ledge then trend left and pull through a small overhang with difficulty to reach another ledge. Finish up the wall behind.

⓭ Artifact . . . . 🔲 **VS 4c**
14m. Follow a thin crack out to the arete and climb this until a short traverse can be made back left under an overhang and finish up the wall. High in the grade.
FA. John Gosling late 1960s

Staffordshire

Whaley Bridge

Kinder

Bleaklow

Chew

Lancashire

Cheshire

Phoenix Buttress Area

Pisa Buttress

The Big Wall

Right

Not much sun

60 min

Descent (dirty)

Descent (awkward)

THE BIG WALL

The smooth north-facing wall towards the right-hand side of the cliff is home to one hard classic and some easier offerings. Although inclined to be a bit scruffy at the start of the season *The Big Wall* is worthy of your attention if you climb at the required grade and are tall enough!

To the right is *Deep Chimney*, a viable if somewhat dirty scrambling descent route.

⑭ Goblin's Crack . . . . ⬜ **VS 4c**
2m. The steep slot in the right-hand wall of the chimney.
A. Con Carey 1988

⑮ Flake Groove . . . . ⬜ **VDiff**
10m. Climb the groove to the big roof (fancy a direct finish?) and escape out right using the big flake.

⑯ Flake Crack . . . . ⬜ **S 4a**
10m. Back-and-foot up behind the big flake to its top then about face and finish as for the last route.

⑰ Toadstool Crack . . . . ⬜ **VS 4c**
10m. The triple overhangs are passed with difficulty.

⑱ Pinnacle Crack . . . . ⬜ **HS 4b**
14m. The crack in the wall behind the pinnacle has awkward initial moves, then trend right up the crack to the arete and finish in a pleasantly exposed position.

The short pinnacle has four climbs - the two best are:

⑲ Ordinary Route . . . . ⬜ **Mod**
4m. The cliff face of the pinnacle is the easiest way up - and of course, down.

⑳ Pinnacle Face . . . . 🔲⬜ **VS 4c**
10m. The valley face is the best way to the top and climbed by a thin crack, the slab and then the left-hand arete.

Hobson Moor

Tintwistle Narr

Laddow

Shining Clough

165

Staffordshire
Whaley Bridge
Kinder
Bleaklow
Chew
Lancashire
Cheshire

The Big Wall

Not much sun   60 min

Descent

SHINING CLOUGH - RIGHT

The right-hand side of the cliff is the least popular section. Despite this fact there are some worthwhile lower grade routes though really the whole area could do with a bit more traffic to get spruced up.

1 Phantom **E3 6a**
14m. A spooky and precarious eliminate up the left-hand side of the face right of the pinnacle. The crucial slab is protected by side-runners and avoiding the next climb is not easy.
FA. Con Carey 1988

2 Nimrod . . . . **S 4a**
14m. Climb the flake and groove in tandem to a block. From a standing position on this, climb discontinuous cracks to the top, finishing with an awkward-feeling layback.
FA. Peter Harding 1947

3 Free Fall **E3 5c**
12m. Climb the middle of the wall to a leftward finger-traverse then swing boldly around the arete to jugs. Climb up until it is possible to transfer back to the front face to finish.
FA. Con Carey 1988

4 Stag Party . . . . **VDiff**
14m. A riotous affair which staggers up the wide crack in the left wall of the groove and finishes up the chimney on the right.

5 Ladies' Day . . . . **S 4a**
14m. Climb a crack until a traverse leads to the chimney on the left. Climb this and hand-traverse back right to a ledge below a hanging groove. Pull into this and finish steeply on good holds.

6 Ladies' Day Direct . . . . **HVS 5**
14m. The arete direct by pleasant climbing and with some long stretches to the ledge. Finish as for *Middleton Groove*.
FA. John Gosling 1960s

7 Middleton Groove . . . . . . **HS 4b**
14m. The steep crack just right leads to the platform. Follow the curving fissure in the back of the groove to the final moves of *Ladies' Day*.

8 Valhalla Crack . . . . . **VS 4c**
14m. A steep groove is jammed to a grassy platform. The imposing continuation requires more jamming, or some rather intimidating laybacking.

9 Sampson **E4 6b**
14m. The impressive arete is followed throughout and is highly technical. Layback and heel-hook until forced left at two thirds height then pull rightwards past the final roof.
FA. Rob Weston 1989

10 Original Route . . . . **VDiff**
14m. The long groove gives a pleasant pitch. Climb initially on the right then left of a flake and finally exit direct.

11 West Ridge . . . . **HVS 5**
14m. The right-hand arete of the groove is another worthwhile outing and is climbed on its right-hand side by laying-away.

12 West Wall Route 1 . . . . . **S 4b**
14m. Follow thin cracks up the steep slab to easier ground then finish up the steep tower directly above.

Hobson Moor
Tintwistle Narr
Laddow
Shining Clough

The Main Cliff

Not much sun | 60 min

THE LOWER TIER

Down the slope from the main cliff, and passed on the approach, is the band of slumped rock that forms the Lower Tier. There are a dozen short offerings here that are especially suitable for those who find the main cliff rather too steep and intimidating. None of the climbs are brilliant but the smattering of stars should point out the best of this particular bunch.

1 Shandy . . . . **VDiff**
10m. The north-facing scoop on the far left.

2 Lager Lout . . . . **HVS 5a**
10m. The left-hand arete of the face is followed on its right-hand side to a finish over a small protruding beak.
FA. Keith Ashton 1989

3 Pint of Beer . . . . **S 4b**
10m. The wide, kinked crack is a bit of a struggle.

4 Omelette Crack . . . . **Diff**
8m. The chimney to the right is okay.

5 The Egg Bowl . . . . **VDiff**
8m. Climb the centre of the concave face to the right, following a thin crack, to a heathery exit.

6 The Vice . . . . **VDiff**
10m. The steep crack in the left-hand side wall; get stuck into it. Above this, wander up easy ground.

7 Main Wall Climb . . . . **VDiff**
12m. Climb to a cracked recess at 6m. Exit from this and finish up a groove containing a thin flake.

8 Captain Zep . . . . **HVS 5a**
10m. Follow a thin seam in the wall to the break below the roof and cross this on the left on a good jug.
FA. Mark Leach 1983

9 Dirtier Groove . . . . **Diff**
10m. The incised groove on the right is partly filled with turf at the moment. The upper half is better.

10 The Rainbow . . . . **Diff**
10m. The sharp (and clean) arete is followed on good holds and is grades easier than the routes on the feature of the same name up on the main cliff.

11 Dirty Groove . . . . **Diff**
10m. The next groove can be a bit of a grubby affair though as the name suggests it is cleaner than its near neighbour.

12 Left Route . . . . **S 4a**
10m. The cracks just right of the arete provide a sustained and delicate pitch.

13 Central Route . . . . **HVS 5a**
8m. The centre of the wall isn't too well-endowed with either gear or holds. Sustained.

14 Right Route . . . . **VDiff**
6m. The crack just before the boulder slope with a tricky move left at mid-height.

Staffordshire · Whaley Bridge · Kinder · Bleaklow · Chew · Lancashire · Cheshire · Hobson Moor · Tintwistle Narr · Laddow · Shining Clough

Staffordshire Whaley Bridge Kinder Bleaklow Chew Lancashire Cheshire Hobson Moor Timwistle Harr Laddow Shining Clough

In the early days of our sport, Laddow Rocks were one of the prime venues visited by climbers at the cutting edge of the sport. Today the place is very much out of fashion, haunted by ghosts and almost always quiet. The place is perhaps Western Grit's equivalent of Wharncliffe Crags; in both cases the nearness of the railway line gave (relatively) easy access, and both places were immensely popular 100 years ago. Since the production of Peak Gritstone East, Wharncliffe has undergone a bit of a renaissance; it would be nice to think we can do the same for Laddow's lofty and lonely buttresses.

The main bulk of the cliff is away on the far right just below the crest of the moor, and from here they straggle leftwards, gradually descending the hillside until they fizzle out close to the point where the approach path climbs onto the plateau.

APPROACH Also see map on page 158

There is extensive parking by Crowden Youth Hostel in Longdendale. The approach path follows the Pennine Way (signed) towards the distant cliff, rising in a series of steps until, having passed by the edge of The Southern Group it reaches the crest of the moor. From here it is usual to head straight to the right-hand side of the cliff, descending past the famous bivvy-cave to then work through the guide backwards! The approach takes about 50 to 60 minutes depending on how many photo-stops you have on the way! The 'old' Pennine Way track runs out onto the flat area below the cliff and although it gives great views it is nearly always unpleasantly boggy - the ridge crest path is a much better bet.

CONDITIONS

A fine but sadly neglected cliff that has become increasingly grassy over the years. Old photographs show extensive nail scratching and little in the way of vegetation, though those days have long since gone. The outlook from the cliff has changed little in the past 100 years and it is easy to see what the pioneers found so attractive about these tall buttresses and their lonely aspect. The cliff faces east and gets the morning sun. The grass tends to slow the drying of the place after rain, though fortunately the great classics of *Long Climb*, *Tower Face* and also the routes around the bivvy-cave are clean enough to dry quickly.

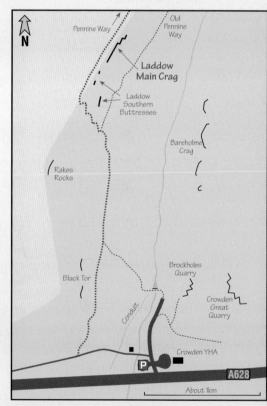

OTHER GUIDEBOOK - A more complete list of routes at Laddow is published in the 1991 BMC *Kinder* guidebook. This also covers the other crags indicated on the map; Rakes Rocks, Black Tor, Brockholes Quarry, Crowden Great Quarry and Bareholme Crag.

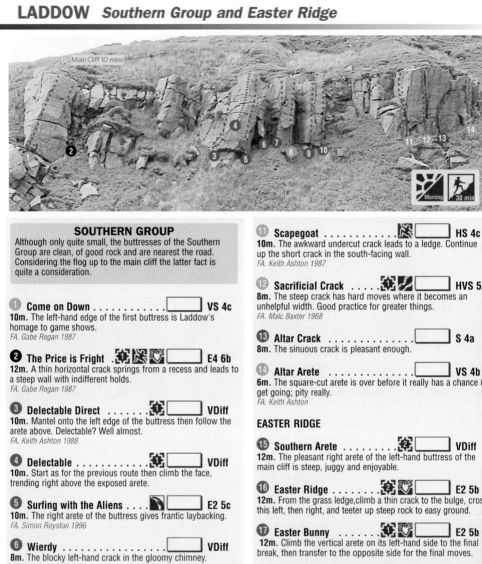

Main Cliff 10 mins

SOUTHERN GROUP

Although only quite small, the buttresses of the Southern Group are clean, of good rock and are nearest the road. Considering the flog up to the main cliff the latter fact is quite a consideration.

1 Come on Down . . . . **VS 4c**
10m. The left-hand edge of the first buttress is Laddow's homage to game shows.
FA. Gabe Regan 1987

2 The Price is Fright **E4 6b**
12m. A thin horizontal crack springs from a recess and leads to a steep wall with indifferent holds.
FA. Gabe Regan 1987

3 Delectable Direct . . . . **VDiff**
10m. Mantel onto the left edge of the buttress then follow the arete above. Delectable? Well almost.
FA. Keith Ashton 1988

4 Delectable . . . . **VDiff**
10m. Start as for the previous route then climb the face, trending right above the exposed arete.

5 Surfing with the Aliens **E2 5c**
10m. The right arete of the buttress gives frantic laybacking.
FA. Simon Royston 1996

6 Wierdy . . . . **VDiff**
8m. The blocky left-hand crack in the gloomy chimney.

7 Poking the Fire **E2 6a**
8m. The technical left-hand arete of the narrow buttress.
FA. Keith Ashton 1994

8 Chimney Breast . . . . **VS 5a**
8m. Climb the front face strenuously, finishing with a couple of 'lifting-a-fridge' type moves.

9 Jammy . . . . **S 4a**
8m. Sadly the clean-cut crack is often a bit gritty.

10 The Tea Drinking Tabby **E1 5b**
8m. The right-hand arete is short and not so sweet - more sugar needed please.
FA. Keith Ashton 1994

11 Scapegoat . . . . **HS 4c**
10m. The awkward undercut crack leads to a ledge. Continue up the short crack in the south-facing wall.
FA. Keith Ashton 1987

12 Sacrificial Crack . . . . . **HVS 5**
8m. The steep crack has hard moves where it becomes an unhelpful width. Good practice for greater things.
FA. Malc Baxter 1968

13 Altar Crack . . . . **S 4a**
8m. The sinuous crack is pleasant enough.

14 Altar Arete . . . . **VS 4b**
6m. The square-cut arete is over before it really has a chance t get going; pity really.
FA. Keith Ashton

EASTER RIDGE

15 Southern Arete . . . . **VDiff**
12m. The pleasant right arete of the left-hand buttress of the main cliff is steep, juggy and enjoyable.

16 Easter Ridge **E2 5b**
12m. From the grass ledge,climb a thin crack to the bulge, cros this left, then right, and teeter up steep rock to easy ground.

17 Easter Bunny **E2 5b**
12m. Climb the vertical arete on its left-hand side to the final break, then transfer to the opposite side for the final moves.

EASTER RIDGE

Up and right, a further five minutes walk, is the start of the Main Cliff, a series of isolated towers left of the stream-bed. All of the rest of the routes are most easily reached from the path along the crest of the ridge - The Pennine Way.

Main Cliff - 5mins

Southern Group - 5mins

GALLIC BUTTRESS

his short and relatively insignificant buttress is situated midway etween Easter Ridge and Pillar Ridge. It does have plenty for the reen spot climber though, and all the routes are worth a look.

1 Route 4 . . . . [ ] **S 4a**
2m. The left-hand arete of the face, skirting the bulge right-ards. Step back left onto the final exposed arete.

2 2nd Holiday . . . . [ ] **Mod**
2m. The left-hand chimney is awkward to start. As it widens, it so eases.

3 Route 3 . . . . [ ] **VDiff**
4m. Climb the slabby wall past a useful 'blob'.

4 Tuppence Ha'penny . . . . [ ] **VDiff**
4m. The kinked crack midway between the two chimneys.

5 Route 2 . . . . [ ] **HVD**
4m. The narrow wall trending right.

6 1st Holiday . . . . [ ] **VDiff**
2m. The peapod-shaped chimney is climbed in classical ashion, passing the outside of the jammed boulder.

7 Route 1 . . . . [ ] **VDiff**
2m. The thin crack left of the arete is good.

8 Route Minus One . . . . . [ ] **E1 5c**
0m. The right arete of the buttress on its left-hand side.

PILLAR RIDGE
To the right is the start of the main section of the cliff. This initial area has a few easier offerings, of a decent length and in a great setting.

9 A Chimney . . . . [ ] **Diff**
6m. The left-hand (and wider) crack to the top of the pillar.

10 A Crack . . . . [ ] **S 4a**
8m. The narrower right-hand crack is tricky towards the top.

11 Omicron Buttress . . . . . . [ ] **HVD**
14m. Climb crusty cracks until it is possible to move left to a large flake. Finish up the left-hand side of this.

12 Staircase . . . . [ ] **Mod**
24m. An excellent route for beginners. Scratched holds lead up the slab to a possible stance on the left. The ridge on the right completes the outing. If in doubt, follow the polish!

13 Pillar Ridge . . . . [ ] **HS 4b**
20m. A classic from way back (the beginning of the 20th century). Climb the crack in the front of the buttress to a possible stance, then step out right and climb the thinner crack that leads rapidly to a groove and then the final arete.
FA. Possibly AE Baker c.1900

Easter Ridge - 50m *Pillar Ridge Area - 50m*

-- Descent

Gallic Buttress - 50m *Long Climb Area - 80m*

Staffordshire · Whaley Bridge · Kinder · Bleaklow · Chew · Lancashire · Cheshire · Hobson Moor · Tintwistle Narr · Laddow · Shining Clough

Pillar Ridge - 80m

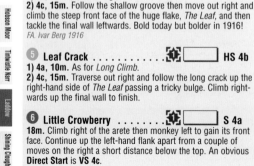

LONG CLIMB AREA

The central part of the main face features a tall clean buttress looking down the valley and tackled centrally by the ever popular *Long Climb*. Other good routes exist here.

① **Priscilla Ridge** . . . . . 🔲🔲 **HVS 5a**
20m. The fine arete is still a lonely lead and was a great effort for its day. Climb the lower arete to a ledge, pull over the overhang and follow the delicate arete (thread) throughout.
FA. Arthur Birtwhistle - of Diagonal fame -1938

② **Priscilla** . . . . 🔲🔲 **HVS 5a**
18m. From the ledge pull over the bulge then climb rightwards up the wall via a scoop to a rest (one-time stance) on the right. Traverse back left to a delicate finish which has one long reach to gain the final crack.
FA. Morley Wood, Fred Pigott (alts) 1921

③ **Long Climb** . . . . 🔲🔲 **S 4a**
A classic which has crept up in grades owing to polish!
1) **4a, 10m.** Climb the slabby buttress on polished holds (a gripper in the wet) trending left then right to a good stance.
2) **15m.** Climb the slippery scoop then follow a series of corners to a grand finale up the crack on the right.
FA. One or more of the Puttrell/Baker mob, early 1900s

④ **Leaf Buttress** . . . . 🔲🔲 **VS 4c**
1) **4a, 10m.** As for *Long Climb*.
2) **4c, 15m.** Follow the shallow groove then move out right and climb the steep front face of the huge flake, *The Leaf*, and then tackle the final wall leftwards. Bold today but bolder in 1916!
FA. Ivar Berg 1916

⑤ **Leaf Crack** . . . . 🔲🔲 **HS 4b**
1) **4a, 10m.** As for *Long Climb*.
2) **4c, 15m.** Traverse out right and follow the long crack up the right-hand side of *The Leaf* passing a tricky bulge. Climb right-wards up the final wall to finish.

⑥ **Little Crowberry** . . . . 🔲🔲 **S 4a**
18m. Climb right of the arete then monkey left to gain its front face. Continue up the left-hand flank apart from a couple of moves on the right a short distance below the top. An obvious **Direct Start** is **VS 4c**.

⑦ **Long Chimney Ridge** . . . . . 🔲🔲 **VDiff**
18m. Climb the right-trending groove right of the crest of the arete until the ledge of *The Pulpit* on the right can be reached. Climb into the twin cracks above with difficulty and finish easily passing a wobbling block with care.

Up and right is a clean(ish) wall above grass fields. There is a selection of short routes here, though the arduous approach and increasingly grassy nature of them means they are only just worth the effort of getting at. A little traffic might return them to their former glory; they were popular 70 years ago!

⑧ **The Blacksmith Climb** . . . . 🔲🔲 **VS 4c**
10m. The wall left of *Straight Crack* is pleasant, if bold. An eminently sensible side-runner can be placed on route.
FA. Herbert Hartley 1928

⑨ **Straight Crack** . . . . 🔲 **S 4a**
10m. The obviously-named crack doesn't have many holds.

⑩ **Little Innominate** . . . . 🔲 **VS 4c**
10m. The narrow wall requires a side-runner - and blinkers.
FA. Herbert Hartley 1928

⑪ **Straight Chimney** . . . . 🔲 **Mod**
10m. The deep groove is better than the grass below!

⑫ **Garden Wall** . . . . 🔲 **S 4a**
10m. The right-hand groove in the wall has an indifferent approach although it improves a little above.

⑬ **Left Twin Chimney** . . . . 🔲 **Diff**
16m. The chimney has some grass, a collection of jammed blocks and a rather grubby finish - but at least it's a good line!

⑭ **Right Twin Chimney** . . . . 🔲 **HVD**
16m. The gradually widening and rather scruffy chimney is included out of historical interest - check the datebelow!
FA. EA Baker 1902

TOWER FACE and CAVE CRACK
The right-hand edge of the cliff is home to the cleanest rock and the best routes here. Many folks head straight to the cave and ignore the green goings-on further to the left!

⑮ Tower Face ..... 🔲 VS 5a
18m. A great pitch; the crag is worth the visit just to do this route. From the cave, pull onto the face (massive thread and just about worth 5a) then climb the centre of the face trending slightly left until it is possible to step back right to the well-positioned final crack. *Photo page 169.*
FA. Harry Kelly 1916

⑯ Modern Times .... 🔲 E3 5c
18m. Takes the rest of the decent rock on Tower Face. Climb the steep right-hand side of the lower wall to mid-height then move left to climb through the overhangs and finish up the left-hand arete in a fine position.
FA. Steve Bancroft 1986

⑰ Tower Arete ..... 🔲 HVS 5a
18m. The exciting and exposed right-hand side of the arete is followed in its entirety.
FA. Albert Hargreaves 1927

⑱ North Climb .... 🔲 VDiff
16m. Take the big groove over easy ground to a possible stance. Then, from a thread in the chimney, shuffle left to reach and finish up a chimney. Traversing further left is the wild **Pongo Finish**. This is perhaps better, a little harder and is certainly more exposed.

⑲ North Wall .... 🔲 HS 4b
16m. Climb the right edge of *North Climb's* groove to the capping overhang and pass this via the steep crack. A stance is available on the left below the roof if the leader needs company on the crux.

⑳ Cave Arete .... 🔲 VS 4b
16m. Follow the scoop delicately out right to the arete and climb to a ledge (possible belay). Take the hugely-exposed top pitch of *Cave Crack* to finish, or creep out right at the roof.

On the far right-hand end of the cliff is a shallow cave much used as a bivouac by the ancients. There are several venerable outings based around this uncomfortable grotto.

㉑ Cave Arete Indirect . 🔲 E1 5b
18m. Climb the left wall of the cave to a good spike then swing left to round the arete and climb to ledges (5a). Continue up the corner to the roof and step left and pull over it rapidly (5c for wimps) to access the easier head wall by a wild move or two.
FA. Ivar Berg 1916. The first E1 ever climbed!

㉒ Cave Crack ..... 🔲 HVS 5a
18m. Climb into the top of the cave and pull out onto the face (the spinning chock can be jammed with judicious use of a sling) and climb to a ledge (possible belay). Climb the corner to the huge roof then skip left and pull over its edge to easier ground - very exposed!
FA. Ivar Berg 1916

㉓ Cave Crack Indirect .... 🔲 S 4a
18m. Start on the right and slant left to join *Cave Crack* above its crux. Continue to the ledge (stance and belay), then follow the groove to the roof and traverse right to escape.

Staffordshire · Whaley Bridge · Kinder · Bleaklow · Chew · Lancashire · Cheshire · Hobson Moor · Tintwistle Knarr · Laddow · Shining Clough

A fine but sadly neglected quarry in an impressive setting with a superb outward view towards the wastes of Bleaklow and the proud buttress of Shining Clough lurking in the shadows. The crag has an excellent set of crack climbs and although the walk up tends to put people off, the effort made to get here is usually repaid in full. There are a dozen routes in the shorter left-hand bay but these are not described here. The Central Bay is better, though turf tufts manage to sprout from the most inconvenient of places; please remove any grass (it is not an endangered species!) you pass in an attempt to keep these great routes clean enough to be climbed. *The Arete* (E2 5c) is especially fine and is worth the walk up alone, as are the classic layback flakes of *The Cornflake* (VS 4c) and the superb finger-wrecking crack of *Kershaw's Krackers* (HVS 5c). The deep groove of *The Old Triangle* (HVS 5a) is also a classic line, well worth doing, though it does take drainage, and next to it the excellent blunt arete of *Sinn Fein* (E3 5c) is only for the really bold.

APPROACH   Also see map on page 158

There is parking for half a dozen cars on the northern side of the A628 road by the edge of the conifer forest and above the reservoir. A good track (the old quarry road) starts at the gate and weaves up the hill to enter the forest and then continues rightwards to end in front of the Central Bay of the quarry; a steady 20 minutes from the car. Leave nothing of value in the vehicle.

CONDITIONS

The quarry is south-facing and gets all the sun that is going, though it takes quite a bit of drainage from the moor behind. Like nearby Laddow, the grass is gradually taking over the place, choking the cracks, covering the ledges and holding moisture so that over time the whole place becomes slower and slower to dry. With a bit more traffic, the best of the climbs here would be rivals to many of Millstone's most popular outings - helping to spread the load a little.

> **OTHER GUIDEBOOK -** A more complete list of routes at Tintwistle Knarr is published in the 1991 BMC *Kinder* guidebook.

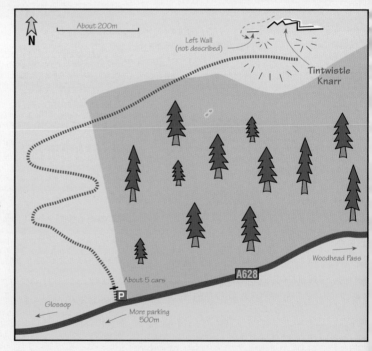

← - - - Descent (down gully)

Staffordshire
Whaley Bridge
Kinder
Bleaklow
Chew
Lancashire
Cheshire

Hobson Moor
Tintwistle Knarr
Ladow
Shining Clough

TINTWISTLE KNARR

The central section of the quarry is dominated by the prominent fewture of *The Arete*, the best route here. Much of the rock is excellent, though the ever-encroaching vegetation is slowly claiming it back.

❶ Levl **E1 5b**
18m. Climb the slab to its left arete then step back into the centre and finish with increasing apprehension.
FA. Mike Simpkins 1962

❷ Leprechaun . . . . **VS 4c**
18m. The groove reached from the left is quite worthwhile but has a crusty finish. Sadly it is rather overgrown at present.
FA. John Gosling 1962

❸ Scimitar . . . . **HVS 5b**
20m. Cut up to the obviously-named thin curving crack and follow it into and up the groove at its end.
FA. Mike Simpkins 1962

❹ Poteen . . . . **HVS 5b**
20m. Stagger up the long right-facing corner/groove. It is worthwhile and proves to be hard work at the overhang.
FA. Mike Simpkins 1962

❺ Sinn Fein **E3 5c**
22m. Serious and scary. Climb the rib on the left and then the crack on the right to a flaky overlap. Pull over this and step left to a spike where a gripping mantel gains the final slab.
FA. Mike Simpkins 1962

❻ The Old Triangle . . . . . . **HVS 5a**
24m. Sustained climbing up the long deep groove leads to a big triangular roof. The most popular exit is to teeter right (**4c**) although going left is possible; harder and more strenuous (**5a**).
FA. Joe Brown 1951

❼ Nil Carborundum Illigitimum **E3 5c**
22m. The smooth face has good moves but is serious and devious. There may be one peg runner in place. It really needs a direct finish.
FA. Loz Francomb 1979

❽ The Arete **E2 5c**
22m. The best route here and worth calling in for. Delicate, sustained and elegant moves throughout with enough gear to allow the experience to be enjoyed to the full. *Photo page 175.*
FA. Pete Crew (2 pegs) 1962. FFA. John Allen 1973

❾ O'Grady's Incurable Itch **E5 6c**
22m. Climb *Little Spillikin* to the traverse then, with gear on the right (wires and RPs), climb the centre of the wall up and left via a hard sequence to better holds. Grade unconfirmed.
FA. Andy Stewart 1999

❿ The Little Spillikin **E3 6a**
22m. Climb thin cracks right of the grassy groove then move out right and climb the shallow groove to a rather unstable exit.
FA. John Gosling 1959. FFA. John Regan 1977

⓫ Kershaw's Krackers . . . . . **HVS 5c**
22m. The finger-knackering cracks are climbed in three stages with the initial section being the crux. One of the purest finger-cracks around and excellent (but excruciating) sport.
FA. Barry Kershaw 1958

Lots of sun | 20 min | Change in viewing angle

12 Stiff Little Fingers E1 5b
22m. The elegant arete is escapable but worth sticking with.
Runners can be placed to the left without too much difficulty.
FA. Malc Baxter 1989

13 Cornflake .... VS 4c
22m. The long left-hand flake gives great laybacking to its top
from where easy (vegetated!) ground leads to the cliff top.
Photo page 3.
FA. Mike Simpkins 1962

14 Soapflake .... VS 4c
22m. The right-hand flake is also well worth doing if you enjoy
the style of climbing. Again the finish is a bit of a spoiler.
FA. Mike Simpkins 1962

15 Knobblekerry Corner .... VS 4c
22m. The long groove in the angle of the bay is strenuous and
sustained, even if you use the iron bar to start. Climb the wide
left-hand crack, then the right-hand one. At its top, swing left
with difficulty and escape up overgrown ledges.
FA. Joe Brown 1951

16 Nosey Parker E4 6a
22m. Climb the tough crack in the side-wall (well-protected but
exhausting) then swing left to a rest in the main groove. Pull up
and right to climb the desperately-thin crack that splits the final
short but impending wall.
FA. Al Parker (3 points) 1973. FFA. Steve Bancroft 1980

17 Black Michael .... VS 4c
22m. The chimney-crack gives a good struggle up to ledges on
the arete. Climb left then right to vegetated ledges then escape
left up a crumbly crack.
FA. Graham West 1958

18 Good Things Come to Those Who Wait E3 5c
26m. Follows the edge of the steep tower left of *Guns and
Drums*. Start to the left of a green wall and climb up and right
on pockets, and then overhanging wall above to a ledge and
flake. Go up the left-hand side of the tower (peg) with a spectacular finish rocking right onto the airy arete.
FA. Andy Stewart 1999

19 Guns and Drums E4 6a
26m. Climb a shallow groove until flakes on the right can be
reached; follow these to the break. Climb the blank groove (old
peg and Friend in a slot) and the bulge to a crusty finish. *Wall
and Groove* makes a better start to the route.
FA. Jim Moran 1983

20 Wall and Groove .... HVS 5a
26m. An early attempt on this part of the face, and a good line
despite suffering from grass-itis. Climb the steep flake-crack to
the break then traverse left to below the base of the shallow
open groove. A short pumpy wall gives access to more pleasant
climbing in the groove above.
FA. Mike Simpkins 1962

21 The Peace Process . E5 6b
26m. Layback up the obvious fin right of *Guns and Drums* to
the overhang. Slap up for a ledge and peg runner. Continue with
fingery and reachy moves, past another peg as far as the last
hold on the blank wall. Escape right to the arete and scramble
up steep grass to finish.
FA. Andy Stewart 1999

22 Fenian Wall E4 6a
12m. The steep and strenuous crack leads via pushy climbing
to the break. The wall above is also hard but turns rapidly to
easy ground and yet more grass scrambling.
FA. Mike Simpkins 1960s. FFA. Jim Moran 1983

23 Republic Groove .... HVS 5a
12m. Climb the acutely overhanging groove that bounds the
wall on the right until forced out right. Take the short corner
then graze-away to the cliff top.
FA. Mike Simpkins 1962

Staffordshire | Whaley Bridge | Kinder | Bleaklow | Chew | Lancashire | Cheshire | Hobson Moor | Tintwistle Knarr | Laddow | Shining Clough

Staffordshire · Whaley Bridge · Kinder · Bleaklow · Chew · Lancashire · Cheshire

Once a bit of a dump (and also used as a dumping ground) the quarry has been cleaned up, landscaped and now provides a valuable resource for local climbers, thanks to the far-sighted attitude of Tameside Council. If you are passing by on the way home from the Lakes or Wales, call in, you might be pleasantly surprised. In the mid-nineties the crag was given a going over, loose rock was removed and a number of fixed pegs were added to make several of the routes into viable leads -though these have since been removed. All the climbs can be adequately protected with a good rack of Friends and a selection of wires. Fixed belays have been placed above many of the routes, for the abseil brigade. For climbers this is designer belaying - just a little continental!

APPROACH

The crag is only 30 seconds from roadside parking, a good place for a quick fix, either in the shape of half a dozen routes or a work-out on the pumpy traverse V4 along the base of the Back Wall. The minor road to the cliff is accessed by turning east off the A6018 at the top of the Mottram cutting (a tight right turn when coming from the Glossop direction) almost opposite the Waggon and Horses pub. Take the left-hand branch where it forks and the quarry soon appears on the left. There is parking for 10 or so cars on the right.

Chris Craggs on *Parker's Eliminate* (HVS 5a) at Hobson Moor. *Page 180*

CONDITIONS

The quarry faces south-west, is well-sheltered and takes little drainage. It dries rapidly and the easy accessibility means the place is ideal for an evening session and is used as such by the locals. Visitors from further afield are less common. The routes on the steep Back Wall are all steep, hard and pumpy, though there is a good range of easier fare to the right including a couple of excellent finger-cracks.

OTHER GUIDEBOOKS - A more complete list of routes at Hobson Moor is published in the 1991 BMC *Kinder* guidebook.

BOULDERING
Hobson Moor is a popular bouldering venue. Full coverage is given in the 1998 Peak Bouldering ROCKFAX.

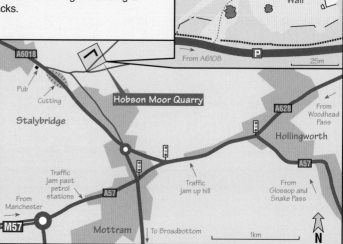

Hobson Moor · Tintwistle Knarr · Laddow · Shining Clough

Staffordshire

Whaley Bridge

Kinder

Bleaklow

Chew

Lancashire

Cheshire

BACK WALL

An excellent wall but not very popular. It might be because the routes are hard and there is little of quality below E4. The *Traverse* sees lots of attention but once you put your head above this chalk-line, you are on your own!

① Back Wall Traverse . . . 🎯🪝 [   ] **V4 (6a)**
The most popular route in the quarry! Traverse the Back Wall, starting on the left, all the way to ledges on the right. Well-pumpy and mighty long. Even better, it can be used as the start to girdling the whole quarry - how much time have you got?

② Eastern Touch . . . . 🪝🎯🪝 [   ] **E4 6a**
14m. Climb past a hanging crack to a niche then head left via a hidden crack to a ledge. Climb up past two good pockets and finish through a shallow niche (2 peg runners).
FA. Sid Siddiqui 1992

③ Apres Midi . . . . 🪝 [   ] **E2 5c**
14m. Use a pocket to reach the horizontal, step right then climb leftwards to a groove and finish up this, or its left arete.
FA. Malc Baxter (solo) 1986

④ Wanna Buy a Bolt Kit? . . . 🪝 [   ] **E4 6b**
16m. The old peg crack is followed until it fades, step left and power up the wall, following the pale streak, to finish through the overlaps.
FA. Nick Plishko 1982

⑤ Heatwave . . . . 🪝 [   ] **E2 5c**
18m. Climb into the open groove and follow it (peg) past the overhang to an awkward exit. Pumpy and with a wild finish.
FA. Al Evans 1989

⑥ Hanging Slab . . . . . . 🪝🪝 [   ] **E1 5b**
18m. Climb the diagonal flake to its end, finish direct. Good gear throughout and high in the grade.
FA. Malc Baxter (1 peg) 1959. FFA. Loz Francomb 1979

⑦ Crock's Climb . . . . 🪝 [   ] **E1 5b**
18m. Climb steeply to ledges which are followed diagonally rightwards to finish up the groove.
FA. Malc Baxter 1975

⑧ The Heat is On . . . . 🪝 [   ] **E4 6b**
18m. Follow *Fingertip Control* but head up and left to a ledge on *Crock's Climb*. Follow the twin cracks above and finish over a small overhang (peg).
FA. Sid Siddiqui 1992

⑨ Fingertip Control . . 🪝🪝🪝 [   ] **E5 6b**
18m. Climb the steep wall from left to right by sustained and fingery moves. 3 peg runners protect one of the better routes in the quarry.
FA. Sid Siddiqui 1992

⑩ Gable End . . . . . . 🪝🪝🪝 [   ] **E4 6a**
18m. The left-hand of the parallel cracks gives fierce finger-jamming to an easy final groove.
FA. (as Rainstorm) Malc Baxter 1961 FFA. Gabe Regan 1976

⑪ Hobson's Choice . . . 🪝🪝🪝 [   ] **E5 6b**
18m. The right-hand parallel crack is more technical and more sustained than its near neighbour.
FA. Greg Rimmer 1989

⑫ Great Expectations . . . . 🪝🪝 [   ] **E3 5c**
18m. Climb the leaning groove to the break. Continue up and right then scale the crucial final wall (two peg runners). Good honest hard work. The finish is often sandy – bloody abseilers!
FA. Chris Hardy 1988

⑬ Monsoon . . . . [   ] **HVS 5b**
18m. Climb the flake to the dubious-looking block, and finish direct up crusty rock.
FA. Al Evans 1989

Hobson Moor

Tintwistle Narr

Laddow

Shining Clough

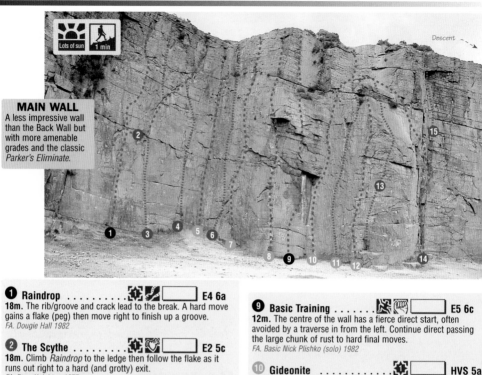

MAIN WALL
A less impressive wall than the Back Wall but with more amenable grades and the classic *Parker's Eliminate*.

❶ **Raindrop** . . . . 🕯🏃⬛ **E4 6a**
18m. The rib/groove and crack lead to the break. A hard move gains a flake (peg) then move right to finish up a groove.
FA. Dougie Hall 1982

❷ **The Scythe** . . . . 🕯🤚⬛ **E2 5c**
18m. Climb *Raindrop* to the ledge then follow the flake as it runs out right to a hard (and grotty) exit.
FA. Dave Knighton 1977

❸ **Sunshine Super Glue** . . 🕯🏃⬛ **E3 6a**
18m. Climb the middle of the wall past a glued side-pull to a peg runner. Join the right-trending flake on *The Scythe* and pull over an overlap to reach a second peg and a steep finish.
FA. Sid Siddiqui 1992

❹ **Bring me Sunshine** . . . . . 🕯⬛ **E2 5b**
16m. Climb the wall left of the big groove up flakes to ledges. Step right and climb the exposed arete. Low in the grade.
FA. Harry Venables 1988

❺ **Epitaph Corner** . . . . 🕯⬛ **VS 4b**
14m. The main groove gives a reasonable, well-protected pitch.
FA. Paul Nunn 1960

❻ **Sunshine Superman** . . . 🕯🤚⬛ **E2 5b**
14m. The wall right of the corner is climbed via a boulder problem up a flake. The upper section is bold and creaky. A runner can be placed in *Parker's*, lowering the grade a notch.
FA. Phil Booth late 1970s

❼ **Parker's Eliminate** . . . . 🕯🎆⬛ **HVS 5a**
14m. The crack in the centre of the wall cuts through an overlap and is a well-protected gem. The best in the quarry and the equal of Millstone's HVS classics, well almost! *Photo page 178.*
FA. Al Parker 1957. FFA. Al Parker 1960

❽ **Gideon** . . . . 🕯⬛ **HVS 5a**
14m. Balance up the steep arete to reach a short (and narrow) jamming-crack. Finish up the left-hand side of the final arete.
FA. Paul Nunn 1960

❾ **Basic Training** . . . . . . 🏃🎆⬛ **E5 6c**
12m. The centre of the wall has a fierce direct start, often avoided by a traverse in from the left. Continue direct passing the large chunk of rust to hard final moves.
FA. Basic Nick Plishko (solo) 1982

❿ **Gideonite** . . . . 🕯⬛ **HVS 5a**
14m. The large groove leads by bridging and finger-jamming to a ledge. Finish up the easy corner behind.
FA. Malc Baxter (2 pegs) 1960 FFA. Jim Campbell 1976

⓫ **Crew's Route** . . . . 🕯⬛ **VS 4c**
12m. The crack gives a good and well-protected pitch. The final overlap can be climbed direct, or bypassed slightly more easily.
FA. Pete Crew 1960

⓬ **Peak Arete** . . . . 🏃⬛ **HVS 5a**
12m. The arete is followed throughout and is steep and quite precarious. A semi-crucial finger-jam is easily blocked by a (bomber) runner, or should you just solo it at E1?
FA. Tom Ellison 1958

⓭ **Steve's Dilemma** . . . . . . 🎆⬛ **E2 6a**
12m. Start just right of the arete and make fingery pocket moves up and rightwards to pass the bulge, where reachy and blind moves reach easier ground. Can be gritty. Finishing up the arete on the right adds a touch of excitement.
FA. Steve Bancroft 1980

⓮ **Evening Ridge** . . . . ⬛ **VDiff**
14m. Climb the groove to a ledge and loose flakes to access the bottom corner of a hanging slab. Climb this diagonally leftwards to a ledge and stance. Finish up the corner.
FA. Paul Nunn 1957

⓯ **Midnight Variation** . . . . ⬛ **S 4a**
12m. From the ledge on the previous route, step right and climb the wall or the groove to its right.
FA. Paul Nunn 1957

DRAGON'S WALL

The right-hand side of the quarry has some quality routes before the walls diminish to bouldering stature. There are old bolt and stake belays on the ledges above all of these climbs. Once fitted with peg runners, these have been been removed though the climbs remain viable leads with Friends in the various horizontal breaks.

① Dragon's Route E3 5c
4m. The thin left-hand crack leads to a break, step left and ower up the crusty flake. Strenuous but not too technical.
. *Loz Francomb 1979*

② Scale the Dragon .. E4 6a
4m. Start right of *Dragon's Route* and crimp to the break then limb powerfully up the shallow groove in the centre of the wall, assing good gear in the break with difficulty. The best route on e wall, but beware the final moves.
. *Jim Burton (with peg runners) 1992*

③ Drizzle E2 6a
4m. The groove on the right leads to a break from where technical and strenuous moves allow the wall to be climbed rapidly. riginally given a pretty hard HVS.
. Loz Francomb 1979

④ Drought E4 6a
4m. The thin crack left of the groove corner leads to a difficult ull to the horizontal. The move over the overlap is not as blank s it looks, but is still strenuous and the upper wall is easier.
A. FA. *Jim Burton (with peg runners) 1992*

⑤ Foghorn Groove ...... VS 4c
4m. The leaning corner is pleasant if somewhat creaky and is ood practice for bigger, looser things! Small wires useful.
A. *Graham West 1959*

⑥ Wind Instrument E1 5b
14m. The nnarrowing wall just right on disposable holds.

⑦ The Harp .... HS 4b
14m. Balance up the wall trending right to a dubious overlap. Pull over this and finish easily. Not too hard or well-travelled, but have your belayer stand aside – just in case!
FA. *Al Parker 1957 FFA. Al Parker 1960*

⑧ Pocket Wall .... VDiff
10m. The narrow face has the expected pocket and makes a good warm-up solo, or a well-protected lead for the timid.
FA. *Malc Baxter 1956*

⑨ Tighe's Arete E1 5a
12m. The arete is delicate and quite low in the grade. A semi-crucial Friend in the slot gets in the way a little, though another out right doesn't!
FA. *Trevor Tighe 1968*

⑩ Ledge Way .... HS 4b
12m. Climb the arete but trend right to the ledge of the amphitheatre. A slim groove on the left-hand side of the wall provides an exit.
FA. *Paul Nunn 1957*

⑪ Grain of Sand .... VS 5a
12m. The bulging centre of the wall to the ledge then the face just right of the upper groove.
FA. *Malc Baxter 1959*

⑫ Amphitheatre Climb .... VDiff
10m. A short steep crack leads to the ledge and a final groove.
FA. *Al Parker 1957*

⑬ Heather Corner .... VDiff
10m. The final groove of any consequence and the arete directly above it are lacking in heather nowadays.
FA. *Malc Baxter 1956*

181

CHEW VALLEY

Mike Appleton and Sherri Davy climbing *Hanging Crack* (E2 5b) Dovestones Edge. *Page 200*

Wimberry is the best of the fine set of cliffs in the Chew Valley, the Cinderella of Peak grit, an unsung gem of a crag with a fantastic collection of routes on an impressive series of buttresses in a dramatic setting, and with superb outward views. The down side (there just had to be one) is that the crag faces north and the approach is a bit of a flog. Here is a superb set of arduous cracks and some particularly thrilling face climbs. The cracks in particular have always had a reputation for being sternly graded - we have upgraded the most glaring of these but be prepared for a tussle. The face climbs include some of the best and hardest in the Peak, though they see a lot less attention then their smaller brethren on Burbage South. The place can be seriously midge-ridden on calm days in July and August. It has been said that if the cliff faced south it would be regarded as the best gritstone cliff in the country - and quite possibly this is true.

APPROACH Also see map on page 182

There is extensive parking (Pay and Display - weekends only) below the huge dam that holds back the Dovestone Reservoir. A metalled road leads past the sailing club boathouse then at the bridge across Chew Brook take the path rightwards into the the trees. This passes through the bouldering area and then starts a steady flog up the side of the stream to reach the left-hand side of the cliff in about 30 minutes from the car. The final ascent is a good test of stamina.

CONDITIONS

North facing, the cliff is not a winter venue, as it stays green for much of the rainy season. Despite this it does dry quickly, is well-sheltered from southwesterly winds and forms a great venue on hot summer days, see the reference to the 'midge alert' above when conditions are especially calm. Grades here are given for perfect conditions and although the superb roughness of the rock can compensate for the green conditions that are prevalent for much of the year, the grades might feel a little stiff at other times.

BOULDERING - There is some superb bouldering at Wimberry on the large boulders passed on the approach walk. Full coverage is given in the 1998 Peak Bouldering ROCKFAX.

OTHER GUIDEBOOK - A more complete list of routes at Wimberry is published in the 1988 BMC *Moorland Gritstone* guidebook.

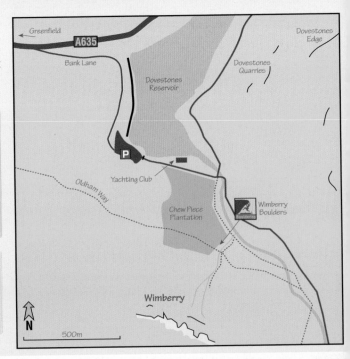

Route I (HS 4b) Wimberry. *Page 189*

FREDDIE'S FINALE AREA

The left-hand side of the cliff has a fine selection of jamming cracks and is a good place to get a feel for the crag and the style of climbing. *Freddie's Finale* is one of the classic hand-and-fist-cracks of the Peak.

❶ Thermometer Crack . . . 🗝️🔏⬜ **VS 4b**
8m. On the far left is a leaning crack which gives good jamming and laybacking. A good one for steamy summer days.

❷ Crack and Slab . . . . 🗝️⬜ **S 4a**
8m. From the foot of the chimney, slant left up the slab to enter and climb the groove at its apex.

❸ Short Crack . . . . 🗝️⬜ **VS 5a**
8m. The bulging chimney and narrower crack above gives technical but well-protected bridging.

❹ Pinball Wizard . . . 🗝️🐾🗝️⬜ **E1 5b**
8m. Follow the finger-crack then the middle of the wall above (slightly bold) on small finger holds, trending leftwards.
FA. Steve Bancroft 1972

❺ Blind Faith . . . . 🗝️⬜ **E2 6a**
8m. The arete has one hard move and then eases with height.
FA. Chris Hardy 1984

❻ Eight Metre Corner . . . . . 🗝️⬜ **Diff**
25ft. The deepening angular groove is pleasant enough.

❼ Poltergeist . . . . ⬜ **VS 4b**
10m. The arete left of the chimney requires tricky balance moves to reach the hanging crack above (and its chockstones).

❽ Blocked Chimney . . . . 🗝️⬜ **VDiff**
10m. Climb the chimney to its blockage and an escape left.

❾ Arete du Coeur . . . . 🗝️⬜ **E4 5c**
10m. A bold arete is climbed direct. Passing the overhang is difficult and requires a heart-in-mouth approach.
FA. J.Fletcher 1981

❿ Ornithologist's Corner . 🗝️🔏⬜ **VS 5a**
12m. Great jamming up the steep crack above the approach path with a strenuous finale rightwards around the overhang.

⓫ Surprise Arete . . . . 🗝️🔩🗝️⬜ **HVS 4**
12m. The delicate arete on its right-hand side to the break then move left to finish up the crack. Harder for the short.
FA. Brian Toase 1970

⓬ One-way Ticket . . . . . 🗝️🗝️⬜ **E2 5b**
12m. The direct finish up the arete is bold.

⓭ Surprise . . . . 🗝️⬜ **VS 4c**
14m. Climb the flaky crack leftwards then follow the groove to tricky moves past the neb.

⓮ The Yellow-bellied Gonk 🗝️🗝️⬜ **E4 6a**
10m. Climb the bulging arete to a break then pull onto the upper slab with difficulty.
FA. Kevin Thaw 1982

⓯ Overhanging Chimney . . . 🗝️⬜ **VDiff**
12m. The leaning and narrowing chimney is steep and awkward as far as the thread, then easier above.
FA. Anton Stoop 1910

⓰ Freddie's Finale . . . 🗝️🔏🗝️⬜ **E1 5b**
14m. Fist-jamming at its best (not the contradiction in terms non-gritstoner's might imagine). Large gear is a must. Climb through the intimidating overhang to an uncomfortable niche then fist-jam and flail until the crack narrows and easier ground gives you a chance to survey the damage - luuverly! A HVS from the days when men were men.
FA. Joe Brown (& Fred Ashton) 1948

⓱ Double Take . . . . 🗝️🗝️🗝️⬜ **E6 6b**
18m. The first of the 'E-big-numbers'. Climb through the first overhang of *Freddie's* then swing right along the break to gain the arete. Slap up this passing the overhang with difficulty. Finish more easily up the superb ramp-in-space.
FA. Dougie Hall 1987

Not much sun | 30 min | Green

Descent

The Trident Area

19
22
23
20
16 18 21 24

HANGING GROOVE
The bulging buttress to the right of Freddie's Finale has several superb hard routes with steep starts and delicate finishes. Further right are two more of Wimberry's fine wide crack climbs - *Hanging Groove* and *Coffin Crack*.

Hanging Groove Area
The Trident Area
Route 1 Area
Freddies Finale Area
Herringbone Slab Area
Northern Ballet Area
Approach
Approach

18 Wimberry Overhang E5 6c
18m. Leap through the centre of the overhangs (2 ancient peg runners may be in place) to gain the hanging slab and an easier finish up the well-positioned ramp above.
FA. 1969/86

19 Space Shuffle E4 6a
22m. From the second thread in *Hanging Groove* tiptoe out left above the overhangs all the way to the distant arete and a finish up a short hanging ramp on the very edge of the world.
FA. Mike Chapman 1983

20 Space Oddity E5 6c
16m. Start left of the groove and traverse left on the lip of the overhang to below a thin crack. Climb this (fingery - crux) to the second horizontal then follow the blunt arete above initially on its right and finally on its left. The slab above is easier.
FA. Dougie Hall 1987

21 Hanging Groove .... VS 4c
16m. Climb steeply and strenuously into the well-named feature, pass the chockstones awkwardly and finish more easily up the left-trending ramp.

22 Hanging Groove Variations .... VS 4c
16m. As for the normal route to the ledge then gain the upper groove on the right using a dynamic approach. Follow this to the top in a fine position.
There are other variations to the left which have been absorbed into the hard routes.

23 The Bad Attitude Brothers E3 6a
16m. Climb *Coffin Crack* to above the recess then traverse the thin break leftwards to the arete. Climb up and round this using an elusive pebble and finish up the scoop above.
FA. Steven Delderfield 1990s

24 Coffin Crack .... VS 4c
16m. Climb the wide fissure past the coffin-shaped recess. Holds on the right allow some rather frantic laybacking to reach the easier upper crack.

Staffordshire | Whaley Bridge | Kinder | Bleaklow | Chew | Lancashire | Cheshire | Den Lane | Running Hill Pits | Alderman | Upperwood Q | Standing Stones | Ravenstones | Dovestones | Rob's Rocks | Wimberry

Staffordshire | Whaley Bridge | Kinder | Bleaklow | Chew | Lancashire | Cheshire | Den Lane | Running Hill Pits | Alderman | Upperwood Q | Standing Stones | Ravenstones | Dovestones | Rob's Rocks | Wimberry

Not much sun | 30 min | Green

Descent

Coffin Crack

THE TRIDENT AREA

The smooth wall capped by impressive overhangs is home to some superb hard routes including the mega-classic *Wristcutter's Lullaby*. As ever the cracks between the blank sections providing easier challenges with the *The Trident* and *Bertie's Bugbear* being the pick. Further right is the fine crack of *Blasphemy* and its excellent left-hand finish - *Piety*.

❶ Berlin Wall **E6 6b**
24m. From the recess on *Coffin Crack* teeter right onto the wall to a pocket. Traverse right again and continue direct in an ever-more committing position to a loose flake in the roof. Traverse right to escape up *The Trident*. Protection includes a (long) hand-placed peg early on and some ancient bolts before things ease.
FA. Nick Plishko 1987

❷ Neptune's Tool **E6 6c**
20m. From the foot of *The Trident* gain and follow the curving flake leftwards out into the middle of the wall (good gear - very hard to place) and climb this trending left again to the edge of the huge overhang and an easier finish. Only 6b for the tall.
FA. Nick Plishko 1986

❸ Wristcutter's Lullaby **E6 6c**
22m. Magnificent. Follow *Neptune's Tool* to the centre of the wall then climb straight up the face on pebbles to the big roofs. Climb through these (a couple of very old bolts can be clipped) finishing leftwards once above the lip. Only 6b for the tall.
FA. (as Desecration)1964. FFA. Nick Plishko 1987

❹ Desecration **E3 6a**
28m. An exciting crossing of the face. From the block on *The Trident* climb down and left to a small ledge then follow poor holds delicately all the way to a finish up *Coffin Crack*. Bold and technical, not for faint-hearted seconds. High in the grade.
FA. Jonny Woodward 1982

❺ The Trident **E1 5b**
20m. Western Grit's answer to *The Peapod*; a classic struggle but a classic nonetheless. The narrow central section is an uphill battle especially for those who are large in the chest, though the final section gives glorious jamming, what relief!
FA. Joe Brown 1948

❻ MaDMAn **E8 6b**
20m. The bald blunt and imposing arete to the right of *The Trident* is hard, harrowing and unprotected as far as a shelf. If you get that far, move left to finish up *The Trident*. Another desperate outing that is probably unrepeated.
FA. Dave Pegg 1990s

❼ Cheltenham Gold Cup **E4 6c**
20m. The left wall of *Bertie's Bugbear* is fiercely technical, especially getting into the the shallow groove in the centre of the face. From the top of the groove trend left up easier ground
FA. Nick Plishko 1985

❽ Bertie's Bugbear . . . . **S 4a**
18m. The best lower-grade route on the cliff climbs the huge central groove. The crucial bulge is climbed using a highly suspicious looking foothold on the left wall. Excellent stuff.
Photo page 42.
FA. Anton Stoop 1910

❾ Sickbay Shuffle **E3 5b**
22m. A terrifying crab-wise expedition across the right-hand wall of the big groove. Protection in the gully becomes increasingly useless, then sprint up the final arete. Gibber gibber.
FA. Nick Plishko 1987

❿ Thorn in the Side-wall **E4 6a**
18m. A bit of an eliminate up the right-hand wall of *Bertie's* to the traverse of *Sickbay Shuffle*, and finishing direct. Somehow side-runners will need to be placed en-route.
FA. Nick Plishko 1987

⓫ Piety **E2 5c**
20m. Bold, delicate and superb. Climb the crack of *Blasphemy* until a delicate scoop leads out left to the arete. Step round the exposed corner, move up and immediately step back right onto an easier slab. Watch that rope drag!
FA. Ian Carr 1982

⓬ Blasphemy **E2 5c**
14m. A superb outing with quality finger-jamming. Gain the sinuous crack from the large block in the corner. The crux occurs where the crack ends, transferring onto the final slab by a tricky mantelshelf - on the left or right - which is best?
FA. Graham West late 1950s. FFA. John Allen 1973

ROUTE 1 AREA

More superlatives are needed as the classics keep on coming. *Blue Light's Crack* may not appeal to all but it is a striking line. *Appointment with Fear* may appeal to all but only the very best need apply. Further right are a couple of easier classics; *Route I* and *Route II* should not be missed.

❸ Blue Light's Crack .... 🔲🔲🔲 **E1 5b**
6m. The wide corner is a titanic struggle for most, wedging-a-ay up is the only option, though macho-men with strong arms nd little imagination can layback although they may well end o regretting it as the top approaches. Said by some to make *reddie's Finale* look like a soft touch and another ancient HVS!
reen Streak, HVS 5a - For those who haven't had enough ake a hand-traverse right to reach the hanging crack.
A. *Don Whillans 1948. FA. (Green Streak) Steve Bancroft 1973*

❹ The Possessed . 🔲🔲🔲🔲 **E7 6b**
0m. A desperate direct on *Sacrilege*. Start up a hairline crack RPs) and gain a broad scoop. Crimp the faint rib on the right o gain the break of *Sacrilege* up which the route finishes.
A. *Dave Pegg 1990*

❺ Sacrilege .... 🔲🔲🔲 **E2 5c**
6m. Climb the chimney for 8m to access the imposing crack n the left wall. Plug in a sustained series of solid jams (except hen green) to final tricky moves way out left.
A. *Tony Howard 1963/FFA. Martin Berzins 1978*

❻ Starvation Chimney ...... 🔲🔲 **HVD**
8m. The compelling narrow rift to a tight exit through the cliff. peaking as one who emerged trouserless from its clutches the imb is well worth exploring.

❼ Appointment With Fear . 🔲🔲🔲 **E7 6b**
4m. The astounding axe-edge arete may by the most impres-ive piece of grit in the Peak, imagine being up there! Gain the rete from 8m up *Route 1* via a 'tricky' mantel and desperate eftwards traverse. The terrifying final section is 'out there' and roves to be only marginally easier. Well-named indeed.
A. *John Hartley (aided as The Prow) 1969. FFA. Dougie Hall 1986*

⑱ Route 1 .... 🔲🔲🔲 **HS 4b**
18m. A great climb up the long groove that is the main feature of the right-hand side of the cliff. A steep initial section leads to a block (the Pulpit) at the foot of the superb curving crack. This can be laybacked by Philistines, the rest of us revel in the quality of the finger and hand-jamming. Protection is bomber throughout. Possibly the best route of its grade in the Peak.
Photo page 185.
FA. L Kiernan 1937

⑲ Route II .... 🔲🔲🔲 **VS 5a**
18m. Climb the tricky initial crack (crux) to the Pulpit then tackle the continuation, by climbing out right to a blobby boss then back left up into the crack. Another fine climb only over-shadowed a little by its neighbour.
FA. L. Kiernan 1937

⑳ Halina .... 🔲🔲🔲 **E2 5c**
16m. Approach the boss of *Route II* from the right then balance up the delicate right-trending ramp to a harrowing exit. A bit of a one-move wonder and harder for the short to flash.
FA. Barry Rawlinson (1 nut) 1972 FFA. John Allen 1975

㉑ Michael Knight
Wears a Chest Wig . 🔲🔲🔲🔲 **E7 6c**
10m. Extremely technical and fingery pebble climbing up the wall and arete left of *Twin Cracks*. Start at the scoop and climb directly using a series of rock-overs on the pebbles to a snatch for a pocket. Move slightly right, then back left to the arete. Finish up the right-hand side of this in a great position.
FA. Nik Jennings 2000

㉒ Twin Cracks .... 🔲 **S 4a**
8m. From the terrace, climb the right-hand twin crack. The left one all the way is a slightly longer **HS 4b**.
FA. Anton Stoop 1910

HERRINGBONE SLAB AREA

The right-hand side of the crag is less spectacular, and less busy, than the rest of the place though it has some worthwhile offerings, including some gripping aretes.

❶ Squirmer's Chimney . . . . . 🔲 **S 4a**
12m. Another Wimberry classical rift. Just as tight as *Starvation* and more of a battle as the tussle goes on longer.

❷ Chockblock . . . . 🔲 **E5 6b**
12m. The slab right of *Squirmer's Chimney*, with runners in the flake to the left of *Squirmer's Chimney*, is an inferior variation to *Consolation Prize*.
FA. Steven Delderfield 1990s

❸ Consolation Prize . . . . 🔲 **E5 6a**
12m. The BOLD arete by some frantic moves (choose a start) to a poor rest on the left, followed by the even BOLDER though easier upper section. The route would probably be E6 without the mid-height 'psyching' ledge.
FA. Jonny Woodward 1981

❹ Slab Gully . . . . 🔲 **VDiff**
12m. The narrow gully bounding the left-hand side of the attractive slab.

❺ Slab Climb . . . . 🔲 **HVD**
10m. The pleasant left-hand side of the slab, may require a runner in the gully for the timid (or should that read 'sensible'). A pleasant pitch.

❻ Herringbone Slab . . . . 🔲 **HVS 4c**
10m. The centre of the slab with a jig right at two thirds-height is pleasant and poorly-protected. Finishing up the left-hand side is bolder again, **E1 5a**.

❼ Groove and Chimney . . . . 🔲 **Diff**
12m. The obviously-named features to the right.

❽ Tap Dance . . . . 🔲 **E3 5c**
8m. Climb the fingery wall to a good horizontal then stretch or teeter to the top.
FA. Chris Hardy 1986

❾ Charm . . . . 🔲 **E3 5c**
8m. The right-hand line. Climb to the break with difficulty then use a poor pocket to reach a delicate finish up a blind flake. Good horizontal wires protect, mild at the grade.
FA. Jonny Woodward 1982

❿ The Climb with No Name . . 🔲 **E5 6a**
10m. The steep arete is approached via a groove and laybacke wildly on its right-hand side.
FA. Johnny Dawes 1984.

⓫ Cooking Crack . . . . 🔲 **HS 4b**
8m. Enter the undercut crack awkwardly.

⓬ Sloping Crack . . . . 🔲 **VDiff**
10m. Climb to the crescent-shaped crack and follow it to a steep and exposed finish.

⓭ Wall and Bulge . . . . 🔲 **E2 5b**
10m. Climb the east-facing wall to the block overhang (poor wires) then scuttle right and finish just left of the arete.
FA. Malc Baxter 1961

⓮ Dream of Blackpool Donkeys 🔲 **E3 5c**
10m. Finger-traverse right to the arete and climb it with increasing trepidation on its exposed valley face. Nasty landing
FA. Adrian Garlick 1973

⓯ Blood, Sweat and Tears . . . . . . 🔲 **E2 5b**
8m. Climb directly up the face to the finish of *Wall and Bulge*.
FA. Chris Hardy 1987

Staffordshire
Whaley Bridge
Kinder
Bleaklow
Chew
Lancashire
Cheshire
Den Lane
Running Hill Pits
Alderman
Upperwood Q
Standing Stones
Ravenstones
Dovestones
Rob's Rocks
Wimberry

NORTHERN BALLET AREA

A collection of smaller routes set above the attractive (and big) boulder of *Northern Ballet*. The whole area sees little attention though it might be worth a visit if you want to escape the crowds -"What crowds?" you might say!

1 The Twilight Zone **E4 5c**
10m. Climb the right edge of the arete to a break and the flying rib above to a gripping exit.
FA. Dougie Hall 1987

2 Cranberry Crack . . . . **VS 5a**
10m. The awkward crack in the upper part of the face is reached via an easy groove. It is berry-filled no longer.

3 Curving Arete . . . . **VDiff**
3m. The curved arete eases with height.

4 Fisher's Chimney . . . . **HVD**
3m. The widening rift.

5 Kvick Chimney . . . . **HS 4c**
3m. The chimney is entered by moves up its right arete.

6 Village Green **E3 6c**
4m. The bulging right-hand arete of the buttress is desperate.
FA. Johnny Dawes 1984

7 Cloudberry Wall . . . . **VS 5b**
5m. The centre of the crinkly wall.

8 Cave Rib **E2 5b**
10m. The outside face of the cave system is climbed up the right rib to a ledge (runners on the left) and a bizarre finale.
FA. Steve Bancroft 1974

Below the right-hand side of the cliff is a very large boulder, severely undercut at its left-hand end.

9 A Walk with Whittaker . . **E3 6a**
10m. The undercut scoop on the left-hand side of the overhang is described as "puzzling and difficult", and is possibly a sandbag! Finish up *Northern Ballet*.
FA. Steven Fisher 1996

10 Northern Ballet **E3 5b**
16m. An easy slab leads to the right-hand edge of the overhang. Step onto it and pad gingerly all the way out to the (rounded) left arete and a harrowing finish above a big drop.
FA. Johnny Dawes 1984

11 Green but Sure **E1 5a**
12m. Follow *Northern Ballet* to the slab then climb it on a set of small rounded bumps: delicate and unprotected.
FA. Kevin Thaw 1983

A pleasant if diminutive south facing outcrop in as wild a setting as you might expect from being opposite the moor called Wilderness. The routes are short but the rock is clean and a couple of hours of pleasant sport is available here for climbers operating in the lower grades. Serious boulderers might be interested in the huge roof that lies to the west of the main cliff; there appears to be no indication that it has ever been climbed. Rob's Rocks gets all the sun that is going and its relatively easy approach makes it a good choice for a short day. It has a better set of lower grade climbs than most cliffs in the area. The classic scramble of Wilderness Gully Easy (150m Mod) lies opposite the cliff and is worth a look at. From its top a right turn leads back along the moor crest to Wimberry and then the parking by the reservoir.

APPROACH Also see map on page 182

From the Pay and Display (weekends only) parking by the Dovestones Reservoir follow the tarmac track up the side of Wilderness Brook, steep initially then easing, until the base of the cliff can be reached by a short scramble up and left, 30 minutes.

CONDITIONS

Despite its altitude the aspect and clean top of the cliff mean that it dries rapidly after rain and is in condition throughout the year whenever the weather is half decent.

Most of the routes with no first ascent details were discovered and recorded by members of The Rimmon Mountaineering Club in the early 1960s.

OTHER GUIDEBOOK - A more complete list of routes at Rob's Rocks is published in the 1988 BMC *Moorland Gritstone* guidebook.

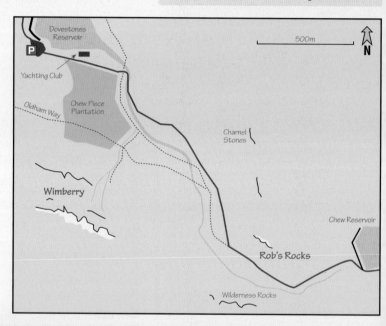

WILDERNESS ROCKS and THE CHARNEL STONES

Halfway up the approach road the straggling outcrop of The Charnel Stones can be seen to the left with the attractive hanging slab of *The Wastelands* **E4 5c**, a classic moorland frightener, one of several Bancroft 1970s 'specials' hereabouts. Worth E5 when dirty which it usually is.
Up right is Wilderness Rocks which is north-facing and often out of condition. When clean and dry there are a number of good routes including some recent hard additions (see ROCKFAX route database). To the east (left) of the Wilderness Rocks is a long gully that runs all the way from the Chew Brook in the bottom, to the crest of the moor. This is the worthwhile:

❶ Wilderness Gully East .... 🗒 ⬜ **Mod**
150m. An excellent scramble (really quite easy for a Mod). It provides a good winter route under the right conditions though care is required as there have been avalanches here.

ROB'S ROCKS

The routes are spread across the crag following good lines on the separate buttresses. The best of the climbs are on the largest 'central' buttress.

Snow Crack . . . . **S 4a**
Drift up the short-lived fissure.
Jeff Sykes 1961

Nice Edge . . . . **S 4b**
The sharp tilted arete is juggy if diminutive fun.
Paul Seddon 1961

Beaky Corner . . . . **VDiff**
The capped corner to a rightward (or leftward - S 4a) exit.

Stairway . . . . **S 4a**
The tilted, inverted staircase is another steep juggy one.

Cascade . . . . **HS 4a**
The centre of the attractive face is short on gear and many he holds are not the most helpful around.
Tony Howard 1961

Zacharias . . . . **VDiff**
The crack right of the arete has a tricky final move.
to page 9.
Tony Howard 1961

Nameless One . . . . **VS 4b**
Climb the crack in the west-facing wall to a leftward exit.
Roy (Chubby?) Brown 1950

Nameless Two . . . . . **HVS 4c**
From the fallen slab, climb the left-hand side of the arete ply and on poor holds. A little harrowing.
an Carr 1985

9 Ylnosd Rib . . . . **HVD**
12m. Pigeon-chested types can squirm the lower crack to ledges and an easier finish. Others will need to start from the right at about the same grade and quality.
FA. J.W.Puttrell 1903

10 Letter-box . . . . **VDiff**
10m. The pleasant slabby face passing a least one useful slot.
FA. J.W.Puttrell 1903

11 Cave Crack . . . . **HS 4c**
10m. The awkward narrowing rift offers a strange kind of 'fun'.

12 Cripple's Way . . . . **VDiff**
10m. Another excellent low-grade route. Finish up the top block for the full effect.

13 Owt . . . . **Mod**
10m. The ribbed-crack and short steep wall above are pleasant.

14 Ice Crack . . . . **VDiff**
8m. The steep groove well to the right gives good bridging.

15 Digital Orbit **E3 5c**
8m. From a block, make a leap-of-faith to pass the nose.
FA. Paul Moreland 1990

16 The Nose . . . . **VS 5a**
8m. Swing on the right edge of the beak, pull to get established and romp on. Alternatively, approach from the right; **Nosey, VDiff**.

17 Freebird **E2 5c**
8m. The bulge and triangular nose to the hanging arete.
FA. Paul Moreland 1990

18 Niche Wall . . . . **VDiff**
Rightwards into the niche and then up and left to finish.

DOVESTONES EDGE
SE 025038 to SE 0290◄

Not to be confused with its even more remote namesake in the Eastern Peak, this fine cliff has a good selection of routes and is rarely busy, the flog to get there being the main reason the place stays so quiet. It faces west and north west and is at its best on warm summer evenings when the many lower grade climbs can be enjoyed to the full.

Below and to the south west of the main Dovestones Edge are three large rambling quarrie on the hillside overlooking the reservoir. All the main lines have been done but the Main Quarry in particular has a habit of falling down big-style. In thirty odd years of climbing in the Peak I have only visited the Main Quarry once, to find the top pitch of our chosen objec tive missing. We did the route anyway - but I vowed never to return, and never have!

APPROACH Also see map on page 182

Park at the Binn Green car park just off the A635, descend to the road, cross over the dam and, either follow the stream to the tunnel then make a steep direct ascent to the cliff via th trackless slope, or do it direct. Alternatively park by the Dovestones Reservoir (page 184), walk round the southern edge of the reservoir, cross the stream and follow the path that slopes up the hill from the Chew Brook bridge. This passes below the quarries before heading resolutely for the cliff high above.

CONDITIONS

A great venue on fine summer evenings when the aspect and position of the cliff can be enjoyed to the full. The cliff dries rapidly after rain and is less green than most here-abouts. On the down-side the left-hand end of the edge can be gritty and it catches south westerly winds in spectacular fashion.

OTHER GUIDEBOOK - A more complete list of routes at Dovestones is published in the 1988 BMC *Moorland Gritstone* guidebook.

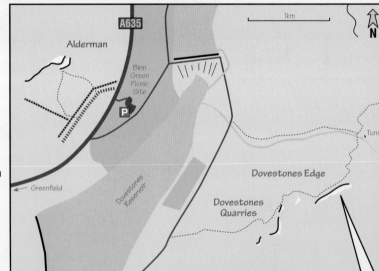

Nasal Buttress Area · Swan Crack Area · Mammoth Slab · Answer Crack Area · Hanging Crack Area

Descent

Staffordshire · Whaley Bridge · Kinder · Bleaklow · Chew · Lancashire · Cheshire · Den Lane · Running Hill Pits · Alderman · Upperwood Q · Standing Stones · Ravenstones · Dovestones · Rob's Rocks · Wimberry

NASAL BUTTRESS AREA

The left-hand side of the cliff has a collection of worthwhile easier climbs although the area tends to be green and gritty after wet weather. It is at its best on late summer evenings when the situation can be enjoyed to the full.

① Route 1 . . . . **HS 4b**
22m. Climb diagonally left out to the arete and on to reach ledges below the pinnacle. Then climb the fingery centre of its face. Other variations are possible and equally good.

② Slab and Saddle . . . . **Diff**
16m. Climb the slabby face until the upper part of the projecting buttress on the right can be reached for an exposed finish.

③ Stirrup . . . . **S 4a**
16m. Climb the slabs straight into the hanging groove then move out right and climb the exposed arete in a fine position.
FA. Tony Howard 1958

④ Double Overhangs . . . . **HVS 5b**
14m. The front face of the buttress passing two roofs is effectively a pumpy direct start to *Stirrup*.
FA. Chris Hardy 1982

⑤ Cooper's Crack . . . . . **S 4b**
12m. The crack splitting the roof eases once past the overhang.

⑥ Sea Route . . . . **VS 4c**
12m. Tackle the face then the thin crack that splits the centre of the slab, crossing the major break of *C Climb* at half-height.
FA. Chris Hardy 1982

⑦ C Climb . . . . **Diff**
14m. Start on the right and climb leftwards along the obvious line to finish up the final two moves of *Cooper's Crack*.

⑧ Green Crack . . . . **VDiff**
12m. The curving groove is a compelling line but not a very edifying experience. It could have been called *Gritty Crack* or *Grotty Crack*.

⑨ Wrinkled Buttress . . . . **VDiff**
18m. Climb the lower buttress right then left to a ledge then the upper face on sloping holds, heading back right again.

⑩ Curving Crack . . . . **VDiff**
12m. Climb the slab to reach the deep crack/groove as it bends back right then follow it to the top.

⑪ Danegeld **E1 5b**
12m. Steep and worthwhile. Climb the face into a scoop then take a crack up the bulging wall. Pull over the left edge of the final overhang or side-step it.
FA. Bill Birch 1986

⑫ Knobbly Wall . . . . **HVD**
12m. The flaky wall to a short crack.

⑬ The Tax Collector **E2 5c**
12m. The centre of the recessed-wall leads to, and through, the capping roof which makes you pay for all favours received.
FA. Rick Hyde 1990s

⑭ The Director's Route . . . . . **HVD**
20m. A long diagonal from the foot of *The Direct Route* to the top left corner of the face involves some good climbing and the odd creaking hold. Exit left under the roof at the end of the wall.

⑮ The Direct Route . . . . **VDiff**
12m. Climb the right-hand side of the wall on flakes (some of which are a bit creaky) - care required.

⑯ Eyebrow . . . . **S 4a**
18m. The northern side of the jutting buttress with a short excursion into the groove on the left and a finish on the exposed arete out to the right.

⑰ Nasal Buttress . . . . . **HS 4b**
16m. The classic of this part of the cliff. Climb the steep arete with the nose being passed on the left by delicate moves; good small wires protect. Finish up the superbly-positioned arete.
Photo page 195.
FA. George Bower early 1920s

Descent

Descent

Descent

Evening | 30 min

Staffordshire
Whaley Bridge
Kinder
Bleaklow
Chew
Lancashire
Cheshire
Den Lane
Running Hill Pits
Alderman
Upperwood Q
Standing Stones
Ravenstones
Dovestones
Rob's Rocks
Wimberry

SWAN CRACK AREA

The central section of the cliff consists of a series of fine jutting buttresses with a good selection of routes. The climbs here tend to be cleaner than those to the left since the good bits of rock protrude from the hillside.

18 Eight Hours! **E1 5a**
16m. Weave a way up the right-hand face of the buttress until it s possible to escape out onto the left-hand arete.
A. Chris Hardy 1984

19 The Changeling . . . . **HS 4b**
16m. The widening-crack is followed past a kink until it is ossible to change to the other side of the chimney and finish p the narrow-faced side-wall. A bit of an oddity.

20 Crack and Chimney . . . . . **Mod**
14m. The widening-rift to an escape over, or under, the chock-tone that blocks the chimney.

21 Palpitation **E1 5a**
14m. Wander up the narrow buttress passing to the left of the verhang before stepping out right to a finish on the arete. Not oo hard but a bit of a shocker unless you seek out all the gear.
A. Jim Campbell 1973

22 Mother's Pride **E1 5b**
14m. The upper half of the rib left of the chimney to a finish ver the block that forms the top of the cliff.
A. Chris Hardy 1980

23 Capstone Chimney . . . . . . **Mod**
14m. Climb the rift to the capstone and and a rightward exit.

24 Kitten Cracks . . . . **S 4b**
10m. Climb the cracks in the right-hand wall of the descent ully to the roof and creep round the right-hand side of this.

25 Square Chimney . . . . **Diff**
12m. Follow the hanging groove in the left-hand side of the uttress to a platform then take the chimney behind. The cracks ust right of the chimney are harder and better (**S 4a**).

26 Central Tower . . . . **VDiff**
18m. A fine climb; long and interesting. Ascend the buttress front with a jig right and left through the bulges, then finish slightly right up the well-positioned final slab.

27 Tower Arete . . . . **VS 4c**
18m. The arete that forms the right-hand edge of the buttress is approached up slabby rock. A pitch of escalating interest.
FA. Rick Gibbon 1986

28 Left Embrasure . . . . . **VS 4b**
16m. The crack rising from the left-hand edge of a shallow recess is pleasant in a graunchy-gritstone kinda-way.
FA. Tony Howard 1958

29 Right Embrasure . . . . . **VS 4c**
14m. The right-hand crack is difficult to access and altogether more of a battle although still enjoyable in a strange way.
FA. Barry Kershaw 1958

30 Matchstick Crack . . . . **S 4a**
10m. The thin crack in the wall, finishing leftwards up the slab.
FA. Tony Jones 1960

31 Maggie . . . . **HVS 5a**
10m. Take the pleasant square-cut arete on its right-hand side.
FA. Tony Jones 1960

32 Grim Wall . . . . **VS 5a**
10m. Climb the overlap and a crack to its end. Finish up the short face above with difficulty.

33 Noddy's Wall . . . . **VS 4b**
12m. The slim buttress gives a pleasant pitch.
FA. John Hadfield (aka Noddy) 1958.

34 Swan Crack . . . . **HVD**
14m. From the toe of the arete cross the face rightwards to the ever-popular crack which doesn't normally require a long neck!

35 Swan Down . . . . **VS 4c**
10m. The wall right of the crack feels a little artificial.
FA.Graham West 1960

DOVESTONES *Mammoth Slab*

Staffordshire · Whaley Bridge · Kinder · Bleaklow · Chew · Lancashire · Cheshire · Den Lane · Running Hill Pits · Alderman · Upperwood Q · Standing Stones · Ravenstones · Dovestones · Rob's Rocks · Wimberry

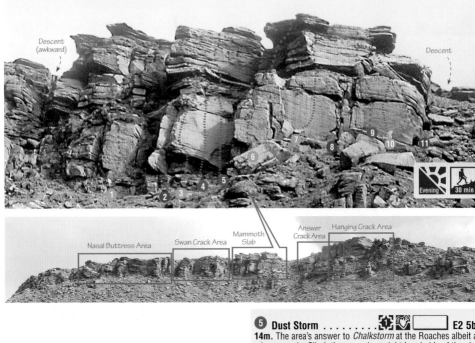

MAMMOTH SLAB

The central section of the cliff has some good routes on a series of fine faces that are generally cleaner than the rock away to the left. *Mammoth Slab* is the best route here but all the others listed are well worth doing.

1 Gnomes' Wall ...... **VS 4c**
14m. Climb the short technical and fingery face to grassy ledges then continue up the buttress above, exiting to the left of the capping snout.
FA. Graham West 1960

2 Rib and Wall .... **S 4a**
16m. Should have been called *Groove and Slab*! Climb into and up the groove in the arete to broad ledges. Then traverse right and finish up the centre of the face above.

3 Mammoth Slab ..... **HVS 5a**
14m. Not the beast you might expect. Swing over the roof to access the left-hand side of the slab (crux) and climb it more easily to the break. Continue up the left-hand side of the buttress above keeping just right of the arete.
FA. Graham West 1960

4 Ferdie's Folly **E1 5b**
14m. The centre of the face is delicate and unprotected, the upper half is much easier, finishing as for *Rib and Wall*.
FA. The first ascent date is not recorded, although it is believed to have been done in the 1940s - good effort!

5 Dust Storm **E2 5b**
14m. The area's answer to *Chalkstorm* at the Roaches albeit at a lower grade. Climb the precarious right-hand side of the slab, initially via a delicate scoop. Step left out of the top of this then make more thin moves to the halfway ledge. Finish direct.
FA. Chris Hardy 1984

6 Kaytoo .... **VS 4c**
14m. Climb onto the block in front of the face then stride left into the thin crack and follow this to ledges. Climb the scoop in the wall behind until an exposed rightward exit is possible.
FA. Barry Kershaw 1958

7 Asinine .... **HVS 5**
12m. Step right of the block and sketch away up the face to the first decent holds. Finish easily.
FA. Ian Carr 1982

8 June Climb .... **Diff**
12m. Take the fissure in the centre of the face to ledges then amble left, pull onto the slab and exit right below the roof.

9 Austin Maxi **E2 5c**
12m. The delicate face to the right of *June Climb* has technical moves to reach the security of the break and one more tricky sequence to reach easy ground.
FA. Chris Hardy 1982

10 June Wall .... **VS 5a**
12m. Start from the useful 'tooth' and climb the slab by thin moves to ledges. Escape off right or extend things a little up and left. A technical tester from the days of bendy boots.
FA. Graham West 1960

11 June Ridge .... **S 4a**
12m. The right-hand arete of the face is started from the right. Gain a ledge on the front then climb to the terrace and finish leftwards as for *June Wall*.

Staffordshire
Whaley Bridge
Kinder
Bleaklow
Chew
Lancashire
Cheshire
Den Lane
Running Hill Pits
Alderman
Upperwood Q
Standing Stones
Ravenstones
Dovestones
Rob's Rocks
Wimberry

ANSWER CRACK AREA

A good collection of climbs including a great VDiff in the shape of *Answer Crack* and a whole bevy of other bits and pieces worth a minute or two of your time

1 Rubber-faced Arete . . . . . **VS 4c**
10m. Climb the thin bending crack in the narrow rib then step right and stretch for better holds and an easier finish.
FA. Malc Baxter 1961

2 Rubber-faced Wall . . . . **VDiff**
12m. The wide right-slanting crack to ledges and easy ground.

3 December Arete . . . . **HVS 5b**
12m. Climb the square-cut arete, initially on its left-hand side, with a strenuous start and precarious finish.
FA. Malc Baxter 1961

4 Layback Crack . . . . **HS 4b**
12m. The classic crack splitting the centre of the buttress eases with height. The lower section is easiest just to the left of the crack, and you can also jam it if you want.

5 Friction Addiction . . **E1 5c**
12m. Balance up the slab (clean those boots) to less precarious ground and a sprint up a short crack. Effectively unprotected.
FA. Chris Hardy 1984

6 Slipoff Slab . . . . **VS 4b**
12m. Balance up the thin crack to the slab which is climbed leftwards on a series of slopers. A direct finish is harder.
FA. Barry Kershaw 1958

7 Double Time Crack . . . . **HVD**
8m. The wide crack on the right-hand side of the slab.

8 Left Chimney . . . . **VDiff**
12m. More of a groove and a rather grassy one at that!

9 Right Chimney . . . . **VDiff**
12m. This one is a proper chimney, awkward but worthwhile. Finish up the steep crack above.

10 'Owd on Arete . . . . **HS 4b**
12m. Get a grip of the arete on its left-hand side, finishing up the left-hand side of the elegant prow above.
FA. Malc Baxter 1961

11 Question Time **E2 5c**
12m. Follow the wall, slab and jutting arete to the left of *Answer Crack* to a well-positioned finale.
FA. Rick Gibbon 1990s

12 Answer Crack . . . . **HVD**
12m. The flake crack is Western Grit's answer to Stanage's *Heaven Crack*, and it's a good effort. Layback to get established and then continue with pleasure. Finish up the wall behind.
FA. Paul Seddon 1960

13 Question Mark . . . . **S 4a**
12m. Climb the obvious, and rather awkward, crack to its end then move left to get the correct answer.
FA. Paul Seddon 1960

14 Full Stop **E1 5a**
12m. The wall and right arete are as well-protected as the grade suggests! Finishing direct is the same grade but manages to feel even bolder.
FA. Steve Bancroft 1973

15 Third Triplet . . . . **Diff**
12m. The unremarkable, wide left-hand, fissure.

16 Yellow Crack . . . . . **HVS 5b**
12m. The short wall and thin crack lead to easier territory.

17 Second Triplet . . . . **Diff**
12m. The narrower central rift of the trio.

18 Loose End . . . . **VS 5a**
10m. The thin crack that was pegged in antiquity leads to the steep arete out to the right and a good finish.
FA. Duggy Banes late 1950s. FFA. Paul Seddon 1960

19 First Triplet . . . . **S 4a**
10m. Climb the crack through an alcove with difficulty and on up the wall above.

20 Scarface . . . . **VS 4c**
10m. The steep groove and curving crack can be dirty and don't see much traffic.

Staffordshire
Whaley Bridge
Kinder
Bleaklow
Chew
Lancashire
Cheshire
Den Lane
Running Hill Pits
Alderman
Upperwood Q
Standing Stones
Ravenstones
Dovestones
Rob's Rocks
Wimberry

HANGING CRACK

The largest buttress on the edge has "the best jamming-crack on grit", or so rumour has it - *Hanging Crack*. There are other oddities as well and the place is especially enjoyable in the evening sun - high summer only though!

① Tower Ridge . . . . VDiff
26m. Start at a lower level and follow a crack and then the blocky ridge to the terrace (belay). Finish up the juggy crack in the upper tier. The star is for the clean upper section.

② The Jester . . . . S 4a
12m. The crack and scoop to a steep juggy exit.
FA. Steve Bancroft 1972

③ Spurt of Spurts E2 5b
20m. An oddity but worth doing if you enjoy being gripped! Follow *The Jester* for 8m then swing rightwards along the break until just left of *Hanging Crack* and finish direct, with difficulty.
FA. Nick Plishko 1983

④ Hymen the Tactless . . . E5 6c
18m. Trend left to reach the left end of the overhang then monkey right and pull over its centre with great difficulty to reach the easier final wall.
FA. Nick Plishko 1983

⑤ Hanging Crack E2 5b
16m. A fine jamming-crack; the crag is worth a visit just to do this route. Climb the crack through a host of overhangs.
Photo page 182.
FA. Joe Brown (a little aid) 1957 FFA. Alan McHardy 1967

⑥ The Gibbet E3 5c
16m. The steep wall is bold (big cams and big balls help) though thankfully things ease with height.
FA. Loz Francomb 1980

⑦ The Catwalk . . . . VS 4a
16m. From the gully on the right shuffle left along the highest break to the arete and an easy finish. Not too difficult but exposed and unprotected; a fall would likely prove very serious.
FA. Graham West 1960

⑧ Strappado E4 6b
10m. The hanging flake is approached from the left and requires plenty of grunt. A harder (E4) version of its near-namesake at Froggatt which is E5.
FA. Nick Colton 1981

⑨ Blank Crack . . . . S 4b
10m. The crack that runs up the buttress front, passing to the right of the overhang.

⑩ Long Ridge . . . . VDiff
28m. Another extended outing. Climb the groove in the lower ridge then scramble to the obvious continuation on the right. Finish up the jutting buttress above.

⑪ Jam and Jug . . . . S 4b
12m. Jam the crescent-shaped crack, then follow jugs on the left to exit.
FA. Tony Howard 1958

To the right are a further 10 or so routes, none is of especial merit so they are not described here.

Dovestones Edge - Hanging Crack Area

Dovestones Main Quarry (not described)

Dovestones Left Quarry (not described)

Bob Hope

Evening | 20 min

Staffordshire
Whaley Bridge
Kinder
Bleaklow
Chew
Lancashire
Cheshire
Den Lane
Running Hill Pits
Alderman
Upperwood Q
Standing Stones
Ravenstones
Dovestones
Rob's Rocks
Wimberry

DOVESTONES QUARRIES - BOB HOPE

The three Dovestones Quarries offer some interesting mountaineering-style routes but really only the lower right quarry has much of interest for more conventional climbers. The seven best routes are described here including the famous finger crack and Chew classic of; *Bob Hope*. Scaffold pipes hammered into the peaty slope above the cliff provide belays - always assuming you can find them!
APPROACH - From the parking by the dam take the good track around the lake and follow the short path that branches into the quarry; an easy 15 minutes stroll.

① Ace of Spades . . . . **HVS 5a**
5m. Similar to *Fox-House Flake* at Burbage but a notch or two arder. Follow the flake-crack all the way.
A. Joe Brown (as Joe's Layback) 1957

② Jet Lag **E5 6b**
5m. The slab and wall left of *Tiny Tim*. From low wires climb he slab to a shelf. Step right to place a runner in *Tiny Tim* then hove back and finish direct.
A. Kevin Thaw 1990

③ Tiny Tim . . . . **VS 4c**
6m. The flake groove leading left from the base of the crack n *Bob Hope* is followed throughout strenuously.
A. Joe Brown 1957

④ Bob Hope **E4 6a**
15m. Miles better than any other route in the Dovestones Quarries. The finger-crack gives super-sustained finger jamming all the way, well-protected, but with little for your feet. Another classic from the raiding Bancroft.
FFA. Steve Bancroft 1978. Previously aided as **Metamorphose**.

⑤ Pedestal Corner . . . . **VS 4c**
15m. Follow the crack to the right of the fissure of *Bob Hope* to reach the top of a pedestal. Climb the corner above, then move out right to pushy exit.
FA. Graham West early 1960s

⑥ Scuttle Buttin' **E7 6c**
15m. The impending arete right of *Pedestal Corner* is climbed without side runners. Bold!
FA. Kevin Thaw 1989

⑦ Five Day Chimney **E2 5c**
15m. The final left-facing corner is gained via a flake. Sustained jamming and awkward corner moves lead to a loose-feeling block. Swing steeply right and up to finish with a flourish.
FA. Bob Whittaker 1977

RAVENSTONES

A fine austere cliff, north facing in a lofty position looking out over Saddleworth Moors, and the steep slopes running down to Holme Clough and the Greenfield Reservoir. The situation of the cliff and the outlook give a remoter feel that almost any other crag in the Peak, with few signs of human activity from the top of the cliff. The likelihood is that, unless the weather is absolutely perfect, you will have the place to yourself. There is a fine set of climbs here, many following good crack-lines, with more arduous undertakings up the dividing walls and aretes.

The cliff continues westwards for a couple of kilometres and the shorter walls here are home to another hundred of so routes, many of which are worth doing but see little traffic - check out the BMC Chew Valley guide for further details.

APPROACH Also see map on page 182

The crag can be reached from the Binn Green picnic/parking area (50 minutes) by dropping down to the reservoir, taking a left turn and walking up the valley until below the left-hand end of the cliff which is reached by a steep ascent. Alternatively, from the top of the A635 take the short tarmac track (see Standing Stones approach) then head over the moor, passing the edge of Standing Stones, dropping down to the stream and scrambling up to the the left edge of the cliff (30 minutes). The latter is shorter but leaves a harder walk out at the end of the day, no minor consideration if you are here for a 'full on' day!

CONDITIONS

The crag is a harsh task-master in all but perfect conditions, and such conditions are pretty uncommon up here. The climbs are graded for such ideal days, but if you are here when things are damp and greasy, be prepared to lower your sights or get ready for a hard time.

OTHER GUIDEBOOK - A more complete list of routes at Ravenstones is published in the 1988 BMC *Moorland Gritstone* guidebook.

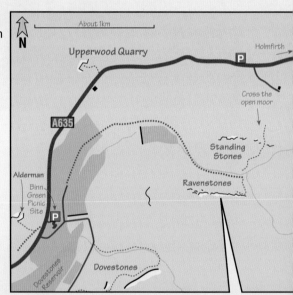

GREEN WALL

The left-hand side of the cliff faces north east and so gets the early morning sun; ideal for early risers. Although not as popular as the cliff further right, it has some worthwhile lower-grade climbs of which *Eastern Slab* is the best. At a higher grade *Green Wall* is worth doing just to see how hot the old guys were, and also because it's good!
Further right *Nil Desperandum* and *Pulpit Ridge* are two striking lines that are well worth doing.

❶ Strenuosity .... VS 4c
6m. The crack leading to an awkward exit around the huge boulder is not mis-named and sees little attention.

❷ Cockney's Traverse ...... HS 4b
10m. Climb a short way up *Strenuosity* then follow the sloping ramp rightwards and up until below the overhangs (thread). Continue in the same line to easy ground.

❸ Hang-glider E2 5b
12m. Climb straight up to the thread on *Cockney's Traverse*. Then tackle the impressive roof direct, or via the thin crack just to the left. Bold moves and/or flexible holds make the route memorable whichever line you take.
FA. Bob Whittaker 1977

❹ Slanter .... VS 4c
10m. Slant up the shallow, leaning groove that sneaks past the right-hand edge of the overhang, to reach easy ground.
FA. Gordon Mason 1977

❺ Alpha .... VDiff
8m. The steep and juggy flake-crack on the left-hand side of the front of the buttress is pleasant if somewhat short-lived.

❻ Beta .... Diff
10m. Cross the jammed boulder to access the constricted rift above then thrash up this.

❼ Grooved Wall .... HS 4b
10m. Balance up the left-hand edge of the slab to the ledge on its crest then continue up the crucial steep and technical groove directly above.

❽ Eastern Slab .... Diff
12m. Start up the centre of the well-scratched slab then trend right to finish up the arete. A worthwhile lower-grade climb.

❾ Deep Chimney .... Mod
12m. The deep, angular rift is very traditional.

❿ Green Wall .... HS 4b
12m. An ancient classic. Climb the shallow groove in the centre of the buttress, to the right of the chimney, to find a tricky exit on the left. A mantelshelf is the traditional way of doing it though there are other (easier!) ways.
FA. Herbert Hartley 1928

⓫ Boy's Own E1 5b
12m. The square right-hand arete of the buttress is worth doing, giving good open moves, even though it feels rather escapable. The chipped hold at the start is avoidable.
FA. Ray Duffy 1982

⓬ Nil Desperandum ...... S 4a
12m. The classic groove that cleaves the centre of this section of the cliff gives an appealing pitch up a striking line and leads to an escape left under the overhangs.

⓭ Pulpit Ridge .... HVS 4
16m. The bold and imposing arete. Climb onto the Pulpit via a traverse from the right then balance up the exciting edge (low gear) to easier ground. Either of the steep twin diagonal cracks below the ridge can be used as a harder **Direct Start (5a)**.
FA. Arthur Birtwhistle 1938

⓮ Over the Moors ... E5 6b
16m. Climb the bold and bald wall, directly above the starting crack of *Pulpit Ridge*, trending slightly left (nut in pocket) then back rightwards to the deep break. Escape up the easy crack.
Photo page 203.
FA. Paul Clark 1990s

THE DRAINPIPE

The central section of the cliff has some worthwhile climbs up a series of impressive corners with *The Drainpipe* and *Nil Desperandum* being a couple of cracking Severes. The smoother rock in between offers some excellent open aretes and some compelling and bold face climbs that don't see much in the way of traffic.

⑮ Black Mountain Collage 　　　　**E7 6c**
6m. Climb the bold and bald right-hand side of the wall tarting off the pedestal. At the top move back left to join *Over he Moors* to finish (without the gear in the pocket!).
A. Andy Popp 1990s

⑯ The Drainpipe 　　　　**S 4a**
6m. A classic line up the steep corner. Good climbing but it is est avoided after (and probably during) wet weather. It can be limbed by secure squirming or rather bolder laybacking. Large ear helps to protect.

⑰ Guerrilla Action 　　　　**E2 5b**
6m. From the spout of *The Drainpipe* head out right to the lunt arete and climb it to a deep horizontal break (gear). From ere make an airy exit up the final section on sloping holds.
A. John Smith 1981

⑱ Unfinished Arete 　　　　**VS 4c**
0m. Devious but interesting. Slant left to the arete and balance p this to the deep break. Wriggle right along the slot to the hort crack in the right side of the upper wall and finish up this.
A. Arthur Birtwhistle 1938

⑲ Welcome to Greenfield, Gateway to the Valley 　　　　**E3 6a**
6m. Climb the centre of the face to a deep slot. It is normal to ave a lie-down here before pulling onto the final wall with diffi-ılty though the climb is considerably easier if you don't get ɔo embroiled with the break, but it is so tempting!
A. Mike Chapman 1982

⑳ Undun Crack 　　　　**VS 4c**
6m. The thin crack on the right-hand side of the wall, and its ider continuation, are inclined to be green and gritty after rain.

To the right is a grassy ledge - Muddy Crack Platform - atop a tall pillar. There are a variety of ways to and off this ledge and they are generally better than their grubby names suggest. The top pitch link-ups described here can be swapped around.

㉑ Slime Crack 　　　　**Diff**
16m. The scruffy corner is included 'because it's there'. Belay on the ledge if required then finish up the chimney on the left.

㉒ Little Kern Knotts 　　　　**S 4a**
16m. Climb the crack in the left wall of the buttress passing the recess. Finish up the wall on the right of the final groove.

㉓ Waterloo Climb 　　　　**HS 4b**
16m. Mount the flake then traverse left to the arete of the buttress and balance up this to the ledge. Choose a finish.

㉔ The Plonker 　　　　**HVS 5b**
12m. From the flake climb straight up the centre of the right wall to access the ledge awkwardly. Choose an exit.
FA. Ian Carr 1982

㉕ Muddy Crack 　　　　**VDiff**
14m. The crack to the ledge and its continuation at the back.

㉖ No Time to Pose 　　　　**E5 6b**
14m. Flash up the steep, leaning arete and double overhang above; rapidly! Not well-protected where it matters.
FA. Speedy Dougie Hall 1987

㉗ Napoleon's Direct 　　　　**E2 5c**
14m. Follow the slanting groove to the overhang and layback through this with difficulty and usually some grunting.
FA. Bill Wilkinson 1970

㉘ Mark I 　　　　**VDiff**
12m. Climb the slabby angle in the left-hand edge of the bay then either take the wide crack direct, or the groove on the left with a quick hand-traverse back right to the final ledges.

Staffordshire
Whaley Bridge
Kinder
Bleaklow
Chew
Lancashire
Cheshire
Den Lane
Running Hill Pits
Alderman
Upperwood Q
Standing Stones
Ravenstones
Dovestones
Rob's Rocks
Wimberry

TRUE GRIT AREA

The right-hand side of the main cliff is composed of two impressive buttresses, divided by a steep grassy gully. On the left are the stacked overhangs of the tall True Grit Buttress and to the right is the free-standing tower of The Trinnacle whose spectacular and photogenic summit can be reached by a short scramble from behind. Almost all the routes here are worth doing. The rock is clean and quick drying and the setting is remote and spectacular - a classic moorland grit experience.

Not much sun · 25 min · Green

1 Mark II .... VDiff
16m. Climb the crack which delineates the left-hand side of the main bulk of the buttress as it narrows and steepens. The interest is maintained throughout.

2 The Derivatives ...... VDiff
18m. Where *Mark II* begins to feel too pushy, escape right to the arete and then follow the short, exposed slab above.

3 Rollup E1 5c
18m. ... if you fancy your chances! Climb right then left through the bulges and into a recess and exit leftwards from this up a crack. Trend right across the exposed and precarious slab above the overhangs to a finish on the flying arete.
FA. Ian Carr 1982

4 Rizla ...... HVS 5a
22m. Follow *Rollup* to the niche then shuffle right below the roof to a ledge (and a possible stance). Finish up the wide (*Wedgewood*) crack in the back of the corner (**4b**).
FA. Paul Seddon 1961

5 Stranger Than Friction E3 5c
20m. Access the undercut slab with difficulty and teeter carefully up it and the blunt arete above. Finish up the exposed hanging arete on its left-hand side using a useful thin crack.
FA. John Smith 1981

6 Wedgewood Crack Direct ...... VS 5a
20m. The awkward flaring and left-leaning crack gives an interesting struggle until the ledge below the *Wedgewood Crack* can be reached. Finish up this with more of the same, only easier.

7 Wedgewood Crack ...... VS 4c
24m. From the gully on the right traverse left along the break to the arete and a little higher a possible stance on a good flat ledge. Wedge the wide and wicked *Wedgewood Crack* to finish.
FA. George Bower early 1920s

8 Wall of China E4 6b
18m. Take the previous climb to the large ledges then head right passing an awkward scoop to reach the exposed arete and climb this boldly to a finish up a crack on the left.
FA. Ian Carr 1987

9 True Grit E3 5c
18m. A great outing up the impressive leaning gully wall, low in the grade but exciting and spectacular. Trend left through the initial bulges then make long reaches to a deep break (large gear). Continue right of the arete in a fine position. *Photo page 7*
FA. John Smith 1981

10 Sniffer Dog E1 5b
14m. Climb the centre of the left-hand wall of the gully passing a useful vertical crack.
FA. Tony Howard (1 point) 1960s FFA. John Smith 1981

11 Trinnacle East ...... HVS 5
12m. Climb out onto the north-facing wall to a groove and climb this passing a wobbly flake.

12 The Left Monolith ...... HS 4b
12m. The front face of the monolith is a classic little pitch, well marked and well-travelled. A short-lived but excellent outing.
FA. Herbert Hartley 1928

13 Trinnacle Chimney ...... Mod
10m. The widening rift that splits the towers is a good easy offering and bags a summit or two along the way.

14 The Right Monolith ...... HVS 5
10m. The centre of the right-hand tower is best climbed without deviation, though it is tempting to trend left and use the arete, in which case the grade drops to **VS 4b**.
FA. Herbert Hartley 1928

15 Trinnacle West E1 5b
8m. The leaning south face is climbed via a prominent crack, passing the overhang with difficulty.
FA. Paul Seddon 1963

Not much sun | 25 min | Green

Right margin tabs: Staffordshire · Whaley Bridge · Kinder · Bleaklow · Chew · Lancashire · Cheshire · Den Lane · Running Hill Pits · Alderman · Upperwood Q · Standing Stones · Ravenstones · Dovestones · Rob's Rocks · Wimberry

THE WESTERN GROUP

Running west from The Trinnacle is a long line of lower rocks, home to almost a hundred routes, many of which are worth doing despite the fact that they see few ascents. The best twenty or so from the first section of cliff are included here. The adventurous might want to explore ever further west, following the setting sun.

1 Nuke the Whale . . . ▨▨▨ ☐ **E4 6b**
m. A bold technical arete, initially on the left, then the right.
A. Ian Carr 1983

2 K. Corner . . . . ☐ **VDiff**
m. The left-facing groove is short and a little awkward.

3 Private Investigations . . ▨▨ ☐ **E3 5b**
m. The unprotected tilted arete on its left-hand side. Don't
low the crucial moves as the landing is especially unsavoury.
A. Con Carey 1982

4 Raven Rib . . . . ▨ ☐ **HVS 5a**
0m. The cracked arete gives a pleasant and well-protected
itch with nice balance climbing throughout.
A. John Allen 1974

5 The Sting . . . . ▨ ☐ **VS 5a**
2m. Climb the flake direct then continue up the short steep
ace above with the predictable sting-in-the-tail.
A. Con Carey 1982

6 Nevermore Arete . . . . ▨▨ ☐ **HVS 5a**
2m. The juggy yet bold arete left of the wide chimney is good.
A. Con Carey 1984

7 Magic Wand . . . . ▨▨ ☐ **E1 5a**
2m. The left-hand arete is precarious and unprotected unless
ou (sensibly!) place side runners in the next climb.
A. Chris Hardy 1985

8 Abracadabra . . . . ▨▨ ☐ **E1 5b**
2m. A delicate face climbed centrally with hard, safe moves
ear the top. Good climbing but much harder for the short.
A. Con Carey 1982

9 Wall and Crack Climb . . . . . . ☐ **S 4a**
2m. From a grassy groove, climb rightwards to a ledge, then
each another ledge awkwardly before the final crack.

10 Colombia Lift-off . . . . ☐ **VS 4c**
14m. Climb up and left to a junction with *Wall and Crack Climb*.
From good runners, move horizontally out right to climb the
exposed wall above the overhang.
FA. Con Carey 1981

11 Impending Crack . . . . ▨ ☐ **HS 4b**
12m. The central crack impends crucially at half height.

12 Toiseach . . . . ☐ **HVS 5a**
12m. Climb the cracked wall, just right of the wide central
fissure, via an overlap near the start and a mid-height ledge.
FA. Con Carey 1982

13 Trio . . . . ☐ **S 4a**
10m. The long groove and cracks left of the main arete are
approached steeply and climbed mainly on their left side.

14 Being Boiled . . . . ▨ ☐ **E1 5b**
12m. The elegant arete gives a pleasing pitch for cool dudes.
FA. Con Carey 1982

15 Under Pressure . . . . . ▨▨ ☐ **E1 5a**
10m. The centre of the slab is approached over an overhang
and is just about as well-protected as the grade suggests.
FA. Con Carey 1982

16 Smilosity . . . . ☐ **Diff**
10m. The oddly-named chimney with a boulder across its top.
FA. Brian Woods 1963

17 Funny Thing . . . . ▨ ☐ **VS 4c**
12m. A humourless crack and the bulging face above.
FA. Paul Seddon 1963

18 The Plin . . . . ☐ **VDiff**
12m. The groove is approached over a small overhang.

19 Plinth Chimney . . . . ▨ ☐ **VDiff**
12m. The widening chimney up the left-hand side of The Plinth.

20 Altered States . . . . ▨▨ ☐ **E3 5b**
12m. The impressive, poorly-protected front face of The Plinth.
FA. Sid Siddiqui 1982

21 Safety Plin . . . . ▨ ☐ **S 4a**
12m. The chimney up the right-hand fissure of The Plinth.

22 Plinth Arete . . . . ▨ ☐ **S 4a**
12m. The right edge of the buttress climbed on its right side.

STANDING STONES

An easily reached cliff, from roadside parking near the high point of the A635 Holmfirth to Greenfield road. It is south facing and has a worthy selection of routes through it is inclined to be a little gritty after rain due to the slope directly above the cliff. The chaotic state of the terrain below the cliff reveals that it was formed by a landslip and it has been suggested that Falling Stones might be better name for the place though the central section of the cliff has stood in its present form for several thousand years. The slope above the cliff is not the crisp clean top of the Eastern Edges; care required when setting up belays. Descents can be made round either edge of the cliff - again care required when wearing slick soled boots on steep grassy terrain. The best of the climbs here such as the fine line of *Twin Crack Corner* (VS 4b) the impressive *Fairy Nuff* (VS 4c) the devious *Ocean Wall* (E1 5b) and the pumpy *Fallen Heros* (E1 5b) would be lauded routes were they on the Eastern Edges; here they don't see much attention at all.

APPROACH Also see map on page 182

From roadside parking just west of the high point of the A635 locate a short tarmaced track on the south side of the road that leads down towards a shooting lodge (the original Rimmon Hut). From here walk down the moor heading to a point at the left end of Ravenstones, clearly visible (unless the clag is down) on the opposite edge of the deep valley that separates the two cliffs. This should take you over the top of Standing Stones! About 10 to 15 minutes from the car to the base of the crag and about double that on the return journey.

OTHER GUIDEBOOK -
A more complete list of routes at Standing Stones is published in the 1988 BMC *Moorland Gritstone* guidebook.

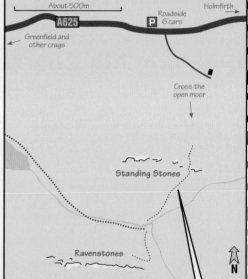

CONDITIONS

A splendid cliff, wild and remote feeling, south facing, ten minutes from the road - and a downhill approach - what more could you want? The cliff has not been especially popular in the past and the wings in particular are inclined to be grassy - a little more traffic would soon clean up the worst of this. The cliff can give good climbing in winter on calm days, but takes a couple of days to dry after rain. Parts of the crag can be sandy with grit washed down from the moor above after rain.

Chris Craggs on *Womanless Wall* (VS 4c) at the Standing Stones. *Page 211*
Photo: Sherri Davy

Staffordshire
Whaley Bridge
Kinder
Bleaklow
Chew
Lancashire
Cheshire
Den Lane
Running Hill Pits
Alderman
Upperwood Q
Standing Stones
Ravenstones
Dovestones
Rob's Rocks
Wimberry

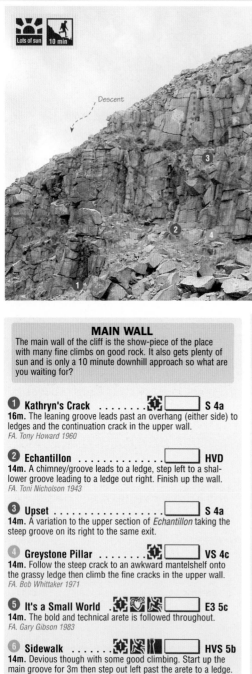

Lots of sun | **10 min**

Descent

MAIN WALL
The main wall of the cliff is the show-piece of the place with many fine climbs on good rock. It also gets plenty of sun and is only a 10 minute downhill approach so what are you waiting for?

① Kathryn's Crack .... **S 4a**
16m. The leaning groove leads past an overhang (either side) to ledges and the continuation crack in the upper wall.
FA. Tony Howard 1960

② Echantillon .... **HVD**
14m. A chimney/groove leads to a ledge, step left to a shallower groove leading to a ledge out right. Finish up the wall.
FA. Toni Nicholson 1943

③ Upset .... **S 4a**
14m. A variation to the upper section of *Echantillon* taking the steep groove on its right to the same exit.

④ Greystone Pillar .... **VS 4c**
14m. Follow the steep crack to an awkward mantelshelf onto the grassy ledge then climb the fine cracks in the upper wall.
FA. Bob Whittaker 1971

⑤ It's a Small World **E3 5c**
14m. The bold and technical arete is followed throughout.
FA. Gary Gibson 1983

⑥ Sidewalk ...... **HVS 5b**
14m. Devious though with some good climbing. Start up the main groove for 3m then step out left past the arete to a ledge. Take the cracked wall rightwards to a ledge and a direct finish.
FA. Bob Whittaker 1971

⑦ Smiler's Corner .... **HS 4b**
14m. A great line. The long and interesting groove at the left end of the area of smoother rock. More traffic would help shift some of the grass that is accumulating on the route!
FA. Toni Nicholson 1943

⑧ Pinocchio .... **VS 4c**
14m. A thin crack leads to a good ledge, then climb the slab to the groove and follow it to a crusty exit out to the right.
FA. Tony Howard 1962

⑨ Digital Dilemma **E2 5c**
14m. The thin cracks in the pillar are finger-wreckers. Follow them slightly leftwards to their end then finish out right.
FA. Nadim Siddiqui 1982

⑩ Guillotine .... **S 4b**
12m. Another good line. The right-facing chimney/corner starting from a ledge which is reached through the overhangs.
FA. Tony Howard 1961

⑪ Fallen Heroes **E1 5b**
12m. The steep hand-jamming crack up the left-hand side of the leaning wall is one of the best hereabouts; sustained and pumpy but well-protected. The moves to access the ledge just above mid-height are a real puzzler.
FA. Allan Wolfenden 1972

⑫ Brainchild **E4 6b**
12m. Climb the wall direct with a huge undercut move where pebbles used to be, or loop onto *Fallen Heroes* (E3 5c) then head to the right side of the wall to finish.
FA. Gary Gibson 1982 and by Paul Clarke 1982 after popping the pebble.

⑬ Vivien .... **S 4a**
16m. Yet another fine line. Climb the wall to a ledge and the base of the excellent parallel cracks. Up these with interest.
FA. Tony Howard 1960

⑭ Prunin' the Duck . . . . [____] **E2 5c**
16m. Climb the arete direct with a difficult start over a bulge.
FA. Bill Birch 1989

⑮ Scratchnose Crack . . . . 🔲🔲 [____] **VS 5a**
16m. The hanging groove is awkward to enter and easier above. The name suggests not to get in too deep at the roof!
FA. Paul Seddon 1960

⑯ Papillon . . . . [____] **E1 5b**
16m. Climb the slender pillar, reaching its base from *Twin Crack Corner* and avoiding any escape routes
FA. Bill Birch 1989

⑰ Twin Crack Corner . . . . . . 🔲 [____] **VS 4b**
16m. Climb *Scratchnose* to the first ledge then step right and follow the excellent twin-cracked groove throughout. Classic.
FA. Paul Seddon 1960

⑱ False Prospects . . . . 🔲 [____] **HVS 5a**
16m. Climb the corner past a roof to reach the hanging arete on the right. Continue up this and the diagonal crack above.
FA. Con Carey 1982

⑲ Fairy Nuff . . . . 🔲🔲 [____] **VS 4c**
18m. A real classic! Climb the wall below the square roof then traverse leftwards to the arete. Follow this before stepping right to enter and finish up the exposed hanging crack.
FA. Paul Seddon 1960

⑳ Leprechauner . . . . . . 🔲🔲 [____] **HVS 5a**
16m. The huge soaring groove is a bit of a battle, especially where the crack is widest. Large gear (the bigger the better) is a good idea. As the name suggests - inclined to be green.
FA. Graham West 1960

㉑ Kremlin Wall . . 🔲🔲🔲🔲 [____] **E1 5c**
14m. The thin crack splitting the centre of the fine smooth wall is approached easily and climbed directly with difficulty especially for short, fat-fingered individuals. The crux is low down.
FA. Mick Wrigley (2 points) 1969. FFA. John Allen 1973

㉒ Layback -a-daisical 🔲🔲🔲 [____] **VS 4b**
14m. Follow a groove rightwards to the roof, move left and climb the bold and strenuous crack to a juggy finish out right.
FA. Tony Howard 1960

㉓ Obyoyo . . . . 🔲 [____] **HVS 5b**
14m. Climb the wall to the roof then gain the hanging crack on the right with difficulty. Once established, finish more easily.
FA. Tony Howard 1961

㉔ The Trouble with Women is.. 🔲 [____] **E1 5b**
14m. Climb directly up the left-hand side of the face, the crux being the upper section. And the trouble actually is.... what?
FA. Chris Hardy 1985

㉕ Womanless Wall . . . . 🔲 [____] **VS 4c**
18m. A fine and open classic. Trend left up the lower wall to a large flake, move up to some big rounded pockets then swing back right to a final steep crack. *Photo page 209.*
FA. Tony Howard 1958

㉖ Stuck . . . . 🔲🔲🔲 [____] **E4 6a**
12m. Climb the right-hand side of the wall via a blind crack and a couple of small flakes to a finish up the easier wall above.
FA. Gary Gibson 1983

㉗ Unstuck . . . . 🔲🔲 [____] **E4 6b**
10m. The pebbly wall is climbed desperately to the twin flakes on *Stuck* hoping they and you both stay stuck.
FA. Paul Clark 1990s

㉘ Diddley Dum Overhang . . . 🔲 [____] **HVS 5b**
10m. Tackle the tough finger-crack above the cave recess. One of those ancient VS's from 'the olden days'!
FA. Graham West 1960s

Staffordshire
Whaley Bridge
Kinder
Bleaklow
Chew
Lancashire
Cheshire
Den Lane
Running Hill Pits
Alderman
Upperwood Q
Standing Stones
Ravenstones
Dovestones
Rob's Rocks
Wimberry

TRANQUILLITY AREA

Two short walls on separate tiers. Although the area looks a bit grotty at first acquaintance there is a collection of worthwhile wall climbs and some testing cracks.

1 Pocked Wall .... VS 4c
10m. Follow the spoor-trail across the face, exiting rightwards.
FA. Tony Howard 1958

2 Touch of Spring .... S 4a
10m. The juggy crack to an awkward but well-protected exit.
FA. Tony Jones 1960

3 Yorkshire Longfellow .. E3 5c
10m. The centre of the face to a break (small runners) and a delicate finish up the steep wall above.
FA. Simon Royston 1996

4 Prolapse E2 5c
10m. Start up *Yorkshire Longfellow* but follow lumps, bumps and dimples rightwards to a finish up the arete.
FA. Gary Gibson 1982

The next two climbs cross both tiers of the crag.

5 Postman's Knock .... S 4a
16m. Follow the arete on the left edge of the lower wall to grotty ledges and its upper continuation via a couple of cracks.
FA. Brian Hodgkinson 1960

6 Pygmy Wall .... HVS 5b
16m. The pocketed wall and tricky layaway moves lead to a shallow groove then ledges. Thin cracks above give the way on.
FA. Bob Whittaker 1977

7 The Ghoul E2 5b
14m. The left-hand of a pair of slanting cracks. Ghoulish indeed.
FA. Bob Whittaker 1977

8 The Slanting Horror ...... VS 4c
14m. The right-hand crack is easier and better, despite its name.
FA. Paul Seddon 1960

9 Wits' End E1 5c
14m. Boulder up the lower wall to the horizontal then sprint up the upper section via a series of long reaches.
FA. Steve Bancroft 1973

10 Tranquillity .... HVS 5a
14m. Mantel onto the niched ledge then climb into and up the steep groove above.
FA. Bill Tweedale 1971

11 Fish-meal and Revenge E4 6a
12m. The centre of the wall on small spaced holds to a gripping slap for the top. A Friend 1.5 is fairly crucial despite being difficult to place.
FA. John Smith 1987

12 The Diamond E2 5b
14m. Climb the wall trending right to a bold finish up the blunt arete on slopers.
FA. Paul Cropper 1982

Lots of sun | 10 min

Change in viewing angle

Recent rockfall

Descent

Staffordshire
Whaley Bridge
Kinder
Bleaklow
Chew
Lancashire
Cheshire
Den Lane
Running Hill Pits
Alderman
Upperwood Q
Standing Stones
Ravenstones
Dovestones
Rob's Rocks
Wimberry

① Wobbling Corner .... HVD
12m. Wobble-a-way up the crack in the west-facing wall to a ledge and short finishing groove.
FA. Tony Howard 1957

② Piece of Pie .... HVS 5a
14m. Climb steeply and swing left to gain a ledge (on *Wobbling Corner*). Step out right onto the arete then follow cracks rightwards to ledges. Escape up or off.
FA. Tony Howard 1964

③ Right of Pie E3 5c
14m. Follow the flake to its end then make hard moves to reach and stand on the one really good hold on the pitch. Continue warily up the steep slab to finish.
FA. Paul Cropper 1982

④ Fat Old Sun E1 5b
12m. Teeter leftwards up the ramp to a thin crack that is tricky to start. The wall above is easier.
FA. Paul Cropper 1982

⑤ Jiggery Pokery E1 5b
12m. Climb the ramp and shallow scoop above it to a long reach for a good ledge. Once stood on this, things ease; finish up the crack above.
FA. Tony Howard 1964

⑥ Small c. E2 5b
12m. Climb the right-hand side of the wall using a shallow groove and make a committing long reach for the ledge. Escape off to the left.
FA. Colin Brooks 1977

⑦ 17 Shades .... HVD
14m. Climb the chimney and trog left along the ledge system at its top to an escape up a crack just short of the left-hand arete.
FA. Tony Howard 1960

⑧ The Annoying Little Man E4 6b
12m. From the base of the large flake (left of the rockfall) climb the face with difficulty. I wonder just who is it referring to?
FA. Steve Delderfield 1993

LEFT TWIN BUTTRESS and OCEAN WALL
The Standing Stones reserve one of the best bits of rock until last. Tucked away on the far right, in a grassy hollow the Right-hand Twin is the excellent venue of *Ocean Wall*. The Left-hand Twin also has some worthwhile climbs.

Across the gully to the right is the final decent bit of rock on the cliff, home to several good routes and well worth a visit.

⑨ Kon-Tiki Korner .... S 4a
12m. Climb easy rock to gain access to the the long groove in the west-facing wall. At its top escape off left, or better, finish up the juggy wall just to the right.
FA. Tony Howard 1961

⑩ Gut Feeling E3 6b
12m. Follow the line of small holds up the diagonal fissure in the steep and narrow side-wall. A side-runner is normal and even sensible at the grade.
FA. Gary Gibson 1982

⑪ The Ocean's Border E3 6a
14m. Climb the roofed-in groove in the arete to its closure then make difficult blind moves up and right past the lip to ledges and a welcome rest. The thin crack in the headwall (*Oceanside*) is the best finish.
FA. Gary Gibson 1983 Oceanside, Paul Cropper 1982

⑫ Dredger E2 6b
14m. The square-cut arete is climbed with difficulty and no gear to ledges at 10m. The *Oceanside* finish is best, though the awkward hanging groove to its right was the original way if you want to be historically correct.
Chris Addy 1977

⑬ Ocean Wall E1 5b
16m. Climb the tricky wall to the upper of a pair of ledges then climb out left to the centre of the wall, up a short crack then swing left again to reach the exposed, juggy arete for a well-positioned finale - sustained. Care with rope work required if you want to enjoy the experience to the full.
FA. Malc Baxter 1960

Not the most prepossessing of quarries although the best of the routes are worth calling in for. The place is only a few minutes from the road, and it also gets the morning sun. Recently the quarry has been given a make-over and now has a good collection of clean climbs, many of which follow strong lines - get them done and help keep them in decent condition!

ACCESS

The quarry is owned by a Mr. Crowther who lives in the farm opposite. He allows climbing if you phone first (01457 870233). The place is occasionally used for clay-pigeon shooting so please make the effort. You can also call at the farm - beware the big baying dogs!

APPROACH Also see map on page 182

The quarry is situated above the A635 Holmfirth to Greenfield road, which is still known as the 'The Isle of Skye road' after a long-gone pub. There is parking for several cars in a lay-by on opposite side of the road to the farm (you did phone didn't you?) just downhill from the gated track that leads up into the quarry. The approach takes less than five minutes from here.

A SPRING CLEAN

Mention should be made of the hard work of Allen Barker and Gordon Mason who gave the whole crag a good cleaning in the summer of 2000, coming up with a selection of new routes in the progress. Thanks to their effort the place is now definitely worth a visit or two.

CONDITIONS

With its east-facing aspect the cliff gets the sun until early afternoon, and as such is a good venue for early risers. Some sections of the quarry take drainage (or even spout impressive waterfalls) and are inclined to be sandy after rain, taking several days to come into prime condition. Fortunately several of the buttresses jut forward enough to stay dry, the great classic of *Renaissance* (E4 6b) is especially notable in this respect so you have no excuse for not calling in and getting it done!

OTHER GUIDEBOOK - A more complete list of routes at Upperwood Quarry is published in the 1988 BMC *Moorland Gritstone* guidebook.

BOULDERING - The quarry isn't a prime bouldering venue but there is one problem worth seeking out. To the left of the quarries is a 6m bullet-scarred wall tackled centrally by the extended boulder problem -
Psycho 2, V4 (6b) (*FA. Chris Hardy 1981*) - said by some to be the best route here!

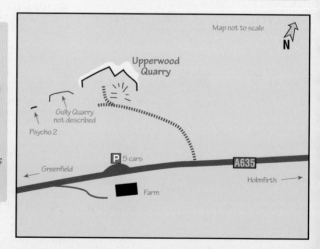

Staffordshire · Whaley Bridge · Kinder · Bleaklow · Chew · Lancashire · Cheshire · Den Lane · Running Hill Pits · Alderman · Upperwood Q · Standing Stones · Ravenstones · Dovestones · Rob's Rocks · Wimberry

Mike Appleton climbing *Renaissance* (E4 6a) Upperwood Quarry. *Page 217*

UPPERWOOD QUARRY *Left*

Morning | 3 min

Descent ◄ - - - - -

Side tabs (left margin): Staffordshire · Whaley Bridge · Kinder · Bleaklow · Chew · Lancashire · Cheshire · Den Lane · Running Hill Pits · Alderman · Upperwood Q · Standing Stones · Ravenstones · Dovestones · Rob's Rocks · Wimberry

UPPERWOOD QUARRY LEFT

The left-hand side of the quarry has some powerful lines and some worthwhile routes. The whole place has been neglected in the past though a little traffic could help keep the place clean.
ACCESS - Phone 01457 870233 and ask! Permission is usually granted if there is no clay-pigeon shooting going on.

①　Little Running Water . . . . . 🔲 **VS 4c**
16m. The frequently water-washed parallel cracks on the far left are approached by a tricky bulge and exited rightwards.

②　Big Heap . . . . 🔲 **HVS 5b**
14m. The steep crack is hardest at the overhangs.
FA. Graham West late 1950s. FFA. Bob Whittaker 1973

③　The Green Meanies . . . . 🔲 **E2 5b**
14m. Gain the square arete from *Big Heap*. Proves to be strenuous and then delicate.
FA. Paul Cropper 1980

④　Heap Big Corner . . . . 🔲 **HVS 5a**
14m. The angular corner gives a worthwhile route when clean and is much less of the dump than the name suggests.
FA. Graham West late 1950s

⑤　Cochise . . . . 🔲 **HVS 5b**
14m. Traverse right from the corner to reach the crack in the wall and power up it. The **Direct Start** is **E'sa**, a dynamic **E3 6a**.

⑥　Blazing Saddles 🔲🔲🔲🔲 🔲 **E4 6a**
16m. Climb the wall to the start of the diagonal crack then continue in a direct line by bold, sustained and reachy climbing. A Friend 3.5 in the crusty break is semi-essential.
FA. Allan Barker 2000

⑦　Little Bighorn . . . . 🔲🔲🔲 🔲 **E5 6a**
20m. The prominent diagonal crack is a bit of a battle! Approach it via the bold and technical wall of *Blazing Saddles* then thug rightwards until a finish can be made up the thin cracks on the left.
FA. Tony Howard 1963. FFA. Steve Bancroft 1978

⑧　Tomahawk . . . . 🔲🔲 🔲 **E4 6a**
16m. The thin once-pegged crack was one of the original routes of the quarry. It is fingery and awkward to protect.
FA. Graham West late 1950s. FFA. Steve Bancroft 1978

⑨　Totem Corner . . . . 🔲 **HVS 5a**
14m. The angular right-facing groove has recently been cleaned up; get it done before it turns back into a greasy pole.
FA. Tony Howard early 1960s

⑩　Hawkwind . . . . 🔲 **E1 5b**
14m. The thin crack just right of the groove is gained from its base. At the top step back into the corner to finish. The gymnastic **Direct Start** makes the route into a worthwhile **E1 5c**.
FA. Brian Cropper 1981. Direct Start - Allen Barker 2000

⑪　Giteche Manitou . . . . 🔲 **E1 5b**
18m. Take either start to *Hawkwind* then move out right to climb the wall and flake trending right to finish.
FA. Paul Cropper 1982

⑫　Cowboys and Indians . . 🔲🔲 🔲 **E1 5c**
24m. Start as for the previous route but continue the traverse all the way out to an exciting finish on the far arete, thrilling.
FA. Allan Barker 2000

⑬　Play it Safe . . . . 🔲🔲 🔲 **E4 6a**
16m. Climb to the bulge then continue up curving groove and slab on an array of indifferent pockets. One ancient peg runner.
FA. Loz Francomb 1980

⑭　Piece of Pipe . . . . . . 🔲🔲 🔲 **HVS 5b**
18m. Climb into the diagonal crack and follow it with difficulty to better holds where the crack widens. Finish steeply.
FA. Graham West late 1950s. FFA. Jim Campbell 1967

⑮　Pipe-line . . . . 🔲🔲 🔲 **E3 5c**
18m. Swarm up the evil narrowing slot (giant cams can be a saviour) until the upper section of *Piece of Pipe* can be gained.
FA. Jim Campbell 1968

Staffordshire
Whaley Bridge
Kinder
Bleaklow
Chew
Lancashire
Cheshire
Den Lane
Running Hill Pits
Alderman
Upperwood Q
Standing Stones
Ravenstones
Dovestones
Rob's Rocks
Wimberry

UPPERWOOD QUARRY RIGHT

The main feature of the quarry is the central jutting overhang that catches your attention on entering the place. Originally bolted (as *The Walum Olum* - A3, Tony Howard 1969) it is now home to three desperate routes including the classic *Renaissance*, arguably the best route in the quarry.

⑯ Waiting for an Alibi 🔲🔲🔲 ⬜ E5 6b
8m. The hairline crack and bold wall are taxing. One poor peg runner and little else to help you along the way.
FA. Dougie Hall 1986

⑰ Pipe of Peace . . . . 🔲 ⬜ VS 4b
8m. Climb across ledgy ground to reach the short-lived crack which was one of the earliest free routes in the quarry.
FA. Tony Howard 1959

⑱ The Screaming Abdabs . 🔲🔲 ⬜ E3 6a
8m. Start from ledges and balance up the bold blunt arete above a worrying drop. One old peg runner just about protects.
FA. Ian Carr 1984

⑲ Turtle . . . . 🔲 ⬜ E1 5b
18m. Climb rock and two veg into the open groove (ancient bolt runner) then follow this to a tricky rightward exit round the capping overhang. The best route of its grade in the quarry. *Photo page 41.*
FA. Bill Birch 1969 FFA. Steve Bancroft 1978

⑳ Edge Your Bets . . . . 🔲🔲🔲 ⬜ E5 6c
18m. The left wall of the great prow with a loop to the right at mid-height to utilise a vital pocket. Two peg runners.
FA. P Kendell 1970 FFA. Dougie Hall 1986

㉑ Renaissance . . . . . 🔲🔲🔲 ⬜ E4 6a
20m. Makes 'El Cap' look like a giant granite monolith! Climb *Forked Tongue* then from a highish runner balance and teeter out left to the arete and a bold finish. The peg on the next route should be avoided if at all possible. *Photo page 215.*
FA. Tony Howard (reached by bolting the huge overhang) 1969
FFA. Steve Bancroft (the best of his Chew classics) 1978

㉒ Give the Dogg a Bone 🔲🔲🔲 ⬜ E5 6b
20m. The technical and fingery right-hand wall of the arete passing stacked (and unclippable) glued pegs. A good climb that had to be done, though its a pity the integrity of *Renaissance* suffered from the placing of the fixed gear.
FA. John Smith 1987

㉓ Forked Tongue . . . . 🔲 ⬜ HVS 5b
16m. The thin cracks are approached easily up grass and are tricky to start but soon ease off. Well-protected by small wires.
FA. Graham West late 1950s FFA. Gerry Peel 1972

㉔ Paleface . . . . 🔲 ⬜ VS 4c
16m. Scramble to the crack and groove and jam it to a short section of laybacking and an awkward mantelshelf exit.
FA. Paul Seddon 1960

㉕ How . . . . 🔲🔲 ⬜ HVS 5a
16m. The big butch groove is approached over mixed terrain.
FA. Graham West late 1950s

㉖ Iron Road . . . . 🔲🔲 ⬜ E3 5c
16m. A diagonal line across the smooth wall right of the big groove. Cross a block (thread), move out to the arete, step back left then right before finishing direct.
FA. Bill Birch 1969 FFA. (by a more devious line) Jonny Woodward 1982

㉗ Renegade . . . . 🔲 ⬜ HVS 5a
16m. The twisting leaning groove, starting from a block (thread) and finishing up the arete on the right.
FA. Graham West late 1950s FFA. Gerry Peel 1972

㉘ Wampum Wall . . . . 🔲 ⬜ S 4a
18m. Climb leftwards into the groove and climb it until the arete on the left can be gained for an exposed finish.
FA. Tony Howard 1959

To the right are about another dozen or so routes, the best of which are General Custard E3 6a (Chris Hardy 1984), up the narrow buttress 15m right, and beyond this Adios Amigo E2 5c (Allen Barker 2000) and Tickled Pink E1 5b (Malc Baxter 1988) using the huge block in the break to access the slab above. The former heads left to the exciting arete and the latter goes direct; both are worth seeking out.

ALDERMAN

This mini-peak is the most popular summit in the area and is home to a small set of generally short climbs, in a superb sunny setting and on great quality rock. The outward view across the Chew Valley reservoirs and into the heart of the Saddleworth and Wilderness Moors is exceptional. The flog from the parking is a bit of a lung-buster (good Alpine training) but only takes a steady 15 minutes and of course it is well worth it. Unusually for grit, most the routes in the centre of the cliff are two pitches in length - split at mid-height by a wide ledge, and this gives an extra attraction to the place.

OTHER GUIDEBOOK -
A more complete list of routes at Alderman is published in the 1988 BMC *Moorland Gritstone* guidebook.

APPROACH Also see map on page 182

There is extensive and free parking in the Binn Green picnic area directly below the conical hill with the cliff just below its crest. Cross the road and follow the cobbly track for 50m to a gap (sheep-feeder in situ early 2003) in the fence on the right, then attack the near vertical grass slopes direct, avoiding the very steepest terrain by looping out right. Alternatively, and just a little easier, continue along the track for a further couple of hundred metres until it descends slightly and there is a collapsed field corner on the right. Cross the fence and zigzag up the slope heading slightly rightwards to the base of the cliff. Both approaches arrive at the well-trodden area right under *The Great Slab*.

CONDITIONS

Although there is only a small selection of routes here, the outlook is a fine as any in the Peak and the fact that several of the climbs run to two pitches makes them worthy of the walk up. It is possible to link a visit here with a walk over to the monument next to Pots and Pans Quarries (home to a reasonable selection of climbs - not described here) giving the prospect of an excellent mountain day out.

The cliff at Alderman faces south east and so is in the sun until mid-afternoon. The rock is clean and takes little drainage and so dries rapidly after rain. On the downside it is very exposed to the west wind.

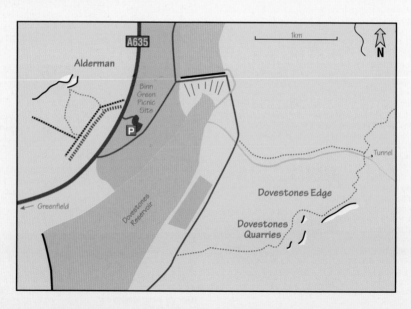

DESCENTS
From the top of the Lower Tier scramble up and left to escape. From the cliff top the easiest descent is down and left to join the route from the Lower Tier.

① Edgehog Flavour . . . . 🏴 [ ] **E1 5b**
m. A tasty treat up the right-hand side of the rounded pebbly rete on the far left-hand edge of the cliff.
A. Carl Dawson 1985

② Pygmy Wall . . . . 🏴 [ ] **HS 4b**
0m. Climb the slabby wall then trend right to finish by ptoeing up the very edge of the undercut face
A. Tony Howard 1958

③ E Route . . . . 🏃 [ ] **S 4b**
m. After a delicate start, the well-scratched slab leads to the vide and easy crack directly above.
A. Brian Hodgkinson 1958

④ F Route . . . . [ ] **S 4a**
m. The main groove and wide crack just to its right give an awkward but short-lived struggle.
A. Brian Hodgkinson 1958

⑤ Golden Wonder . . . . 🏴 [ ] **E1 5b**
3m. From a flat block swing out right to access the right-hand side of the arete then layback smartly (or jibber) up this. Jnprotected and with a pretty poor landing.
A. Chris Hardy 1982

⑥ Crispy Crack . . . . 🏴1 [ ] **HVS 5a**
3m. The attractive shallow seam/runnel that crosses the slab diagonally rightwards gives a good little pitch that surprisingly s easier to foot-traverse than to hand-traverse.
A. Tony Howard 1958

⑦ Rib and Face . . . . 🏴2 [ ] **VDiff**
l) 10m. Climb the easy angled rib in the back of the wide roove to a series of ledges then step left to a good stance.
2) 10m. The well-protected crack in the centre of the west-acing continuation wall gives a fine second pitch.
A. Tony Howard 1958

⑧ Cleft and Chimney . . . . . . 🏴1 [ ] **VDiff**
1) 10m. The rather green recessed groove leads without incident to the mid-height terrace and a stance.
2) 10m. The narrow chimney just above is awkward to enter due to its undercut base but then soon eases.
Malc's Flaky Finish - takes the flying flake left of the chimney and has some wild moves at **E2 5c**.
FA. Brian Hodgkinson mid 1950s. Flake Finish - Malc Baxter 1960s

⑨ Great Slab Arete . . . . 🏴1 [ ] **S 4a**
10m. Weave through the bulges (or pull over the lowest one - 4b) to gain and then climb the well-positioned arete on its right-hand side throughout.
FA. Brian Hodgkinson mid 1950s

⑩ Great Slab . . . . 🏴3 [ ] **VS 4c**
A fine climb though many teams only do the first pitch, earning themselves a 2-star tick.
1) 4c, 10m. The centre of the attractive slab gives good climbing with escalating interest with final tricky moves (good runners in the horizontal break) to reach its crest.
2) 4c, 10m. Move right to the fist crack in the upper wall and follow this until it is possible to swing left and mantel into the base of the wide finishing cleft.
A **Direct Finish** above the fist crack is a pumpy **HVS 5a**.
FA. Tony Howard mid 1950s

⑪ Great Slab Chimney . . . . [ ] **Diff**
10m. The rift to the right of *Great Slab* gives pleasant climbing up a good line. A worthwhile beginners' route
FA. Brian Hodgkinson mid 1950s

⑫ Great Slab Right . . . . [ ] **HVS 4c**
10m. The right-hand arete of the chimney is delicate and the nose directly above is strenuous - not well-protected.

⑬ Pebble Mill . . . . 🏴 [ ] **E2 5b**
8m. The rather crusty centre of the right-hand slab. Don't pull too hard on those pebbles
FA. Bill Birch 1986

Staffordshire
Whaley Bridge
Kinder
Bleaklow
Chew
Lancashire
Cheshire
Den Lane
Running Hill Pits
Alderman
Upperwood Q
Standing Stones
Ravenstones
Dovestones
Rob's Rocks
Wimberry

The Pits is a smallish set of quarries (8 in all) looking out over the Upper Tame Valley. Although individually quite small there are almost 150 routes here, pretty much covering the grade spectrum. Despite their name and the fact that they're rarely busy, their westerly aspect and quality rock make them worth a visit from afar when conditions are right. There are a number of excellent crack climbs here, some fine bold face routes, and some high quality fingery bouldering. Of the quarries, 1 and 2 are the prime venues after a dry spell, and there are some worthwhile routes in 5, 6, and 8. Number 4 (Back Quarry) is worth a visit just to see how neat and tidy the quarrymen can be when they really want to!

APPROACH Also see map on page 182

From the centre of Uppermill (when travelling north on the A670) take a right turn by the off licence and follow the road that climbs steadily uphill, passing a crossroads by Saddleworth Church. Continue uphill passing the Cross Keys to arrive at limited parking at a cross-road (two of the roads - the right-hand and straight on branches - are no more than grass tracks). Follow the deeply incised track ahead uphill for ten minutes to a gate. Number 1 and 2 quarries are here on the right, whilst No 8 lies leftwards diagonally down the bank another three minutes away. Nos 7, 6 and 5 are reached by the old track that leads past the entrances to the quarries.

CONDITIONS

The Pits are a series of quarries cut socket-like, into the edge of Broadstone Hill. They are best avoided if the weather is poor, as the cloud tends to hug the hillside here. Under these conditions the quarries make a dreary venue and the lichen is at its worst. They might have been OK for aid climbing in days gone by but are no good for serious free climbing when these conditions prevail. Much better is to choose a fine summer's evening and enjoy these 'holes in the ground' when they are filled with glowing golden light and the rock is in prime condition, the outlook from the various quarries is superb and the place can then be enjoyed to the full.

BOULDERING - Although not a great venue there is some decent bouldering to be found in the quarries, especially in number Eight.

OTHER GUIDE-BOOK - A more complete list of routes at Running Hill Pits is published in the 1988 BMC *Moorland Gritstone* guidebook.

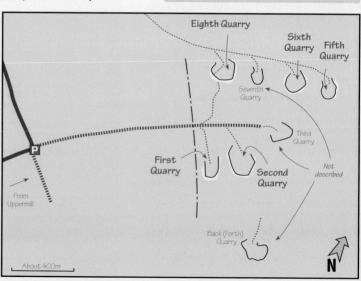

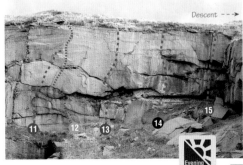

FIRST QUARRY

The first quarry reached from the car has some worthwhile crack climbs. The classic pumpy *Calamity Crack* is especially worthwhile, if somewhat arduous in execution.

1 Spider Crack . . . . **HVS 5c**
m. The thin crack just right of the left arete of the quarry to a nish up the proper jamming-crack on the right.
A. Bob Whittaker 1977

2 Nora Batty **E1 6a**
m. Attack the thinner, finger-shredding crack leading right out o the arete then back left to the solid jams of *Spider Crack*.
A. Clive Maybury 1983

3 Acarpous **E2 5b**
2m. Climb into the recess, pull out right for a breather on the rassy ledge then finish back leftwards up the slanting crack.
A. Chris Hardy 1987

4 Maquis **E1 5b**
2m. Take the steep and pumpy jamming-crack to the niche here it joins and finishes as for *Acarpous*.
A. Bill Tweedale 1966

5 Flush Pipe **E1 5c**
0m. Climb the tricky arete than make a swift mantel to reach he rest on *Maquis*. Finish direct up the short-lived crusty crack.
A. Bob Whittaker 1977

6 Gull-wing **E2 5c**
4m. Start up the wider left-hand crack then swing left on a line f flat holds to access a steep groove. Climb this past the roof nd the strength-sapping wall on the right to the top.
A. Paul Braithwaite 1978

7 Mimosa **E2 5c**
2m. Climb the main right-trending crack strenuously passing a seful hole a short distance from the top. Use the thinner right-hand crack when needed.
A. Tony Howard (1 point of aid). 1966 FFA. John Smith 1980

8 Calamity Crack **E4 6a**
4m. Short but action packed. The thin leaning crack is an phill struggle on thin-hand-jams and fat finger-locks though rotection is superb; which way to face is the real conundrum. he old wooden wedges manage to get in the way and the crux s where you don't want it, just below the top! *Photo page 225.*
A. Tony Howard (aid) 1962. FFA. Steve 'that man again' Bancroft 1972

9 Gargantua **E1 5b**
14m. Bridge the groove to a niche. Pull out of this into another niche and then escape rightwards. Steep and strenuous.

10 Godzilla **E3 6a**
8m. Start up the groove then layback the right-hand side of the arete until a bit of a 'pop' is need to reach the slab. Exit left.
FA. Chris Hardy 1987

11 Kaptain Klepton **E1 5c**
8m. Climb a flake to reach the horizontal jams then tackle the blank wall, trending right to finish.
FA. Chris Hardy 1987

12 Mickey Thin . . . . **HVS 5a**
8m. Climb to a hanging flake then follow it leftwards to a slim-tips crack. Up this to a mantel and easier finish.
FA. Mick Shaw 1974

13 It Only Takes Two to Tango . **E2 5b**
8m. Climb out of the left side of the grotty recess to reach a narrow ramp then finish direct via thin cracks. Often wet.
FA. Gary Gibson 1982

14 Tin Man **E4 6b**
7m. The right-hand side of the undercut wall passing a peg.
FA. John Smith 1989

15 Flue Pipe **E1 5c**
6m. The hanging crack on the far right is okay, though sadly, escape is too easy an option.
FA. Gordon Mason 1977

Staffordshire
Whaley Bridge
Kinder
Bleaklow
Chew
Lancashire
Cheshire
Den Lane
Running Hill Pits
Alderman
Upperwood Q
Standing Stones
Ravenstones
Dovestones
Rob's Rocks
Wimberry

SECOND QUARRY - LEFT
An open aspect and worthwhile routes make this quarry the most popular in the complex. The left-hand wall is the showpiece of the quarry with the clean *Spanner Wall* attracting most attention.

❶ Tighten Up Yer Nuts — **E4 6a**
10m. A fiercely-thin finger-traverse with a particularly hard move to reach the jugs and a sprint finish. Memorable.
FA. Dougie Hall (onsight solo) 1987

❷ Iguanodon — **E5 6b**
10m. Bold and fierce. The blank wall is climbed rightwards by committing moves to better holds where more hard (and even more committing) moves allow access to a shallow groove. Climb this to safety.
FA. Jonny Woodward (onsight solo) 1980

❸ Folies Bergeres — **HS 4b**
12m. The first crack right of the main angle gives a short tussle and is especially awkward at the start.
FA. Bill Tweedale 1966

❹ Lolita — **HS 4b**
12m. A precocious little number up the wall and crack.
FA. Pete Oldham 1966

❺ Harvest Moon — **E4 6b**
12m. Climb into the hanging groove (ancient peg) swing right to another, then make desperate moves to reach good flat holds in the open groove above. Finish up this carefully.
FA. Chris Hardy 1984

❻ The Connection — **E4 6b**
14m. The obvious link-up gives the best way up the wall which is both bold and committing. Replacing the pegs with decent fixed gear would lower the grade to a stiff E3.
FA. Mike Watson 1987

❼ Spanner Wall — **E2 5b**
14m. From *Dead Dog Crack* traverse to the spanner (its base is a bit thin, but threading it is better than nothing) then balance up the precarious shallow groove above and right.
FA. Dougie Hall 1978

❽ Dead Dog Crack — **VS 4c**
8m. The left-hand of the cracks that form an inverted Y.
FA. Graham West 1962

❾ Cave Crack — **VS 4c**
8m. The right-hand arm of the inverted Y.
FA. Graham West 1962

❿ Midsummer — **S 4a**
8m. The flaky right arete of the wall starting just to the right.
FA. Bob Whittaker 1972

⓫ Hazy Groove — **VDiff**
8m. The deep groove stepping right into its extension to finish.
FA. Bob Whittaker 1972

⓬ The Cracks — **S 4a**
8m. Climb the cracks to an exit left or right.

⓭ Breakdown — **HVS 5**
8m. The thin crack in the steep slab is pleasantly technical.
FA. Brian Cropper (1 peg) 1974 FFA Bob Whittaker 1975

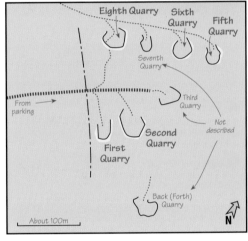

SECOND QUARRY - CENTRE

Short walls of quality rock. The cliff faces into the setting sun and the location is tranquil; add this to the other sections of the quarry and the place is well worth a visit.

❶ Yorick's Crack **E5 6c**
0m. The thin right-trending seam is superbly desperate. It was only pegged a few times in antiquity and so, alas, has maintained its cruel razor-sharp edges.
A. Dougie Hall 1988

❷ Overhanging Chimney .... **VS 4c**
10m. The main groove develops from cracks to a wider rift which leads to a rightward exit over the bulge.
A. F. Farrar (2 pegs) 1972. FFA. Brian Cropper 1974

❸ Sagittarius Flake .. **E5 6b**
10m. The hairline crack leads with great difficulty to a final lunge or massive stretch for the top edge.
A. Paul Cropper (1 peg) 1978. FFA. Nick Colton 1979

❹ Scoop de Grace **E5 7a**
12m. A stunningly technical wall leads into the precarious scoop which is followed rightwards to easy ground. The tall may find the start 'only' 6c and the short might consider it impossible although the block to the left may be a help. Scooptastic!
A. Dougie Hall 1987

❺ Phaestus **E4 5c**
8m. 'Walk' up the ramp leftwards and climb the blunt arete into more harrowing territory and a tough mantel above a big drop.
A. Bob Whittaker 1972

❻ Windbreaker **E2 5b**
6m. From the toe of the ramp blast up the centre of the 'blank' slab on a continuously surprising set of holds.
A. Bob 'the blaster' Whittaker 1974

❼ Cochybondhu **E2 5c**
6m. The rib on the right-hand side of the slab gives precarious laybacking; once committed, do or fly!
A. Bob Whittaker 1974

❽ Kneepad .... **HVS 5b**
6m. The awkward groove is ... awkward! Knees might well help.
A. Bob Whittaker 1974

❾ Crosstie .... **VS 5a**
12m. Mantel onto the tip of the slab with difficulty then trend right until a precarious move accesses the V-groove of *Groove-V Baby* and a rightward exit.
FA. Bob Whittaker 1974

❿ Pipe Spanner **E1 5c**
8m. Climb the centre of the slab to a hard sloping exit.
FA. Dougie Hall 1980

⓫ Pipe Inspector **E3 5c**
10m. Start as for *Pipe Spanner* but move right then climb direct to a hard exit balancing up into the tiny left-facing groove.
FA. Chris Booth 1985

⓬ Groove-V Baby .... **VS 4c**
10m. Follow the groove on the right-hand side of the slab (small wires) as it leads pleasantly to a rightward exit.
FA. Tony Howard 1969

Staffordshire

Whaley Bridge

Kinder

Bleaklow

Chew

Lancashire

Cheshire

Den Lane

Running Hill Pits

Alderman

Upperwood Q

Standing Stones

Ravenstones

Dovestones

Rob's Rocks

Wimberry

Not much sun | **10 min** | **Sheltered**

Iron Bar

SECOND QUARRY - RIGHT

The final wall lies beyond a grass slope and faces north. It is split by a fine set of cracks, most of which are worth doing when in condition and well worth steering clear of when not!

❶ Dusty Arete . . . . ⚡ **Diff**
12m. The ledgy wall is climbed close to the arete. It has a useful iron bar runner and not too much else in the way of gear.
FA. Pete Oldham 1966

❷ Midgebite Express . . . . . . 🪨 **E2 6a**
12m. The arete on its right-hand side.
FA. Kevin Thaw 1989

❸ William the Conkerer **E1 5b**
12m. Climb the wall 2m right of the grotty groove (*Sardonicous* HVS 5b). It is often rather green hence its original moniker.
FA. Chris Hardy as Green Wall 1984

❹ Paradise Crack . . . . **HS 4b**
12m. The first crack in the long north-facing wall is not a patch on its Stanage namesake and is probably a grade harder!
FA. Pete Oldham 1966

❺ Cameo . . . . **VS 4c**
12m. The central crack of the trio is a little less of a gem than its Wilton twin though still worth doing when clean.
FA. Bill Tweedale 1966

❻ Riddler . . . . ⚡ **HVS 5a**
12m. The right-hand crack is the pick of the trio. Passing the mid-height niche is the crux though the interest is well-maintained throughout.

❼ Pantagruel . . . . ⚡🔧 **HVS 5a**
12m. The parallel cracks give gruelling jamming that might well leave you panting. Starting up the right and finishing up the left is the easiest combination.
FA. Bill Tweedale 1966

❽ Mangled Digit . . . . . . ⚡🖐 **E3 6a**
14m. The thin wiggling crack is hard on the fingers and gives reachy moves between sketchy jams. Protection is excellent.
FA. Ian Carr 1982

❾ Plumb Line . . . . ⚡🔧 **VS 4c**
14m. An excellent straight jamming crack swallows all the gear you can carry. Despite the picture in the 1988 Moorland Grit guide, it isn't an overhanging horror.
FA. Mick Quinn 1966

❿ Passport to the Pits . . . 🪨🖐 **E5 6b**
14m. An eliminate up the wall right of *Plumbline*.
FA. Dougie Hall 1989

⓫ Liquor, Loose Women and Double Cross . . . . . . ⚡🪨 **E5 6c**
12m. Direct up the thin balancy wall past a peg.
FA. John Smith 1989

⓬ Sodom . . . . ⚡🪨 **HVS 5c**
12m. Boulder up the wall to reach the left-hand crack which gives pleasant jamming. It can also be approached from the next climb at a lower grade.
FA. 1966 Bill Tweedale (4 pegs). FFA. Bob Whittaker 1972

⓭ Gomorrah . . . . ⚡🖐 **E1 5b**
12m. The right-hand crack gives good finger jamming on solid lockers with the quality of runners you might hope for.
FA. Ian Lonsdale 1977

⓮ Breakin' for a Bogey ⚡🖐🔧 **E6 6c**
12m. The thin and fingery wall past a peg.
FA. Kevin Thaw 1989

⓯ Cosmic Enforcer . . . . 🪙🕳 **E2 5c**
6m. From the bank on the right, swing left and climb the short but exposed left-hand side of the arete. A runner up and right is a good idea (hard for the short to place).
FA. Colin Brooks 1983

⓰ Unctious . . . . 🕳🪨 **S 4c**
4m. A short wall with a fingery start and a myriad harder variations for those of a bouldering bent.
FA. Ian Lonsdale 1977

Eighth Quarry

EIGHTH QUARRY

Good rock with worthwhile mini-routes or bouldering.
APPROACHES - From the gate just before the First Quarry,
cross the fence and head downhill, slightly rightwards, to
enter the back of the Eighth Quarry. From the front of this a
track leads past Seven and Six and on round to Five.

❶ Firefly . . . . **HVS 6a**
8m. The the left-hand side of the wall via a crack climbed on
'tips' jams. Short but sweet, keep your nails filed for this one.
FA. Bob Whittaker 1983

❷ Duckdoo . . . . **S 4b**
8m. The wide leaning crack is a struggle. Starting up the cracks
to the right is an alternative **4c** variation.
FA. Chris Hardy 1979

❸ A Fist Full of Daggers **E2 6b**
8m. Another searingly thin crack-line giving technical finger
jamming of the 'ouch' kind and a l-o-n-g reach to finish.
FA. Chris Hardy 1987

❹ Deliver Us From Evil . . . . . . **HVS 5b**
6m. The pair of converging cracks are climbed left then right.
FA. Gordon Mason 1983

❺ Black Watch . . . . **VS 4c**
6m. The crack passing a flake with mega-jugs on its crest.
FA. Chris Hardy 1980

❻ Talliot . . . . **HVS 5b**
8m. The crack and groove are harder than they appear from
below; finger jam, layaway and tarry not.
FA. Bob Whittaker 1983

❼ Eye-catcher . . . . **HVS 5**
10m. Climb the right-hand crack in this section of the wall and
at its top scoot leftwards to finish above *Black Watch*.
FA. Bob Whittaker 1983

❽ Repetition **E1 5c**
5m. The thin crack-line has a reachy move.
FA. Bruce Goodwin 1983

❾ Fall Guy **E1 5c**
5m. A green crack. Move left at the top to *Repetition*.
FA. Bob Whittaker 1983

❿ Chew Grit . . . . **VS 4b**
5m. Climb the short groove and the slab above.
FA. Bob Whittaker 1983

⓫ A Day Too Late **V2 (5c**
Traverse the handrail from the base of *Chew Grit*.
FA. Dave Hinton 1989

⓬ The Groove **V7 (6c**
The steep blank groove. Finish left at the roof.
FA. Kevin Thaw 1991

⓭ Legacy **V0 (5b**
The thin crack gets easier with height.
FA. Bob Whittaker 1983

⓮ Chalkie **V0 (5a**
Climb the short arete right of the corner.
FA. Steve Marshall 1980

⓯ Tomintool **V1 (5c**
The wall just right of the arete. Right again is also V1.
FA. Steve Marshall 1980

SIXTH QUARRY

The left-hand side of this quarry has a short wall of decent rock that faces south.

Sixth Quarry - Left

⓰ Reachy . . . . **VS 5b**
4m. The short problem, with a good landing, on the left.

⓱ Intro Wall . . . . **HS 4b**
6m. The left-hand crack is tricky to exit - stretch for the top.
FA. Tony Howard early 1960s

⓲ Summary . . . . **HVS 5**
6m. Zigzag up the next crack-line, an awkward little number.
FA. Chris Hardy 1984

Fifth Quarry

Sixth Quarry - Right

19 Seconds . . . . [ ] **VS 4c**
m. Jam the crack to its end at the shelving break then swing
ft to access the continuation and jam on.
A. Bob Whittaker 1974

5m to the right is a wall split by some cracks.

20 Parallax . . . . [ ] **E3 6a**
0m. Climb the left-hand side of the blunt arete. A runner on
ne right is a good idea and should really be placed on the lead.
A. Chris Hardy 1987

21 Sticky Fingers . . . . [ ] **E1 5b**
0m. The left-hand of a pair of cracks is of an awkward width,
ffering well-protected exercise. Easier for the small-handed.
A. Bob Whittaker 1977

22 Widfa . . . . [ ] **HVS 5a**
0m. The right-hand crack is easier though it widens awkwardly
ith height. Exit left above the useful chockstone on good jams.
A. Bob Whittaker 1974

23 Sunstroke . . . . [ ] **HVS 5b**
m. Climb the arete of the groove throughout, with a tricky
nitial mantelshelf. The groove can be bouldered direct at **6a**.
A. Bob Whittaker 1974

24 Cosmo Smallpiece . . . . [ ] **E1 6a**
m. The narrow wall is eliminatish but worthwhile; a somewhat
linkered approach is best to enjoy it to the full.
A. Chris Hardy 1985

25 Puffin . . . . [ ] **HS 4b**
m. Follow the groove with a useful crack in its left wall to the
dge of the hanging slab and pull over the roof to finish.
A. Bob WHittaker 1974

26 Delicate Wall . . . . [ ] **HS 5a**
0m. Climb the slab leftwards to the arete and a finish over the
oof as for *Puffin* without panting.
A. Tony Howard early 1960s

27 White Honkey . . . . [ ] **VS 5a**
8m. Climb the slab then head for the edge of the roof. Above
scape or cross easy ground to thin cracks in the final wall.
A. Bob Whittaker 1977

FIFTH QUARRY
The main feature of this quarry is a fine pale wall that faces
south and has a couple of excellent technical offerings.

28 Swing-up . . . . [ ] **HS 4b**
6m. Climb the narrow west-facing wall until is is possible to
swing rightwards around the arete (instant exposure) and finish
up the edge of the steep slab.
FA. Graham West early 1960

29 Yarn Spinner . . . . [ ] **E5 6c**
8m. The left-hand side of the face is climbed with considerable
difficulty. Start up the disappearing-crack and crank direct to
reach some proper holds just below the top. Unfeasible moves
linking unhelpful holds; a likely tale!
FA. Dougie Hall (solo) 1982

30 Weaver's Wall . . . . [ ] **E3 5b**
8m. Weave-a-way up the wall right of centre linking a series of
useful spaced holds, to a final bold mantelshelf.
FA. Bob Whittaker 1976

31 Weaver's Crack . . . . [ ] **HS 4b**
6m. The crack that bounds the right-hand side of the smooth
wall gives some good, if awkward, jamming.
FA. Bob Whittaker 1977

32 Norah Batty . . . . [ ] **S 4a**
8m. The wider left-slanting crack to the right. The second route
with this name in the quarries.
FA. Clive Maybury 1983

33 The Virgin . . . . [ ] **VDiff**
8m. The next crack is not popular judging by the tufts.
FA. Clive Maybury 1983

34 Cool Fool . . . . [ ] **VS 4c**
8m. The thin left-leaning fissure is over far too soon.
FA. Clive Maybury 1983

35 Kiss My Arm . . . . [ ] **VS 4c**
8m. ....and the same can be said about its right-leaning twin.
FA. Clive Maybury 1983

Staffordshire
Whaley Bridge
Kinder
Bleaklow
Chew
Lancashire
Cheshire
Den Lane
Running Hill Pits
Alderman
Upperwood Q
Standing Stones
Ravenstones
Dovestones
Rob's Rocks
Wimberry

Den Lane Quarry is an easily-approached outcrop just to the west of the pleasant small town of Upper Mill - birthplace of Troll, the outdoor company. The quarry has the usual smattering of graffiti and the odd bits of abandoned cars, though despite this the old spoil heaps hide the nearby town and the setting is quite tranquil. Many of the routes follow strenuous cracks and the rock is of reasonable quality. The best climbing is on the impressive Rake Wall though sadly the upper section of this is heathery and loose. The Long Wall is shorter but has some good strenuous climbs and the potential for some excellent fingery bouldering - the exits from the top of the wall are best described as 'problematical'!

ACCESS

Climbing on the right-hand section is not permitted due to being on private land (an industrial estate). The climbs on this section are not covered here.

OTHER GUIDEBOOK - A more complete list of routes at Den Lane is published in the 1988 BMC *Moorland Gritstone* guidebook.

APPROACH Also see map on page 182

When entering Uppermill from the south take a left turn into the narrow walled lane of Moorgate and follow this as it swings right into Den Lane. About 500m down here there is parking on the left for a couple of cars and further on room for a couple more on the right. muddy track leads under the railway line and up into the quarry only minutes away - arrivin just to the right of the right-hand end of Long Wall. The more impressive Rake Wall is located up the slope to the right.

CONDITIONS

The crag faces east and is well-sheltered from the prevailing winds. It gets the morning sun and can be a pleasant escape from the heat on stuffy summer days. The sheltered nature of the cliff, and the trees that grow in the quarry, make it a potentially midgy venue on humid days. Despite the slopes above the quarry, the faces do not take a lot of drainage and it is usually possible to get something done here even when the weather is poor.

BOLT BELAYS ON GRIT?

Many of the worthwhile climbs here are spoilt by the dangerous unstable and overgrown exits. There are some old peg belays and some fixed threads in the centre of the Rake Wall. The addition of a few discrete fixed-bolt-belays below the grot would make the climbing here much safer and perhaps a little more popular.

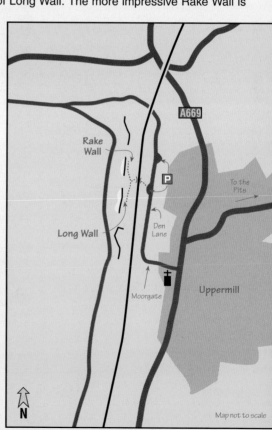

DEN LANE *The Long Wall*

Staffordshire
Whaley Bridge
Kinder
Bleaklow
Chew
Lancashire
Cheshire
Den Lane
Running Hill Pits
Alderman
Upperwood Q
Standing Stones
Ravenstones
Dovestones
Rob's Rocks
Wimberry

THE LONG WALL
The left-hand section is the well-named Long Wall, which is home to some reasonable short (and not so short) routes, mostly with grotty exits. An abseil descent is normal from the old fixed gear - care required. There is some good bouldering on the lower section of the face.

1 Irish Jig . . . . ☐ **VS 4c**
8m. The zigzagging crack to a choice of (dirty) exits.
FA. Jeff Sykes 1959

2 Hadrian's Wall . . . . ☐ **E1 5c**
8m. From the fallen block pull past the right edge of the 'cave' and use broken flakes to power up to the tree.
FA. Jim Campbell 1973

3 Ash Tree Direct . . . . ☐ **S 4b**
6m. Take the crack to above the roof then head left to the tree.
FA. Tony Howard 1958

4 The Ramp . . . . ☐ **VS 5b**
8m. The fingery wall eases as soon as 'the ramp' is reached.
FA. Mike Pilling mid 60s

5 Cancan . . . . ☐ **VS 5a**
8m. A good jamming-crack leads to a slanting slab. Escape left up this or tackle the thin crack above to a sea of grot.
FA. Jeff Sykes 1960

6 Elderberry Slab . . . . ☐ **VDiff**
10m. The diagonal ramp leads left all the way to the tree.
FA. Tony Howard 1957

The next three routes all have poor finishes, best escape right.

7 Calypso Crack . . . . ☐ **VS 5a**
6m. The sinuous and disjointed crack is tough to start.
FA. Barry Kershaw 1958

8 Quickstep . . . . ☐ **VS 5b**
6m. Pull over the overlap and climb the crack to tricky moves onto the slab above.
FA. Barry Kershaw 1958

9 Fire-power . . . . ☐ **E1 6b**
6m. The thin crack on tips jams and one good locker.
Pass Me That Araldite... Please (E1 6b) is the flake just right.
FFA. Steve Bancroft 1984. FA. (Pass Me That Araldite) Ian Carr 1986

10 Jive . . . . ☐ **HS 4b**
12m. Climb onto a ledge then take the crack as it bends left towards the roof. Escape right round this to an awful exit.
FA. Tony Howard 1959

11 Palais Glide . . . . ☐ **VS 4c**
14m. Steep and pumpy. Climb the groove to the roof then layback round it. At the second roof move right again to finish. Iron hoop (and nut) belays. Alternate finishes are poorer.
FA. Jeff Sykes 1959

12 Fox-trot . . . . ☐ **HVS 5a**
14m. Climb straight into the leaning groove, at its top step out left and teeter across to the steep crack above and a sprint finish. Belay as for *Palais Glide*.
FA. Tony Howard 1960, FFA. Roy Brown 1961

13 Mississippi Dip . . . . ☐ **VS 4c**
14m. Follow the ramp to the groove on Fox-trot but pull onto a slab then exit out right to reach a crack. Up this to awkward final moves. Belay as for *Palais Glide*.
FA. Brian Hodgkinson 1959

14 A Stretch Named Desire . . . ☐ **E5 6b**
14m. Climb direct through the traverse of *Long Wall Eliminate*. Slink right at the top to the finish of *Orchestral Crack*.
FA. Kevin Thaw 1988

15 Long Wall Eliminate . . . . . ☐ **E3 6a**
14m. Climb the groove the tackle the fierce left-slanting crack to join and finish (with luck) up *Mississippi Dip*.
FA. John Allen 1973

16 Orchestral Crack . . . . . ☐ **HVS 5a**
14m. The groove that bounds the wall, steeply, to an awkward exit at an old piece of angle iron. The better belay as for *Three Notch Slab* is down and right - back it up!
FA. Jeff Sykes 1960. FFA Bill Tweedale mid 1960s

17 Three Notch Slab . . . . . . ☐ **VS 4c**
12m. The classic of the crag - well sort of. Skip onto the ledge then cross the slab rightwards and layback up the arete to a multi-peg (and nut) belay. Abseil off.
FA. Barry Kershaw 1957

RAKE WALL

The most impressive section of the cliff is situated 80m to the right, and up a slope, from the Long Wall. It has some good and strenuous left-leaning crack climbs that lead to 'The Rake'. From here upward progress doesn't add a lot to the climbing experience. The orange scar of the rock fall on the right, and the small memorial, under *The Popple*, point to the fact that care is required when climbing here! Bolt belays below the grot would make the climbing much safer!

DESCENT - One way to avoid having to top-out is to belay on the good stance in the centre of the wall (big flake, nuts and Friends) then use the fixed threads to abseil from.

❶ Noah's Crack . . . . VS 4b
22m. The leaning groove and tricky layback above leads to easy ground. Head up and right for a choice of escapes; either direct up the straightforward but grotty groove, or over to the right and a fixed belay. A good start but an awful upper section.
FA. Barry Kershaw 1959

❷ Sunset Crack . . . . ▨▨ VS 4c
22m. From a large block pull onto a ledge then climb the sharp-dged crack to a leftwards exit under the capping flake. Select a inish as for *Noah's Crack*. Again spoilt by the rock/grot mix.
FA. Tony Howard 1957

❸ Tony's Terror . . . . VS 4b
18m. Climb the steepening groove then exit right to a rest on a hanging slab. Continue up the steep crack to easy ground on the right and cross this to a stance above the threads. Abseil descent or finish up the groove through the overhangs.
FA. Tony Howard 1958

❹ Midgebite Crack . . . . . ▨▨ HVS 5a
16m. Climb the deep groove, left then right, to its apex and pull out right to reach a rest with difficulty (crux). Jam the good crack above more easily, then pass the left-hand side of the large hanging block by more tricky climbing. Pull right to easier ground and just a little higher the stance. *Photo page 229.*
FA. Tony Howard 1959

❺ The Popple . . . . ▨▨ HVS 5b
18m. From just right of the memorial, climb the steep jamming crack to a triangular niche then follow the thinner finger-crack (the one to the right with an ancient thread may also be found of use), to reach better holds and one more strenuous pull to easy ground. Traverse carefully left and up to reach the stance.
FA. Tony Howard 1959, FFA. Malc Baxter 1962

❻ The Drooper . . . . . ▨▨▨ E2 5c
20m. The main angle is bridged to the overhang then power past this (old peg) to reach a jug in the wider crack above. Get established with difficulty then follow the easier crack as it runs leftwards to join *The Popple*. Follow this to the fixed belay.
FA. Tony Howard 1958 (as Milk Crate Crack) and Barry Roberts (1 peg) 1962. FFA. Jim Campbell 1968

❼ The Wilter . . . . . ▨▨▨ E1 5b
24m. The crack running up the left-hand side of the orange scar has some of the best climbing here though it is spoilt by the grubby exit. It has difficult, but well-protected, moves to pass the overhang where wilting arms is a common phenomenon. Above this the difficulties ease. Select a way on carefully.
FA. Tony Howard 1958. FFA. Tony Jones 1963

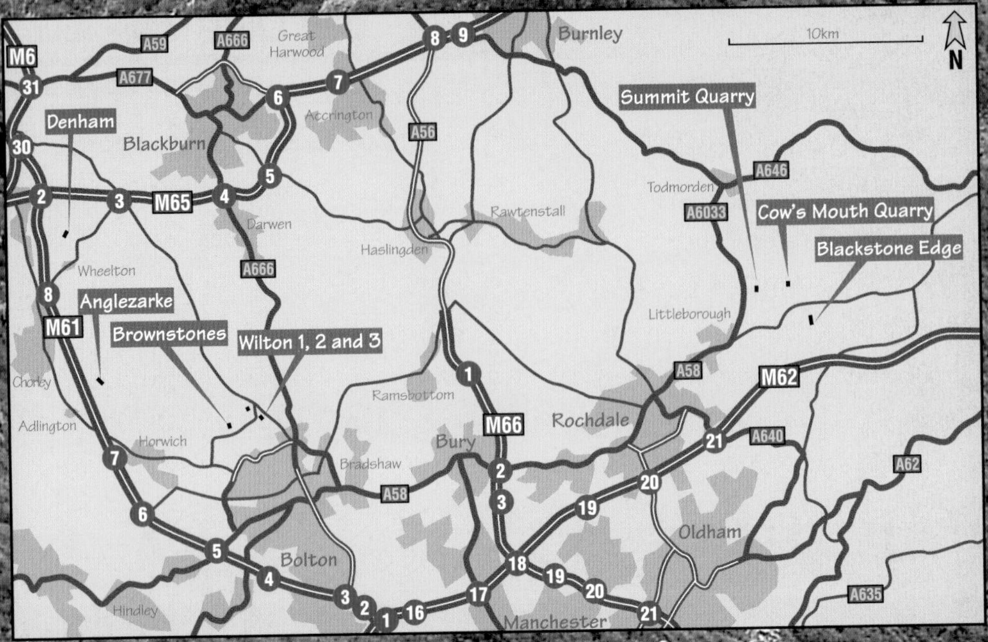
Burnley
10km
N
Great Harwood
M6
A59
A666
A677
31
8
9
7
6
Summit Quarry
Denham
Accrington
A56
Blackburn
30
5
A646
2
3
M65
4
Todmorden
Darwen
Rawtenstall
A6033
Cow's Mouth Quarry
Haslingden
Blackstone Edge
Wheelton
A666
8
Anglezarke
Littleborough
M61
Brownstones
Wilton 1, 2 and 3
1
A58
M62
Chorley
Ramsbottom
M66
Rochdale
Adlington
21
A640
Horwich
Bury
7
Bradshaw
2
A62
20
A58
3
19
6
Oldham
18
5
Bolton
19
4
20
A635
3
17
21
2
1
16
Hindley
Manchester

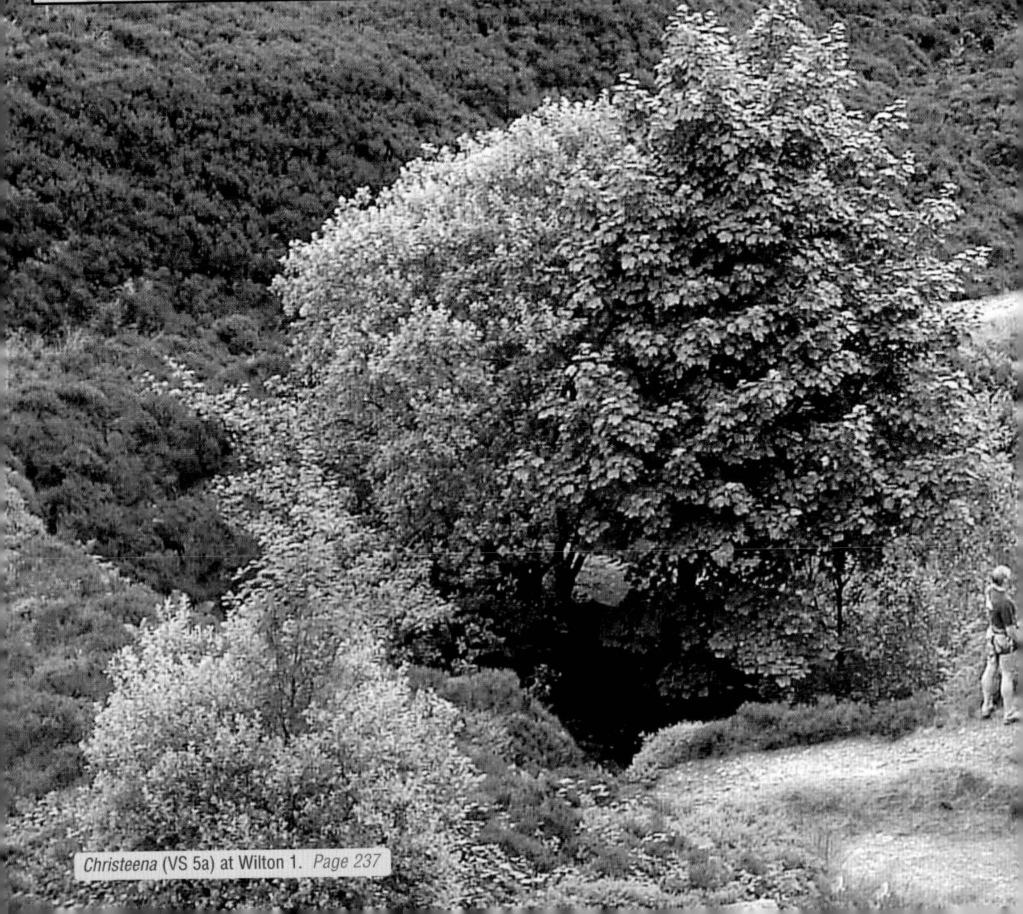

Christeena (VS 5a) at Wilton 1. *Page 237*

LANCASHIRE

The Wilton complex of quarries (from 1 through to 4) overlooks Egerton, to the north of Bolton and is reached in minutes from a collection convenient parking places. Wilton 1 is arguably the finest cliff in Lancashire with well over 200 routes many of which are hard or very hard. Although the thin cracks, with which the place abounds, were originally climbed with aid, the area was never the popular practice-ground that the eastern Peak became. Because of this many of the cracks are in near-pristine condition, making them worthy of the attention of any visiting thin-crack-meister. Scattered amongst the hard routes is a reasonable selection of more moderate fare that give the chance to look at the harder routes and imagine - maybe one day! Those who find Wilton 1 a bit intimidating should enjoy Wilton 2 and 3 where the setting and the spread of grades are a little more amenable as is the angle of much of the rock.

APPROACH Also see map on page 232

There is dedicated parking just down the slope from the Wilton Arms (the Wilting Arms would surely be more appropriate). Steps lead through the bushes in the left-hand corner of this to a wide quarry track that loops right then left to arrive opposite the conspicuous fin of rock that is The Prow. More direct approaches are steeper and save only seconds.

To the left of The Prow the quarry descends into the overgrown depths of The Allotment and to its right the steep walls of The Pit Face. These are home to 60 or so routes, many of which are worth seeking out - see the definitive Lancashire guide. From the approach path minor tracks lead up and right to the White Slabs and Grey Walls, home to many fine climbs and rarely busy.

CONDITIONS

The cliff faces the morning sun and, although in the shade after midday, is sheltered from the prevailing westerly winds. The place is inclined to be green in the winter, or after rain, but if the day turns sour then the sunny delights of Anglezarke or bouldering of Brownstones are not too far away. The exception to the rule is the west face of The Prow that gets the afternoon sun (until it sets below the quarry rim) and is almost always in climbable condition.

On rare hot summer days the quarry makes an ideal shady retreat.

> **OTHER GUIDEBOOK** - A more complete list of routes at the Wilton Quarries is published in the 1999 BMC *Lancashire* guidebook.
> **Egerton Quarry** has almost 180 routes, many of which are steep, hard and worthwhile, despite the grotty setting!
> **Ousel's Nest** has 30 routes in a pleasant location and, although only 10-12m high, many are hard work.

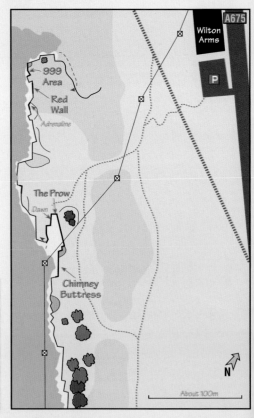

The Prow

Morning | 5 min | Green | Sheltered

CHIMNEY BUTTRESS

The left-most popular piece of rock is split right of centre by the shallow cleft of *Wombat Chimney*. All the routes here are steep, strenuous and well worth doing. The crack climbs are well-protected, though the gear is often hard-won. In contrast the face routes tend to be bold and harrowing with gear offered only by the horizontal breaks and the odd peg.

❶ Paradox **E2 5b**
12m. A fine and varied pitch with an interesting start followed by steep jamming to a teetering exit. The pitch follows the slanting crack in the south-facing wall until a short traverse right leads to easy ground. Well-protected where you need it.
FA. Hank Pasquill 1968

❷ Parasite **E5 6b**
16m. The left arete of the front face is technical and bold. Various old bits of metal provide the protection.
FA. Jerry Peel/Hank Pasquill 1980

❸ Leucocyte Left-hand . . . **E3 5c**
16m. Climb past an iron ring to a good ledge out right then step left and enter a hanging crack. Finish more easily.
FA. Ray Evans 1964

❹ Leucocyte Right-hand . . **VS 4c**
16m. From a ledge on the *Leucocyte Left-hand* climb the groove above then the continuation crack past an old peg. Steady ground remains.
FA. Hank Pasquill 1967

❺ The Hacker **E4 6b**
16m. Climb the wall past twin overlaps then finish up the bold and technical wall above.
FA. Hank Pasquill 1973

❻ Central Route **E1 5b**
16m. A great route which is not as pumpy as it looks but requires concentration right to the last move. It follows the continuous crack-line past a ledge at 6m. Take care with a couple of rattling holds.
FA. Hank Pasquill 1967

❼ Max **E3 5c**
18m. Climb straight up the wall to the overlap (poor rest in a niche) then follow the thin, pumpy crack above. The start is serious; the hard moves near the top can be well-protected.
FA. Hank Pasquill 1968

❽ Wombat Chimney **E2 5b**
18m. The narrow hanging fissure is approached via a steep crack. Take a rest before the chimney then struggle up it to an awkward but well-protected exit.
FA. Ray Evans 1966

❾ The Soot Monkey . . **E6 6c**
18m. Climb the thin wall to a peg then continue right and left boldly to the break. Climb the wall above via a little diversion to the arete of *Wombat*.
FA. Paul Pritchard 1985

❿ Toxic Bilberrys **E8 7a**
18m. Bold face work, giving powerful, technical and pushy climbing up the face to the left of *Loopy*. There is a long run-out start and a then a crucial section protected (well maybe just) by skyhook runners!
FA. Gareth Parry 1998

⓫ Loopy **E4 6a**
14m. An intimidating pitch, strenuous then delicate and always bold. Climb cracks to some hanging blocks. Pull up into the groove on the left then balance delicately leftwards up a scooped slab. The direct finish up the groove is hard, safe but less good. There is also a right-hand finish up the dirty groove.
FA. Hank Pasquill 1968 and 1970

THE PROW
The outer face of The Prow has a couple of popular lower grade climbs and some bold routes at a higher grade plus the classic *Cameo*.

The Hook

① **Horrock's Route** . . . . 🔟 [ ] **VS 4b**
14m. Start below a corner and climb right and up to reach a edge. Take the groove behind to reach easy ground.
Horrock's Route Direct - E1 5b, follows the corner direct and the crack above to the top.
FA. Ken Powell 1964. FA. John Hartley (The Direct) 1983

② **Fingernail** . . . . 🔟 [ ] **HS 4b**
18m. Climb a crack to the prominent hook then traverse left on your fingernails before climbing straight up to a ledge (peg). Step out right and traverse the face to a shallow groove, which leads to the top on positive holds.
FA. Mick Pooler 1962

③ **Orange Peel** . . . . 🔟 [ ] **HS 4b**
18m. From the hook stride right then climb straight up to join the upper part of *Fingernail*.
FA. Ray Evans 1964

④ **Flingle Bunt** . . . . 🔟 [ ] **VS 4c**
20m. Layback the pointed flake then climb straight up the wall to *Eastern Terrace*. Move left along ledges then step back right to enter and climb the upper groove.
FA. Ray Evans 1964

⑤ **Spider Crack** . . . . 🔟 [ ] **HVS 5a**
18m. Layback round the roof then climb the wall to ledges. Take the wide crack in the wall just to the right to finish.
FA. Ken Powell 1963

⑥ **Jubilee Climb** . . . . 🔟 [ ] **E1 5c**
18m. Climb straight up the wall just to the right of *Spider Crack*. Step left and tackle the thin crack in the upper wall. The route feels like two boulder problems separated by a terrace.
FA. Ian Lonsdale 1977

⑦ **Lazy Friday** . . . . 🔟 [ ] **E4 5c**
18m. The wall left of *Cameo* has bold climbing but if you can crimp then you'll find it OK! It may need a clean and a side-runner in *Spider Crack* is probably no bad idea. A tiny 'nubbin' can be tied-off, and who knows - it might even hold a fall!
FA. Jerry Peel 1977

⑧ **Cameo** . . . . 🔟 [ ] **E1 5a**
18m. The seam left of the arete gives superb steep wall climbing, although the gear (small wires) is a little spaced. One for a steady leader but not really too hard for E1. *Photo page 235*.
FA. Ray Evans 1964

⑨ **Pathetique** . . . . 🔟 [ ] **E5 6b**
18m. Bold wall climbing on tiny holds. A side-runner in *Cameo* gives the only real protection.
FA. Paul Pritchard 1985

⑩ **Christeena** . . . . . . 🔟 [ ] **VS 5a**
14m. Climb the narrow front of the Prow (crux!) to a ledge. Move up to a good hold on the left arete and use this to swing (low) or teeter (high) round the edge and across into the groove. Climb this pleasantly to the top. *Photo page 232*.
FA. Mick Pooler 1962

Descent: reverse down the awkward ramps (*Max's Dilemma*)

Christeena

Afternoon | 5 min | Sheltered

THE PROW - INSIDE FACE

The sunniest piece of rock in the quarry has a small collection of excellent routes and, not surprisingly, it is one of the most popular bits of rock here. The routes tend to be strenuous and bold in places, and the rock is exceptionally clean. Belaying on top of The Prow, requires a little care (there are various fixed bits of iron work) as does the exposed escape along its crest - all very Culm Coast!

❶ Christine Arete E4 5c
14m. Bold and fingery climbing up the left-hand arete of the face. No side-runners at this grade. Wires in the upper left-hand crack of *Dawn* knock the grade down to a still scary **E3 5c**.
FA. Hank Pasquill 1967

❷ Dawn . . . . HVS 5b
14m. A steep crack climb which is high in the grade. Jam your way up to a sit-down rest on a sloping ledge. Continue up the draining upper crack past some small wire runners. The left-hand crack throughout is a good pump at E2 5c.
Photo opposite.
FA. Graham Kilner 1961. FFA. Mick Pooler 1963

❸ Innominate E4 6b
14m. A bouldery start (a side-runner brings it down to E3) leads a break. Follow the upper break to gain the thin crack left of the upper section of *Ann*.
FFA. Hank Pasquill early 1980s

❹ Eliminate . . . . VS 4c
18m. An indirect line but with good climbing. Climb the groove then make a tricky traverse right along the narrow undercut ledges to *Rambling Route*. Finish up its left arete.
FA. Rowland Edwards 1963

❺ Ann E1 5b
14m. Two good sections split by a big ledge. Climb the thin once-pegged crack to ledges. Power up the twin cracks in the groove to finish. Eschewing all use of the left-hand crack is a touch harder and also more strenuous.
FA. Les Ainsworth 1967

❻ Cheat E3 5b
14m. Steady climbing with a bold feel. Gear in the midway break gives protection that is just about adequate. Climb the reachy lower wall via a thin crack to ledges then attack the upper face by a line of (small) chipped holds. The route is at least **E4 5c** for the short.
FA. Hank Pasquill 1967

❼ Rambling Route . . . . VDiff
14m. Ramble up the chimney on the right to the ledge out left then take the groove above to finish, or the arete to the left.
FA. Graham Kilner 1961

❽ Flywalk . . . . VS 4c
12m. Climb strenuously across small ledges to a (well-jammed - well maybe) block. Finish through a small roof.
FA. Graham Kilner 1961

Staffordshire | Whaley Bridge | Kinder | Bleaklow | Chew | Lancashire | Cheshire | Littleborough | Denham | Anglezarke | Brownstones | Wilton 2 and 3 | Wilton 1

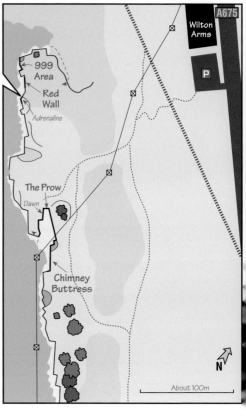

ADRENALINE

The tall right-hand end of the Grey Wall rises from behind a heap of grassed-over quarry spoil. All the routes start indifferently but things improve dramatically on the better rock above the mid-height break. Here are a couple of the very hardest offerings in the area, *Gigantic* and *Chocolate Girl*, plus the classic overhanging groove of *Adrenaline*.

❶ Adrenaline — E4 6a

24m. Despite an inauspicious start up a poor crack and past a grubby cave, the upper groove offers superb well-protected climbing which is unrelenting and technical on an ever-uphill line. Just keep pushing on and the holds keep arriving but so does the adrenaline. Protection is good once you reach the crack, though the 'easy' bottom wall is a bit worrying!
FA. Jim Fogg 1969. FFA. Hank Pasquill 1981

❷ Chocolate Girl — E7 6c

26m. This arduous outing takes the lower of a pair of thin, tilted cracks in the impressive pillar to the right of the groove of *Adrenaline*. Climb the groove to the cave then exit right to gain access to the base of the withering crack. Power up this, sustained, fingery and technical, passing four peg runners until a semi-rest is reached in the groove of *Adrenaline*. Finish up this much more easily.
FA. Hank Pasquill 1969. FFA. Gareth Parry 1996

❸ Gigantic — E8 6c

16m. The upper of the pair of hanging cracks in the wall was shamefully neglected by the aid climbers, resulting in there being barely a place that will admit a fingertip in its entire length! Climb a flaky crack in the right-hand wall of the main groove to ledges out right and a good stance. From the stance swing around the arete to gain the crack-line and follow it desperately to a final hideous sequence which allows the last couple of moves on *Adrenaline* to be reached - phew!
FA. Ken Powell 1964. FFA. Dave Pegg 1990

Staffordshire

Whaley Bridge

Kinder

Bleaklow

Chew

Lancashire

Cheshire

RED WALL

A neglected part of the quarry but with some quality rock. The best routes tend to be in the higher grades although the intimidating VS classic of *Blackout* is excellent.

❶ Blackout .... **VS 4c**
26m. Another wandering and intimidating classic on which care is required to protect the second adequately. Climb to the top of the pillar then the groove above until its is possible (essential?) to head left to the first of a series of ledges. Move left to a peg belay. Move up and left to more ledges then follow these back right to an exposed and grotty exit.
FA. Dave Brodigan 1963

❷ Master Spy **E4 6a**
20m. A pumpy Wilton classic, powerful and devious, though with good gear throughout. Rope work can be a little problematical. From *Blackout* climb strenuously to the 'seagull-shaped' roof then compose yourself before launching right long this to a bridged rest at it far end. Just when you thought it was all over you find that the final short crack takes no prisoners.
Master Spy Direct E4 6a - Starting up *Counter Intelligence* and finishing up *Master Spy* gives a superb three star combination.
FA. Hank Pasquill 1970. FA. (Direct) Paul Clarke mid 1980s

❸ Counter Intelligence **E5 6b**
18m. Climb the long and sustained crack that falls from the right-hand edge of the 'seagull-shaped' roof to reach a bridged rest on its right. Pull leftwards onto the hanging face then make a daunting and crucial mantel/rock-over way out in space to reach the final thin crack.
FA. John Hartley 1982

❹ Wipe Out **E2 5b**
18m. Another great route at a (slightly) more amenable grade. The next long crack-line gives excellent climbing with sustained and well-protected climbing and more difficult (or at least more pumpy) moves to reach the top.
FA. Les Ainsworth 1966

999

The last section of the cliff has a small selection of worthwhile routes on good rock, and once again they see little traffic. *999* is one of the best lower grade routes in the quarry following an excellent natural line and with good protection throughout.

❺ Knock Out .... **VS 4c**
16m. Climb awkwardly onto the slab and trend left, passing a big blob of rust to a stance on the arete. Step back right and follow the thin crack just right of the arete and the pleasant groove directly above.
FA. Ray Evans 1966

❻ Virgin's Dilemma ..... **HVS 5a**
20m. A rare thing indeed - a Wilton slab - what else? Climb the centre of the lower slab to the sandy break then continue up its centre, passing a peg, to enter the shallow open groove splitting the upper face. Follow this throughout by sustained moves.
FA. Hank Pasquill 1967

❼ 999 .... **HS 4b**
18m. The long clean groove that bounds the slab gives a fine piece of climbing, sustained and well-protected up an excellent line. The crux, as they always say is 'where it should be'.
FA. Ken Powell 1963

❽ Left Edge .... **HVS 4c**
14m. From the grass on the right (reached by a grotty scramble) step left and balance up the fine and poorly-protected arete. Short but well-positioned and worthwhile.
FA. Ray Evans 1964

Littleborough

Denham

Anglezarke

Brownstones

Wilton 2 and 3

Wilton 1

On the crest of the hill above the deep slash of Wilton 1 are three more quarries, numbered from left to right 4, 2 and 3! Number 4 is short, overgrown and unpopular, but both 2 and 3 are well worth a visit and, because of their proximity to each other, a useful day can be spent between the pair of them. The rock is not the most impressive but the routes are more friendly than Wilton 1 and especially of interest if you operate in the green and orange grade zones. Wilton 2 tends to have the harder routes, offering steep, fingery and challenging climbing whereas, in Wilton 3, there are more routes of an amenable angle and grade. The well-battered areas below the Orange and Rappel Walls is an indication of how popular these areas are with supervised groups; be prepared to share the objects of your desire!

APPROACH Also see map on page 232

Wilton 2 and 3 (and 4) quarries are set behind Wilton 1 and are most easily reached by driving up the hill - the A675 - past the Wilton Arms and the parking for Wilton 1. After a kilometre or so take the first left turn and continue up the hill to where the quarry tracks can be seen on the right - though the cliffs themselves remain hidden until you are actually inside them. Both quarries are reached by short gated tracks and there is roadside parking on the left opposite the entrances. Leave nothing valuable in the car.

CONDITIONS

The cliffs face north and east and so are in the sun until early afternoon. They take little drainage and dry rapidly after rain, though many of the climbs tend to be gritty from sand washed down from above. There are belay stakes in place above many of the climbs, checking their solidity before using them is a sensible idea.

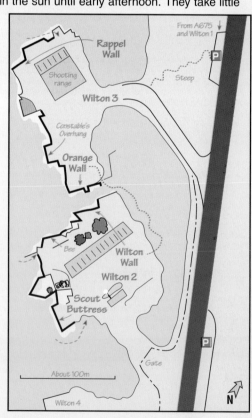

ACCESS RESTRICTION

WIlton Two and Three are used by a rifle club and are closed to climbers on Wednesdays, Fridays and Sundays, as well as Boxing Day. Climbers are asked not to visit on these days even if shooting appears not to be taking place (i.e. no red flag is flying) as gun club members may turn up at any time.

OTHER GUIDEBOOK - A more complete list of routes at Wilton 2 and 3 is published in the 1999 BMC *Lancashire* guidebook.

SCOUT BUTTRESS

The left-hand side of the cliff has a series of short steep walls with routes that make up in impact what they lack in stature. Many of the climbs tend to be quite fierce for their given grade, but they don't go on too long!

ACCESS - Shooting takes place here on Wednesdays, Fridays and Sundays so please avoid these days.

① Concrete Crack . . . 〓〓〓 E2 6a
8m. The thin and technical crack is gained from *Cement Mix.* The gear is good, but only if you can stop to place it!
FA. Ian Lonsdale 1982

② Cement Mix E1 5b
8m. The shallow crusty groove left of the main angle could have done with a bit more cement to hold it together!
FA. Dave Cronshaw 1971

③ Short Corner . . . . 〓 E1 5c
8m. The groove on the right-hand side of the wall has a stubborn exit (old peg runner).
FFA. Ian lonsdale 1981

④ Start . . . . Diff
8m. The shot holes lead to a grassy exit up a corner.
FA. Rowland Edwards 1964

⑤ Boomerang . . . . Diff
8m. Climb onto a shelf at 3m then take the slab rightwards and finish through a notch.
FA. Rowland Edwards 1964

⑥ Shallow Groove . . . . . . 〓〓 HVS 5b
10m. The shallow left-facing groove is worth seeking out, being well-protected, quite technical and pretty steep.
FA. Rowland Edwards 1964

⑦ Shallow Green . . . . . 〓〓 E2 5c
10m. Pad rightwards up the slab to a peg, pull rightwards through the small overhang to a welcome jug then finish up the centre of the bold wall above. High in the grade.
FA. Nigel Bonnett 1976

⑧ Shukokia . . . . 〓〓 E3 6a
8m. The groove and ensuing thin crack-line give good climbing to a tough exit through the overlap.

⑨ Kung Fu . . . . 〓 HVS 5a
8m. The crack leads to a deep slot and then a steeper finish.
FA. Rowland Edwards late 1960s

⑩ The Bod . . . . 〓〓 E1 5b
10m. Despite being awkward the shallow left-facing corner-groove is worthwhile.
FA. Hank Pasquill mid 1970s

⑪ Disappearing Aces . . . . 〓〓 E3 6a
10m. Also known as *Ace of Spades*. Despite good climbing the vicious leaning groove sees little attention, hence the herbage!
FA. Terry Waring 1967. FFA. Dennis Gleeson 1982

⑫ Tweeker . . . . 〓〓 E3 5c
12m. Climb the crack of *Throsher* then traverse out left and pull into an awkward groove. Up this to a peg then make crucial moves to pass the centre of the overhang using a 'wart' to gain the final wall and a sprint finish.
FFA. Ian Lonsdale 1978

⑬ Throsher . . . . 〓 VS 4c
12m. The crack up the right-hand side of the tallest face in this part of the quarry is the best VS hereabouts. Nice climbing, fine positions and good protection ensure its continued popularity and 'throshing' should not be necessary. The bore-hole is a 'cool' feature.
FA. Rowland Edwards 1964

Staffordshire · Whaley Bridge · Kinder · Bleaklow · Chew · Lancashire · Cheshire · Littleborough · Denham · Anglezarke · Brownstones · Wilton 2 and 3 · Wilton 1

Descent

5m gap

Not much sun

Morning | 3 min | Sheltered | Restrictions

Staffordshire
Whaley Bridge
Kinder
Bleaklow
Chew
Lancashire
Cheshire
Littleborough
Denham
Anglezarke
Brownstones
Wilton 2 and 3
Wilton 1

S-GROOVE and THE BEE

The left-hand side of the Main Wall wall has a small selection of short routes on good rock with some surprisingly technical outings. On most occasions you are more than likely to have the routes here to yourself.

ACCESS - Shooting takes place here on Wednesdays, Fridays and Sundays so please avoid these days.

❶ The Axe Wound **E6 7a**
6m. The well-brushed wall on the right of the recess. Only short but savagely technical. The only 'sport route' in the guide!
FA. Gareth Parry 1992

❷ The S-Groove **E7 6c**
8m. The attractive sinuous groove in the pale wall at a lower level. Originally climbed with side runners at E5 6c; it has now been soloed. Also known as *Against all Odds* - apt really!
FA. Mark Leach (side-runners) 1984. FA. Gareth Parry 1990s

❸ Frostbite **E2 5c**
7m. Steep climbing up the corner past a low overlap.
FA. Hank Pasquill 1964

Past an overgrown descent gully is a slabby wall.

❹ The Bee **E1 5b**
8m. Climb the crack to a ledge then step out left past the overlap and balance up to a horizontal break, runners and an easier finish. Better and much more feasible than it looks, giving very neat wall climbing, with a bold feel due to the distant runners out right.
FA. Hank Pasquill mid 1970s

❺ The Wasp **E3 6a**
8m. The balancy right arete throughout. In the upper section a thin crack is useful, leading to a sting in the tail - or not?
FA. John Hartley 1982

❻ Laying the Ghost **E2 6b**
8m. The thin crack in the left wall is approached from a short way up *Slanting Slab* and climbed tenuously passing a peg runner to a desperate finale.
FFA. John Hartley 1982

❼ Slanting Slab . . . . **S 4a**
8m. The pleasant right-slanting slab is climb right to left then back right to a reach a grassy exit.
FA. Ray Evans 1964

❽ Savage Stone **E4 6c**
8m. From a couple of moves up the groove of *Direct*, monkey left into the hanging groove and levitate up it using the one decent hold. A vital peg protects. Originally given 7a.
FA. John Hartley 1982

❾ Direct . . . . **HVS 5a**
8m. The leaning groove is best taken at a gallop. Laybacking is the best approach though stopping to place gear can be a touch problematical!
FA. Rowland Edwards 1964

❿ Kukri Crack . . . . **HVD**
8m. The clean-cut crack running right then cutting back left is pleasant at the grade. Protection is good.
FA. Rowland Edwards 1964

⓫ Three Corner Climb . . . . **Mod**
10m. The rather grassy three stepped corners can be used as a beginners' route or more usually as a quick way down.

Descent →

← --- Descent

Starts obscured by shooting mound

Wilton 3 - 2 minutes walk, over the ridge or round by the track

WILTON WALL

The smooth face on the right-hand side of the quarry, and behind the firing range, is the showpiece of the place offering superb fingery routes on impeccable rock. Most of the routes are poorly protected so best arrive with your bold head on!

ACCESS - Shooting takes place here on Wednesdays, Fridays and Sundays so please avoid these days.

① Deep Groove . . . . ☐ **Diff**
10m. The groove to a ledge and the continuation from here.
FA. Rowland Edwards 1964

② Meandering Molly . . . . ☐ **VDiff**
10m. From *Deep Groove* access the arete on the right and follow it to ledges. Finish up the short wall behind.
FA. Rowland Edwards 1964

③ Cross Tie . . . . 🔲☐ **S 4a**
10m. Climb the arete until *Meandering Molly* rolls up then step out left to the centre of the face and climb this.
FA. Rowland Edwards 1964

④ Flake Crack . . . . 🔲☐ **S 4a**
10m. The flake-crack right of the grotty corner.
FA. Rowland Edwards 1964

⑤ Big Dorris . . . . . . 🔲🔲🔲 **E2 5c**
12m. Interesting climbing which is bold but safe. Towards the centre of the wall is a thin hanging crack, gain this from the left and make some thin crimpy moves to a good rest. The top is delicate but easier in comparison.
FA. Ian Lonsdale 1977

⑥ Falling Crack . . . . 🔲🔲☐ **E2 5b**
14m. Often well-named! The fine fissure cleaving the centre of the face has good gear but is pumpy enough. Gaining the mid-height niche is the crux but interest is well-maintained.
FA. Rowland Edwards 1964 FFA. Hank Pasquill 1974

⑦ Wilton Wall . . . . . . 🔲🔲🔲 **E3 6a**
14m. The classic of the quarry. From *Falling Crack* swing right to the thin seam in the smooth face and climb this with difficulty as it develops into a shallow groove, to ledges and an easy escape. The **Direct Start** is also 6a and adds to the pump.
FA. Ken Powell 1964 FFA. Hank Pasquill 1969

⑧ Pigs Direct . . . . 🔲🔲🔲🔲☐ **E6 6c**
12m. Steep and intense. Climb *PotW* to the jugs (gear) then head up the wall above by bold, fingery and sustained climbing.
FA. Mark Leach 1985

⑨ Pigs on the Wing . . 🔲🔲🔲 **E5 6b**
14m. Great climbing, crimpy, technical and bold. Climb leftwards then direct to jugs and runners. Step right and follow a thin seam to the top. A superb outing.
FA. John Hartley 1982

⑩ The Swine . . . . . 🔲🔲🔲☐ **E3 6a**
14m. Boulder rightwards up the wall left of the arete to good holds. Continue up in the same line past a peg.
FA. Hank Pasquill mid 1970s

⑪ Iron Orchid . . . . . 🔲🔲🔲 **E4 6b**
14m. The square-cut arete of the wall is technical and airy. Climb the arete to a peg, swing right to a second peg below a shallow scoop. Finish up its right arete with increasing trepidation.
FA. John Hartley 1982

⑫ Saturday Crack . . . . . . 🔲🔲☐ **HVS 5a**
10m. The butch groove/jamming-crack in the side wall is a change from all the fingery chicanery on the front face.
FA. Rowland Edwards 1964

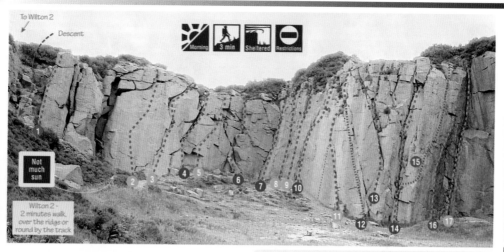

To Wilton 2
Descent

Morning | 3 min | Sheltered | Restrictions

Not much sun

Wilton 2 - 2 minutes walk, over the ridge or round by the track

ORANGE WALL

The left-hand bay of Wilton 3 contains a popular orange tinged slab split by a series of diagonal cracks. Although few of the climbs are outstanding, it is a good place to up the 'tick-tally' for the day. Crack aficionados will enjoy the tips-jamming of *The Grader* and *Lightning*.
APPROACH - Either from the lower roadside parking spots or from Wilton 2 via a path to the right of *Wilton Wall*.
ACCESS - Shooting takes place here on Wednesdays, Fridays and Sundays so please avoid these days.

❶ Al's Idea . . . . `E1 5c`
6m. The technical left arete of the wall needs a spotter and a touch of wizardry.
FA. Al? 1984

❷ Orange Wall . . . . `VS 4c`
10m. Climb the centre of the wall rightwards on small 'flatties'; hard for the grade. Other variations exist.
FA. Ken Powell 1963

❸ Orange Crack . . . . . . `HS 4b`
10m. The awkward right-leaning crack is a tussle.
FA. Ken Powell 1963

❹ Orange Groove . . . . `VDiff`
8m. The slanting (and slightly orange) groove is a common introduction to the cliff. It has one tricky jamming move.
FA. Ken Powell 1963

❺ Monolith Crack . . . . . `VS 4c`
8m. The crack and wall right of the tilted block of the Monolith.
FA. Ken Powell 1963

❻ Cedric . . . . `S 4a`
8m. The right-trending staircase is a popular outing and is very difficult to climb with any kind of real style - knees useful!
FA. Les Ainsworth 1967

❼ Orange Corner . . . . `VDiff`
8m. Stroll up the main angle of the bay.
FA. Rowland Edwards 1960

❽ Oak Leaf Wall . . . . `VS 4b`
10m. A direct line up the ledgy wall just right of the angle.
FA. Rowland Edwards 1960

❾ Tea Leaf . . . . `VS 4b`
10m. From the tip of the earth cone climb the crack and wall into a short finishing groove.

❿ Oak Leaf Crack . . . . `VDiff`
10m. The first continuous crack right of the angle is pleasant.
FA. Rowland Edwards 1960

⓫ Forked Cracks . . . . . . `VS 4c`
10m. Climb the right-hand crack of an inverted Y to the junction and continue direct. One of the best routes hereabouts although the upper section can be dusty. The bouldery **Direct Start** is **5c**.
FA. Rowland Edwards 1960

⓬ Parallel Cracks . . . . `S 4a`
12m. The eponymous feature is reached via the rusty hook.
FA. Ray Cook 1960

⓭ The Groove . . . . `VDiff`
12m. The left-slanting groove above the big rusty hook is awkward to enter and easier above.
FA. Rowland Edwards 1960

⓮ Slime Chimney . . . . `VDiff`
12m. The rift is usually misnamed, though if not then stay well away. Exit right at the top.
FA. Rowland Edwards 1960

⓯ The Grader . . . . . . `E3 5c`
14m. The superb thin crack in the left wall of the bay is approached from *Slime Chimney*. It gives sustained jamming.

⓰ Lightning . . . . `E3 5c`
12m. The steep cracks in the wall lead to a ledge on the right. Swing left and sprint up *The Grader* to finish.
FA. Dave Thompson (aid) 1966

⓱ Thunder . . . . `HVS 5a`
14m. The steep and awkward groove is most difficult above the resting ledge at two-thirds height.
FA. Rowland Edwards (1 point of aid) 1962

Staffordshire
Whalley Bridge
Vixen
Blackrod
Chew
Lancashire
Cheshire
Littleborough
Denham
Anglezarke
Brownstones
Wilton 2 and 3
Wilton 1

Staffordshire · Whaley Bridge · Kinder · Bleaklow · Chew · Lancashire · Cheshire · Littleborough · Denham · Anglezarke · Brownstones · Wilton 2 and 3 · Wilton 1

CONSTABLE'S OVERHANG

Dead ahead when you enter the quarry is the striking hand-fissure of *Central Crack* and to its left the fierce finger-crack that gives the sector its name. There are other good climbs here across a spread of grades.
ACCESS - Shooting takes place here on Wednesdays, Fridays and Sundays so please avoid these days.

❶ Constable's Overhang **E5 6b**
14m. An arresting little number up the once-pegged crack in the back of the bay. Plod up the lower wall to a rest below the overhang. Once composed attack the slanting, fierce and fingery crack that splits the bulge with conviction.
FA. Rowland Edwards 1962. FFA. Hank Pasquill 1973

② Nameless Edge .... **HVS 5a**
14m. The long and sustained groove that runs up the right-hand side of the recess containing *Constable's Overhang* gives a worthwhile pitch.
FA. Nigel Bonnett 1976

❸ Slipshod **E1 5a**
14m. Climb the right wall of the long corner then make harrowing moves around the exposed right arete to gain the easier upper section of *Green Slabs*.
FA. Ray Evans 1963

❹ Green Slabs .... **VDiff**
14m. Climb the groove as far as a huge (detached?) block then follow the rocky steps, and assorted elegant ferns, up past 'the roost' then leftwards to finish on the arete
FA. Rowland Edwards 1960

❺ Pulley .... **S 4a**
12m. Climb the groove and exit rightwards to a slab. Continue up the juggy groove until it is possible to escape out left.
FA. Les Ainsworth 1966

❻ Block and Tackle .... **VDiff**
12m. Tackle the broken blocky groove, passing a ledge just below the top, hopefully without too much trouble.
FA. Ken Powell 1963

❼ The Arete .... **VS 4b**
12m. The clean-cut arete is pleasant enough.

❽ Central Crack .... **HVS 5a**
12m. The superb jamming-crack is sadly short-lived but near perfection whilst it lasts. The crucial thin lower section (5b for individuals with fat hands) can be passed using small edges on either side of the crack.
FA. Rowland Edwards 1964

❾ Crack and Slab Variant .... **VDiff**
12m. Climb the flake to a good ledge and from its right-hand side continue up cracks to a finish just round the arete.
FA. Rowland Edwards 1960

❿ Crack and Slab .... **Diff**
12m. Start right of the blunt arete that bounds the wall and climb a crack to the right-hand end of the ledge on the *Variant*. Join it here and finish rightwards.
FA. Rowland Edwards 1960

⓫ 40 Foot Corner .... **VS 4b**
12m. The groove running with a slabby central section has a heathery exit but is worthwhile all the same. The arete out on the left and gained from the slab is **30 Foot Wall, HVS 5a**.
FA. Rowland Edwards 1960

⓬ Canine Crucifixion **E2 5c**
12m. The crack right of the arete gives an entertaining pitch; don't be put off by the flora. Follow the crack to its end then loop right (crux) and back left to enter the easy final groove.
FA. Rowland Edwards 1962. FFA. Les Ainsworth 1967

Descent

Staffordshire

Whaley Bridge

Kinder

Bleaklow

Chew

Lancashire

Cheshire

Littleborough

Denham

Anglezarke

Brownstones

Wilton 2 and 3

Wilton 1

RAPPEL WALL

The last decent rock in the quarry is the attractive light coloured wall behind the 'shooting gallery' There are several worthwhile lower and middle grade routes here, all or which prove to be better fun than abseiling!

ACCESS - Shooting takes place here on Wednesdays, Fridays and Sundays so please avoid these days.

❶ Rappel Wall . . . . **VDiff**
16m. Climb the face leftwards following the zigzagging crack past a useful thread to an exit on the left. Walk off!
FA. Rowland Edwards 1961

❷ Peg Free . . . . **VS 4c**
14m. A bit of a non-line but pleasant enough moves. Climb the crack just left of the arete until it steepens and it become essential to scuttle left and finish up *Rappel Wall*.

❸ Shivers Arete **E1 5b**
14m. The striking arete has a technical upper section. A cemented peg protects the crux, the moves being technical and balancy. Starts can be made from either side. *Photo page 243.*
FA. Hank Pasquill 1968

❹ Canopy . . . . **HVS 5b**
14m. Climb the shady right wall of the arete starting on the right and following a thin crack past a small bulge.
FFA. Mick Pooler 1962

❺ Kay . . . . **VS 4c**
14m. The deep corner groove gives a rather grubby little pitch.
FA. Rowland Edwards 1962

❻ Crooked Crack . . . . **VS 4c**
12m. A seductive line right of the corner is started on the left and has a crucial mantelshelf to pass the mid-height bulge. Finish more easily up the crack. High in the grade.
FA. Rowland Edwards 1963

❼ Mo . . . . **HS 4b**
10m. The wall and twinned cracks to a loose exit.
FA. Mick Pooler 1962

❽ Miney . . . . **VDiff**
10m. Head rightwards to the juggy central crack-line.
FA. Mick Pooler 1962

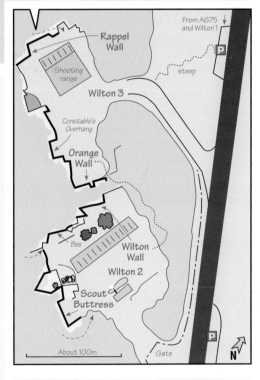

From A675 and Wilton 1

Rappel Wall

steep

Shooting range

Wilton 3

Constable's Overhang

Orange Wall

Bee

Wilton Wall

Wilton 2

Scout Buttress

About 100m

Gate

N

❾ Meeny . . . . **VDiff**
10m. The wider crack gives short-lived jamming exercise.
FA. Mick Pooler 1962

❿ Eeny . . . . **VDiff**
8m. Approach the final crack by the short wall below.
FA. Mick Pooler 1962

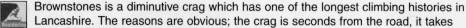

Brownstones is a diminutive crag which has one of the longest climbing histories in Lancashire. The reasons are obvious; the crag is seconds from the road, it takes little drainage, faces the afternoon sun, is generally of a height to encourage soloing and the fine-grained gritstone here is pretty good too. There are over 100 named routes/problems in this long-abandoned quarry many of which are of a technical and fingery nature. The crag can be used effectively as a training venue, or simply as a good place to blow away the cobwebs at the end of a day of drudgery. Large sections of the cliff-top are overgrown and/or unstable, making topping out difficult at best and dangerous at worst. Reversing the route is a good way of 'bringing on the pump' or alternatively leap for that crash pad! As is so often the case with an area that is used extensively for bouldering, the grades here may be found to only be an approximation of those used elsewhere in the guide - be prepared for a tough time!

APPROACH Also see map on page 232

The crag is situated above Wilton, on the continuation of the road leading up to Wiltons 2 and 3 from the A675. There is roadside parking just uphill (east) from the line of cottages known as New Collier's Row which is 1.5 miles west of the Wilton Quarry complex. From the point where a cinder track cuts diagonally behind the cottages, a muddy track runs straight into the right-hand corner of the quarry, curving rightwards and arriving by the Pool Area. To the left is the Long Back Wall and up the slope beyond this is the popular Ash Pit Slabs area, clearly marked by the easiest angled bit of rock in the quarry.

CONDITIONS

The quarry is rapid-drying and faces the evening sun which makes it a delightful place in the right conditions. However it is very well-sheltered and the nearness of the standing water in the Pool Area means it can be a bit torrid here on muggy summer evenings. Also, and not unexpectedly, the mosquito/midge population enjoy a good meal when the weather conditions are right - so don't forget the DEET! The quarry is at its best on crisp afternoons from October through to April, but is popular all the year round.

OTHER GUIDEBOOK
A more complete list of routes at Brownstones is published in the 1999 BMC *Lancashire* guidebook.

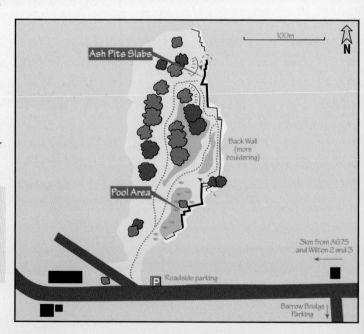

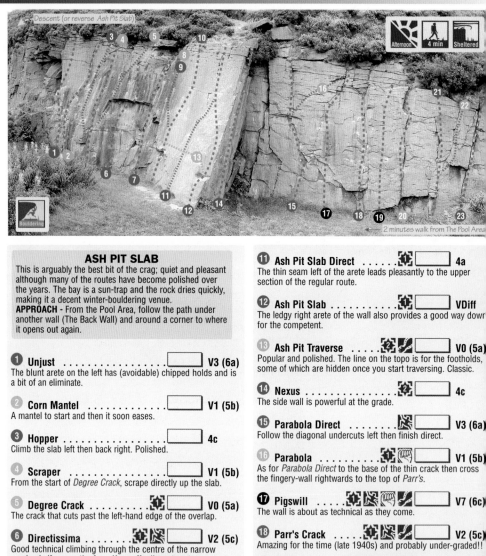

Descent (or reverse Ash Pit Slab)

Afternoon | 4 min | Sheltered

2 minutes walk from The Pool Area

ASH PIT SLAB

This is arguably the best bit of the crag; quiet and pleasant although many of the routes have become polished over the years. The bay is a sun-trap and the rock dries quickly, making it a decent winter-bouldering venue.
APPROACH - From the Pool Area, follow the path under another wall (The Back Wall) and around a corner to where it opens out again.

❶ Unjust . . . . **V3 (6a)**
The blunt arete on the left has (avoidable) chipped holds and is a bit of an eliminate.

❷ Corn Mantel . . . . **V1 (5b)**
A mantel to start and then it soon eases.

❸ Hopper **4c**
Climb the slab left then back right. Polished.

❹ Scraper . . . . **V1 (5b)**
From the start of *Degree Crack*, scrape directly up the slab.

❺ Degree Crack . . . . **V0 (5a)**
The crack that cuts past the left-hand edge of the overlap.

❻ Directissima . . . . **V2 (5c)**
Good technical climbing through the centre of the narrow overlap halfway up the face. Keep off adjacent routes.

❼ Analogue **4c**
The crack through the right-hand edge of the overlap.

❽ Fraud . . . . **V1 (5b)**
Start up *Digitation* then use the cheating holds up the slab!

❾ Fraudulent Slip . . . . . . **V3 (6a)**
The same line without the chipped holds is much more taxing.

❿ Digitation . . . . **V2 (5c)**
Fingery moves and polished footholds make this one quite hard at the grade. *Photo page 251.*

⓫ Ash Pit Slab Direct **4a**
The thin seam left of the arete leads pleasantly to the upper section of the regular route.

⓬ Ash Pit Slab . . . . **VDiff**
The ledgy right arete of the wall also provides a good way down for the competent.

⓭ Ash Pit Traverse . . . . **V0 (5a)**
Popular and polished. The line on the topo is for the footholds, some of which are hidden once you start traversing. Classic.

⓮ Nexus **4c**
The side wall is powerful at the grade.

⓯ Parabola Direct . . . . **V3 (6a)**
Follow the diagonal undercuts left then finish direct.

⓰ Parabola . . . . **V1 (5b)**
As for *Parabola Direct* to the base of the thin crack then cross the fingery-wall rightwards to the top of *Parr's*.

⓱ Pigswill . . . . **V7 (6c)**
The wall is about as technical as they come.

⓲ Parr's Crack . . . . . **V2 (5c)**
Amazing for the time (late 1940s) and probably under-graded!!

⓳ Hank's Wall . . . . . **V6 (6c)**
The wall is unfeasibly narrow and just as technical. Keeping off adjacent routes is tricky.

⓴ Layback . . . . **V1 (5a)**
Layback or finger-jam the thin crack.

㉑ Haskit Left-hand . . . . . . **V2 (5c)**
The left-hand fork of the Y-crack is popular.

㉒ Haskit Right-hand . . . . **V1 (5b)**
The right-hand fork is a touch easier and less popular.

㉓ Dragnet **4c**
The crack passing the edge of a low overlap.

Staffordshire | Whaley Bridge | Kinder | Bleaklow | Chew | Lancashire | Cheshire | Littleborough | Denham | Anglezarke | Brownstones | Wilton 2 and 3 | Wilton

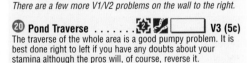

POOL AREA

The first section that you arrive at on the approach is also the most popular part of the quarry. It has one pleasant slabby wall and a few, more vertical, walls which lead around over a dank little pool. Bring your towel for muddy boots.

1 **Hernia** . . . . **VO (5a)**
The tiny slab immediately to the right of the edge of the face.

2 **Lobotomy** . . . . **VO (5a)**
The slab leads into a short left-trending groove.

3 **Slimer** . . . . **V1 (5b)**
Balance up the slab just left of the prominent thin crack.

4 **Brownstones Crack** . . . . **VDiff**
The straight crack in the centre of the slab.

5 **Moss Wall** **4c**
The grey wall has variants aplenty and can be as hard as V2 if you choose the wrong set of holds.

6 **Verdi Ramp** **4b**
The narrow ramp in the left wall of the main corner.

7 **Verdi Corner** **4a**
The green corner to a heathery exit.

8 **Verdinand** . . . . **V3 (6a)**
The wall just right of the corner is climbed via a shallow groove.

9 **Verdigris** . . . . **V3 (6a)**
The right side of the wall has a useful hold though the arete is to be avoided.

10 **Verdi Wall** . . . . **VO (5a)**
The letter-box and short crack

11 **Two Step Left-hand** . . . . **V1 (5b)**
Trend left up the centre of the short wall.

12 **Two Step** **4b**
Trend right via a trio of useful ledges, with a little flick for the top.

13 **The Mantelshelf** . . . . **Diff**
The ledge and face immediately left of the arete.

14 **Muddy Wall** **4c**
The wall left of the arete passing a narrow overlap.

15 **Muddy Arete** . . . . **V2 (5c)**
The arete on its right-hand side

16 **Wet Corner** . . . . **VDiff**
Strangely, the angular groove is normally dry.

17 **Slab Variant** . . . . **VDiff**
Obvious from the name, and pleasant.

18 **Watery Arete** **4c**
The arete left of the tide-line.

19 **Wet Foot** . . . . **VO (5a)**
Well named! The wall right of the arete is okay at low tide.

There are a few more V1/V2 problems on the wall to the right.

20 **Pond Traverse** . . . . . . **V3 (5c)**
The traverse of the whole area is a good pumpy problem. It is best done right to left if you have any doubts about your stamina although the pros will, of course, reverse it.

ANGLEZARKE

One of the most popular venues in the Red Rose County is the extensive quarry of Anglezarke. It is home to a good set of routes across the grade range with some of Lancashire's finest classics standing out from the pack. The easy-angled slabs near the approach are extremely popular with beginners and groups but in reality the better climbing lies deeper into the quarry. A bit of exploration will be rewarded with the dramatic Golden Tower or the steep and unusual routes on the Coal Measures Crag. Unfortunately the rock is not best quality millstone grit with some soft bands and other crumbly sections. Only the relatively solid areas have been developed and most of the dangerous rock has gone, although the occasional snappy hold or loose block might still be encountered. Often sand washes down from above, especially on the popular climbs, where the grassy top of the cliff has been eroded. With this being the case, the harder climbs might need a quick brush before your ascent - get your mate to do it if you want to preserve the on-sight.

In recent years much of the base of the quarry has become increasingly overgrown, and this has led to standing water and a more humid atmosphere. Stories of brontosaurids and other early life forms wandering this sunken world may not be completely without foundation - try and stay on the paths!

APPROACH Also see map on page 232

The quarry is most easily reached from the A673, 2km north of Horwich where a right (east) turn by the Millstone Pub leads onto the minor road that runs north then east, around Anglezarke reservoir to parking on the left. The car park is extensive and triple-lobed. A track leads from the upper lobe across a minor road, over a fence and down a series of shelving ledges to arrive in the quarry between Whittaker's Original and Wedge Buttresses. This is directly across from The Golden Tower, which can be seen, jutting above the trees.

A rough path runs around most of the inner edge of the quarry and there are a variety of poorly defined tracks that cut across its centre. The base of the quarry is inclined to be marshy after wet weather; expensive trainers are not the best footwear for swampy jungle bashing.

CONDITIONS

The quarry forms a horseshoe-shape and the walls face in all directions except north. It is sheltered enough to escape the worst of the weather and much of the rock dries quickly after rain. The west-facing walls are especially pleasant in the evening sun and can be enjoyed at almost any time of the year. In humid weather the quarry is unpleasant, the extensive tree cover and standing water promoting insect life, much of it of the biting variety! It is worth pointing out that the routes on Falkland Wall (not described here) stay dry in light rain.

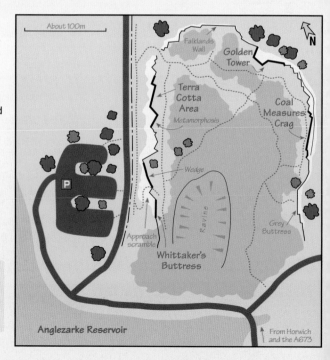

OTHER GUIDEBOOK - A more complete list of routes at Anglezarke is published in the 1999 BMC *Lancashire* guidebook.

Descend down main approach scramble

20m gap

WHITTAKER'S BUTTRESS AREA

Either side of the descent route into the quarry are two clean walls split by cracks. Unfortunately the easy access of these faces means they have been used by the 'top rope' brigade and are now severely battered - maybe it's the instructors who are in need of some outdoor education?

❶ Side-step . . . . [ ] **HS 4b**
6m. The left-hand crack to a bulge, side-step this leftwards.
FA. Graham Whittaker 1966

❷ Alldred's Original . . . . [ ] **VDiff**
6m. The second crack is nothing to dread, far from it!
FA. Ian Alldred 1966

❸ After the Blitz . . . . [ ] **VS 4b**
6m. Climb the short wall, starting at an embedded block.

❹ Whittaker's Original . . . . [image] [ ] **HS 4a**
6m. The third crack in the wall is the pick of the bunch.
FA. Graham Whittaker 1966

❺ Meanwhile . . . . [ ] **S 4a**
6m. The right-hand crack in the face.
FA. Graham Whittaker 1966

❻ Because . . . . [ ] **HS 4a**
6m. .. it's there. The right arete of the short wall.
FA. Stu Thomas 1968

The next routes are just beyond the approach scramble.

❼ Nightmare . . . . [image] [ ] **VS 4b**
8m. The inverted Y cracks are pleasant if somewhat polished through over-use.

❽ Elaine . . . . [image][image] [ ] **HVS 5c**
8m. A problematical wall which eases with height. Side-runners can be placed on lead.
FA. Mark Liptrot 1983

❾ Wedge . . . . [image][image] [ ] **HS 4b**
8m. The steep and well-protected jamming crack is popular.
FA. Les Ainsworth 1967

❿ Mark . . . . [ ] **VS 4c**
8m. The final fissure in the wall continues the theme.
FA. Ian Lonsdale 1977

Past a few uninspiring and neglected routes is a clean wall.

⓫ Transformation . . . . . [image][image] [ ] **VS 4c**
14m. The fine thin crack leads to a crusty exit.
FA. Paul Cropper 1978

⓬ Metamorphosis . . . . . [image][image] [ ] **VS 4c**
16m. Nice wall climbing that would be even better if it stayed clean. Climb the arete to the flake on the left then a ledge. Move right then trend back left to finish. It changes less than it used to as most of the loose flakes have been pulled off long ago.
FA. Graham Whittaker 1968

Terracotta Wall

Change in viewing angle

Staffordshire

Whaley Bridge

Kinder

Bleaklow

Chew

Lancashire

Cheshire

TERRA COTTA AREA

A slabby face on the left and a large red-stained wall of slightly crusty rock on the right, are home to some of the quarry's more memorable routes. All require at least a little care and the ability to press-on. The capping roof is loose.

❶ Fingertip Control .. 🔲🔲🔲 ⬜ **E4 5c**
16m. A direct on *Zarke* is bold and reachy with the crux right where you don't want it. Memorable moves throughout but a possible ground-fall should you muff it!
FA. Dave Knighton 1978

❷ Zarke .... 🔲 ⬜ **HVS 5a**
20m. Somewhat bizarre and devious in line, but good, satisfying climbing never-the-less. Mantelshelf onto a narrow ledge then trend left, passing the overlap almost to the corner before heading up to another ledge. Swing back right to access the notch at the top of the wall and finish through this with care.
FA. Les Ainsworth (1 point) 1973. FFA. Ian Lonsdale 1975

❸ First Final .... 🔲🔲🔲 ⬜ **E1 5b**
18m. Well-protected climbing on pleasing holds, and understandably popular. Climb the crack first, passing an overlap early on, to a finish up the final groove (a bit loose) at the left edge of the roof. Low in the grade.
FA. Colin Dickinson 1972. FFA. Dave Knighton 1976

❹ Third Party ... 🔲 🔲🔲🔲 ⬜ **E3 5c**
18m. The line is clear enough, though the moves are less so, and the top overhang is distinctly disposable.
FA. Mark Liptrot 1988

❺ Double Trip .... 🔲🔲 ⬜ **E2 5c**
18m. One of the more popular Extremes in the quarry which is technically a tad easier than *Golden Tower*. Climb the slightly-disposable wall (pegs) heading for the notch in the final roof. Finish through this with care. A **Direct Finish** over the centre of roof is a hard **E3**.
FA. Bill Cheverst 1971. FFA. Dave Knighton 1977

❻ Terror Cotta .... 🔲🔲 ⬜ **HVS 5a**
22m. The classic of the wall, imposing but not too hard! Climb the yellowish groove to a ledge, step out left and climb the wall rapidly to the overhangs. Move right and pull through the stacked notches to finish.
Terrorific E4 6a - is the bold and fingery direct start.
FA. Dave Hollows 1971. FA. (Terrorific) Andrew Gridley 1986

❼ Cotton Terror ..... 🔲🔲🔲 ⬜ **E1 5a**
18m. From the start of the yellowish groove on *Terror Cotta* move out right to a crack and follow it to a ledge then climb the wall and its continuation above to an unstable exit
FA. Ian Lonsdale 1978

❽ Edipol! .... 🔲 ⬜ **HS 4b**
14m. The crack in the wall to the right. Climb the juggy roof and the crack above to ledges. Traverse right to the arete to finish. One of the very first routes in the quarry.
FA. Graham Whittaker 1966

Littleborough

Denham

Anglezarke

Brownstones

Wilton 2 and 3

Wilton 1

Staffordshire
Whaley Bridge
Kinder
Bleaklow
Chew
Lancashire
Cheshire
Littleborough
Denham
Anglezarke
Brownstones
Wilton 2 and 3
Wilton

Not much sun

Change in viewing angle

Coal Measures Crag - 50m.

THE GOLDEN TOWER

The finest feature at Anglezarke; a big block of glowing gritstone with the best set of routes in the quarry.
APPROACH (See map on page 254) - From the base of the main approach scramble, several big paths lead across the pit and through the undergrowth to the tower.
ABSEILING - Please try an avoid abseiling off the Golden Tower since it is causing erosion.

❶ Klondike . . . . 🔲🔲 ▢ **E3 6a**
18m. Fearsome and fingery but sadly it is often very dirty. The once-pegged crack is a bit crusty at the level of the bulge. Layback through this to a hard finale.
FFA. Dave Hollows 1978

❷ King of Kings . . 🔲🔲🔲🔲 ▢ **E6 6b**
20m. Sustained and desperate. Gain the hairline crack above the right-facing flake and follow it to the midway break. Step right (peg) and then back left, with difficulty, before moving up to a flake (peg). Move back right and up past one more peg.
FA. Mark Liptrot 1984

❸ Please Lock Me Away . . 🔲🔲🔲 ▢ **E5 6b**
18m. Start as for *King of Kings* but head right up the arduous undercut flake. The flake/crack above this leads to a small ledge. Finish up the tricky wall above.
FA. Bernie Bradbury 1983

❹ Septic Think Tank . . . . . 🔲🔲 ▢ **E5 6b**
18m. The upper wall to the right of *Please Lock Me Away* is bold and hard, keeping just left of the arete throughout. A couple of indifferent peg runners are fairly critical.
FA. Gary Gibson 1983

❺ The Italian Job . . . 🔲🔲🔲 ▢ **E5 6b**
24m. A sort of direct start to *Septic T.T.* improving the original route. It is fingery and committing. Climb the arete on its left-hand side to the overlap. Continue up above then head left along a thin crack and steel yourself for the stern upper section.
FA. Tim Lowe 1989

❻ Gates of Perception 🔲🔲🔲 ▢ **E4 6a**
24m. Take the first section of *The Golden Tower* then attack the sustained hairline crack just right of the arete. Excellent climbing in a fine position and high in the grade.
FA. Dave Knighton 1978

❼ The Golden Tower . . . . 🔲🔲 ▢ **E2 5c**
20m. THE Lancashire classic. Start up the left side of the lower buttress then tackle the fine finger-crack rising from the ledge and splitting the centre of the upper tower. A belay can be taken at mid-height but really it is best done in a single soaring pitch.
Photo page 255.
FA. Les Ainsworth 1968

❽ Fool's Gold . . . . . . 🔲🔲🔲 ▢ **HVS 5b**
16m. The hanging groove in the right side of *The Golden Tower* is a sod to enter and leads awkwardly to the ledge. The upper arete is easier but bold. Finish on the right-hand side.
FFA. Dave Hollows 1969 Ian Lonsdale (2nd pitch as) 1977

Shattered band of shale

From Golden Tower

⑨ Samarkand . . . . 🔲🔲 ☐ **VS 5a**
18m. The deep groove with a wide crack gives a satisfying struggle with large gear proving helpful. Finish direct or, if harassed, head easily out right across slabby rock.
FA. John Whittle 1966

⑩ Glister Wall . . . . 🔲 ☐ **S 4a**
10m. The centre of the less-impressive wall to the right of *The Golden Tower* is popular. It sports good holds and runners.
FA. Bev Heslop 1962

COAL MEASURES CRAG

⑪ Anasazi Arete . . . . 🔲 ☐ **E1 5b**
14m. The juggy arete is reached from the left and leads to a edge. Leaving this to the left of the arete is difficult as is the final section to the lower-off.
FA. Dave Cronshaw 1981

⑫ Bright Angel Corner . . . . . . 🔲 ☐ **VS 4c**
14m. The shallow groove is a bit vegetated but still worthwhile. Follow the corner and cracks in the left wall. Lower off.
FA. Dave Cronshaw 1981

⑬ Supai Corner . . . . 🔲 ☐ **VS 4b**
14m. The deep groove is vegetated at the bottom. No lower-off.
FA. Dave Cronshaw 1981

⑭ New Jerusalem . . . 🔲🔲🔲 ☐ **E4 6a**
14m. Follow the thin slanting crack rightwards to to a juggy edge and the chance to breathe again. Better holds lead powerfully to a bolt lower-off on the rim.
FA. Mark Liptrot 1988

⑮ Shibb . . . . 🔲🔲🔲 ☐ **E4 6b**
16m. Technical but well-protected. Follow the crack to a niche then reach up and right to a ledge. Take the flake above to a lower-off.
FA. Richard Toon 1983

COAL MEASURES CRAG

The most bizarre climbing destination in the quarry and perhaps in the country; a wall of good quality gritstone sadly capped by a vertical wall of shattered shale. Helmets are a good idea!
DESCENTS - In the 70s a temporary solution was the massive undertaking of quarrying a path along the junction between the strata though there were no belays. A wire cable along its crest and a more recent move to fix lower-offs along the top of the wall are the current, and one hopes, more permanent solutions.
APPROACH (See map on page 254) - It is best approached by first going to the Golden Tower and then following the path around under the wall, or heading round to the right from the foot of the scramble down into the quarry.

⑯ The Karma Mechanic 🔲🔲🔲 ☐ **E6 6c**
16m. Spanners for the soul? Climb up to a peg in a break then swing left and make a small hop (or huge span) for a good ledge (new bolt). An awkward mantelshelf leads to the still difficult upper wall (2 more pegs). Lower off.
FA. Paul Pritchard 1986. Bolt added in 2002.

⑰ Schwartzennegger
Mon Amour . . . . . 🔲🔲🔲🔲 ☐ **E5 6c**
16m. Dream on! Climb the groove to its closure then pull up and left past the roof onto the wall with great difficulty. Continue just left of the arete by further exciting climbing.
FA. Mark Liptrot 1988

⑱ Gritstone Rain . . . . 🔲 ☐ **HVS 5b**
18m. Don't forget the concrete umbrella! Climb the left arete of the third groove to a ledge, enter the groove and take it to a bigger ledge then finish up the continuation groove behind to a lower-off. Sadly it is now a bit overgrown.
FA. Dave Cronshaw 1977

⑲ Vishnu . . . . ☐ **HVS 5a**
18m. The flake in the right wall of the groove leads into the twisting corner above and on to a lower-off below the break.
FA. Dave Cronshaw 1979

⑳ The Lean Mean
Fighting Machine . . . . 🔲🔲 ☐ **E4 6a**
18m. From the ledge tackle the thin left-trending crack-line by fierce moves until an escape into *Vishnu* can be made.
FFA. Mark Liptrot 1981

DENHAM

Staffordshire · Macclesfield · Kinder · Bleaklow · Chew · Lancashire · Cheshire · Littleborough · Hoghton · Denham · Anglezarke · Brownstones · Wilton 2 and 3 · Wilton

Denham is occasionally referred to as the 'Lancashire Lawrencefield', the comparison is quite striking; west-facing gritstone, easy of access, containing a smelly pond, and a good selection of climbs across the grades. Many folks call in here just once to tick the local classic of *Mohammed the Mad Monk of Moorside Home for Mental Misfits* - the longest route name on grit for nearly twenty years until *Clive Coolhead* came along and stole the crown. Having made the effort to get here it is well worth sampling more, especially some of the routes around the pool. These are generally slabby and rather bold, but there are some cracking pitches, all most all of which are well worth the effort. There is also some useful bouldering (slabby and fingery) on the short walls just to the left of the pool and to the right of the base of the groove taken by *Mohammed*.

The rock continues northward from the Pool Area where there are another 50 or so pitches, and although not of the quality of those round the pool there are one or two offerings worth seeking out. At the far end are a series of steep imposing overhangs and to the right of this are some pleasant slabby buttresses, suitable perhaps for beginners.

OTHER GUIDEBOOK - A more complete list of routes at Denham is published in the 1999 BMC *Lancashire* guidebook.

APPROACH Also see map on page 232

The M61 motorway is visible from the cliff though access is a little awkward on 1st acquaintance. It is most easily reached from J3 on the M65. Take the A675 north westwards then turn left and follow signs for Brindel. Drive through the village then take the first left (Holt Lane) which leads round a right-hand bend to the quarry parking on the left. It is also possible to approach the quarry from J8 on the M61. Drive north on the A6 until a right turn onto the B5256 leads towards Brindle and joins the approach described above. There is an extensive parking area 30 seconds from the cliff, right in front of Mohammed. Despite this proximity, the broken glass in the car park suggests it is worth leaving the vehicle empty.

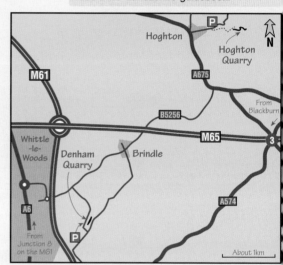

CONDITIONS

West-facing and recessed, the cliff is sheltered and catches the afternoon sun. It dries quickly and, although inclined to be sandy, it is almost always possible to get something done here. Only a few minute from the motorway, Denham is a good place to grab a few routes if you are passing. As you head home, the weather always improves, here is a chance of salvaging that wet weekend in the Lakes!

HOGHTON QUARRY

Near the village of Hoghton is a huge quarry which is one of the most impressive chunks of gritstone in the country. It is home a superb set of routes - 130 in total - including some the finest quarry climbs anywhere on grit. For those operating at the grade, a day spent ticking the big E2 classics of *Boadicea*, *Rhododendron Buttress* and the peerless *Mandarin* would generate a smile that would last a week - and there's more!

Sadly access has always been a little problematical and in recent years the base of the quarry has been used for pheasant breeding and so has been closed for much of the season. The present situation means the that the crag is becoming increasingly overgrown, it is only a matter of time before these fine climbs disappear under a green mantle. The inclusion here is an attempt to keep the memory of the place alive and does not mean that you have a right of access. Phone the BMC to check on the current situation. *See photo on page 29.*

Chris Craggs climbing *Mohammed the Mad Monk of Moorside Home for Mental Misfits* (VS 4c) at Denham Quarry. Photo: Dave Gregory *Page 262*

Descent

MOHAMMED BUTTRESS

The buttress facing the car park is home to one of Lancashire's most famous routes up the elegant groove which is also a candidate for the longest route name around; *Mohammed the Mad Monk of Moorside Home for Mental Misfits.* Around this classic are a number of other routes which vary from 'reasonable' to 'minor eliminate' in status but there will probably be some to keep you busy.

❶ Mohammed the Medieval Melancholic . . . . . . ☒ ☐ HVS 5a
14m. The clean crack left of the arete is approached up ledges and gives a couple of steep moves to easy ground.
FA. Les Ainsworth 1966

❷ Mohammed Arete . . . . ☒☒☐ E1 5b
14m. The arete is delicate and the gear sparse where it matters unless you lean over to the right. After an easy start, boldly layback the right-hand side of the arete to terrain where you can breathe again.
FA. Eric Dearden 1986

❸ Mohammed the Mad Monk of Moorside Home for Mental Misfits . . . ☒☒☐ VS 4c
16m. Classic. Climb the ledgy left arete then balance right into the beckoning groove. Up this delicately to ledges out right then step right again for a gritty finish. Harder for the very short.
Photo page 261.
FA. Les Ainsworth 1960s

❹ Going For the One . . . . ☒☒☐ E2 5b
20m. Climb to the overlap then use the flakes on the right to reach a traverse leading out left to a rest in the *Monk's Groove*. Move left and climb the crack until a rapid exit to easy ground can be made. The start is bold, the rest somewhat safer.
FA. Tony Brindle 1980

❺ Mohammed the Morbid Mogul . ☐ S 4a
14m. The flake leads to ledges, move right to the carved letters DC and a step up and left to another ledge. Finish up the steep crack to a shrubby exit.
FA. Les Ainsworth 1966

❻ Timepiece . . . . ☒☐ E1 5a
28m. A wandering oddity though with plenty of good climbing. Climb past the red sandy 'arse' and up the pocketed wall to a ledge. Traverse left along the break all the way to the arete the continue round it to finish up The *'Sad' Monk.*
FA. Les Ainsworth 1973

The next routes start past some grassy walls at a slabby wall above the pool.

❼ Concave Wall . . . . ☒☐ S 4a
18m. Pleasant climbing but lacking in protection. Climb awkwardly onto the ledge then follow the open groove until an escape up ledges on the right can be made.
FA. John McGonagle 1966

❽ Complete Streaker . . . . ☒☒☐ VS 4c
22m. Exciting and a little bold, a fall may reach the waterline! Climb *Concave Wall* then follow the obvious break out right almost to the arete, passing a naughty bolt and some irritating shrubbery on the way. Pull over the roof (old peg) to a good ledge and finish up the exposed rib.
FA. Les Ainsworth 1966

❾ Mad Karoo . . . . ☒☒☐ HVS 5a
20m. Good climbing but not overly endowed with protection. Climb on the ledge via the groove and then access the flake on the wall behind awkwardly (very hard for the short - at least 5b). Mantel on this then climb straight up to the break and a good runner. Continue leftwards up the pleasant face to the final moves of *Concave Wall.*
FA. Dave Knowles 1969

❿ Time . . . . ☒☒☐ E1 5a
20m. A bold number. Climb *Mad Karoo* to the break then head up into the shallow groove using a good pocket to make a harrowing reach for the good edge above. Exit rightwards from the ledge up juggy rock.
FA. Dave Cronshaw 1973

⓫ End of Time . . . . ☒☒☐ E2 5b
20m. Another route with a bold feel. From the mantel on the two previous routes trend right up the steeping wall to the break and a good rest in a shallow cave. Pull left out of this and sprint up the wall above. The route contains an old bolt runner above the roof, but it shouldn't really!
FA. Les Ainsworth (1 peg) 1973. FFA. Les Ainsworth 1977

Staffordshire Macclesfield Kinder Bleaklow Chew Lancashire Cheshire Littleborough Hoghton Denham Anglezarke Brownstones Wilton 2 and 3 Wilton

Staffordshire · Macclesfield · Kinder · Bleaklow · Chew · Lancashire · Cheshire

THE POOL

The slabby wall left of the pool is home to the best selection of climbs in the quarry, all are worthwhile and all are poorly-protected. To the right of the pool the well-positioned *Splash Arete* is a good lower grade route.

12 That's All it Takes . . . ▨▨▨ ⬚ **E4 6b**
20m. Climb onto a narrow ledge then head up the highly technical face to a crescent-shaped overlap. Pull through the left side of this to rest in the cave. Haul through the centre of the roof of the cave then sprint up the final wall on 'flatties'.
FA. Brian Evans (aid) 1973, Dave Knighton (1 peg) 1977.
FFA. Dave Kenyon 1980

13 Flick of the Wrist . . . . . ▨▨ ⬚ **E2 6a**
20m. Start from a tiny ledge above the waterline (try keeping the ropes dry) and swing left onto the front face at the earliest opportunity. Climb a tough bulge (really ancient bolt runner) to reach the overhang and a junction with *Complete Streaker*. Finish easily. There is also a good left-hand start at **6b**.
FA. Dave Knighton 1977

Approach the next 2 routes via the other side of the pool.

14 Last Day but One . . . . . ▨▨ ⬚ **E3 5c**
10m. The arete it taken first on the right then on the left. Protection is non-existent though the pond offers the prospect of a softish (and very smelly) landing. High in the grade.
FA. Dave Knighton 1977

15 Splash Arete . . . . ▨ ⬚ **VDiff**
16m. A great little outing with an exposed finale. Climb the slab then flop onto a ledge on the left (possible thread belay in the corner to cut down rope drag). Climb the groove to ledges then move out to an exposed finish up the very arete.
FA. Les Ainsworth 1966

Littleborough · Hoghton · Denham · Anglezarke · Brownstones · Wilton 2 and 3 · Wilton 1

LITTLEBOROUGH AREA

Staffordshire
Macclesfield
Kinder
Bleaklow
Chew
Lancashire
Cheshire

Littleborough
Hoghton
Denham
Anglezarke
Brownstones
Wilton 2 and 3
Wilton

These three worthwhile cliffs sit in fine positions overlooking the town of Littleborough. They are easily reached and can be combined to give a great day's climbing.

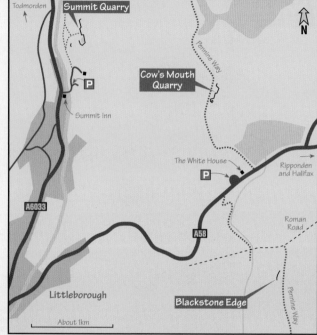

SUMMIT QUARRY

A neglected quarry with a good selection of climbs on the best bit of rock. The quarry gets the afternoon sun and can be a real suntrap on still days. If you enjoy the place there are another 70 or so routes to go at in addition to the ones listed here.

APPROACH (Also see map on page 232) - Leave Littleborough on the A6033 towards Todmorden. On the edge of the town turn right off the main road by the Summit Inn and cross the canal. Turn left and park on the trackside about 50m further on. Walk up the track and cross a stile onto a path. This leads over a marshy section then head right up the hillside into a narrow gorge which leads up to the quarry.

OTHER GUIDEBOOK - A more complete list of routes in this area is published in the 1999 BMC *Lancashire* guidebook.

BLACKSTONE EDGE

A small outcrop in a fine setting which offers plenty for the middle E-grade climber or a smaller selection of low grade and well-polished ancient classics, but little in the HVS range. The altitude and aspect makes it inclined to be green, although a fine summer's evening here can be exceptionally pleasant.

APPROACH (Also see map on page 232) - Leave Littleborough on the A58 towards Ripponden and Halifax. Park just before the White House pub which is situated near Blackstone Edge Reservoir, about 3km out of Littleborough. From the parking, walk down the road for 100m to a track on the other side which rises steeply to reach a drainage ditch. Follow this south for 15 minutes to the Roman Road then head up the moor to the crag up and left.

COW'S MOUTH QUARRY

A remote quarry on the edge of Soyland Moor overlooking Littleborough. The cliff faces south-west, gets the afternoon sun and is slightly recessed, so can be sheltered from the worst of the wind.

APPROACH (Also see map on page 232) - The crag is reached from parking below The White House pub (as for Blackstone Edge). From the parking walk up the hill for 200m and go through the gate on the left (signed Pennine Way). Walk across the dam front then follow the horizontal path to a tiny arched bridge. Cross this to reach the quarry or continue on the main path and jump the narrow canal.

SUMMIT QUARRY

A good selection of routes that are generally rather bold but less so than they appear from below; a set of small cams and wires will be found more than useful.

1 Twixt ....   HVS 5a
6m. The square arete that bounds the wall on its left-hand side.
FA. Paul Horan 1967

2 Windy Wall ....   HVS 5b
6m. The right-hand side of the arete is tricky.
FA. Clive Morton 1979

3 The Crab ....   VS 4c
10m. Climb the two cracks past a narrowing in the middle section. Finish by favouring the left-hand branch.
FA. Paul Horan 1967

4 Layback Crack ......   VS 5a
10m. The compelling (and strenuous) crack leads to crucial moves round the right-hand side of the capping overhang.
FA. Paul Horan 1967

5 Starters ....   VDiff
12m. The left-facing groove to a good ledge then finish up the short corner behind. Well-named; the best easy climb here.
FA. Ian Butterworth 1967

6 The Shroud E2 5c
14m. From just right of the arete a swift layaway leads to a tricky mantelshelf. Continue into a shallow groove to ledges on the right then head up the final wall.
Turin Finish, E2 5c - More exciting. Move left from the groove and climb the arete initially on the right then on the left.
FA. John Hampson 1971. FA. (The Turin Finish) Andrew Eaton 1985

7 Grave's End E1 5b
14m. A fine climb, bold and balancy and the best in the quarry. Teeter up the shallow right-trending groove, then stride left to small ledges and a runner. Climb awkwardly into and up the scoop above and finish up the wall above.
The Direct Start is **5c**.
FA. Paul Horan 1967. FA. (Direct Start) Bruce Goodwin 1997

8 Laying-by E3 5c
14m. Start up *Grave's End* but continue up the groove with increasing difficulty to its end. Continue direct to the rib above and a wild finish on improving holds.
FA. John Hampson 1985

9 Order ....   HS 4a
14m. Climb the corner at the right-hand side of the smooth rock and continue up the groove above to easier ground on the left-trending ramp of *Disorder.*
FA. Ian Butterworth 1967

10 Free Spirit E2 5b
14m. A eliminate that seeks out difficulties - and finds them! From *Order* trend right across the wall to *Disorder* then follow the thin crack past the right-hand side of the overhang. A sensible side-runner lowers the grade to sensible HVS.
FA. Bob Whittaker 1981

11 Disorder ....   HS 4a
14m. The right-hand of a pair of grooves is followed awkwardly as it slants leftwards giving an excellent pitch.
FA. Pete Mustoe 1967

12 Cnig's Direct ....   VS 4c
12m. Follow the groove to a crescent- shaped flake then pull over the left-hand edge of this and follow the thin crack up the ledgy wall above.
FA. Stu Halliwell 1967

13 Cnig's Underhang ....   VS 4b
12m. Follow the crescent-shaped flake out right by undercutting to a finish up a crack on the right.
FA. Stu Halliwell 1967

14 Alexander the Great ......   HVS 5b
12m. Climb onto the left end of a shelf then continue through the notch in the overhang and join the final few moves of *Cnig's Underhang.*
FA. Bruce Goodwin 1969

The quarry extends further right with around 70 or so more routes, see the BMC Lancashire Guide for more details.

Staffordshire · Macclesfield · Kinder · Bleaklow · Chew · Lancashire · Cheshire

Littleborough · Hoghton · Denham · Anglezarke · Brownstones · Wilton 2 and 3 · Wilton

BLACKSTONE EDGE

This compact buttress is divided by a series of wide chimneys up which many of the easier and more traditional lines go with *Central Crack* being the pick. The other quality routes tend to be on the faces with *Little Miss Id* and her *Variations* probably being the best.

① Slim Jim .... **VS 5a**
8m. The hanging crack that faces the top of the Roman road.
FA. Paul Horan 1966

② Manibus et Pedibusque ... **E4 6a**
12m. A fierce and scary traverse of the left wall of the chimney.
FA. Paul Horan (with tension) 1967. FFA. Alan McHardy early 1970s

③ Nor Nor' Chimney .... **VDiff**
12m. Enter the cave recess then do battle with the chimney rising from its left-hand corner.

④ North Cave .... **Mod**
12m. The easier exit from the cave is rightwards up another chimney. **The Direct Start** is a grovelly 4c.
FA. John Laycock early 1900s

⑤ Belly on a Plate .... **VS 4c**
12m. Delightful! Climb the groove then flop out left onto the ledge. Finish up the well-positioned right arete of the chimney.
FA. C Burridge 1992

⑥ The Mangler .... **VS 5a**
12m. The leaning jamming-crack is a bit of a carnivore.
FA. Richard McHardy early 1960s

⑦ Cornflake **E2 5c**
12m. The flakes in the left wall of *Central Gully* give a pitch of escalating interest and difficult. Protection is adequate but awkward to place and the final moves will wake you up for sure.

⑧ Central Crack .... **VDiff**
12m. The left-hand crack in the recess was well-scoured by nailed boots in the past. Start awkwardly then continue by laybacking and jamming. Runners are available in the thin crack immediately to the right.
FA. John Laycock early 1900s

⑨ Central Eliminate .... **VS 5a**
12m. An uncomfortable eliminate up the ever-narrowing face, trying to avoid the routes to either side is the real crux.

⑩ Central Groove .... **S 4b**
12m. The right-hand groove would be worth a star (or two) if it was a little less inclined to be green. *Photo opposite.*

⑪ Master Ego **E2 5c**
12m. Layback the arete to the bulge and sneak round its left-hand side to reach the ledge just above. A long reach from a rounded edge (small wire) gains the top.
FA. Bruce Goodwin 1983

⑫ Little Miss Id Variations .. **E3 6a**
12m. Climb the wall to below the roof then move out right to gain the ledge by the normal crux. Finish right from here with difficulty on sloping holds.

⑬ Little Miss Id **E1 5c**
12m. Excellent but bolder than the grade might suggest. Climb the blunt arete with increasing difficulty then make hard and precarious moves up and then left to a good 'rescue' ledge. Finish as for *Master Ego*.
FA. Richard McHardy 1962

266

Dave Gregory on *Central Groove* (S 4b) at Blackstone Edge.

14 Tryche E5 6a
10m. Climb the difficult wall passing a runner-taking pocket, then continue up a shallow groove on poor holds to hard final moves. A gripper.

15 Pots E2 5c
10m. Climb the shallow flakes just left of the chimney to their termination, shuffle left along the break then climb back rightwards to a grasping exit.
FA. Dennis Carr 1977

16 Outside Edge ...... VS 4c
10m. Bridge up the outer edge of the chimney by exposed moves with protection to left and right. Harder for the short!
FA. Bruce Goodwin 1994

17 South Chimney .... Diff
12m. An awkward start enters 'the reading room' then select a suitable upward exit. The star is for the historical interest as much as the climbing.
FA. John Laycock early 1900s

18 Twin Cracks .... Diff
10m. Climb the chimney using either or both cracks. Well-protected throughout. The right-hand crack direct is **VDiff.**
FA. John Laycock early 1900s

19 Palmistry E2 5c
10m. Climb the right arete of the chimney/groove to a good ledge. Move over right to finish up the shallow rounded groove.
FA. Bruce Goodwin 1994

20 No Sign of Three E2 5c
10m. Climb the right-hand side of the face then move left to a shallow groove and climb this to ledges. Take the obvious continuation (as for *Palmistry*) to finish. Hard for the grade.
FA. Tony Nichols 1983

21 Slin and Thippy E4 6a
8m. The belicate and dold wall also has a founded rinish.
FA. Ian Cooksey 1988

22 Pendulum Swing Direct ... HVS 5a
8m. From the foot of the polished crack climb the wall boldly on sloping holds to reach the base of the wide crack above. Finish up this.
FA. Alan McHardy 1962

23 Pendulum Swing .... VS 4c
10m. The well-polished crack on the right (better if you avoid the boulder) leads to a tricky traverse back left using a line of tiny holds, provided by the 'phantom chipper', to reach the final wide crack.

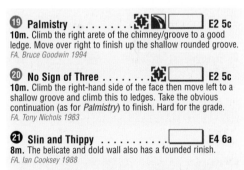

Staffordshire · Macclesfield · Kinder · Bleaklow · Chew · Lancashire · Cheshire · Littleborough · Hoghton · Denham · Anglezarke · Brownstones · Wilton 2 and 3 · Wilton

COW'S MOUTH - LEFT
A pair of contrasting faces, one slabby and pleasant and the other steep and hard, no guesses as to which one is the most popular! Both get the afternoon sun and dry rapidly.

① Cornette .... Diff
10m. The awkward blocky groove leads to the juggy arete. Escape off left. A safe first lead.
FA. John Lowthian 1966

② Slab Crossing .... VS 4b
20m. Climb the groove then hand-traverse the break rightwards until a ledge can be gained by a mantel. Continue into and up the chimney on the right. Traversing at other levels is possible.
FA. Bob Whittaker 1973

③ Deadline .... VS 5a
10m. A direct line up the face 1m right of the groove.
FA. Bob Whittaker 1987

④ Route 1 .... HS 4c
10m. Balance up and right to good holds then runners in the break. Finish up the left-hand groove above to a rounded mantel - a perfect grit finish.
FA. Ian Butterworth 1966

⑤ King B E1 5c
10m. Make a bold start up the centre of the slab to the break. Then climb the shallow groove above avoiding *Route 1*.
FA. Bob Whittaker 1981

⑥ Route 2 .... HVS 5a
10m. Climb the shallow groove (Rock 1 on the right) then balance left and right to the break and more wires. Finish up the right-hand groove. A traditional VS that is just a bit too bold.
Photo page 30.
FA. Paul Horan 1966

⑦ Slabmaster .... VS 4c
10m. Climb the groove to a ledge then the slotted wall above until it becomes necessary to move left and join *Route 2*.
FA. Bob Whittaker 1981

⑧ Route Right .... HS 4b
10m. Trend right from the start of *Slabmaster* until forced off the slab. Finish up the easy chimney; a bit of an anticlimax.
FA. Paul Horan 1966

⑨ Daytona Wall E5 6a
10m. A bold outing that weaves across the impressive buttress. Rumoured to be unprotected since the demise of an ancient bolt runner! Start under the arete and climb up and right through the bulge to a slot, then move right to another. Take a deep breath and finish direct.
FA. Al Evans 1977

⑩ Daytona Wall Direct E5 6b
10m. Climb a faint crack up the lower wall to joint the regular route at the bulge. Pull up to the pocket and finish direct.
FA. (Start) Phil Kelly 1984 (Finnsh) Jerry Peel

⑪ Boldness Through Ignorance E7 6c
10m. From the *Direct* sketch up and right (peg) to some small finger-pockets and a scary finish.
FA. Gareth Parry 1991

⑫ Overlapper .... HVS 5b
10m. Climb the flaky groove to the bulge then pull left to gain a good pocket, the continuation crack and a sprint finish.
FA. Bob Whittaker 1973

⑬ Lapper E1 5b
10m. Follow the groove throughout then make a pumpy hand-traverse out right to finish.
FA. Bob Whittaker 1981

⑭ Dessers .... VS 4c
10m. The thin crack has an awkward moves to overcome the initial crucial section.
FA. Paul Horan 1967

⑮ Sard .... HVS 5a
8m. After a tricky start head up the fingery wall, or access it from the next route at a more amenable **VS 4c**.
FA. Bob Whittaker 1981

⑯ Seazy .... HS 4c
8m. The thin crack with a triangular niche at 3m. Passing this is the crux though it is steep above.
FA. Stu Halliwell 1966

COW'S MOUTH - RIGHT

An interesting set of varied routes, sheltered from the worst of the wind, though inclined to be green after wet weather.
APPROACH - Walk right from under the central section of the crag (home to a set of less inspiring climbs).

① Groovin' . . . . ☐ **HS 4b**
8m. From a block climb the shallow groove and escape left.
FA. Paul Horan 1967

② The Romeo Error . . . . . 🔲🔲 ☐ **E1 6a**
10m. Sketch up the slab to a sloping mantel, hop onto it precariously then sneak off left to avoid the grass cornice. A sneaky start from the left is a grade easier.
FA. Al Evans 1977 Direct Start Andrew Unsworth 1984

③ Screwy . . . . 🔲🔲 ☐ **E2 5c**
10m. More thin climbing up the face just right of the unclippable in-situ gear (they look like nails to me). An ancient peg just below the top might help if you have a rope on!
FA. Ras Taylor 1964. FFA. Bob Whittaker 1966

④ Groundhog . . . . 🔲🔲 ☐ **E1 5b**
10m. The face is climbed on small holds to a grubby exit. A side-runner drops the grade a notch. Just keep trying until you get it right!

⑤ Sandy Crack . . . . ☐ **VS 5a**
10m. The crack just left of the chimney/corner is usually clean. No bridging allowed at this grade.
FA. Pete Mustoe 1964

⑥ Curving Chimney . . . . ☐ **Diff**
8m. The rift is 'orrible and desperate!
FA. Pete Mustoe 1964

⑦ Jumping Jive . . . . 🔲 ☐ **E1 5b**
8m. Leap for the ledge then finish leftwards.
FA. Bruce Goodwin 1985

⑧ Pavanne . . . . ☐ **HVS 5a**
8m. Crawl on to the ledge then trend right to the top.
FA. Al Evans 1977

⑨ Overhanging Crack . . . . . 🔲 ☐ **VS 4c**
8m. The excellent but short hand-crack has a tricky exit.
FA. Pete Mustoe 1964

⑩ Z Crack . . . . 🔲🔲 ☐ **VS 5a**
10m. A little classic and well-protected throughout. Finish direct with a long reach or follow the logical line leftwards at **HVS**.
FA. Pete Mustoe 1964

⑪ The Don . . . . 🔲 ☐ **E2 6a**
10m. The blank and bold wall right of *Z Crack*.
FA. John Ellis 1980

⑫ Los Endos . . . . 🔲 ☐ **HVS 5a**
8m. A problem start up the arete leads to easier ground.
FA. Al Evans 1972

⑬ Scree? Pain! . . . . 🔲 ☐ **E3 6a**
6m. Nasty. Climb the wall, using a slot, to a scary finish.
FA. Bruce Goodwin 1985

⑭ Flupper . . . . ☐ **VS 5a**
6m. Climb the scooped wall until forced right to easier ground.
FA. Bruce Goodwin 1976

⑮ Flipper . . . . ☐ **S 4b**
6m. Polished holds just right of the arete are pleasant.
FA. Pete Mustoe 1964

⑯ Flopper . . . . ☐ **VS 4c**
6m. Use an undercut to reach rounded holds and a quick pull.
FA. John Hampson early 1980s

Staffordshire · Macclesfield · Kinder · Bleaklow · Chew · Lancashire · Cheshire · Littleborough · Hoghton · Denham · Anglezarke · Brownstones · Wilton 2 and 3 · Wilton 1

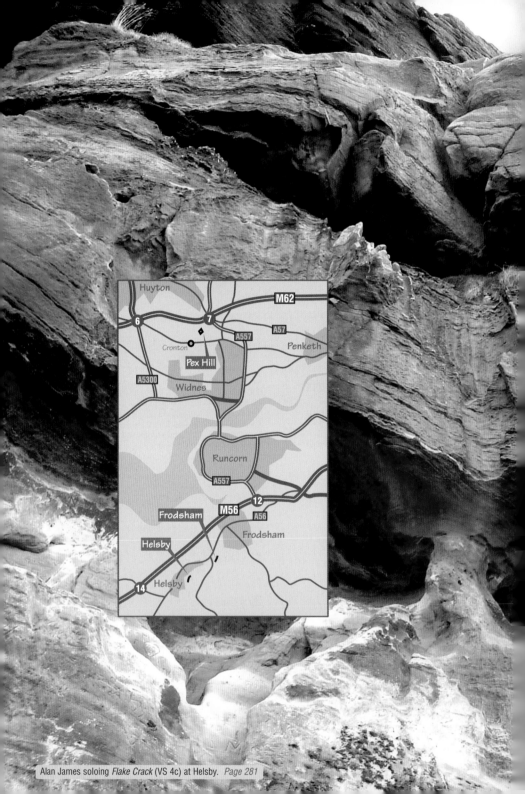

Alan James soloing *Flake Crack* (VS 4c) at Helsby. *Page 281*

CHESHIRE

Staffordshire Whaley Bridge Kinder Bleaklow Chew Lancashire Cheshire

A fine two-tiered cliff of New Red Sandstone, overlooking the River Mersey and the M56 motorway. Uninformed climbers often glance up and scorn the place as they speed by on their way to North Wales. Perhaps they should consider taking the time to have a closer look since most will be pleasantly surprised by the compact and clean walls offering some superb routes on great rock. From below, the dark overhangs appear to dominate the view and the fine pink walls tend to blend into the hillside. In reality there is a lot of good climbing here, so next time you are zipping by call in for an hour, enjoy the fine outward views and do *Grooved Slab*, *Flake Crack* and *Eliminate 1*; the chances are you will be back at Helsby sooner rather than later.

APPROACH Also see map on page 270

The best approach for most climbers is from junction 14 of the M56. Follow the signs for Helsby village off the motorway and turn left onto the A56 at the first junction. As you arrive in the village fork right. Follow this road for about 2km to a point where there is wide junction with houses on the left and steep wooded slopes on the right. The road on the left here is called Crescent Drive. Park sensibly somewhere on the roadside, there is always plenty of space, then cross the road towards the wood and pick up a path which winds uphill to the crag. This starts off diagonally to the right, then heads back left along a wide track and finally turns up a narrow path through the bushes to arrive at the right-hand end of the cliff; about 5 minutes steep walk from the parking.

CONDITIONS

Helsby is a crag full of surprises and it is not unknown to arrive here in the middle of winter to find the place bone dry and as clean as a whistle. The western (right-hand) side receives late afternoon sun and the lower sections tend to escape the worst of the greenness. However for the majority of the routes you are better advised to turn up at a warmer time of year preferably after a short dry spell. The eastern side of the crag (not covered here) receives very little sun and only comes into condition rarely. Since the crag is made of sandstone, it is worth keeping away immediately after rain even if the place appears to be dry. Sandstone is porous and once the rock has absorbed rainwater it is prone to snapping suddenly. A badly-timed pull on one of the small flakes could damage a route irreparably and not do a lot for your health! It is worth pointing out that the view from the cliff out across the Stanlow refinery and the Mersey estuary is superb and spectacular sunsets here are common.

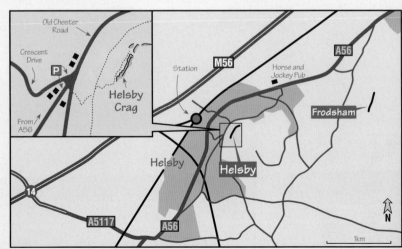

Pex Hill Frodsham Helsby

ark Hounslea on *Eliminate 1* (E1 5b) at Helsby. *Page 281* Photo: Pete Chadwick

Staffordshire

Whaley Bridge

Kinder

Bleaklow

Chew

Lancashire

Cheshire

Pex Hill

Frodsham

Helsby

Clashooks Gully

Upper Central Buttress

The Broadwalk

Grooved Slab Area

Lower Central Buttress

Golden Pillar

Flake Crack Area

Eliminate 1 Area

Evening | 10 min

Descent down gully

UPPER CENTRAL BUTTRESS
This fine wall is perched high above the valley at the point where the crag changes angle (the routes further left are both difficult to get to and often very green.) This spot is often very windy and the routes feel much more exposed than their lengths would suggest.

1 Central Climb .... VDiff
15m. Climb the wall to the right of a niche then move left onto a rib and continue to the top.

2 Easy Buttress .... Diff
15m. Start on the right-hand end of the ledge and follow a crack up into a corner.

3 The Illegitimate E3 5c
15m. Make committing moves up the superb flying arete. Once at the top of this sidle left through the narrowing in the roofs.
FA. Hugh Banner 1960s

4 Carsten's Variant E2 5b
15m. An eliminate up the wall left of the corner.
The **Forceps Finish** over the roof is **E2 5c**.

5 Carsten's Abortion E2 5b
15m. The steep corner-cracks past a potential nesting site. Exit rightwards at the top. **Keep away if the nest is occupied.**
FA. Arnold Carsten early 1950s

6 Downes' Doddle E2 5b
12m. Pull up into the hanging scoop. Then move delicately right to a crack which is followed past a rocking block.
Clockwork Orange, E3/4 5c - A good direct finish which can be protected by two slings on horns and a Friend in the roof.
FA. Hugh Banner 1960s, named after Bob Downes who had failed on it

7 Technicolour Yawn .... NL 6a
12m. The elegant slim groove gives a good technical problem.

8 The Cornice .... VDiff
12m. Climb the groove to a bulge, from which the climb presumably gets its name.

9 The Cornice Indirect ..... S 3c
15m. Traverse right across the face to finish up the blunt arete.

10 Deception .... HVS 5a
10m. Good climbing past a small overlap and up the blunt arete.

11 Mossy Slab .... VDiff
12m. Follow the curving flake/groove across the slab which has long been moss-less.

12 Gather No Moss E3 6b
7m. A short and technical high-ball boulder problem.

Not much sun | 10 min | Descent | Green | Sheltered

LOWER CENTRAL BUTTRESS

This wall is well-hidden from above but is worth a look, especially if it is blowing a gale since it is reasonably sheltered by the trees. The routes are only short although *Crumpet Crack* will be found long enough for most.
APPROACH - Scramble easily down a steep path which leaves the base of the main crag below Clashooks Gully.

1 Blue Light . . . . **HVS 5b**
8m. The left-hand side of the wall, using the arete.

2 In the Pie **E2 6a**
10m. An eliminate up the centre of the wall trending left.
FA. David Ranby 1980s

3 Pigeonhole Wall . . . . **VS 5a**
10m. The slanting groove is entered steeply using the holes.
FA. C.W.Marshall 1920s

4 Pigeonhole Arete **E1 5c**
10m. The blunt rib is steep and worthwhile.

5 Crack of Doom . . . . **S 3c**
10m. Enter at your peril. 'Off-width' it, facing right, or bridge.

6 Whimper **E2 5c**
10m. The wall just right of the corner past some pockets.

7 Wafer Wall **E2 5c**
10m. Bold with thin moves and little in the way of gear.

8 Z Route . . . . **VDiff**
18m. A long diagonal along the overlap to a finish above the roof.

9 Z Route Direct . . . . **S 4a**
12m. Climb direct to the traverse of the previous route and then finish along it.

10 Oblique Crack . . . . **VDiff**
11m. Climb the diagonal crack left of the big roof to meadows.

11 Muffin Crack . . . . **HVS 5b**
11m. The big roof is split by two prominent cracks. This route tackles the lesser left-hand crack.

12 Crumpet Crack **E4 6b**
11m. The central crack is a classic and crusty struggle but lay off the crumpets before you give it a go.
FA. Hugh Banner 1960s

13 Hades Crack . . . . **HS 4b**
10m. The slashing diagonal line right of the roof is awkward.
FA. C.W.Marshall 1920s

14 Wild Oat Wall . . . . **HVS 5b**
10m. Step left out of *Two Step Crack* onto the tricky wall.

15 Two Step Crack . . . . **VDiff**
10m. Climb the corner via a step or two, to a grassy exit.

16 Honeycomb Wall . . . . . **VS 4c**
9m. Follow big but crusty holds up the steep wall.

17 Nameless Wall . . . . **VS 5a**
8m. Just off the topo. Climb the wall over the narrow right-hand edge of the low bulge.

18 Nameless Crack . . . . **S 4a**
7m. The short thin crack just before the end of the wall.

Staffordshire · Whaley Bridge · Kinder · Bleaklow · Chew · Lancashire · Cheshire · Pex Hill · Frodsham · Helsby

Staffordshire

Whaley Bridge

Kinder

Bleaklow

Chew

Lancashire

Cheshire

Pex Hill

Frodsham

Helsby

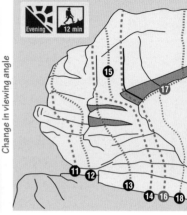

Change in viewing angle

THE BROADWALK
At the tallest part of the cliff a wide ledge runs across the upper section of the crag from the diagonal Clashooks Gully. This ledge is a popular hang-out for local youths but also has a few steep and nasty climbs on compact black rock.
APPROACH - From the centre of the crag, Scramble up Clashooks Gully and double back right onto the ledge.

① Hemingway's Wall .... 🔲🔳 **E3 5c**
8m. Start above a boulder in the gully and climb the bulging wall using a rounded shelf. Starting just right is **6a**.

② Late-nite Greenhaigh .. 🔲🔳 **E3 6a**
8m. Steep moves on horizontal holds up the bulging wall.

③ The Missing Font ..... 🔳🔳 **NL 5c**
8m. An eliminate with thin moves on flakes.

④ Senile Saunter .... 🔳 **E1 5b**
11m. Start up *West Wall Chimney* and traverse left (exposed) to reach the hanging flake/corner. The steep **Direct Start** is **5c**.

⑤ West Wall Chimney ... 🔳🔳 **VDiff**
9m. The chimney has a steep start. At the top step left onto the wall for a less-enclosed finish.

⑥ Windy Corner .... 🔳🔳 **VDiff**
15m. From a short way up *West Wall Chimney*, traverse right-wards in a fine and exposed position. Keep going until you can walk to the top. Mild but wild!

⑦ Windy Corner Nose Finish .. 🔳 **HS 4b**
9m. Finish up the wall above the traverse on the previous route.

⑧ Diopera .... 🔳 **HVS 5a**
9m. Climb the edge of the buttress, through a weakness just left of the bigger roofs, often windy.

⑨ Eroica .... 🔳 **HVS 5a**
9m. The first route through the roofs has some friable holds.

⑩ Erotica .... 🔳 **NL 6b**
9m. More dodgy rock. Climb the scoop and pockets just right of *Eroica*. Best set a rope up first!

⑪ Coward of the County .. 🔳🔳 **E4 6a**
10m. The roofs get bigger and the quality picks up. Make a hard move to gain a good hold on the right. Move back left and finish direct up the steep wall.
FA. Pete Chadwick 1990s

⑫ Spooky .... 🔳🔳🔳 **E5 6b**
10m. Start 4m right of *Coward*. Make a long reach from a small pocket to gain some good holds. Move left and continue up the wall joining *Coward* near the top.

**⑬ Brandenburg
Wall Direct** ...... 🔳🔳🔳🔳 **NL 6c**
10m. The direct start is a serious proposition, even on a top-rope! Make a big reach from some small pockets to gain a little prow. Pull up into the parent route above.

⑭ Brandenburg Wall . 🔳🔳🔳 **E4 5c**
12m. A great route in a spectacular position. Start down and right of the flakes on the upper wall. Climb to the roof (good Friends) then hand-traverse left to below the flakes. Finish up these.

⑮ Stingray .... 🔳🔳🔳 **E4 6a**
10m. A direct finish to *Brandenburg Wall* on small holds.
FA. Mike Collins

⑯ The Mangler ..... 🔳🔳🔳 **E3 6a**
10m. A good old-fashioned roof crack which succumbs to a typical struggle. Those with an aversion to jamming can use finger-holds but that misses the point really!
FA. Hugh Banner 1960s

⑰ Gorilla Wall .... 🔳🔳 **E3 5c**
12m. Start as for *The Mangler* but traverse right along a flake until you can pull over onto the upper wall.
FA. Hugh Banner 1960s

⑱ Gorilla Wall Direct .🔳🔳🔳 **E4 5c**
10m. The direct start begins at big holds about 2m to the right

Descent down gully

The Broadwalk

Evening | 10 min

Staffordshire | Whaley Bridge | Kinder | Bleaklow | Chew | Lancashire | Cheshire

GOLDEN PILLAR

At the left-hand end of the main section of the face is the long diagonal gash of *Clashooks Gully*, a useful descent from the cliff top. To the right of this is a fine pillar and a broad slab, both home to a good selection of climbs across the grades though hard and scary ones out-number easy and safe ones by quite a margin.

① Cloister Traverse . . . . `S 4a`
30m. The horizontal gash can be gained from *Clashooks Gully* and followed rightwards until the ground rises gently up to meet you. If only it was always so!

② Chromium Crack . . . . . 🔲🔲 `E2 5c`
14m. The black, bulging crack in the arete is approached easily and then gives a good pumpy battle with friendly protection.

③ Golden Pillar . . . . 🔲🔲 `E1 5b`
14m. A spooky lead up the front of the rounded pillar. Easy ground leads up the centre of the buttress then make bolder moves up and left into a scoop. Follow this with increasing apprehension. Low in the grade but still harrowing.

④ The Overhanging Crack . 🔲🔲 `VS 4c`
14m. Follow the easy chimney into a cave/recess then bridge and strenuously jam the steep crack that splits the roof of the cave to reach easy ground.
FA. Laycock c1910. The hardest route on grit at the time.

⑤ Agag . . . . 🔲🔲 `VS 4c`
14m. Take *The Overhanging Crack* to the cave then exit right-wards by sustained jamming. Follow the continuation crack to the terrace.

⑥ Cadaver Eyes . . . . . 🔲🔲🔲 `NL 6b`
14m. Climb the rib right of the chimney to the black overhangs and pull through these with difficulty then scale the steep slab above. Awaits a lead ascent?

⑦ Magical Charm . . . . . 🔲🔲 `E5 6a`
14m. Climb the slab left of the diagonal fissure of *Morgue Slab* to the bulges. Stretch through these and make a crucial mantel up the steep slab. Gear under the bulge is your lot!

⑧ Morgue Slab . . . . 🔲🔲 `E2 5b`
14m. A classic heart-stopper. Climb slanting cracks to the bulges. Psyche, then pull through these and climb the steep slab rightwards, carefully, to reach easy ground.

⑨ Mogadon's Good for You 🔲🔲 `E3 5c`
14m. Climb the face right of *Morgue Slab*, past a crucial undercut move, to join its final moves.

⑩ Necrophiliac . . . . 🔲🔲 `E5 6a`
14m. A stiff little number. Climb the rounded rib to the bulges, step out right and gain the upper slab with difficulty. Finish direct to the terrace.

⑪ Time Regained . 🔲🔲🔲 `E7 6c`
14m. The black, tilted wall is climbed on tiny holds trending left then back right for a sprint finish. A very low, and very thin, thread provides the only protection.
FA. Andy Popp 2001. Formerly the top-rope problem Dog on a String.

Pex Hill | Frodsham | Helsby

Meadow Terrace

Staffordshire | Whaley Bridge | Kinder | Bleaklow | Chew | Lancashire | Cheshire

GROOVED SLAB AREA

A fine slab of sandstone. Its open aspect and a great picnic area make this Helsby's most popular destination. *Grooved Slab* is the best lower grade route on the cliff and *Beatnik* is a long-standing test-piece.

⑫ Beatnik **E5 6a**
14m. A classic sandstone test-piece. Climb the short crack then balance up the near vertical slab using the tiny half-moon flake to reach better holds under the overhang. Scuttle left then right to finish up an easy crack. **Right-hand Finish** is **E5 6a**.
FA. Jim O'Neill 1960s (TR). FA. Alan Rouse (solo) late 1960s
FA. (Right-hand) Andy Popp 2000s

⑬ 240 Volt Shocker . . . **E5 6c**
14m. Trend up the steep face making strenuous use of the 'light bulb' hold to reach relief at the deep break.
FA. Andy Popp 2000s

⑭ Twin Scoops **E1 5c**
14m. Bold and delicate. Climb the pair of crescent-shaped grooves to runners in the break then the ever-steeper scoop trending right to finish.
FA. Hugh Banner 1960s

⑮ The Gangway . . . . **VS 4b**
24m. Teeter up the crescent-shaped crack then at its top climb the shallow groove leftwards to the break. Upward progress is problematical so follow the horizontal out left until a crack in a short corner offers a means of escape.

⑯ Grooved Slab . . . . **VS 4a**
14m. One of the classics of the crag, although protection could be better. From the grass ledge climb the groove to its end then step left and take the continuation all the way to the terrace and a tree belay. *Photo page 277.*

⑰ The Brush Off Direct . . . **E4 6a**
14m. Climb the steep slab 2m to the right of *Grooved Slab* to a breather at the break. Step right and finish up the steep upper face using some useful pockets.

⑱ The Brush Off **E4 5c**
14m. Climb past the useful chipped 'R' then trend left up the steep slab to the break and a junction with the *The Direct*. Finish as for this.

⑲ The Brush Off Direct Finish **E6 6a**
14m. Climb *The Brush Off* to the break then step right and sketch up the centre of the bold steep and tenuous wall. The only gear is a wire in a slot on *Jim's Chimney*. Seriously serious! It is possible to avoid the regular route completely, and all the chipped holds, by staying left at the start - **6b (NL)**.

⑳ Jim's Chimney **E2 5c**
14m. A misnomer if ever there was one. Climb through the shallow oval groove then on up the bulging face above to the ledge. A second pitch up the wall above is available at **5b**.

㉑ Little by Little . . . . **VS 4b**
14m. A tricky number. Follow the slippery chipped ladder then sidle right into the left-leaning groove which leads to the ledge of Meadow Terrace. *The Notch* provides a logical way to the cliff top at a lower grade or the juggy direct version is worth **VS 4b**.

㉒ Oyster Slab Super Direct . . . **VS 5a**
14m. Climb the slab to the base of the groove of *Little by Little* then continue steeply just to the right of the arete. The original **Oyster Slab (S)** starts here and wanders across to *Trojan Crack*.

㉓ Oyster Slab Direct . . . . **VS 4b**
14m. Take the centre of the rippled slab to the break in the overhangs. Pull right through this and finish up the face.
FA. Dave Price early 1950s

㉔ Oyster Slab Route III . . . . . **VS 5b**
14m. A couple of metres left of the grotty groove of *Trojan Crack* climb straight up the slab to the bulges, undercut through these and finish up the slab above.

㉕ Trojan Crack . . . . **S 4a**
14m. The dirty crack is poor.

㉖ Trojan Nose . . . . **S 4a**
10m. The blunt nose just right of *Trojan Crack*.

Starting from Meadow Terrace a logical finish to many of the previous routes is:

㉗ The Notch . . . . **Diff**
10m. Climb the juggy rib to ledges then traverse left and climb steeply to and through the eponymous feature.

Pex Hill | Frodsham | Helsby

279

HELSBY *Flake Crack Area*

④ Wood's Climb . . . . 〔3〕 [ ] **HVS 5a**
12m. The long shallow groove is a fine route. Climb it to the block overhang and exit leftwards under this.
FA. C.W.Marshall 1920s

⑤ The Unknown Quantity . 〔〕 [ ] **E4 6a**
12m. The stretchy and rounded arete bounding the groove.
FA. Andy Popp 1990s

⑥ Lipalongago . . . . . 〔1〕 〔〕 〔〕 [ ] **E4 6b**
12m. Climb straight up to the overlap and pass it with difficulty making vigorous use of the short diagonal crack

⑦ Unknown . . . . 〔〕 〔〕 [ ] **NL 6b**
12m. Tussle with the tiny crack in the overlap.

⑧ The Runnel . . . . 〔2〕 [ ] **NL 6b**
14m. Make desperate but short-lived moves up the runnels. Finish over the roof above.

⑨ Greenteeth Gully . . . . 〔1〕 [ ] **Mod**
14m. Obvious from the name, it provides one of the easiest outings on the cliff and a suitable way down for the expert.

⑩ Greenteeth Crack . . . . [ ] **HS 4b**
14m. Squirm up the undercut hanging slot with gusto!

⑪ Dinnerplate Crack . . . . . . 〔2〕 [ ] **S 4b**
14m. The left-hand flake on the front face is approached steeply and gives thrilling juggy climbing. Sadly the 'dinnerplate' was smashed years ago.

⑫ Ho Ho Ho . . . . [ ] **E3 6a**
14m. Between the two cracks.
FA. Mike Collins 1990 (Christmas Day)

FLAKE CRACK AREA
The conspicuous fissure of *Flake Crack* is probably Cheshire's most famous route and with good reason, great rock, a cracking line and a long history - just do it!

① Waterloo Wall . . . . 〔〕 [ ] **E2 5c**
12m. Gain the tiny ledge on the wall right of *Trojan Nose*.

② Fragile Wall . . . . 〔2〕 〔〕 [ ] **E3 5c**
12m. Climb up into the right-facing curving groove and balance carefully up it using the small flakes that are referred to in the name! The left-hand finish is only **E2 5b** but **E2 6a** if you climb it direct from the ground.
FA. Hugh Banner 1960s

③ Jugged Forest . . . . [ ] **E2 5c**
12m. The wall just left of the corner past two layaways.

ELIMINATE 1 AREA

This tall buttress is the first significant bit of rock you come to on the approach to the crag. It is home to the superb *Eliminate 1* - an amazingly bold offering from the 1940s, surely one of the hardest climbs around at that time. Its poorly protected final sections still commands respect.

⑬ Twin Caves Crack . . . . 🔲🔲 | S 4b
14m. Climb up the pillar between the two caves then make a steep pull into the groove. This gives great juggy climbing.

⑭ Pathfinder . . . . 🔲 | E3 6a
14m. Climb direct over the big bulges and up the blunt flake to join the top section of *Flake Innominate*.
FA. Mark Hounslea 2001

⑮ Flake Innominate . . . . . . 🔲 | E2 5c
14m. The small buttress on the left of the final section of *Flake Crack* has a couple of pleasant moves and good positions, although the best climbing is still on the parent route.

⑯ Flake Crack . . . . 🔲 | VS 4c
14m. The finest route on the cliff! If you are passing at least call in and tick this one! The upper section is a classic layback although those in the know will jam it. *Photo page 270.*
FA. Colin Kirkus early 1920s. Climbed on-sight by Menlove Edwards 1931.

⑰ Licentious Jug . . . . 🔲🔲🔲 | E5 6a
16m. Climb *Flake Crack* to the base of the crack then balance across the right wall and climb the harrowing left-hand side of the arete. Originally done without recourse to *Flake Crack*.

⑱ Foolish Finish . . . . 🔲🔲🔲 | E4 5c
16m. Take *Flake Crack* to a point halfway up the layback then crimp along the bubbly break to join *Licentious Jug*.

⑲ Flake Wall . . . . 🔲🔲🔲🔲 | E5 6a
16m. A cracking hard route but with some crumbly holds. Climb the curving flake under the roof (or the wall to its left) until forced into *Flake Crack*. Place a runner then balance out right and boldly climb the centre of the pitted wall. Exciting stuff.

⑳ Black Hole Arete . . . . 🔲🔲 | NL 6b
16m. Use jugs to reach the lip of the roof then traverse left out to the exposed arete. Make hard moves to an easier finish.

㉑ Calcutta Wall . . . . . . 🔲🔲 | E4 5c
16m. Start up the pillar of *Eliminate 1* but trend left across the bulging wall using the black hole of the route's name.
FA. Hugh Banner 1960s

㉒ Eliminate 1 . . . . 🔲 | E1 5b
16m. The other great classic of the crag. Climb the pillar and a short pocket-wall to the break and some rounded spike runners. Traverse out left into ever-more exposed terrain then make a tricky move (elusive finger holds) to easy ground. Perhaps only HVS 5a for those used to the vagaries of sandstone.
Photo page 273.

㉓ Pratabout . . . . . . 🔲🔲🔲 | E5 6b
14m. Climb the centre of the wall left of the gully. Pull onto the wall and continue in a direct line to a rounded exit.
FA. Dave Ranby 1980s

㉔ Easy Chimney . . . . 🔲 | Mod
14m. The deep rift behind the jutting proboscis.

㉕ The Wendigo . . . . . 🔲🔲🔲 | E3 5c
16m. From halfway up *Easy Chimney* make a committing and difficult traverse along the bubbly break all the way out to the spikes on *Eliminate 1*. Finish direct.

㉖ End Crack . . . . 🔲 | S 4b
10m. The short crack in the bulge is accessed up scoops and leads to a tricky exit.

㉗ The Umbrella . . . . . . 🔲🔲 | E2 5c
10m. Climb the pumpy leaning wall to the left of the cave rapidly to reach easy ground.

㉘ Parapluie . . . . 🔲🔲 | E1 5b
10m. The blocky roof crack out of the cave is hard work. A parachute might be more use than a poncy French umbrella!

Frosdsham consists of a small set of west-facing buttresses on the crest of the wooded slopes of Frodsham Hill. The rocks are hidden in a beech forest overlooking the Mersey estuary and are ideal for a short work-out session. The crag receives the afternoon sun and several of the buttresses are steep enough to stay dry in light summer rain. Although relatively diminutive the cliffs are fairly easy to reach from the Liverpool conurbation, or from the M56 if you are Wales-bound. Interestingly, many of the climbing world's luminaries have left their mark here.

The cliff is a very popular bouldering venue and most of the better problems are chalked throughout the year. The climbing is generally steep and juggy; power pays more dividends here than fancy footwork ever will. The routes are almost invariably soloed, though the bigger routes on Cinema Screen and Great Buttress are BOLD. The slightly soft nature of the rock and the steep slope below the cliff all add up to make these particularly serious undertakings.

APPROACH

To the west of Frodsham (heading towards Helsby) on the A56 and just west of the Netherton Arms, turn left onto the B5393 (Tarvin Road). Drive up the hill for 1.5km until opposite a farm where there is limited parking space. If this is full (2 or 3 well-parked cars) continue up the road for another couple of hundred metres to more parking. Opposite the farm a steep track runs straight up the hill, follow this (try jogging up it!) until it bends right. Go through the gate then head straight up towards the crest of the hill. Just before the top, a narrow track leads left to the first - or is it the last - buttress; 10 minutes from the car.

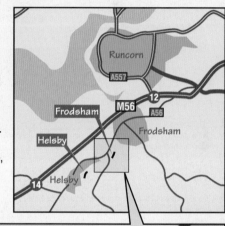

CONDITIONS

The rocks are well-sheltered from the weather because of the extensive tree cover. Some the sections of the cliff capped by overhangs (e.g. Hoopla Buttress) give ever-dry bouldering, though, as with all the sandstone in the area, climbing in damp conditions is not a good idea as the humidity softens the rock. The crag is perhaps at its best on warm spring and autumn evenings when the atmosphere is magical and the foliage doesn't interfere too much with the view. Ticking as many of the routes as possible before heading down to the pub to sooth sore fingers, is a great way of blowing away the days cobwebs!

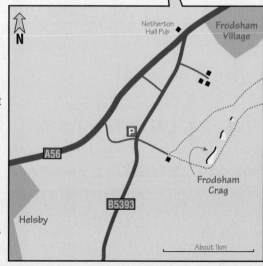

The first routes are on the diminutive beak of St.Stephen's Buttress, just beyond the Great Wall.

❶ St Stephen's Wall 4b
4m. The centre of the north-facing wall.

❷ Left Wall V2 (5c)
4m. The wall just left of the arete.

❸ Mexican Bob V3 (6a)
4m. The left-hand arete of the front face and roof direct.

❹ The Long Lurch V1 (5b)
4m. Climb the middle of the overhang via a l-o-n-g lurch.

❺ Rick's Reach V2 (5c)
4m. The right-hand arete of the front face.

❻ Right-hand Route . . . . VO (5a)
4m. The blunt rib at the right-hand edge of the face.

❼ Big Wall 4c
4m. Right of the easy groove is a small wall.

❽ Deep Crack 4b
4m. The wide, awkward and over-grown fissure.

❾ Twin Cracks . . . . Diff
4m. The crack, if you can get to it.

Across the slope is the Great Wall.

❿ Left Arete V1 (5b)
12m. The leaning left-hand arete of the impressive face.

⓫ Tom's Roof V6 (6b)
12m. The lower wall leads directly to the huge triangular roof that caps the wall. Cross this with conviction.

⓬ Unknown V2 (5c)
12m. Climb the wall passing the right edge of a smaller roof to the big one then do the sensible thing and leg-it out right.

⓭ Left-hand Route V2 (5c)
16m. Head up into the prominent hanging groove in the right-hand side of the wall then make a long exposed traverse away left to outflank the banks of overhangs.

⓮ Great Wall V2 (5c)
14m. Follow *Left-hand Route* into the hanging corner but at its top exit rightwards to reach the easier upper wall.

⓯ Iron Dish Wall V2 (5c)
14m. The bulging wall right of the big tree is excellent.

⓰ Frodsham Crack . . . . . VO (5a)
12m. The prominent deep crack on the right gives classic fist jamming - not quite the contradiction that might appear.

⓱ Unknown Wall V3 (6a)
12m. The bold and fierce wall just right of *Frodsham Crack.*

GREAT WALL

The most impressive piece of rock at Frodsham is The Great Wall. Perched high above a steep slope the routes here are imposing undertakings and are only soloed by the terminally confident. Respectable E-grades would apply elsewhere!

Change in viewing angle

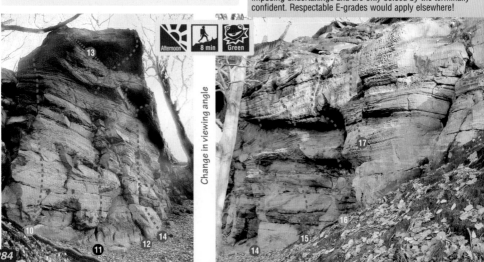

Staffordshire · Whaley Bridge · Kinder · Bleaklow · Chew · Lancashire · Cheshire

CINEMA SCREEN WALL and CAVE BUTTRESS

The Cinema Screen is an imposing and well-named piece of rock which unfortunately doesn't provide climbing of the quality that you might expect. Further right along the slope, Cave Buttress has better quality rock and routes.

CINEMA SCREEN WALL

① Slanting Crack . . . . **Diff**
10m. The left-slanting break that bounds the buttress.

② Slab Route . . . . **V0 (5a)**
10m. Climb the green slab to steep rock then jig left through these to get onto the upper slab.

③ Cinema Arete **4c**
10m. The bulging but juggy arete gives a popular pitch.

④ Birch Tree Corner **4a**
10m. The left-hand groove bounding the screen and escaping left at the capping overhang.

⑤ Multi-Screen . . . . . **V3 (6a)**
10m. The left-hand side of the smooth section of the screen is climbed on brittle holds to a steep juggy finish.

⑥ Central Route . . . . . **V2 (5c)**
10m. The right-hand line on the wall.

⑦ Cracked Corner **4b**
8m. The right-bounding groove of the central screen can be bridged to an escape out right.

⑧ Arete Route . . . . **V1 (5b)**
8m. Lay-away to start the blunt arete on the right-hand side of the face then sprint to the top.

CAVE BUTTRESS

⑨ Corner and Traverse . . . . . **VDiff**
6m. A groove in the north-facing wall, exiting up the right arete.

⑩ Left Wall . . . . **V0 (5a)**
6m. The crimpy centre of the north-facing wall is worthwhile.

⑪ Crew's Arete Left-hand . . **V2 (5c)**
6m. The left-hand arete of the narrow buttress on the left is steep and pumpy.

⑫ Crew's Arete . . . . . **V1 (5b)**
6m. The centre of the overhangs give a classic tussle - easier for the talented. *Photo page 283.*
FA. Pete Crew 1960s

⑬ Superdirect . . . . **V0 (5a)**
6m. The right-hand arete to a bulging finish.

⑭ Superwall . . . . **V1 (5b)**
6m. Take the narrow side-wall directly

⑮ Leo's Traverse . . . . . . **V0 (5a)**
10m. Climb into the undercut crack on *Ordinary Route* then make a gripping traverse out to the right below the big roof.
FA. Leo Dickinson 1960s

⑯ Ordinary Route . . . . **VDiff**
8m. Climb leftwards into the corner then continue in the same direction to outflank the capping roof.

**⑰ I Was a Teenage
Caveman** . . . . **V7 (6c)**
8m. The centre of the big roof is approached directly from below and is crossed with trepidation on holds that are not above suspicion.

Pex Hill · Frodsham · Helsby

Afternoon | 8 min | Green

Change in viewing angle

LONG BUTTRESS

A short but wide buttress spit centrally by an awkward chimney which breaks an almost continuous line of overhangs and bulges providing the entertainment.

① Arete Route . . . . **V1 (5b)**
6m. The left arete of the buttress is reached via a taxing bulge.

② Jimmy's Crack . . . . **V2 (5c)**
6m. The hanging crack above the roof is approached across the roof using the expando-flakes with trepidation.

③ Direct Route . . . . **V1 (5b)**
6m. The juggy right-hand side of the roof is fun.

④ Heather Wall Direct . . . . **V0 (5a)**
6m. Climb past the right-hand edge of the roof where it fades.

⑤ Donkey Route Direct . . . . **V1 (5b)**
6m. Through the centre of the bulges.

⑥ Heather Variant **4c**
6m. The right-hand side of the bulges.

⑦ Heather Wall **4a**
6m. Climb left along a hanging slab to a tricky, exposed exit.

⑧ Chimney Route **3c**
6m. The grubby rift that splits the buttress.

⑨ Tank Top . . . . **V3 (6a)**
6m. The right-hand arete of the chimney on its left-hand side.

⑩ Sweater . . . . **V1 (5b)**
6m. Tackle the arete on its right-hand side via the overhang and the best of the pockets above.

⑪ Pullover . . . . **V1 (5b)**
6m. The centre of the overhangs is beefy, the wall above much more delicate. Trend left to finish.

⑫ Jumper . . . . **V2 (5c)**
6m. The right-hand side of the roof is a bit of an eliminate though the moves are good.

⑬ Thin Crack Superdirect . . . . . . **V2 (5c)**
6m. An eliminate which gains the thin crack directly and avoids any contamination with the ledge on the right.

⑭ Thin Crack **4b**
6m. Using the projecting ledge on the right to access the thin crack is easier and a lot more sensible!

⑮ Left-hand Crack . . . . **VDiff**
6m. The short left-hand crack is approached over a bulge and gives a couple of jamming moves.

⑯ Right-hand Crack . . . . . . **VDiff**
6m. The slightly thinner right-hand fissure.

⑰ Flake Route . . . . **VDiff**
6m. Pull through the bulges and climb the crack to a tricky exit.

NEB BUTTRESS

⑱ Wall and Traverse . . . . **VDiff**
6m. The left-hand wall of the buttress trending left.

⑲ Intermediate Route **4b**
6m. The juggy left-hand arete of the front face.

⑳ Direct Route . . . . **V0 (5a)**
6m. The centre of the front face passing double overhangs.

㉑ Neb Route . . . . **V2 (5c)**
6m. The right-hand arete of the buttress. Trending left across the face reduces the grade to **5b**.

HOOP-LA BUTTRESS

㉒ Pants . . . . **V1 (5b)**
6m. The left-hand buttress is better than the name suggests!

㉓ The Overhanging Wall **4c**
6m. The well-endowed wall just to the left of the overhangs can be climbed by a variety of lines.

㉔ Colton's Crack . . . . **V6 (6b)**
8m. Approach the thin hanging crack directly below then climb it with great difficulty.
FA. Nick Colton 1970s

Staffordshire | Whaley Bridge | Kinder | Bleaklow | Chew | Lancashire | Cheshire | Pex Hill | Frodsham | Helsby

NEB BUTTRESS

Just beyond the bouldering of Hoop-La buttress is this short protruding neb of rock, good for a quick workout.

28 The Hoop-La V1 (5b)
8m. The crack splitting the centre of the buttress is a classic tussle and forms a good warm-up for the harder roof problems.

29 Boysen's Route ... V3 (6a)
8m. Cross the roof to the right of the crack looping right then left to reach jugs then pull over to easy ground.
FA. Martin Boysen 1960s

30 Banner's Route ... V2 (5c)
8m. Climb the right-hand side of the overhang heading for the juggy flake on the lip.
FA. Hugh Banner 1950s

31 Tradesman's Entrance . V3 (6a)
8m. From the juggy flake above all difficulties on *Banner's*, lurch right to locate a finish on slopers to the right of the arete.

32 The Overhanging Crack ...... Diff
6m. The groove to the right of the overhangs provides a descent or a little something for the timid.

33 The Right Wall V0 (5a)
6m. The juggy wall is the last (or first) route on the cliff.

25 Dave's Roof V7 (6c)
8m. The desperate bulge 1m right of the crack on a poor set of pockets and slopers.
FA. Dave Johnson 1990s

26 Mike's Route .. V7 (6c)
8m. Cross the roof left of the deep crack of *Hoop-La* to a pocket on the lip then finish leftwards with extreme difficulty.
FA. Mike Collins 1990s

27 Pearce's Route V3 (6a)
8m. Follow *Mike's Route* to the pocket on the lip then cop-out and (sensibly) pull rightwards to better holds. Stretch to finish.
FA. Dave Pearce 1960s

HOOP-LA BUTTRESS

Hoop-La Buttress is the first piece of rock reached from the parking. This roof gives the best bouldering on the cliff, with countless eliminates. The choicest problems are always well-chalked up. many of the problems require cunning foot-hooks which can leave you flat on your back if your hands fail. Bring a mat, a friend or both.

Afternoon · 8 min · Green

PEX HILL

This small hole in the ground holds an important place in the hearts of Merseyside climbers; it has easy access, great rock and is home to a myriad of problems and mini-routes. I lived in Liverpool for a year way back in the 1970s and a short apprenticeship at Pex Hill served me well, the steep and fingery style of the climbing here translating well to Welsh volcanics. Have no doubt, time spent honing finger strength and technique at Pex will be repaid in full. Many of the routes are soloed by the competent (with or without mats) although top-roping is also quite popular here (please don't belay to the railings) despite the fact that the majority of the climbs are less then 10 metres high. The reason is obvious - except for a few exceptions the routes here are effectively unprotected and often very blank with no rest ledges.

APPROACH Also see map on page 270

Pex Hill Country Park is located 15km to the east of the Liverpool conurbation, and is most easily reached from the A5080 as it runs between Widnes and Cronton. Opposite the brick buildings of Widnes 6th Form College are the old cast-iron gateposts that mark the park entrance. Follow the road (speed-bumps) as it loops round to the right then turns left into the parking area by the Visitors Centre. The entrance to the quarry is five minutes downhill walk away from the parking and is sometimes tricky to find on first acquaintance. Take the central track until you hit the railings then follow these round to the entrance.

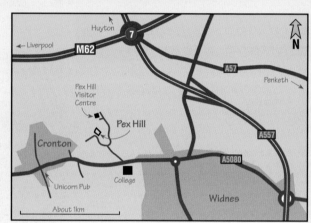

CONDITIONS

Over the years the main part of the quarry has gradually filled with trees. These enhance the pleasant nature of the place but reduce the airflow in the quarry and add to the humidity. This appears to be directly responsible for some of the walls being greener than they used to be. Despite this, the quarry dries fast, takes no drainage (well except when NW Water fill it to the brim) and due to its facing in all directions it is usually possible to get something done here in summer or winter.

Climbers are asked not to use wire brushes here as this abrades the sandstone; if you must, a once-over with a toothbrush should be adequate.

GRADES, GRADES, GRADES

Most of the climbs here tend to be either soloed or top-roped and leading isn't common. Over the years this has led to Pex Hill developing a grading system all of its own with technical grades only being used in past guides despite the fact that some of the routes deserve impressive E-grades. In consultation with the local climbers, particularly Pete Chadwick and Andy Farnell, we have come up with a set of grades that hopefully sets the record straight; E-grades for the big routes and V-grades for the shorter ones. This is a first attempt so there may well be inconsistencies. Let us have your feedback at www.rockfax.com and we will try to make sure the grades are even more accurate next time. Where there is gear on a route this is usually mentioned and the grade given in these instances is for a lead ascent.

Staffordshire · Whaley Bridge · Kinder · Bleaklow · Chew · Lancashire · Cheshire

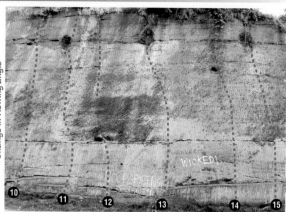

Change in viewing angle

Early morning | 5 min | Sheltered

LADY JANE WALL

The long wall to the left of the entrance has many good routes though a high percentage are hard. The holds on the blanker sections are often so small that they are often invisible unless chalked by previous climbers. There are easier offerings towards either end of the wall. Running along the top of the wall are a series of nine bee-hive-shaped niches that aid route identification.

1 Too Bold for Steve Boot . . . . . . ☐ **V1 (5b)**
A typically deceptive Pex route. Harder than it looks.

2 Set Square . . . . ☐ **VS 4c**
The direct start is **V2 (5c)**.

3 Tequila Sunrise . . . . ☐ **V2 (5c)**
Head straight through the right-hand triangular slot.

4 Harvey Wallbanger . . . . . . ☐ **V3 (5c)**
The wall 1m right on small holds. Requires an udge.

5 Black Russian . . . . ☐ **V4 (6a)**
A direct line 1m right again heading straight to the step at the top of the cliff; interesting

6 Lew's Leap . . . . ☐ **V1 (5b)**
Climb straight to the first of the niches. A short hop for its base is normal. The left-hand direct (?) start is **V2 (5c)**. Tricky.

7 Finger-Ripper . . . . ☐ **V6 (6b)**
An eliminate just right of the first niche. Gnarly in the extreme.

8 Bermuda Triangle . . . . ☐ **V4 (6a)**
A brilliant problem past the second niche. A hard, reachy start leads to a rest and then another crux. The top out is steady.

9 Cosine Alternative . . . . ☐ **V4 (6b)**
A forgotten counter line to *Bermuda Triangle*. Can be used to gain the upper section of *Bermuda Triangle* for shorties.

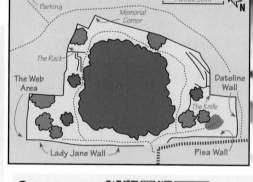

About 50m

Parking

Memorial Corner

The Rack

The Web Area

The Jungle

Dateline Wall

The Knife

Lady Jane Wall

Pisa Wall

N

10 Breakaway . . . . ☐ **V8 (6c)**
Straight up the wall on a series of tiny, tiny holds. Utterly desperate with steel tendons the minimum requirement. *Photo page 289.*

11 Catalepsy . . ☐ **V7 (6c)**
Reach the third niche by a sustained series of pulls. Very reachy and balancy with a high crux.

12 Monoblock . . . . . . ☐ **V10 (7a)**
Said to be 'The Hardest Route in the World', with holds little bigger than decent-sized atoms - and spaced ones at that!.

13 Bernie . . . . ☐ **V6 (6b)**
The easiest line on this section of wall! Start right of old bolts. More like E4 6b if the bolts are clipped.

14 Termination . . . . . ☐ **V7 (6c)**
Make a desperate move to reach the large pocket.

15 Philharmonic . . . . . ☐ **V4 (6b)**
Tall climbers can by-pass the crux.

16 Algripper . . . . . . ☐ **V2 (5c)**
The wall is climbed via two good pockets, linking them (a rockover) proves to be the crux which is higher than you want it.

17 Jurassic Pork . . . . . . ☐ **V6 (6b)**
A blank wall with a hard move using a pebble.

Pex Hill · Frodsham · Helsby

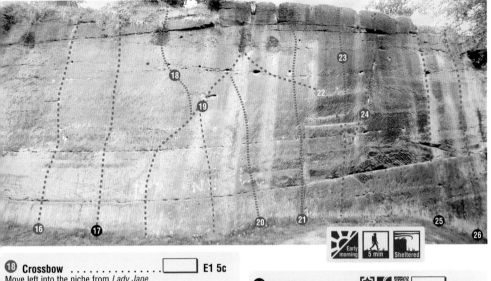

Staffordshire

Whaley Bridge

Kinder

Bleaklow

Chew

Lancashire

Cheshire

18 Crossbow . . . . [ ] **E1 5c**
Move left into the niche from *Lady Jane*.

19 Lady Jane . . . . [ ] **E1 5c**
Climb the right-trending ramp; swing right and follow the
pockets to the top passing the left-hand of a pair of niches.
Direct Start - V3 (5c).

20 Side step . . . . [ ] **E1 5c**
Climb straight up the the final section of *Lady Jane*.

21 Twin Scoops Direct . . [ ] **E1 6a**
Climb straight up the wall to the right-hand niche by a balancy
mantelshelf and a bit of stretch. Especially reachy for the short.

22 Twin Scoops . . . . [ ] **HVS 4c**
At last an easier offering. Climb the ledgy wall then follow the
holds leftwards past *Twin Scoops Direct* to finish up *Lady Jane*.
Much used as a quick way down by local hot-shots.

23 Twin Scoops Right-hand . . . . [ ] **E2 5c**
Direct above the start of *Twin Scoops*.

24 Creeping Jesus . . . . [ ] **E1 5b**
Climb *Twin Scoops* to the last decent ledge then step right to a
good finger-jam (wire) and a sprint finish. Direct start is **V2 (5c)**.

25 Kitt's Wall . . . . [ ] **E5 6b**
Link the three pockets by hard moves. **V4**.

**26 The Black Pimp
from Marseilles** . . . . . [ ] **E6 6b**
The wall to the left of the low relief blunt rib which is the main
feature of this part of the face. **V6**.

27 Unicorn . . . . [ ] **E3 5b**
Climb straight up the blunt rib to a recess just below the cliff
top, exit left to avoid the prickles.

28 Cave Route Right-hand . . . [ ] **E6 6b**
An eliminate via the square pocket. **V6**.

29 Ladytron . . . . [ ] **E4 5c**
The bold wall midway between the two blunt ribs.

30 Cardiac Arete . . . . [ ] **E4 6b**
Boulder up to the break then from the jug make crucial moves
to marginally easier ground. **V5**.

31 Hart's Arete . . . [ ] **E4 6b**
The bold, blunt arete feels big for its size and is suffering from
polish. The grade given is for a lead since there is gear.

32 Zigger Zagger . . . . [ ] **E2 5b**
The stretchy wall has a gripping sloping exit.

33 Big Greenie . . . . [ ] **E3 5c**

34 The Hulk . . . . [ ] **E2 5c**
Left of the crack. You won't like it when you are angry!

35 Hart's Arete Traverse . . [ ] **V5 (6a)**
Start at the crack (*Crack and Up*) and traverse left to *Unicorn*.
The higher break is **V3** and the ultra-low level is **V9**.

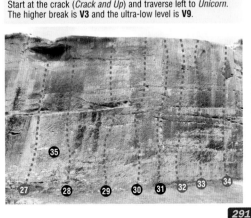

Pex Hill

Frodsham

Helsby

Staffordshire | Whaley Bridge | Kinder | Bleaklow | Chew | Lancashire | Cheshire

Change in viewing angle

THE WEB AREA
The walls either side of the long right-angled corner have a fine selection of routes across the grades. The face right of the corner is one of the sunnier walls in the quarry.

① **Crack and Up** **E1 5b**
The prominent crack gives a good route with solid gear.

② **Corner and Overhang** **E2 5b**
Start up *Crack and Up* but step right to climb the wall just to its right by sustained moves on reasonably sized holds for once. A **Direct Start** is **V3 (6a)** and well worth doing.

③ **McArthur Park** **E3 5b**
Climb the pocketed wall past the twin slots.

④ **Eliminate One** **E2 5b**
The first of four tightly-packed routes.

⑤ **The Abort** **E1 5a**
A high crux on sloping holds feels very bold.

⑥ **Eliminate Two** **E2 5b**

⑦ **One Step** **E1 5a**
2m left of the corner through the slot near the top

⑧ **Eliminate Three** **E3 5c**
Just left of the corner.

⑨ **The Web** **E1 5b**
Spiderman's fave route. The long corner gives a fine pitch. It can be damp but it is normally possible to bridge past the worst of this.

⑩ **Pex Wall** **E3 6a**
Follow the long, slightly-rising break until it fizzles out. A great work-out. Finish rightwards.

⑪ **Eliminate Four** **E3 5c**
Just right of the corner.

⑫ **The Witch** **E2 5b**
The wall 3m right of the corner to a trickier finish.

⑬ **Four Jays** **E2 5b**

⑭ **The Wizard** **E2 5b**
Start at a set of pockets.

⑮ **Green Monster** **E4 6a**

⑯ **Alchemy** **E4 6a**

⑰ **Warlock** **E3 5c**
The wall behind and left of the tree, trend right at the top.

⑱ **Warcry** **E5 6b**

⑲ **Warmonger** **E5 6b**

⑳ **Cobweb Crack** **E3 5c**
The oft-damp crack can be led and has decent gear.

㉑ **Spiderman** **E5 6b**
Don't touch *Cobweb Crack*.

㉒ **Warlord** **E4 6a**
Trend right at the break to finish.

㉓ **The Pacifist** **E5 6b**
A counter line to *Warlord*.

㉔ **Innocent** **E4 6a**

To the right are more routes but most are overgrown. the prominent arete is Gaming Club, a loose and crumbly 5a.

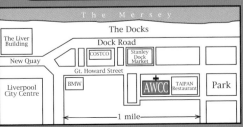

Lots of sun | 5 min

30m gap

Bouldering

OUTLYING AREAS

Many of the walls opposite the quarry entrance are short and overgrown. In amongst them are one or two good sections. Things improve once you reach *The Knife*.

1 Ramble **4c**

2 Short Crack **4b**

3 Heather Wall . . . . **V1 (5b)**

4 Bon Ami . . . . **V0 (5a)**

5 Master Race **E5 6b**
A scary mantel high up.

6 The Rack **E1 5a**
A classic which isn't that hard but don't fall off the top move!

Past some overgrown routes is an open corner with a prominent arete on its left-hand side.

7 Sweeney Arete . . . . **V0 (5a)**
The wall just left of the corner.

8 Headstone . . . . **V4 (6a)**
A scary and blank wall.

9 Memorial Wall **4b**
Wander left then right up the wall via good pockets.

10 Memorial Corner **4b**
The corner is often wet. Just left is **Tombstone, 5a**.

11 Hunter's Walk . . . . **V2 (5c)**

12 St Paul . . . . **V2 (5c)**
Gain a big pocket and finish either left or right.

Past an area of easy-angled rock is a dramatic arete.

13 The Knife **E4 6a**
The arete that forms the edge of the bay was once cutting edge and it remains quite superb. Amigos in pockets protect.

14 Catemytes Crack **E5 6b**
The shallow groove in the wall. Can be led with Amigos.

15 Main Wall **E5 6b**
From a little way up *Catemytes*, move right across the wall using pockets to a groove. Climb this to a rightward exit.

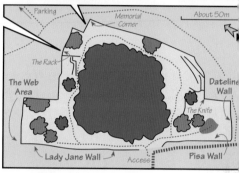

Parking
Memorial Corner
About 50m
The Rack
The Web Area
Dateline Wall
The Knife
Lady Jane Wall
Access
Pisa Wall

Afternoon

Dateline Wall

16 Staminade **E6 6b**
Climb the hard wall straight into the base of the shallow groove, layback up this then exit to the right. The grade is for leading using the old bolts for protection.

17 Lemonade . . . . **NL 6b**
The dirty wall 3m right of *Staminade*.

18 Pernod and Black . . . . . **NL 6b**
Another dirty wall climb. Might be good with a brushing.

19 Rum and Cocaine . . . . **NL 6b**
2m left of the corner.

Staffordshire | Whaley Bridge | Kinder | Bleaklow | Chew | Lancashire | Cheshire | Pex Hill | Frodsham | Helsby

Alan James on *Eliminate* (4b) at Pex Hill. *Page 297*

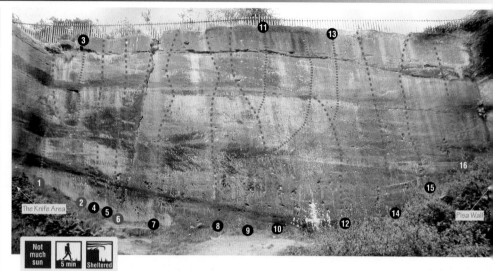

Not much sun · 5 min · Sheltered

DATELINE WALL
The recessed bay to the right of the entry has a whole series of hard and bold face climbs plus the classic crack of *Dateline*. The climbs are soloed by the talented, though the rest of us are inclined to top-rope them although leading is possible if you know the tricks. The bay is home to many of the hardest climbs in the quarry, the amount of chalk on them shows how many good climbers there are out there.

❶ One of These Days
Direct Start **E3 5c**
Bridge the angular corner that bounds the left-hand edge of the back wall. Finish up the parent route.

❷ One of These Days **E3 5c**
Climb the right wall of the corner starting at a slot and trending left to enter the corner halfway up it.

❸ One of These Days
Direct Finish **E4 6a**
Follow the regular route then continue up the wall above passing a small triangular overhang.

❹ The Famous Alto
Sax Break . . . . **NL 6c**
Climb the smooth wall with great difficulty.

❺ Padarn Dance **E5 6b**
Climb the wall left of the crack. No touching the crack! A side-runner in *Dateline* is required at this grade.

❻ Dateline **E2 5c**
The once-pegged crack is a classic pumpy pitch. It can be soloed by the talented and led by the merely good.
FA. Rick Newcombe 1960s

❼ Sinbad **E6 6b**
The technical wall just right of the crack on tiny holds. **E5** with an easy-to-place side runner in *Dateline*. Hard **E6** without.

❽ Depression . . . **E6 6b**
A couple of slopy slots allow the start of a depressingly-difficult sequence up the wall just right.

❾ Exit On Air **E7 6b**
Climb the wall to a bubbly break then traverse right, crossing *Black Magic*, to join *Acid Test* just in time to tackle its crux.

❿ Black Magic . . . **E5 6b**
Magic indeed. Climb the fingery and technical wall, easing with height. Sadly the route was chipped by some half-witted technical dunce, though the worst of the damage was repaired a few years back. This grade is for leading over the old bolts, and Friends in the top break. *Photo page 40.*
FA. Phil Davidson late 1970s

⓫ Black Magic Direct . . . **E6 6c**
Continue trending slightly right where the regular route starts to follow the better holds out to the left.

⓬ Acid Test . . **E5 6b**
The right-hand of the popular lines on this section of wall. Trend gradually left with the crux move up and left from a slot which is well-protected by a bomber Friend.

⓭ Parker's Mood **E6 6b**
The direct finish to *Acid Test*.

⓮ Euphoria . . . **E6 6b**
The wall right of *Acid Test*.

⓯ Never Mind the Acid **E4 5c**
The wall 3m left of the corner. Trend right at the top to a crack.

⓰ Treadmill **E3 5c**
2m left of the corner.

Routes 24 to 26

PISA WALL

The most popular section of the quarry with the polish and the chalk to prove it. The 'proper' routes are almost all well worth doing, as are the variations on the low-level traverse.

❶ The Widow .... ☐ **V1 (5b)**
The scruffy corner on the left could do with a spruce up.

❷ Polar Bear .... ☐ **V5 (6b)**
Start 2m right of the corner and reach the deep horizontal slot with difficulty. Finish between the encroaching vegetation.

❸ Time Passages ...... ☐ **V4 (6b)**
Climb the wall above a rib to the break, swing right and sprint to finish.

❹ Cyclops .... ☐ **V1 (5b)**
The wall left of the twin slots.

❺ Two Eyes .... ☐ **4c**
Climb past the sightless sockets. Finish up a shallow groove.

❻ Cornea .... ☐ **V2 (5c)**
The wall to the right of the sockets.

❼ Willy Simm's Silly Whim ☐ **V6 (6b)**
Climb the tiny arete.

❽ Retina .... ☐ **V1 (5b)**
Head left towards the left-hand side of the shrubbery.

❾ Nameless .... ☐ **4c**
Take a direct line into the right-hand side of the hanging gardens.

❿ Eliminate .... ☐ **4b**
The vague groove leads to a rightwards exit. *Photo page 295.*

⓫ Goliath .... ☐ **V2 (5c)**
Climb the wall heading for the right-hand side of the beehive and with a crucial stretch for the break.

⓬ Square Four .... ☐ **4b**
Climb to the four neatly square-cut holes and then use the left-hand pair to finish. The wall just to the right is a popular **V1**.

⓭ Greeting .... ☐ **V1 (5b)**
Tricky moves below the break. Avoiding using the right-hand pair of holes is difficult.

⓮ Handshake .... ☐ **V1 (5b)**
Climb the wall to the useful pinch-grip just below the top.

⓯ Pisa Wall .... ☐ **4a**
The short wall into the left edge of the notch at the cliff top.

⓰ Straight Crack .... ☐ **4a**
The rather battered pseudo-crack is the easiest offering on the wall. Oddly it would probably get 4c on Stanage!

⓱ Eliminate Wall ...... ☐ **V2 (5c)**
The bulging wall between the two ill-defined cracks is short but manages to be quite pumpy.

⓲ Mankey Road ...... ☐ **V2 (5c)**
The vague right-hand crack is pushy and keeps going.

⓳ Monkey Grip .... ☐ **V1 (5b)**
Climb the smooth wall passing a useful hole early on and finishing over a small overhang. Pleasant.

⓴ Green Streak .... ☐ **V1 (5b)**
Twin parallel bogey-lines mark the line.

㉑ Fingers .... ☐ **V2 (5c)**
Trend right up the wall to a good break, then stretch.

㉒ Bushy Tale .... ☐ **V1 (5b)**
Climb straight up the wall to another tricky finish.

㉓ One Move .... ☐ **V2 (5c)**
The wall below the end of the railings a bit more than a one move wonder.

㉔ Thumb Screw .... ☐ **V3 (6a)**
Use a bore-hole to start.

㉕ Commando .... ☐ **V3 (6a)**
2m left of the edge of the wall. Use a sharp slot on the left for the last move to the top. A dyno from the break to the top is superb.

㉖ Gorilla .... ☐ **V2 (5c)**
Just left of the edge of the wall.

㉗ Pisa Traverse ...... ☐ **V3 (5c)**
The pumpy low-level traverse is the most popular piece of climbing here and sees constant horizontal traffic. From *Gorilla* to *Two Eyes* ..... and back again if you feel like it. The crossing is possible at (at least) three different levels.

ROUTE INDEX

ROUTE INDEX

ROUTE INDEX

GENERAL INDEX